11 Years

CBSE

Class 12

Chemistry

Previous Year-wise Solved Papers

(2013 - 2023) Powered with Concept Notes

DISHA™
Publication Inc

DISHA Publication Inc.

45, 2nd Floor, Maharishi Dayanand Marg,
Corner Market, Malviya Nagar, new Delhi –110017
Tel: 49842349/ 49842350

Edited by : Kalpana Bhargav

Typeset By
DISHA DTP Team

Buying books from DISHA

Just Got A Lot More Rewarding!!!

We at DISHA Publication, value your feedback immensely and to show our apperciation of our reviewers, we have launched a review contest.

To participate in this reward scheme, just follow these quick and simple steps:
• Write a review of the product you purchase on Amazon/Flipkart.
• Take a screenshot/photo of your review.
• Mail it to **disha-rewards@aiets.co.in**, along with all your details.

Each month, selected reviewers will win exciting gifts from
DISHA Publication. Note that the rewards for each month
will be declared in the first week of next month on our website.

https://bit.ly/review-reward-disha.

**Write To
Us At**

feedback_disha@aiets.co.in

CONTENTS

Chapterwise Division of Questions

The table below presents the chapter-wise division of the questions of the 19 papers. So this book can be put to dual usage-yearwise as well as chapter-wise. To find questions of a chapter just follow the question numbers in its row against the 19 papers. This table also depicts the Trend Analysis of 2023-2013 papers.

CH. No.	Chapter Name	Year of Examination				2021				
		2023		2022			2020		2019	
		All India	Delhi	Term-I	Term-II		All India	Delhi	All India	Delhi
1.	The solid state *			2, 8, 11, 22, 32, 48, 50			—	—	1,14	1,15
2.	Solutions	7, 15, 23, 30	7, 34	1, 9, 10, 16, 25, 26, 35, 38, 45			6, 22 & OR, 32, 34	22,16,29	8 &OR ,13	7,16
3.	Electrochemistry	8, 16, 24, 34	2, 3, 8, 12, 24, 31		3, 11 & OR		7,8, 35 & OR	11,12,17, 31	7,11,16 & OR	25 &OR
4.	Chemical Kinetics	4, 12, 22, 29	4, 16, 23, 29		12		20, 23, 33	13, 35 & OR	27 & OR	8,13
5.	Surface Chemistry *				8 & OR		14	24 & OR, 32 & OR	2,15	3 & OR,14
6.	General Principles and Processes of Isolation of Elements *			—	—		16, 31	21&OR, 15, 23	19 & OR	17
7.	The *p*-Block Elements *			3, 7, 13, 18, 19, 21, 24, 30, 31, 34, 37, 39, 46, 49, 51			4, 17, 24, 30 & OR	1,2,3,4,5	6&OR, 25 & OR	6 & OR,27 & OR
8.	The *d* and *f*- Block Elements	13, 17, 35	6, 13, 35		4, 9		13, 36 & OR	36&OR	18 & OR	9,18
9.	Coordination Compounds	2, 14, 25, 28	5, 18, 19, 23		10		18, 25	20,14,26	3 & OR,17	4,10 & OR,11
10.	Haloalkanes and Haloarenes	1, 6, 18, 26	22, 32	5, 15, 17, 23, 29, 33, 42, 43, 44, 47			1, 2, 3	6,28	4,24&OR	21 (i,ii)
11.	Alcohols,Phenols and Ethers	10, 27	11, 20, 26	4, 12, 28, 53, 54, 55			5, 37 & OR		12,23	21(iii),26 & OR
12.	Aldehydes,Ketones and Carboxylic Acids	9, 11, 20, 21, 31	1, 17, 33	2, 5 & OR, 7 & OR			12, 15, 26	19,37 & OR	26 & OR	12,23 & OR
13.	Amines	3, 33	9, 14, 21, 30		1, 6		11, 29	7,34	5& OR,22	2,22
14.	Biomolecules	5, 19, 32	10, 15, 25, 28	6, 14, 20, 27, 36, 40, 52			19, 27 & OR, 29	8,30	21	5& OR,24 & OR
15.	Polymers *			—	—		9	10,25	9,10	19 & OR
16.	Chemistry in Everyday Life *			—	—		10, 21 & OR	9,27	20	20 & OR
	Total	35	35	55	12		37	37	27	27

Exam not held in 2021 due to Covid-19 pandemic

Note:
*** These Chapters are removed from the NCERT**

Chapterwise Division of Questions

Chapter Number	Chapter Name	Year of Examination		
		2018	2017	
		All India	All India	Delhi
1.	The solid state	2, 13	10 , 14	25 & OR
2.	Solutions	7,14,	26 & OR	7, 11
3.	Electrochemistry	26 & OR	7,13	9, 12
4.	Chemical Kinetics	10,12	2,22	3, 15
5.	Surface Chemistry	5,15,	4,12 &OR	5, 14
6.	General Principles and Processes of Isolation of Elements	16	15	17
7.	The p-Block Elements	6, 25 & OR	3,6,18	6 & OR , 8, 21
8.	The d and f- Block Elements	9, 22	25 & OR	1, 24 & OR
9.	Coordination Compounds	1,19	9,11	13
10.	Haloalkanes and Haloarenes	3, 11(b,c)	1 , 21	4, 16
11.	Alcohols,Phenols and Ethers	4,11(a),21(ii,iii)	5,8 & OR	26 & OR
12.	Aldehydes,Ketones and Carboxylic Acids	8&OR,17 ,21(i)	24 & OR	10, 18 & OR
13.	Amines	24 & OR	16,17	2, 22
14.	Biomolecules	20 & OR	23	23
15.	Polymers	23	20	19,
16.	Chemistry in Everyday Life	18	19	20
	Total	**26**	**26**	**26**

Chapterwise Division of Questions

Chapter Number	Chapter Name	Year of Examination			
		2016		2015	
		All India	Delhi	All India	Delhi
1.	The solid state	4,17	3 ,12	18	5, 13
2.	Solutions	8 , 22	26 & OR	10, 17	9 & OR, 11
3.	Electrochemistry	25 & OR	6 , 16	3, 24 & OR	10, 16
4.	Chemical Kinetics	6, 19	9 ,13	8, 21	26 & OR
5.	Surface Chemistry	3, 21	5, 14	4, 22	4, 17
6.	General Principles and Processes of Isolation of Elements	14	15	11	12
7.	The p-Block Elements	5, 10 & OR, 15	2, 24 & OR	6, 12	1, 24 & OR
8.	The d and f- Block Elements	26 &OR	7 & OR, 17	1, 25 & OR	6, 14
9.	Coordination Compounds	9, 16	8, 22	7 & OR, 13	9, 15,
10.	Haloalkanes and Haloarenes	2,12 & OR	1,11,	2, 19	3, 22
11.	Alcohols,Phenols and Ethers	1 , 11	10, 18	5, 20	2,20 & OR
12.	Aldehydes,Ketones and Carboxylic Acids	24 & OR	25 & OR	26 & OR	8, 19
13.	Amines	7, 20	4, 19	9, 14 & OR	25 & OR
14.	Biomolecules	13,	21	16	21
15.	Polymers	18	20 & OR	15	18
16.	Chemistry in Everyday Life	23	23	23	23
	Total	26	26	26	26

Chapterwise Division of Questions

Chapter Number	Chapter Name	Year of Examination			
		2014		2013	
		All India	Delhi	All India	Delhi
1.	The solid state	9 ,10 & OR	9, 10	9, 10	1, 19
2.	Solutions	28 & OR	6, 11, 12	28 & OR	9, 20
3.	Electrochemistry	11, 19	28 & OR	11, 26	10, 21
4.	Chemical Kinetics	4, 20	13	12, 19	28 & OR
5.	Surface Chemistry	1, 21	1, 19	1, 20	11 & OR, 12
6.	General Principles and Processes of Isolation of Elements	13, 2	2, 14	2, 13	2, 13
7.	The p-Block Elements	3, 14, 15, 22	15 & OR, 20, 21	3, 14, 15, 21	3, 14, 29 & OR
8.	The d and f- Block Elements	29 & OR	16, 18, 29 & OR	22, 29 & OR	15, 22 & OR
9.	Coordination Compounds	23	3	22 (OR)	23
10.	Haloalkanes and Haloarenes	4	17, 18, 27 (i)	4, 23	4, 5, 16
11.	Alcohols,Phenols and Ethers	16, 17,24	5, 26	16, 17	6, 17, 18
12.	Aldehydes,Ketones and Carboxylic Acids	8, 30 & OR	4, 27 (ii), 30 & OR	5, 30 & OR	30 & OR
13.	Amines	6, 25 & OR	7, 27 (OR)	6, 24	7, 24
14.	Biomolecules	7, 26	8, 24	7, 27	8
15.	Polymers	5, 18	25	8, 18 & OR	25
16.	Chemistry in Everyday Life	27	23	25	26,27
	Total	**30**	**30**	**30**	**30**

All India *2023*

CBSE Board Solved Paper

Time Allowed : 3 Hours   *Maximum Marks : 70*

General Instructions:

(i) This Question Paper contains **35** questions. All questions are compulsory.

(ii) Question Paper is divided into **FIVE** sections. Section **A, B, C, D** and **E**.

(iii) In section A – question number **1** to **18** are Multiple Choice (MCQ) type questions carrying **1** mark each.

(iv) In section B – question number **19** to **25** are Very Short Answer (VSA) type questions carrying **2** marks each.

(v) In section C – question number **26** to **30** are short Answer (SA) type questions carrying **3** marks each.

(vi) In section D – question number **31 & 32** are case based questions carrying **4** marks each.

(vii) In section E – question number **33** to **35** are Long Answer (LA) questions carrying **5** marks each.

(viii) There is no overall choice. However, an internal choice has been provided in 2 questions in Section **B**, 2 questions in Section **C**, 2 questions in Section **D** and 2 questions in Section **E**.

(ix) Use of calculator is NOT allowed.

SECTION - A

1. Auto oxidation of chloroform in air and sunlight produces a poisonous gas known as

  (a) Tear gas   (b) Mustard gas

  (c) Phosgene gas   (d) Chlorine gas

2. Which of the following ligands is an ambidentate ligand?

  (a) CO   (b) NO_2

  (c) NH_3 (d) H_2O

3. Among the following which has the highest value of p^Kb?

  (a) ⬡—NH_2

  (b) ⬡—$CH_2 - NH_2$

  (c) H_3C—⬡—NH_2

  (d) O_2N—⬡—NH_2

4. The slope in the plot of $\log \dfrac{[R]_0}{[R]}$ vs. time for a first order reaction is

  (a) $\dfrac{+k}{2.303}$ (b) $+k$

  (c) $\dfrac{-k}{2.303}$ (d) $-k$

5. When D-glucose reacts with HI, it forms

  (a) Gluconic acid

  (b) n-hexane

  (c) Saccharic acid

  (d) Iodohexane

6. Inversion of configuration occurs in

  (a) S_N2 reaction

  (b) S_N1 reaction

  (c) Neither S_N2 nor S_N1 reaction

  (d) S_N1 as well as S_N2 reaction

7. Solubility of gas in liquid decreases with increase in

  (a) Pressure

  (b) Temperature

  (c) Volume

  (d) Number of solute molecules

8. Which of the following relations is incorrect?

  (a) $R = \dfrac{1}{k}\left(\dfrac{l}{a}\right)$ (b) $G = k\left(\dfrac{a}{l}\right)$

  (c) $G = k\left(\dfrac{l}{a}\right)$ (d) $\wedge_m = \dfrac{k}{c}$

9. The reagent that can be used to distinguish acetophenone and benzophenone is

  (a) 2, 4-dinitrophenyl hydrazine

  (b) aqueous $NaHSO_3$

  (c) Fehling solution

  (d) I_2 and NaOH

10. Which of the following reactions are feasible?

 (a) $CH_3CH_2Br + Na^+ O^-C(CH_3)_3 \rightarrow CH_3CH_2-O-C(CH_3)_3$

 (b) $(CH_3)_3C-Cl + Na^+ O^-CH_2CH_3 \rightarrow CH_3CH_2-O-C(CH_3)_3$

 (c) Both (a) and (b)

 (d) Neither (a) nor (b)

11. Which of the following compounds will undergo self-condensation in the presence of dilute NaOH solution?

 (a) C_6H_5CHO (b) CH_3CH_2CHO

 (c) $(CH_3)_3C-CHO$ (d) $H-CHO$

12. For the reaction $3A \rightarrow 2B$, rate of reaction $-\dfrac{d[A]}{dt}$ is equal to

 (a) $\dfrac{+3}{2}\dfrac{d[B]}{dt}$ (b) $\dfrac{+2}{3}\dfrac{d[B]}{dt}$

 (c) $\dfrac{+1}{3}\dfrac{d[B]}{dt}$ (d) $\dfrac{+1}{2}\dfrac{d[B]}{dt}$

13. Which of the following transition metals shows 4.1 and 4.2 oxidation states?

 (a) Mn   (b) Zn

 (c) Sc   (d) Cu

14. The formula of the complex Iron (III) hexacyanidoferrate (II) is

 (a) $Fe_2[Fe(CN)_6]_3$ (b) $Fe_1[Fe(CN)_6]_3$

 (c) $Fe[Fe(CN)_6]$ (d) $Fe_3[Fe(CN)_6]_2$

For Questions 15-18: Given below are two statements labelled as Assertion (A) and Reason (R). Select the most appropriate answer from the options given below:

 (a) Both (A) and (R) are true and (R) is the correct explanation of (A).

 (b) Both (A) and (R) are true, but (R) is not the correct explanation of (A).

 (c) (A) is true, but (R) is false.

 (d) (A) is false, but (R) is true.

15. Assertion (A) : The enthalpy of mixing $\Delta_{mix} H$ is equal to zero for an ideal solution.

 Reason (R) : For an ideal solution the interaction between solute and solvent molecules is stronger than the interactions between solute-solute or solvent-solvent molecules.

16. Assertion (A) : Molar conductivity decreases with increase in concentration.

 Reason (R) : When concentration approaches zero, the molar conductivity is known as limiting molar conductivity.

17. Assertion (A) : Transition metals show their highest oxidation state with oxygen.

 Reason (R) : The ability of oxygen to form multiple bonds to metals.

18. Assertion (A) : Chlorobenzene is resistant to nucleophilic substitution reaction at room temperature.

 Reason (R) : C-Cl bond gets weaker due to resonance.

SECTION - B

19. What are nucleic acids? Why two strands in DNA are not identical but are complementary?   **1 × 2**

20. Do the following conversions in not more than two steps: **2 × 1**

 (a) CH_3COOH to CH_3COCH_3

 (b) benzene$-CH_2CH_3$ to benzene$-COOH$

21. Write the chemical equation involved in the following reactions: **2 × 1**

 (a) Reimer-Tiemann reaction

 (b) Acetylation of Salicylic acid

22. (a) The conversion of molecule A to B followed second order kinetics. If concentration of A increased to three times, how will it affect the rate of formation of B?   **2 × 1**

 (b) Define Pseudo first order reaction with an example.

23. The vapour pressure of pure liquid X and pure liquid Y at 25 °C are 120 mm Hg and 160 mm Hg respectively. If equal moles of X and Y are mixed to form an ideal solution, calculate the vapour pressure of the solution.   **2**

24. (a) Give reasons: **2 × 1**

  (i) Mercury cell delivers a constant potential during its life time

  (ii) In the experimental determination of electrolytic conductance Direct Current (DC) is not used.

       OR

 (b) Define fuel cell with an example. What advantages do the fuel cells have over primary and secondary batteries?   **2**

25. (a) Write the IUPAC names of the following: **2 × 1**

  (i) $[Co(NH_3)_5(ONO)]^{2+}$

  (ii) $K_2[NiCl_4]$

       OR

 (b) (i) What is a chelate complex? Give one example.

  (ii) What are heteropletic complex? Give one example.

       2 × 1

SECTION - C

26. Answer any 3 of the following: **3 × 1**

 (a) Which isomer of C_5H_{10} gives a single monochloro compound C_5H_9Cl in bright sunlight?

 (b) Arrange the following compounds in increasing order of reactivity towards S_N2 reaction:

  2-Bromopentane, 1-Bromopentane, 2-Bromo-2-methylbutane

(c) Why p-dichlorobenzene has higher melting point than those of ortho-and meta-isomers?

(d) Identify A and B in the following:

$$\text{(Cyclohexyl-Br)} \xrightarrow[\text{Dry ether}]{\text{Mg}} A \xrightarrow{H_2O} B$$

27. (a) (i) Write the mechanism of the following reaction:

2×1

$$2CH_3CH_2OH \xrightarrow[413K]{H^+} CH_3-CH_2-O-CH_2-CH_3 + H_2O$$

(ii) Why ortho-nitrophenol is steam volatile while para nitrophenol is not?

OR

(b) What happens when 3×1

(i) Anisole is treated with CH_3Cl anhydrous $AlCl_3$?

(ii) Phenol is oxidised with $Na_2Cr_2O_7/H^+$?

(iii) $(CH_3)_3C-OH$ is heated with CuI 573 K ?

Write chemical equation in support of your answer.

28. (a) Draw of geometrical isomers of $[Co(en)_2Cl_2]^{2+}$. Which geometrical isomer of $[Co(en)_2Cl_2]^{2+}$ is not optically active and why?

(b) Write the hybridisation and magnetic behaviour of $[CoF_6]^3$. $2 + 1$

[Given : Atomic number of Co = 27]

29. A first order reaction is 50% complete in 30 minutes at 300 K and in 10 minutes at 320 K. Calculate activation energy (E_a) for the reaction. [R = 8.314 J K^{-1} mol^{-1}]   **3**

[Given : log 2 = 0.3010. log 3 = 0.4771. log 4 = 0.6021]

30. When 19.5 g of F $- CH_2 - COOH$ (Molar mass = 78g mol^{-1}). is dissolved in 500 g of water, the depression in freezing point is observed to be FC. Calculate the degree of dissociation of $F-CH_2-COOH$.   **3**

[Given : K_f for water = 1.86 K kg mol^{-1}]

SECTION - D

The following questions are case based questions Read the passage carefully and answer the questions that follow:

31. The carbon - oxygen double bond is polarised in aldehydes and ketones due to higher electronegativity of oxygen relative to carbon. Therefore they undergo nucleophilic addition reactions with a number of nucleophiles such as HCN, $NaHSO_3$, alcohols, ammonia derivatives and Grignard reagents. Aldehydes are easily oxidised by mild oxidising agents as compared to ketones. The carbonyl group of carboxylic acid does not give reactions of aldehydes and ketones. Carboxylic acids are considerably more acidic than alcohols and most of simple phenols.

Answer the following:

(a) Write the name of the product when an aldehyde reacts with excess alcohol in presence of dry HCl.

1

(b) Why carboxylic acid is a stronger acid than phenol?

1

(c) (i) Arrange the following compounds in increasing order of their reactivity towards CH_3MgBr:

$$CH_3CHO,\ (CH_3)_3C-\underset{\underset{O}{\|}}{C}-CH_3,\ CH_3-\underset{\underset{O}{\|}}{C}-CH_3$$

(ii) Write a chemical test to distinguish between propanal and propanone. 2×1

OR

(c) Write the main product in the following:

(i)

$$\text{(3-formylcyclohexanone)} \xrightarrow{[Ag(NH_3)_2]^+}$$

(ii)

$$\text{(benzaldehyde)} \xrightarrow{H_2NCONHNH_2} \qquad 2 + 1$$

32. Carbohydrates are optically active polyhydroxy aldehyde and ketones. They are also called saccharides. All these carbohydrates which reduce. Fehling's solution and Tollen's reagent are referred to as reducing sugar Glucose, the most important source of energy for mammals is obtained by the hydrolysis of starch. Vitamins are necessary food factors required in the diet. Proteins are the polymers of a acids and perform various structural and dynamic functions in the organisms. Deficiency of vitamins leads to many diseases.

Answer the following:

(a) The penta-acetate of glucose does not react with Hydroxylamine. What does it indicate?   **1**

(b) Why cannot vitamin C be stored in our body?   **1**

(c) Define the following as related to proteins.

(i) Peptide linkage

(ii) Denaturation 2×1

OR

(c) Define the following as related to carbohydrates:

(i) Anomers 2×1

(ii) Glycoside linkage

SECTION - E

33. (I) Give reasons: **3 + 2**

    (i) Aniline on nitration gives good amount of m-nitroaniline, though $-NH_2$ group is o/p directing in electrophilic substitution reactions.

    (ii) $(CH_3)_2 NH$ is more basic than $(CH_3)_3N$ in an aqueous solution.

    (iii) Ammonolysis of alkyl halides is not a good method to prepare pure primary amines.

(II) Write the reaction involved in the following:

    (i) Carbyl amine test

    (ii) Gabriel phthalimide synthesis

OR

(b) (I) Write the structure of A, B and C in the following reactions: **3 + 1 + 1**

(i)
$$\text{C}_6\text{H}_5-N_2^+Cl \xrightarrow{\text{CuCN}} A$$

$$\xrightarrow{H_2O/H^+} B \xrightarrow[\Delta]{NH_3} C$$

(ii)
$$\text{C}_6\text{H}_5\text{NO}_2 \xrightarrow{\text{Fe/HCl}} A \xrightarrow[273\ K]{NaNO_2 + HCl} B$$

$$\xrightarrow{C_2H_5OH} C$$

(II) Why aniline does not undergo Friedal-Crafts reaction?

(III) Arrange the following in increasing order of their boiling point:

$$C_2H_5OH, C_2H_5NH_2, (C_2H_5)_3 N$$

34. (a) Conductivity of 2×10^{-3} methanoic acid is 8×10^{-5} cm^{-1}. Calculate its molar conductivity and degree of dissociation of $\wedge_m^o$ for methanoic acid is 404 S cm^2 mol^{-1}.   **3 + 2**

(b) Calculate the $\Delta_r G^o$ and log K_c for the given reaction at 298 K:

$$Ni_{(s)} + 2Ag^+_{(aq)} \rightleftharpoons Ni^{2+}_{(aq)} + 2Ag_{(s)}$$

Given: $E^o_{Ni^{2+}/N_1} = -0.25V$, $E^o_{Ag^+/Ag} = +0.80V$

$1\ F = 96500\ C\ mol^{-1}$.

35. (I) Account for the following: **3 + 2**

    (i) E^o value for Mn^{3+}/Mn^{2+} couple is much more positive than that for Cr^{3+}/Cr^{2+}.

    (ii) Sc^{3+} is colourless whereas Ti^{3+} is coloured in an aqueous solution.

    (iii) Actinoids show wide range of oxidation states.

(II) Write the chemical equations for the preparation of $KMnO_4$ from MnO_2.

OR

(b) (I) Account for the following: **2 + 2 + 1**

    (i) Transition metals form alloys.

    (ii) Ce^{4+} is a strong oxidising agent.

(II) Write one similarity and one difference between chemistry of Lanthanoids and Actinoids.

(III) Complete the following ionic equation:

$$Cr_2O_7^{2-} + 2OH^- \longrightarrow$$

Solutions

SECTION - A

1. **(c)** Phosgene gas;

$$2CHCl_3 + O_2 \xrightarrow{\text{sunlight}} 2COCl_2 + 2HCl$$
$$\text{Carbonyl chloride}$$
$$\text{or Phosgene} \qquad \textbf{(1 Mark)}$$

2. **(b)** NO_2; $M \longleftarrow N \underset{O}{\overset{O}{\lessgtr}}$ and $M \longleftarrow O - N = O$

Two donor atoms of NO_2 are 'O' and 'N' are ligating with central metal atom (M) at a time. **(1 Mark)**

3. **(d)** $O_2N - \langle\!\!\langle \rangle\!\!\rangle - NH_2$; $K_b = \dfrac{[R\overset{+}{N}H_3][OH^-]}{[RNH_2]}$

Larger K_b value $\rightarrow$ smaller pK_b value $\rightarrow$ higher basicity.
$-NO_2$ group exerts $-$ I effect on the lone pair of $-NH_2$ group. This results into the difficulty of lone pair towards acid. Therefore, K_b value becomes smaller, pK_b value larger. **(1 Mark)**

4. **(a)** $\dfrac{+K}{2.303}$;

For 1st order reaction, $[R] = [R]_0\, e^{-kt}$

or, $\dfrac{[R]_0}{[R]} = e^{kt}$

or, $2.303 \log\dfrac{[R]_0}{[R]} = kt$

or, $\log\dfrac{[R]_0}{[R]} = \dfrac{k}{2.303}t$ **(1 Mark)**

5. **(b)** n-hexane;

$$\begin{array}{c} CHO \\ | \\ (CHOH)_4 \\ | \\ CH_2OH \end{array} \xrightarrow{HI,\,\Delta} \begin{array}{c} CH_3 \\ | \\ (CH_2)_4 \\ | \\ CH_3 \end{array}$$
D-Glucose   n-Hexane **(1 Mark)**

6. **(a)** S_N2;

S_N2 reaction always produces the product with inversion of configuration in comparison to the reactant. **(1 Mark)**

7. **(b)** Temperature;

The solubility of gas in the decreases with increase in temperature as the kinetic energy of the gas increases. Which is increases the escaping tendency from liquid. **(1 Mark)**

8. **(c)** $G = K\left(\dfrac{l}{a}\right)$

Conductance (G) is directly proportional to area (a) of the conductor, conductivity of the medium and inversely proportional to the length of the conductor. **(1 Mark)**

9. **(d)** I_2 and NaOH;

This is the reagent of iodoform reaction. At least one methyl group to attached to $\overset{}{\underset{}{>}}C = O$ group is required to occur this reaction.

Acetophenone $(C_6H_5\overset{O}{\overset{\|}{C}}CH_3)$ has $- CH_3$ group but

benzophenone $(C_6H_5\overset{O}{\overset{\|}{C}}C_6H_5)$ has no $- CH_3$ group.

$$C_6H_5\overset{O}{\overset{\|}{C}} - CH_3 \xrightarrow{I_2/NaOH} C_6H_5\overset{O}{\overset{\|}{C}} - O\,Na + CHI_3$$
(1 Mark)

10. **(b)** $CH_3CH_2 - Br + Na^+\,\overset{-}{O}C(CH_3)_3 \xrightarrow{S_N2}$
Bulky t-butoxide

$$CH_3CH_2 - O - C(CH_3)_3 + Br^- + Na^+$$

Although primary alkyl halide favours the S_N2 reaction but the bulky t-Butoxide nucleophile acts as strong base instead of nucleophile.

$$Br - CH_2 - CH_2 + \overset{-}{O}C(CH_3)_3 \longrightarrow$$
$$H \qquad H_2C = CH_2 + (CH_3)_3COH$$

Whereas in (b) the substrate facilitates the carbocation stability and therefore, S_N1 mechanism as the attacking nucleophile is not bulky one. **(1 Mark)**

11. **(b)** CH_3CH_2CHO

It undergoes aldol condensation in presence of dil. NaOH and in order to occur this reaction at least one α $-$ H has to be present.

$$2CH_3CH_2CHO \xrightarrow[\text{(ii) }\Delta]{\text{(i) dil. NaOH}}$$
$$CH_3 - CH = CH - CHO \textbf{ (1 Mark)}$$
But$-2-$enal

12. **(a)** $\dfrac{+3}{2}\dfrac{d[B]}{dt}$;

$3A \longrightarrow 2B$

Rate of the reaction $= -\dfrac{1}{3}\dfrac{d[A]}{dt} = \dfrac{1}{2}\dfrac{d[B]}{dt}$

$\therefore\ -\dfrac{d[A]}{dt} = \dfrac{3}{2}\dfrac{d[B]}{dt}$ **(1 Mark)**

13. **(d)** Cu;

Cu shows (+1) and (+2) oxidation states **(1 Mark)**

14. **(b)** $Fe_4^{III}[Fe^{II}(CN)_6]_3$;

Counter ion : $4Fe\,(III) \longrightarrow (+3) \times 4 = +12$

Complex ion :

$$\overset{\text{II}}{[\text{Fe(CN)}_6]_3} \longrightarrow [(+2) + \{(-6)\times 1\}]\times 3 = -12$$

Unidentate
ligand (CN$^-$)

(1 Mark)

15. (c) For ideal solution, $\Delta_{\text{mix}}\text{H}=0$

Solute – Solvent interaction = Solute – solute or
      Solvent – solvent interaction   **(1 Mark)**

16. (b) Molar conductivity (Λ_{m}) decreases with increase in concentration can be explained by Debye – Huckel – Onsager equation.

$$\Lambda_C = \Lambda_0 - \Lambda\sqrt{C}$$

Limiting
molar conductivity   Concentration

As the concentration of the electrolyte increases the ion-cloud surrounding the a' particular ion increases as the ion-cloud is created by oppositely charged ions. Therefore, the movement of desired ion towards the electrode gets hindered. As the dilution increases the counter ion-cloud is simultaneously decreases and conductivity increases.   **(1 Mark)**

17. (a) Oxygen forms double bonds to metals in order to stabilize the highest oxidation states of metal. e.g.

$$[\text{MnO}_4^-] \longrightarrow \text{Mn in (+7) oxidation state.}$$

Structure ::

(1 Mark)

18. (c)

Due to the delocalization of lone pair of 'Cl' atom in the benzene ring the electron density enhances, which is not favourable for nucleophilic substitution reaction. Further, the C – Cl bond gets stronger due to resonance. **(1 Mark)**

SECTION - B

19. Nucleic Acids, the long chain polymeric biomolecules, are one of the components of chromosome present in the nucleus of the cell. These are responsible for transmitting the genetic information. The monomer of the biopolymer is known as nucleotide.   **(1 Mark)**

The two strands in DNA are complementary to each other because the H-bonds form between specific pairs of bases belong to different chains.   **(1 Mark)**

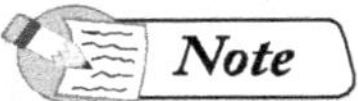

Adenine forms H-bonds with Thymine : 2H-bonds

[Adenine (A)]

Thymine (T)

Guanine pairs with cytosine : 3H-bonds

Cytosine (C)

Guanine (G)

20. (a) $$\text{CH}_3\text{COOH} \xrightarrow{\text{Ca(OH)}_2} (\text{CH}_3\text{COO})_2\text{Ca}$$

$$\xrightarrow[\text{distillation}]{\text{Dry}} \text{CH}_3 - \overset{\overset{\text{O}}{\|}}{\text{C}} - \text{CH}_3 \;\; \textbf{(1 Mark)}$$

(b)

$$\text{CH}_2\text{CH}_3 \xrightarrow[\Delta]{\text{KMnO}_4 - \text{KOH}}$$

COOK $\xrightarrow{\text{H}_3\text{O}^+}$ COOH

(1 Mark)

21. (a) Reimer-Tiemann Reaction:

OH $\xrightarrow{\text{CHCl}_3,\text{ aq NaOH}}$ ONa, CHCl$_2$ $\xrightarrow{\text{NaOH}}$

Benzal Chloride

ONa, CHO $\xrightarrow{\text{H}^+}$ OH, CHO

(1 Mark)

Salicylaldehyde

This reaction is specifically used for ortho-formylation.

(b) Acetylation of Salicylic acid:

$$CH_3COOC_2H_5 + H_2O \xrightarrow{H^+} \text{(Salicylic acid)} \xrightarrow{(CH_3CO)_2O,\ H^+} \text{(Acetylacetic acid) (Aspirin)} + CH_3COOH$$

(Salicylic acid)   (Acetylacetic acid) (Aspirin)

(1 Mark)

22. (a) $A \longrightarrow B$

Rate of the reaction : $r_1 = k[A]^2$ ($\because$ 2nd order kinetics)

Increasing concentration of A by 3 times:

$$r_2 = k(3[A])^2$$
$$= 9k[A]^2$$
$$= 9r_1$$

$\therefore$ Rate of the reaction enhances by 9 times.

The formation of 'B' enhances by 9 times. **(1 Mark)**

(b) The order of the reaction is sometimes, of higher order but appears as a first order reaction due to the presence of one of the components in excess. Such reactions are known as pseudofirst order reaction. e.g. Acid catalysed hydrolysis of ester, **(½ Mark)**

$$CH_3COOC_2H_5 + H_2O \xrightarrow{H^+} CH_3COOH + C_2H_5OH$$
$$Rate = k[CH_3COOC_2H_5][H_2O]$$

H_2O is present in the reaction mixture in excess. Therefore, there is hardly any change happens in the concentration of water in the end of reaction.

$\therefore \quad Rate = k'[CH_3COOC_2H_5]$

Rate becomes dependent on the concentration of ester.

(½ Mark)

23. $p_x^0 = 120$ mm Hg, $p_y^0 = 166$ mm Hg at 25°C

Equal moles of X and Y.

$\therefore \quad \chi_x$ = mole fraction of X = $\dfrac{1}{2}$

χ_y = mole fraction of Y = $\dfrac{1}{2}$ **(½ Mark)**

$P_{Total} = p_x + p_y$ **(½ Mark)**

$\qquad = \chi_x p_x^0 + \chi_y p_y^0$

$\qquad = \left(\dfrac{1}{2} \times 120 + \dfrac{1}{2} \times 160 \right)$ mm Hg   **(½ Mark)**

$\qquad = 140$ mm Hg   **(½ Mark)**

The vapour pressure of the solution = 140 mm Hg.

24. (a) (i) Mercury cell delivers a constant potential, ~1.35 V during its life time as the overall reaction does not involve any ion in solution whose concentration can change during its life time. **(1 Mark)**

(ii) Passing the direct current (DC) in the electrolyte changes the composition of the solution. **(1 Mark)**

OR

(b) Fuel Cell: The galvanic cells which are designed to convert the energy of combustion of fuels like hydrogen, methane, methanol etc. directly into electrical energy are called fuel cells. **(1 Mark)**

Advantages:

(a) It produces electricity with an efficiency of about 70% compared to thermal plants whose efficiency is about 40%.

(b) Fuel cells are pollution free.

(c) The H_2–O_2 fuel cell produces water vapour which can be, further, condensed and reused as a drinking water. **(1 Mark)**

25. (a) (i) $[Co(NH_3)_5(ONO)]^{2+} \Rightarrow$ Pentaamminenitrito-O-Cobalt(III) **(1 Mark)**

(ii) $K_2(NiCl_4) \Rightarrow$ Potassium tetrachloridonickelate (II) **(1 Mark)**

OR

(b) The complex which is formed by ligating more than one donor sites of a multidentate ligand simultaneously to the metal centre is known as chelating complex. e.g. **(1 Mark)**

$\Rightarrow$ Ethylenediamminetetraacetate ion (EDTA^{4-}) is a hexadentate ligand. It uses all 6 donor site to form a chelating complex. **(1 Mark)**

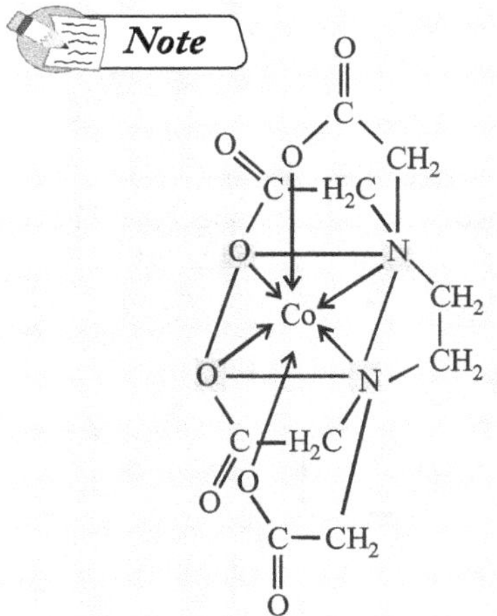

Note

$\Rightarrow$ *[Co(EDTA)]; a chelating complex.*

25. (b) (ii) The complexes in which a metal is bound to more than one kind of donor groups, are known as heteroleptic complex. **(1 Mark)**

e.g. $[Co(NH_3)_4Cl_2]^+$ **(1 Mark)**

SECTION - C

26. (a) To produce single monochloro compound all the 'H' atoms have to be equivalent. That is possible only in the following structure.

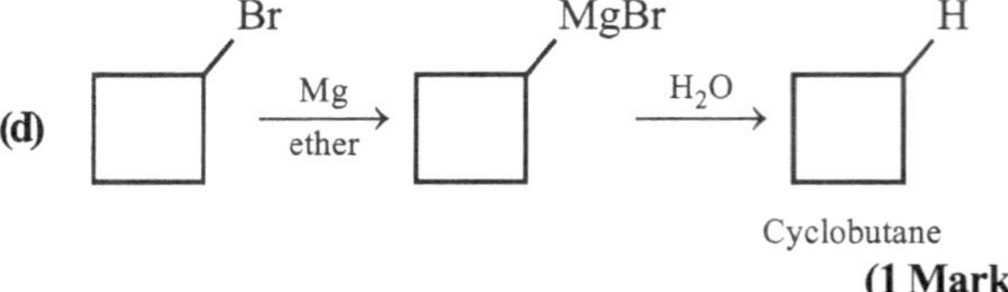

C_5H_{10} = Cyclopentane

(1 Mark)

(b) 2-Bromopentane :

(I)

$CH_3\ CH_2\ CH_2\ \underset{\underset{Br}{|}}{C}HCH_3 \Rightarrow 2°$ substrate

1-Bromopentane :

(II)

$CH_3\ CH_2\ CH_2\ CH_2\ \underset{\underset{Br}{|}}{C}H_2 \Rightarrow 1°$ substrate

2-Bromo-2-methylbutane :

(III)

$CH_3CH_2 - \underset{\underset{Br}{|}}{\overset{\overset{CH_3}{|}}{C}} - CH_3 \Rightarrow 3°$ substrate

order of reactivity towards S_N2 reaction:

$3° < 2° < 1° \Rightarrow$ (III) < (I) < (II)   **(1 Mark)**

(c)

p-dichloro benzene   m-dichloro benzene   o-dichloro benzene

p-dichlorobenzene is symmetric in structure in comparison to o- or m-dichlorobenzene. Therefore, the packing of p-dichlorobenzene in crystal lattice is highly ordered and compact in comparison to other two isomers.   **(1 Mark)**

(d)

Cyclobutane

(1 Mark)

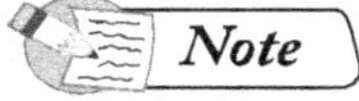 *Note*

The 'c' atom attached to – MgBr always have more electron density as Mg is the electropositive elements. So, the Grignard agent always acts as nucleophile.

27. (a) (i) $CH_3CH_2\ddot{O}H \xrightarrow{H^+} CH_3CH_2\overset{+}{O} - H$ **(½ Mark)**
$\quad\quad\quad\quad\quad\quad\quad\quad\quad\quad\quad\quad\quad\underset{H}{|}$

$CH_3CH_2\ddot{O}H + CH_3CH_2 \overset{+}{\underset{\underset{H}{|}}{O}} - H \longrightarrow$

$CH_3CH_2 - \overset{+}{\underset{\underset{H}{|}}{O}} - CH_2CH_3 \xrightarrow{-H^+}$ **(1 Mark)**

$CH_3CH_2 - O - CH_2CH_3$

(½ Mark)

(ii) Ortho-nitrophenol is steam volatile while para-nitrophenol is not due to intermolecular Hydrogen bonding present in p-nitrophenol.   **(1 Mark)**

OR

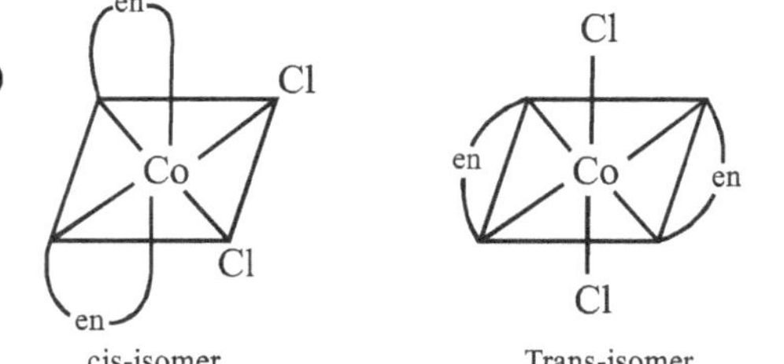

(i) $\xrightarrow{CH_3Cl/Anhy.\ AlCl_3}$

(1 Mark)

(ii) $\xrightarrow{Na_2Cr_2O_7/H^+}$

Benzoquinone

(1 Mark)

(iii) $H_3C - \underset{\underset{CH_3}{|}}{\overset{\overset{CH_3}{|}}{C}} - OH \xrightarrow[\text{Dehydration}]{Cu,\ 573k} CH_3 - \overset{\overset{CH_3}{|}}{C} = CH_2$

(1 Mark)

t-alcohol gives alkene by dehydration whereas p- and s-alcohols undergo dehydrogenation resulting into aldehyde and ketone, respectively.

28. (a)

cis-isomer   Trans-isomer

(1 Mark)

Trans - isomer is not optically active as it has plane of symmetry and axis of symmetry.   **(1 Mark)**

(b) $[CoF_6]^{3-} \Rightarrow$ Co is in (+3) oxidation state.

$Co^{3+}(24) \Rightarrow 3d^6\ 4s^0 \Rightarrow$ ⇅ ↑ ↑ ↑ ↑ __
$\quad\quad\quad\quad\quad\quad\quad\quad\quad\quad\quad\quad\quad 3d \quad\quad 4s$

Since F^- is a weak field ligand, the outer d-orbital participates in the hybridization to form 6 equivalent bonds. Hence, the hybridization of the central metal atomic orbitals is **sp^3d^2**.

Co^{3+} has 4 unpaired electrons which imparts the spin magnetic moment of the complex. Therefore $[CoF_6]^{3-}$ is a paramagnetic complex.

$$\mu_{s.o} = \sqrt{n(n+2)} = \sqrt{4(4+2)} = 2\sqrt{6} \approx 4.9\ B.M.$$

(1 Mark)

29. For 1st order reaction, $t_{1/2} = \dfrac{0.693}{k}$

At 300k, $(t_{1/2})_1 = \dfrac{0.693}{k_1}$; $k_1 = Ae^{-Ea/RT_1}$ **(½ Mark)**

$\therefore\ k_1 = \dfrac{0.693}{30 \times 60}$; $k_1 = Ae^{-Ea/R.320}$ ... (i) **(½ Mark)**

At 320k, $(t_{1/2})_2 = \dfrac{0.693}{k_2}$; $k_2 = Ae^{-Ea/RT_2}$

$\therefore\ k_2 = \dfrac{0.693}{10 \times 60}$; $k_2 = Ae^{-Ea/R.320}$ ... (ii) **(½ Mark)**

$\therefore$ Eq. (ii) $\div$ Eq. (i)

$$\dfrac{k_2}{k_1} = \dfrac{Ae^{-Ea/R.320}}{Ae^{-Ea/R.300}} = \dfrac{\dfrac{0.693}{10 \times 60}}{\dfrac{0.693}{30 \times 60}}$$

(½ Mark)

or $e^{\frac{Ea}{R}\left(\frac{1}{300} - \frac{1}{320}\right)} = 3$

or $\dfrac{Ea}{R} \times \dfrac{\cancel{20}}{300 \times \cancel{320}_{16}} = 2.303 \log 3$ **(½ Mark)**

or $Ea = 8.314 \times 4800 \times 2.303 \times 0.4771 \times 10^{-3}\ kJ$
$= 43.848\ kJ \approx 43.85\ kJ$ **(½ Mark)**

30. 19.5 g of $F-CH_2-COOH : n_1 = \dfrac{19.5}{78} = 0.25\ mol$

(½ Mark)

Molality of solution (m) $= \dfrac{0.25}{0.5} = 0.5\ (m)$

Depression of freezing point due to dissociation $= 1°$

$\therefore\ \Delta T_f = imK_f$

$\therefore\ i = \dfrac{1}{0.5 \times 1.86} = 1.075$ **(½ Mark)**

$F-CH_2-COOH \rightleftharpoons FCH_2COO^- + H^+$
$0.25\ mol$
$0.25(1-x)\ mol \quad 0.25x\ mol \quad 0.25x\ mol$

[Suppose x is the degree of dissociation]

$\therefore$ Total no. of particles
$= 0.25(1-x) + 0.25x + 0.25x$ **(½ Mark)**
$= 0.25 + 0.25x$

$i = \dfrac{\text{Total no. of moles of particles after dissociation}}{\text{Total no. of moles of particles before dissociation}}$ **(½ Mark)**

$\therefore\ i = \dfrac{0.25(1+x)}{0.25} = 1.075$ **(½ Mark)**

or $1 + x = 1.075$

or $x = 1.075 - 1 = 0.075$

$\therefore$ Degree of dissociation of $F-CH_2-COOH = 0.075$.

(½ Mark)

SECTION - D

31. (a) Aldehyde + Alcohol (excess) $\xrightarrow[\text{HCl}]{\text{Dry}}$ Acetal

$$R-CHO \xrightleftharpoons{R'OH_2HCl\ gas} \left[R-C \begin{matrix} \diagup OR' \\ \diagdown OH \end{matrix} \right]$$

Hemiacetal

$$\xrightleftharpoons[H^+]{R'OH} R-C \begin{matrix} \diagup OR' \\ \diagdown OR' \end{matrix}$$ **(1 Mark)**

Acetal

(b) Acidity of a substance is judged by the stability of its conjugate base.

$$R-COOH \longrightarrow R-C \begin{matrix} \diagup\!\!\!= O \\ \diagdown O^- \end{matrix} + H^+ ;$$

Conjugate base

$$R-C \begin{matrix} \diagup\!\!\!= O \\ \diagdown O^- \end{matrix} \longleftrightarrow R-C \begin{matrix} \diagup O^- \\ \diagdown\!\!\!= O \end{matrix}$$

Two equivalent cannonical structures of conjugate base

Further, in these two cannonical structures, the negative charge is symmetrically distributed over the more electronegative atom 'O'.

Therefore, carboxylic acids are the most acidic organic compound among the other organic substances. **(1 Mark)**

(c) **(i)** $CH_3CHO,\ (CH_3)_3C-\underset{\underset{O}{\|}}{C}-CH_3,\ CH_3-\underset{\underset{O}{\|}}{C}-CH_3$

    (I)   (II)   (III)

Increasing order of reactivity toward CH_3MgBr

(II) < (III) < (I)

+I effect of alkyl group(s) reduces the electrophilicity of carbonyl carbon. **(1 Mark)**

(ii) The mild oxidizing agents, e.g. Tollen's reagent, Fehling's reagent can easily oxidize aldehydes but not ketones.

$$R-CHO + 2\left[Ag(NH_3)_2\right]^+ + 3OH^- \longrightarrow$$
(Freshly prepared ammoniacal silver nitrate solution)

$$RCOO^- + 2Ag + 4NH_3 + 2H_2O$$

$$R-\underset{\underset{O}{\|}}{C}-R + \left[Ag(NH_3)_2\right]^+ \xrightarrow{OH^-}$$

no reaction **(1 Mark)**

OR

(c) **(i)**

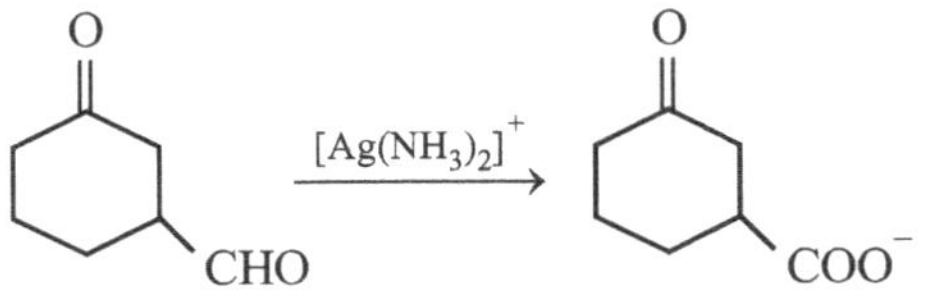

$$\text{(cyclohexanone with CHO)} \xrightarrow{[Ag(NH_3)_2]^+} \text{(cyclohexanone with COO}^-)$$

(keto group remains unaffected with mild oxidizing agent)

(1 Mark)

(ii)

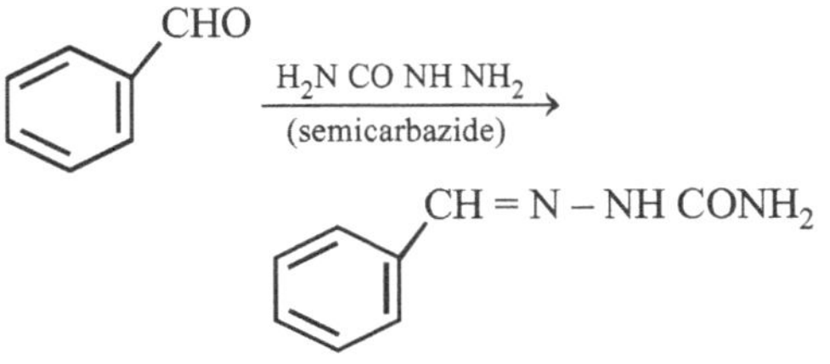

$$\text{(benzaldehyde, CHO)} \xrightarrow[\text{(semicarbazide)}]{H_2N\,CO\,NH\,NH_2} \text{(CH}=N-NH\,CONH_2\text{)}$$

semicarbazone.

(1 Mark)

32. **(a)** Pentacetate of glucose does not react with hydroxylamine (NH_2OH). This indicates the absence of aldehyde (–CHO) group.   **(1 Mark)**

(b) Vitamin C is a water soluble vitamin. That is why it cannot be stored in body but excreted in urine.

(1 Mark)

(c) **(i)** Peptide linkage is nothing but the amide linkage which is formed between – COOH group and – NH_2 group of two same or different amino acid molecules. This results to the elimination of a water molecule and formation of a peptide bond – CO – NH – .

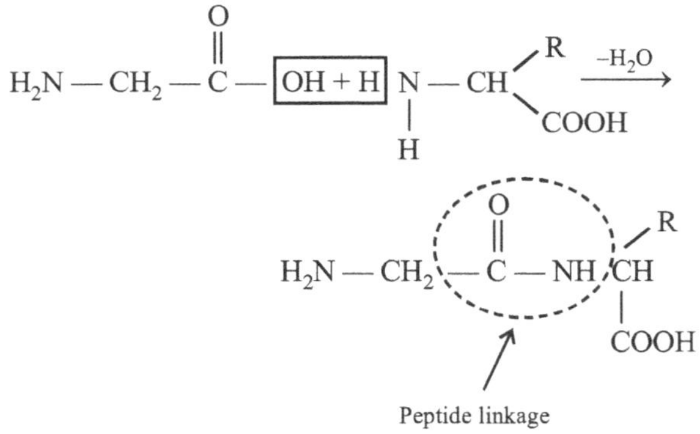

$$H_2N-CH_2-\overset{\overset{O}{\|}}{C}-\boxed{OH+H}\underset{H}{N}-CH\overset{R}{\underset{COOH}{}} \xrightarrow{-H_2O}$$

$$H_2N-CH_2-\overset{\overset{O}{\|}}{C}-NH\,CH\underset{COOH}{\overset{R}{}}$$

Peptide linkage

(1 Mark)

(ii) Denaturation: When a protein, in its native form, is subjected to a physical or chemical change like change in temperature, or pH, the native conformation of the molecule is disrupted as the secondary and tertiary linkages get destroyed but primary linkage remains intact. This phenomenon is known as denaturation of protein.   **(1 Mark)**

OR

(c) **(i)** Anomers: Carbohydrates which differ in configuration at the glycosidic carbon (i.e., C_1 in aldoses and C_2 in ketoses) are called anomers. e.g. α-D-Glucose and β-D-Glucose are anomers.

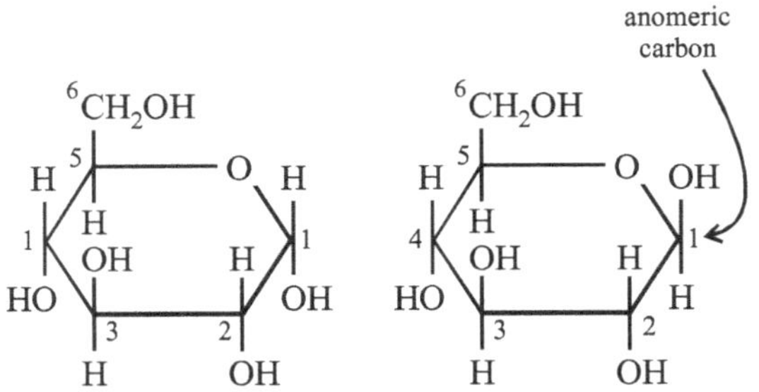

α-D-Glucose   β-D-Glucose

(1 Mark)

(ii) Glycosidic Linkage:

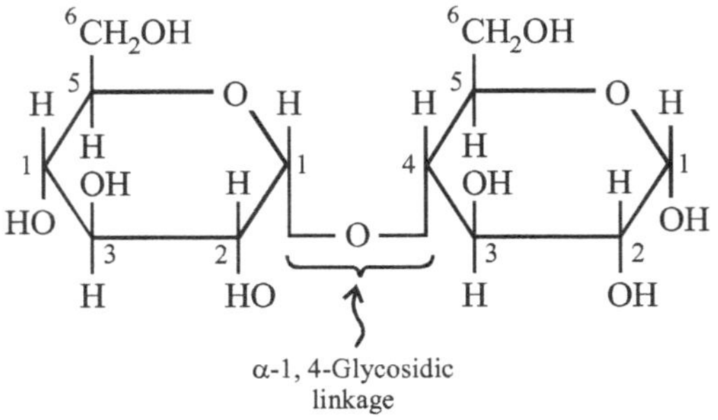

α-1, 4-Glycosidic linkage

The two monosaccharides are joined together by an oxide linkage formed by the loss of a water molecule. Such a linkage between two monosaccharide units through oxygen atom is called glycosidic linkage.   **(1 Mark)**

SECTION - E

33. **(a)** **(i)**

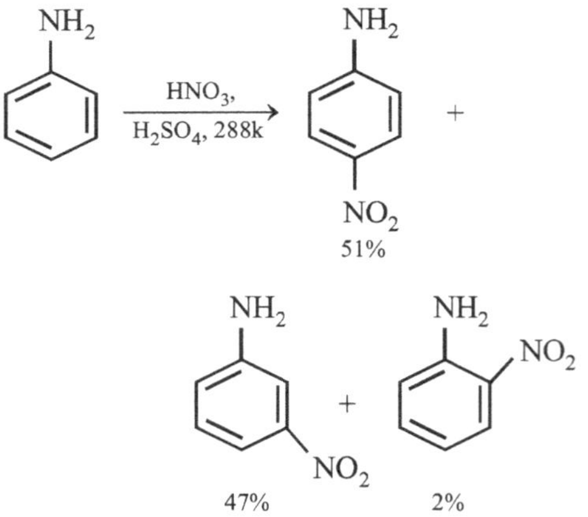

$$\text{(aniline, }NH_2\text{)} \xrightarrow[H_2SO_4,\,288k]{HNO_3,} \text{(p-nitroaniline, }NO_2\text{)} \; 51\% \; +$$

$$\text{(m-nitroaniline) } 47\% \; + \; \text{(o-nitroaniline) } 2\%$$

In a strong acidic medium, aniline gets protonated to form anilinium ion $\left(\text{C}_6\text{H}_5-\overset{+}{N}H_3\right)$ which is meta directing.   **(1 Mark)**

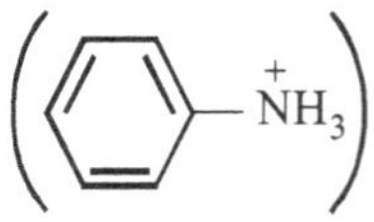

(ii) In aqueous solution $(CH_3)_3N$ is less basic than $(CH_3)_2NH$ due to the difficulty in solvation of tertiary amine group than secondary amine after protonation. Therefore, the instability of conjugate acids of t-amines leads to the less basicity.

So, $(CH_3)_2NH$ is more basic than $(CH_3)_3N$.

(1 Mark)

(iii) $R\!-\!X + \overset{\cdot\cdot}{N}H_3 \longrightarrow R\overset{+}{N}H_3X^- \longrightarrow RNH_2$ (1° amine)

Primary amine or 1° amine obtained by ammonolysis of alkyl halide further reacts as nucleophile to react with alkyl halide and leads to the formation of secondary and tertiary amines and finally, quaternary amines.

$$R\!-\!NH_2 \xrightarrow{RX} R_2NH \xrightarrow{RX} R_3N \xrightarrow{RX} R_4\overset{+}{N}X^-$$

(1 Mark)

(II) (i) Carbylamine Test or Isocyanide Test:
This reaction is used for primary amine test.

$$R\!-\!NH_2 + CHCl_3 + 3KOH \xrightarrow{\Delta} RNC + 3KCl + 3H_2O \quad \textbf{(1 Mark)}$$

(ii) Gabriel Phthalimide Synthesis:

N-alkylphthalimide $R\!-\!NH_2$ (1°-amine)

(1 Mark)

 **Note**

Aromatic primary amines cannot be prepared by this method.

OR

(b) (I) (i)

(1½ Marks)

(ii)

(1½ Marks)

(II) Aniline acts as Lewis base and forms salt with Lewis acid $(AlCl_3)$ used in Friedel Craft reaction. **(1 Mark)**

(III)

C_2H_5OH	$C_2H_5NH_2$	$(C_2H_5)_3N$
(I)	(II)	(III)
78.37°C	16 – 20°C	88.6 – 89.8°C

Boiling pt. $\propto$ molecular wt.; $\propto$ H-bonded substance

$\therefore$ order = (II) < (I) < (III)   **(1 Mark)**

34. (a) $HCOOH \rightleftharpoons HCOO^- + H^+$

$K = 8 \times 10^{-5}\,S\,cm^{-1}$ for concentration $= 2 \times 10^{-3}\,M$

$\therefore$ Molar conductivity $(\Lambda_m) = \dfrac{K}{C} = \dfrac{8 \times 10^{-5}}{2 \times 10^{-3}}$ **(1 Mark)**

$$\begin{aligned}
&= 4 \times 10^{-2}\,S\,M^{-1}\,cm^{-1}\\
&= 4 \times 10^{-2}\,S\,mol^{-1}\,L\,cm^{-1}\\
&= 4 \times 10^{-2} \times 10^{3}\,S\,mol^{-1}\,cm^{2}\\
&= 40\,S\,cm^{2}\,mol^{-1} \quad \textbf{(½ Mark)}
\end{aligned}$$

$\therefore \alpha = \dfrac{\Lambda_m}{\Lambda_m^0} = \dfrac{40}{404} \approx 0.099$ **(1 Mark)**

Degree of dissociation $= 0.099$ **(½ Mark)**

(b) $Ni\,(s) + 2Ag^+\,(aq) \rightleftharpoons Ni^{2+}\,(aq) + 2Ag\,(s)$

Anodic reaction: $Ni \longrightarrow Ni^{2+} + 2e$

Cathodic reaction: $2Ag^+ + 2e \longrightarrow 2Ag$ **(½ Mark)**

$$\begin{aligned}
\Delta_r G^0 &= -nFE^0_{cell}\\
&= -2 \times 96500 \times 1.05\,J\,mol^{-1}\\
&= -202{,}650\,J\,mol^{-1}\\
&= -202.65\,kJ\,mol^{-1} \quad \textbf{(½ Mark)}
\end{aligned}$$

$$E^0_{cell} = E^0_{Ni/Ni^{2+}} + E^0_{Ag^+/Ag}$$

$$= (0.25 + 0.80)\,V$$
$$= 1.05\,V \quad \textbf{(½ Mark)}$$

$\therefore \quad \Delta_r G^0 = -RT \ln K_C = -202.65$

$$\text{or,} \quad \log K_C = \frac{202.65 \times 10^3}{2.303 \times 8.314 \times 298} = 35.52$$

$\Delta_r G^0 = -202.65 \, \text{kJ mol}^{-1}$

$\log K_C = 35.52$ **(½ Mark)**

35. (a) (I) (i) The third ionization energy of Mn is very large compare to Cr. The 3rd ionization of Mn corresponds to Mn^{2+} (d^5) $\longrightarrow$ Mn^{3+} (d^4) which implies the stability of d^5 (half - filled) system, hence, more positive Mn^{3+}/Mn^{2+} reduction potential. **(1 Mark)**

(ii) Sc (21) $\longrightarrow 3d^1 4s^2$; $Sc^{3+} \longrightarrow 3d^0 \, 4s^0$

Ti (22) $\longrightarrow 3d^2 4s^2$; $Ti^{3+} \longrightarrow 3d^1 \, 4s^0$

Ti^{3+} shows the d-d transition in its aqueous complex, $[Ti(H_2O)_6]^{3+}$ and this is responsible for colour of the aqueous solution. **(1 Mark)**

(iii) Actinoids show in general (+3) oxidation state. The elements, in the first half of the series frequently exhibit higher oxidation states because they have 5f, 6d, 7s orbitals of comparable energies. **(1 Mark)**

(II) $KMnO_4$ is prepared by fusion of MnO_2 with an alkali metal hydroxide and an oxidizing agent like KNO_3.

$$2MnO_2 + 4KOH + O_2 \longrightarrow 2K_2MnO_4 + 2H_2O$$
$$\text{(dark green)}$$
$$3K_2MnO_4^- + 4H^+ \longrightarrow 2KMnO_4 + MnO_2 + 2H_2O$$

(1 Mark)

OR

(b) (I) (i) Alloys are solid solutions. The transition elements have minimal difference in their atomic sizes. So, the lattice points are replacable by atoms of different elements in solid states. **(1 Mark)**

(ii) Ce^{4+} ($4f^0$) has a tendency to form Ce^{3+} ($4f^1$).

$$\left(E^0_{Ce^{4+}/Ce^{3+}} = +1.74 \, V \right)$$

It has very high positive standard electrode potential which favours the formation of Ce^{3+}. However, $Ce^{4+} \longrightarrow Ce^{3+}$ conversion is slow enough to use as oxidizing agent in analytical chemistry. **(1 Mark)**

[**Note:** $4f^0 \to$ the empty orbital gets extra stability like half-filled and full filled subshells]

(b) (II) Similarities:

(i) Both series of elements experience contraction in atomic sizes from left to right.

(ii) The general oxidation state shown by these elements (+3). **(1 Mark)**

Differences:

(i) Most of the actinoids are radioactiars in comparison to lanthanoids.

(ii) Actinoids are highly reactive metals why they are finely divided.

(iii) Magnetic properties of actinoids are more complex than lanthanoids. **(1 Mark)**

(b) (III) 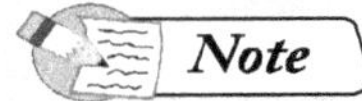 $Cr_2^{+6} O_7^{2-} + 2OH^- \longrightarrow 2Cr^{+6} O_9^{2-} + H_2O$
(dichromate) (chromate)

This reaction is dependent on pH. **(1 Mark)**

Note

$$\begin{bmatrix} & O & \\ & \| & \\ & Cr & \\ O & | & O \\ & O & \end{bmatrix}^{2-} : \text{Tetrahedral ;}$$

Chromate

$$: \text{Two tetrahedral}$$

Dichromate

Delhi *2023*

CBSE Board Solved Paper

Time Allowed : 3 Hours   *Maximum Marks : 70*

General Instructions:

(i)   This Question Paper contains **35** questions. All questions are compulsory.

(ii)   Question Paper is divided into **FIVE** sections. Section **A, B, C, D** and **E**.

(iii)   In section A – question number **1** to **18** are Multiple Choice (MCQ) type questions carrying **1** mark each.

(iv)   In section B – question number **19** to **25** are Very Short Answer (VSA) type questions carrying **2** marks each.

(v)   In section C – question number **26** to **30** are short Answer (SA) type questions carrying **3** marks each.

(vi)   In section D – question number **31 & 32** are case based questions carrying **4** marks each.

(vii)   In section E – question number **33** to **35** are Long Answer (LA) questions carrying **5** marks each.

(viii)   There is no overall choice. However, an internal choice has been provided in 2 questions in Section **B**, 2 questions in Section **C**, 2 questions in Section **D** and 2 questions in Section **E**.

(ix)   Use of calculator is NOT allowed.

SECTION - A

1. Which one of the following has lowest pK_a value?   1

    (a) CH_3-COOH (b) O_2N-CH_2-COOH

    (c) $Cl-CH_2-COOH$ (d) $HCOOH$

2. Which of the following cell was used in Apollo space programme?   1

    (a)   Mercury cell   (b)   Daniel cell

    (c) H_2-O_2 Fuel cell   (d)   Dry cell

3. Consider the following standard electrode potential values: 1

$$Fe^{3+}_{(aq)} + e^- \rightarrow Fe^{2+}_{(aq)} \quad E° = +0.77\,V$$
$$MnO_4^-{}_{(aq)} + 8H^+ + 5e^- \rightarrow Mn^{2+}_{(aq)} + 4H_2O_{(l)} \quad E° = +1.51\,V$$

What is the cell potential for the redox reaction?

    (a) $-2.28\,V$ (b) $-0.74\,V$

    (c) $+0.74\,V$ (d) $+2.28\,V$

4. The following experimental rate data were obtained for a reaction carried out at 25°C: 1

$$A_{(g)} + B_{(g)} \rightarrow C_{(g)} + D_{(g)}$$

Initial $[A_{(g)}]$/ mol / dm^{-3}	Initial $[B_{(g)}]$/ mol / dm^{-3}	Initial rate / mol / dm^{-3}g^{-1}
3.0×10^{-2}	2.0×10^{-2}	1.89×10^{-4}
3.0×10^{-2}	4.0×10^{-2}	1.89×10^{-4}
6.0×10^{-2}	4.0×10^{-2}	7.56×10^{-4}

What are the orders with respect to $A_{(g)}$ and $B_{(g)}$?

	Order with respect to $A_{(g)}$	Order with respect to $B_{(g)}$
(a)	Zero	Second
(b)	First	Zero
(c)	Second	Zero
(d)	Second	First

5. The magnetic moment of $[NiCl_4]^{2-}$.   1

    (a)   1.82 BM   (b)   2.82 BM

    (c)   4.42 BM   (d)   5.46 BM

(Atomic number : Ni = 28)

6. Which of the following ions has the electronic configuration $3d^6$? (Atomic number : Mn = 25, Co = 27, Ni = 28)   1

    (a) Ni^{3+} (b) Co^{3+}

    (c) Mn^{2+} (d) Mn^{3+}

7. Which of the following aqueous solution will have highest boiling point?   1

    (a)   1.0 M KCl   (b)   1.0 M K_2SO_4

    (c)   2.0 M KCl   (d)   2.0 M K_2SO_4

8. A voltaic cell is made by connecting two half cells represented by half equations below: 1

$$Sn^{2+}_{(aq)} + 2e^- \rightarrow Sn_{(a)} \quad E° = -0.14V$$

$$Fe^{3+}_{(aq)} + e^- \rightarrow Fe^{2+}_{(aq)} \quad E° = +0.77V$$

Which statement is correct about this voltaic cell?

    (a) Fe^{2+} is oxidised and the voltage of the cell is -0.91 V

    (b)   Sn is oxidised and the voltage of the cell is 0.91 V

    (c) Fe^{2+} is oxidised and the voltage of the cell is 0.91 V

    (d)   Sn is oxidised and the voltage of the cell is 0.63 V.

9. Amides can be converted into amines by the reaction named **1**

(a) Hoffmann degradation
(b) Ammonolysis
(c) Carbylamine
(d) Diazotisation

10. Which of the following statements is not true about glucose? **1**

(a) It is an aldohexose
(b) On heating with HI it forms n-hexane
(c) It is present in pyranose form
(d) It gives 2, 4 DNP test

11. Which of the following alcohols will not undergo oxidation? **1**

(a) Butanol   (b) Butan-2-ol
(c) 2-Methylbutan-2-ol   (d) 3-Methylbutan-2-ol

12. Four half reactions I to IV are shown below: **1**

I. $2Cl^- \rightarrow Cl_2 + 2e^-$
II. $4OH^- \rightarrow O_2 + 2H_2O + 2e^-$
III. $Na^+ + e^- \rightarrow Na$
IV. $2H^+ + 2e^- \rightarrow H_2$

Which two of these reactions are most likely to occur when concentrated brine is electrolysed?

(a) I and III   (b) I and IV
(c) II and III   (d) II and IV

13. Which property of transition metals enables them to behave as catalysts? **1**

(a) High melting point
(b) High ionisation enthalpy
(c) Alloy formation
(d) Variable oxidation states

14. Which of the following would not be a good choice for reducing nitrobenzene to aniline? **1**

(a) $LiAlH_4$ (b) H_2/Ni
(c) Fe and HCl   (d) Sn and HCl

For Questions number 15-18, two statements are given - one labelled as Assertion (A) and the other labelled as Reason (R). Select the correct answer to these questions from the codes (a), (b), (c) and (d) as given below:

(a) Both Assertion (A) and Reason (R) are true and Reason (R) is the correct explanation of the Assertion (A).
(b) Both Assertion (A) and Reason (R) are true, but Reason (R) is not the correct explanation of the Assertion (A).
(c) Assertion (A) is true, but Reason (R) is false.
(d) Assertion (A) is false, but Reason (R) is true.

15. Assertion (A) : Vitamin C cannot be stored in our body.
Reason (R) : Vitamin C is fat soluble and is excreted from the body in urine. **1**

16. Assertion (A) : The half life of a reaction is the time in which the concentration of the reactant is reduced to one half of its initial concentration.
Reason (R) : In first order kinetics when concentration of reactant is doubled, its half life is doubled. **1**

17. Assertion (A) : Bromination of benzoic acid gives m-bromobenzoic acid.
Reason (R) : Carboxyl group increases the electron density at the meta position. **1**

18. Assertion (A) : EDTA is a hexadentate ligand.
Reason (R) : EDTA has 2 nitrogen and 4 oxygen donor atoms. **1**

SECTION - B

19. (a) Which of the following species cannot act as a ligand? Give reason.   **2 × 1 = 2**

OH^-, NH_4^+, CH_3NH_2, H_2O

(b) The complex $[Co(NH_3)_5(NO_2)]Cl_2$ is red in colour. Give IUPAC name of its linkage isomer.

20. For the pair phenol and cyclohexanol, answer the following: **2 × 1 = 2**

(a) Why is phenol more acidic than cyclohexanol?
(b) Give one chemical test to distinguish between the two.

21. (a) (i) Draw the zwitter ion structure for sulphanilic acid
(ii) How can the activating effect of $-NH_2$ group in aniline be controlled? **2 × 1 = 2**

OR

(b) (i) Complete the reaction with the main product formed: **2 × 1 = 2**

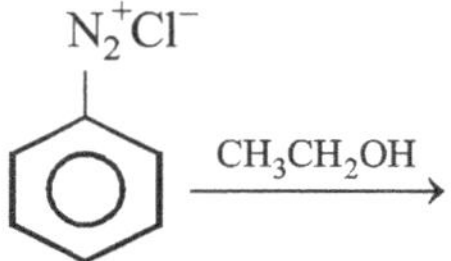

(ii) Convert Bromoethane to Propanamine.

22. Write equations for the following: **2 × 1 = 2**
(a) Oxidation of chloroform by air and light
(b) Reaction of chlorobenzene with CH_3Cl/anhyd. $AlCl_3$.

23. What happens to the rate constant k and activation energy E_a as the temperature of a chemical reaction is increased? Justify. **2**

24. (a) (i) What should be the signs (positive/negative) for E°_{Cell} and ΔG° for a spontaneous redox reaction occurring under standard conditions? **2 × 1 = 2**
(ii) State Faraday's first law of electrolysis.

OR

(b) Calculate the emf of the following cell at 298 K:
$Fe_{(s)}| Fe^{2+} (0.01M)\|H^+_{(1M)}|H_{2(g)}$ (1 bar), $Pt_{(s)}$
Given $E^{\circ}_{Cell} = 0.44$ V.   **2**

25. Give the reaction of glucose with acetic anhydride. Presence of which group is confirmed by this reaction?   **2**

SECTION - C

26. (a) (i) Why is the C–O bond length in phenols less than that in methanol? $3 \times 1 = 3$

(ii) Arrange the following in order of increasing boiling point:

Ethoxyethane, Butanal, Butanol, n-butane

(iii) How can phenol be prepared from anisole? Give reaction.

OR

(b) (i) Give mechanism of the following reaction: $2 + 1 = 3$

$$CH_3CH_2OH \xrightarrow[413K]{H_2SO_4} CH_3CH_2 - O - CH_2CH_3 + H_2O$$

(ii) Illustrate hydroboration - oxidation reaction with an example.

27. (a) On the basis of crystal field theory write the electronic configuration for d^5 ion with a weak ligand for which $\Delta_0 < P$. $1 + 2 = 3$

(b) Explain $[Fe(CN)_6]^{3-}$ is an inner orbital complex whereas $[FeF_6]^{3-}$ is an outer orbital complex.

[Atomic number : Fe = 26]

28. Give reasons for any 3 of the following observations: $3 \times 1 = 3$

(a) Penta-acetate of glucose does not react with hydroxylamine.

(b) Amino acids behave like salts.

(c) Water soluble vitamins must be taken regularly in diet.

(d) The two strands in DNA are complimentary to each other.

29. (a) For the reaction

$$2N_2O_{5(g)} \rightarrow 4NO_{2(g)} + O_{2(g)} \text{at } 318 \text{ K} \quad 1 + 2 = 3$$

calculate the rate of reaction if rate of disappearance of $N_2O_{5(g)}$ is $1.4 \times 10^{-3} \text{ ms}^{-1}$.

(b) For a first order reaction derive the relationship $t_{99\%} = 2t_{90\%}$.

30. (a) Illustrate Sandmeyer's reaction with an equation. $1 + 2 = 3$

(b) Explain, why $(CH_3)_2NH$ is more basic than $(CH_3)_3N$ in aqueous solution.

SECTION - D

The following questions are case based questions. Read the passage carefully and answer the questions that follow:

31. Rahul set-up an experiment to find resistance of aqueous KCl solution for different concentration at 298 K using a conductivity cell connected to a Wheatstone bridge. He fed the Wheatstone bridge with a.c. power in the audio frequency range 550 to 5000 cycles per second. Once the resistance was calculated from null point he also calculated the conductivity K and molar conductivity Λ_m and recorded his readings in tabular form.

S.No	Conc. (M)	k S cm^{-1}	Λ_m S cm^2 mol^{-1}
1.	1.00	111.3×10^{-3}	111.3
2.	0.10	12.9×10^{-3}	129.0
3.	0.01	1.41×10^{-3}	141.0

Answer the following questions :

(a) Why does conductivity decrease with dilution ?   **1**

(b) If Λ_m^0 of KCl is 150.0 S cm^2 mol^{-1}, calculate the degree of dissociation of 0.01 M KCl.   **1**

(c) If Rahul had used HCl instead to KCl then would you expect the Λ_m values to be more or less than those per KCl for a given concentration. Justify. $2 \times 1 = 2$

OR

(c) Amit a classmate of Rahul repeated the same experiment with CH_3COOH solution instead of KCl solution. Give one point that would be similar and one that would be different in his observations as compared to Rahul. $2 \times 1 = 2$

32. **Nucleophilic Substitution**

Nucleophilic Substitution reaction of haloalkane can be conducted according to both S_N1 and S_N2 mechanisms. S_N1 is a two step reaction while S_N2 is a single step reaction. For any haloalkane which mechanism is followed depends on factors such as structure of haloalkane, properties of leaving group, nucleophilic reagent and solvent.

Influences of solvent polarity : In S_N1 reaction the polarity of the system increases from the reactant to the transition state, because a polar solvent has a greater effect on the transition state than the reactant, thereby reducing activation energy and accelerating the reaction, In S_N2 reaction, the polarity of the system generally does not change from the reactant to the transition state and only charge dispersion occurs. At this time, polar solvent has a great stabilizing effect on Nu than the transition state, thereby increasing activation energy and slow down the reaction rate. For example, the decomposition rate (S_N1) of tertiary chlorobutane at 25°C in water (dielectric constant 79) is 300000 times faster than in ethanol (dielectric constant 24).

The reaction rate (S_N2) of 2-Bromopropane and NaOH in ethanol containing 40% water is twice slower than in absolute ethanol. Hence the level of solvent polarity has influence on both S_N1 and S_N2 reaction, but with different results. Generally speaking weak polar solvent is favourable for S_N2 reaction, while strong polar solvent is favourable for S_N1. Generally speaking the substitution reaction of tertiary haloalkane is based on S_N1 mechanism in solvents with a strong polarity (for example ethanol containing water).

Answer the following questions:

(a) Why racemisation occurs in S_N1 **1**

(b) Why is ethanol less polar than water ?   **1**

(c) Which one of the following in each pair is more reactive towards S_N2 reaction?

    (i) $CH_3 - CH_2 - I$ or $CH_3CH_2 - Cl$

    (ii) ⬡—Cl or ⬡—$CH_2 - Cl$ **2 × 1 = 2**

OR

(c) Arrange the following in the increasing order of their reactivity towards S_N1 reactions:

    (i)   2-Bromo-2-methylbutane, 1-Bromopentane, 2-Bromopentane

    (ii)   1-Bromo-3-methylbutane, 2-Bromo-2-methyl-butane, 2-Bromo-3-methylbutane   **2 × 1 = 2**

SECTION - E

33. (a) (i)   Write the reaction involved in Cannizaro's reaction   **1 + 1 + 3 = 5**

      (ii)   Why are the boiling point of aldehydes and ketones lower than that of corresponding carboxylic acids?

      (iii)   An organic compound 'A' with molecular formula $C_5H_8O_2$ is reduced to n-pentane with hydrazine followed by heating with NaOH and Glycol. 'A' forms a dioxime with hydroxylamine and gives a positive Iodoform and Tollen's test. Identify 'A' and give its reaction for Iodoform and Tollen's test.

O R

(b) (i)   Give a chemical test to distinguish between ethanal and ethanoic acid.   **1 + 1 + 3 = 5**

      (ii)   Why is the α-hydrogens of aldehydes and ketones are acidic in nature?

      (iii)   An organic compound 'A' with molecular formula $C_4H_8O_2$ undergoes acid hydrolysis to form two compounds 'B' and 'C'. Oxidation of 'C' with acidified potassium permanganate also produces 'B'. Sodium salt of 'B' on heating with soda lime gives methane.

(1)   Identify 'A', 'B' and 'C'.

(2)   Out of 'B' and 'C', which will have higher boiling point? Give reason.

34. (a) (i)   Why is boiling point of 1M NaCl solution more than that of 1M glucose solution?   **1 + 2 + 2 = 5**

      (ii)   A non-volatile solute 'X' (molar mass = 50 g mol^{-1}) when dissolved in 78g of benzene reduced its vapour pressure to 90%. Calculate the mass of X dissolved in the solution.

      (iii)   Calculate the boiling point elevation for a solution prepared by adding 10g of $MgCl_2$ to 200g of water assuming $MgCl_2$ is completely dissociated.
(K_b for Water = 0.512 K kg mol^{-1}. Molar mass $MgCl_2$ = 95g mol^{-1})

OR

(b) (i)   Why is the value of Van't Hoff factor for ethanoic acid in benzene close to 0.5?   **1 + 2 + 2 = 5**

      (ii)   Determine the osmotic pressure of a solution prepared by dissolving 2.32×10^{-2}g of K_2SO_4 in 2L of solution at 25 °C, assuming that K_2SO_4 is completely dissociated.
(R = 0.082 L atm K^{-1} mol^{-1}, Molar mass K_2SO_4 = 174g mol^{-1})

      (iii)   When 25.6g of Sulphur was dissolved in 1000g of benzene, the freezing point lowered by 0.512 K. Calculate the formula of Sulphur (S_x).
(K_f for benzene = 5.12 K kg mol^{-1}. Atomic mass of Sulphur = 32g mol^{-1})

35. (a)   A transition element X has electronic configuration [Ar] $4s^2 3d^3$.   **1 + 1 + 3 = 5**
Predict its likely oxidation states.

(b)   Complete the reaction mentioning all the products formed:

$$2KMnO_4 \xrightarrow{\Delta}$$

(c)   Account for the following:

    (i)   In the 3d transition series, zinc has the lowest enthalpy of atomisation.

    (ii) Cu^+ ion is unstable in aqueous solution.

    (iii)   Actinoids show more number of oxidation states than lanthanoids.

Solutions

SECTION - A

1. **(b)** $pK_a = -\log K_a$ so the species with the highest K_a value will have the lowest pK_a value.

Highest K_a value indicates the **strongest** acid among the given options.

The presence of an electron - with drawing group increases the acidic strength of the species as it stabilizes its conjugate base. The order of acidic strength effect is $I < Br < Cl < F < NO_2$.

Thus, $NO_2 - CH_2 - COOH$ is the strongest acid and therefore its K_a value is highest or pK_a is lowest.

(1 Mark)

Thus, option **(b)** is correct.

2. **(c)** The Apollo space programme had used a fuel cell that would convert chemical energy into electrical energy and it was an $H_2 - O_2$ fuel cell.

Overall reaction : $2H_2\,(g) + O_2\,(g) \longrightarrow 2H_2O\,(l)$

Cathode : $O_2\,(g) + 2H_2O\,(l) + 4e^- \longrightarrow 4OH^-\,(aq)$

Anode : $2H_2\,(g) + 4OH^-\,(aq) \longrightarrow 4H_2O\,(l) + 4e^-$

Thus, option **(c)** is correct. **(1 Mark)**

3. **(c)** Cell potential (standard) of a cell reaction:

$$E^0_{cell} = E^0_{cathode} - E^0_{anode} = E^0_{Right} - E^0_{Left}$$

Now, among the two reactions, the one with the higher value of the standard electrode potential will act as the cathode and vice-versa.

Thus, the second reaction (reduction of manganate ion) will be the reduction half-cell reaction and therefore the E^0_{cell} will be:

$$E^0_{cell} = E^0_{MnO_4^-/Mn^{2+}} - E^0_{Fe^{3+}/Fe^{2+}}$$

$$= (+1.51\,V) - (+0.77\,V)$$

$$= +0.74$$

Therefore, option (c) is correct. **(1 Mark)**

4. **(c)** From the given data, it is apparent that when the concentration of $A(g)$ is kept constant and that of $B(g)$ is doubled, the rate of the reaction **does not change**. Thus, the reaction is of **zero order** with respect to $B(g)$. When the concentration of $B(g)$ is kept constant and that of $A(g)$ is doubled, the rate of the reaction is **quadrupled**. Thus, the reaction is of **second order** with respect to $A(g)$.

Therefore, option **(c)** is correct. **(1 Mark)**

5. **(b)** Ni in $[NiCl_4]^{2-}$ exists as Ni^{2+} ion as there are four Cl^- ligands and the net charge on the complex is -2.

The configuration for Ni^{2+} is $4s^0\,3d^8$ or just $3d^8$. The weak Cl^- ligands are unable to pair up the electrons in

the 3d - subshell of Ni^{2+} and therefore its configuration will be $\boxed{\uparrow\downarrow}\ \boxed{\uparrow\downarrow}\ \boxed{\uparrow\downarrow}\ \boxed{\uparrow}\ \boxed{\uparrow}$ that has **two** unpaired electrons.

Thus, magnetic moment $(M_s) = \sqrt{n(n+2)}$ B.M.

$$= \sqrt{2(2+2)}\ \text{B.M.}$$

$$= \sqrt{8}\ \text{B.M.} = \textbf{2.82 B.M.}$$

Therefore, option **(b)** is correct. **(1 Mark)**

6. **(b)** $Mn = 4s^2\,3d^5$, so $Mn^{2+} = 3d^5$ and $Mn^{3+} = 3d^4$

$CO = 4s^2\,3d^7$, so $CO^{3+} = \textbf{3d}^\textbf{6}$

$Ni = 4s^2\,3d^8$, so $Ni^{3+} = 3d^7$

Thus, option **(b)** is correct. **(1 Mark)**

7. **(d)** All the given species are strong electrolytes so they dissociate completely in the aqueous solution.

The species that gives the highest number of particles upon dissociation will have the highest boiling point.

$1.0\,M\ KCl = 1$ mole K^+ ions $+ 1$ mole Cl^- ions.

$2.0\,M\ KCl = 2$ moles K^+ ions $+ 2$ mole Cl^- ions.

$1.0\,M\ K_2SO_4 = 1 \times 2 = 2$ moles K^+ ions $+ 1$ mole SO_4^{2-} ions.

$2.0\,M\ K_2SO_4 = 2 \times 2 = 4$ moles K^+ ions $+ 2$ moles SO_4^{2-} ions.

Therefore, $2.0\,M\ K_2SO_4$ will give the highest number of particles and therefore its boiling point will be highest.

Therefore, option **(d)** is correct. **(1 Mark)**

8. **(b)** Among the two half-cell reactions, the half-cell reaction having a higher value of the standard electrode potential will be the reduction half-cell reaction and vice-versa.

Thus, cathode half-cell reaction is $Fe^{3+} + e^- \longrightarrow Fe^{2+}$ and the anode half-cell reaction is $Sn^{2+} + 2e^- \longrightarrow Sn$ which takes place is $Sn \longrightarrow Sn^{2+} + 2e^-$.

So, Sn is oxidized and Fe^{3+} is reduced.

$$E^0_{cell} = E^0_{cathode} - E^0_{anode} = E^0_{Fe^{3+}/Fe^{2+}} - E^0_{Sn^{2+}/Sn}$$

$$= (+0.77\,V) - (-0.14\,V)$$

$$= \textbf{+0.91 V}$$

Therefore, option **(b)** is correct. **(1 Mark)**

9. **(a)** Amides are converted into primary amines by the reaction called Hoffmann bromamide degradation reaction.

$$\underset{\text{Amide}}{R - \overset{\overset{\displaystyle O}{\|}}{C} - NH_2} + Br_2 + 4NaOH \longrightarrow \underset{1°\ \text{amine}}{R - NH_2} +$$

$$Na_2CO_3 + 2NaBr + 2H_2O$$

Therefore, option (a) is correct. **(1 Mark)**

Ammonolysis, carbylamine reaction and Diazotization are all reactions of amines and for their preparation from amides.

10. **(d)** The molecular formula of glucose is $C_6H_{12}O_6$ and it contains an aldehydic (–CHO) functional group.

Thus, it is an aldohexose.

On prolonged heating with HI, it forms n-Hexane suggesting a straight chain form.

It exists in a six-membered pyranose ring form.

Due to the cyclic structure, it does not give 2, 4–DNP test.

Therefore, option **(d)** is correct. **(1 Mark)**

11. **(c)** Tertiary alcohols do not undergo oxidation due to the absence of an α-hydrogen atom.

Among the given options, **2-Methyl butan-2-ol** is a tertiary alcohol that would not undergo oxidation.

$$H_3C - H_2C - \underset{\underset{CH_3}{|}}{\overset{\overset{CH_3}{|}}{C}} - OH$$

3° alcohol

Therefore, option **(c)** is correct. **(1 Mark)**

12. **(b)** Brine solution is an aqueous solution of NaCl.

Electrolysis of NaCl (aq.):

$$NaCl\,(aq.) \xrightarrow{\ H_2O\ } Na^+\,(aq.) + Cl^-\,(aq.)$$

Now, we have the following reactions occurring at cathode and anode:

Cathode:

$$Na^+ + e^- \longrightarrow Na\ (E^0 = -2.71\ V)$$

$$H^+ + e^- \longrightarrow \frac{1}{2}H_2\ (E^0 = 0.00\ V)$$

Thus, reduction of H^+ to H_2 is preferred due to higher E° value.

Anode:

$$Cl^- \longrightarrow \frac{1}{2}Cl_2 + e^-\ (E^0 = 1.36\ V)$$

$$2H_2O \longrightarrow O_2 + 4H^+ + 4e^-\ (E^0 = 1.23\ V)$$

Thus, oxidation of H_2O should be preferred but due to the over potential of O_2, oxidation of Cl^- is preferred. Therefore, reactions I and IV are preferred with brine solution and option **(b)** is correct. **(1 Mark)**

13. **(d)** Transition metals act as good catalysts due to their ability to exhibit variable oxidation states.

This property allows them to bond with and form different compounds and therefore participation in various chemical reactions.

Therefore, option **(d)** is correct. **(1 Mark)**

14. **(a)** Using $LiAlH_4$ for reduction of nitrobenzene to aniline is not a good choice because it converts nitrobenzene to diazobenzene. (Ph – N = N – Ph).

Therefore, option **(a)** is correct. **(1 Mark)**

15. **(c)** Vitamin C is a **water - soluble** vitamin that is released from our body through urine and therefore cannot be stored in our body.

Therefore, Assertion (A) is **true** but Reason (R) is **false.**

Therefore, option **(c)** is correct. **(1 Mark)**

16. **(c)** The half life of a reaction is defined as the time taken for the initial concentration of a reactant to be reduced to half of its value.

Thus, Assertion (A) is **true**.

For, a first order reaction, $t_{1/2} = \dfrac{0.693}{k}$ which shows that the half-life is independent of the concentration of the reactant.

Thus, Reason (R) is **false**.

Therefore, option **(c)** is correct. **(1 Mark)**

17. **(a)** Benzoic acid has a – COOH group on the benzene ring. Now, the – COOH is a **meta-directing** and **ring-deactivating** group due to its electron-withdrawing nature.

Thus, bromination of benzoic acid gives m-bromobenzoic acid and the ring is deactivated for electrophilic substitution due to decreased charge density.

The charge density is increased at the meta-position due to which meta-bromination happens.

Therefore, both, Assertion (A) and Reason (R) are **true** and Reason (R) correctly explains Assertion (A).

Therefore, option **(a)** is correct. **(1 Mark)**

18. **(a)** EDTA stands for Ethyline Diamine Tetra Acetate which is a **hexadentate ligand** indicating that it has **six** donor atoms.

The donor atoms are two N-atoms and four O-atoms.

$$HOOC-H_2C \diagdown \diagup CH_2-COOH$$
$$N-CH_2-CH_2-N$$
$$HOOC-H_2C \diagup \diagdown CH_2-COOH$$

Therefore, both, Assertion and Reason are **true** and Reason correctly explains the assertion.

Therefore, option **(a)** is correct. **(1 Mark)**

SECTION - B

19. **(a)** The species that does not have an atom with a lone pair (donor atom), cannot act as a ligand. Among the given choices, NH_4^+ is the species that cannot act as a ligand. **(1 Mark)**

(b) The linkage isomerism results in two complexes with the same molecular formula but different linkages of an ambidentate ligand to the central metal atom or ion.

In the given complex, $-NO_2^-$ is an ambidentate ligand that gives red $[CO(NH_3)_5\,(NO_2)]Cl_2$ complex and yellow $[Co(NH_3)_5\,(ONO)]Cl_2$ complex. **(½ Mark)**

The IUPAC name of $[CO(NH_3)_5\,(ONO)]Cl_2$ is:

Pentaamminenitrito-o-Cobalt (III) chloride. **(½ Mark)**

20. **(a)** Phenol is more acidic than cyclohexanol because the conjugate base of phenol, which is phenoxide ion, is much more stable than the conjugate base of cyclohexanol which is cyclohexoide ion due to resonance stabilization.   **(1 Mark)**

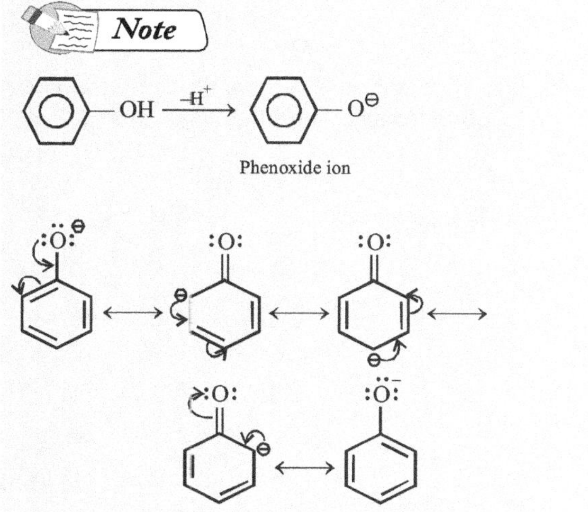

Note

$$\text{Ph–OH} \xrightarrow{-H^+} \text{Ph–O}^{\ominus}$$
Phenoxide ion

(b) Phenol being an aromatic alcohol, gives positive $FeCl_3$ test and gives violet solution while cyclohexanol gives negative $FeCl_3$ test.   **(1 Mark)**

21. **(a)** **(i)** The zwitter ion structure of an amino acid is a di-polar ion and has both, amino and carboxylic groups (acidic) ionized.

The ionized form of sulphanilic acid has the following structure:

$$SO_3^{\ominus}$$
                                (1 Mark)
$$\overset{\oplus}{N}H_3$$

(ii) The activating effect of $-NH_2$ group in aniline can be controlled by protecting it by acetylation.   **(1 Mark)**

$$\underset{NH_2}{\bigcirc} \xrightarrow[\text{Pyridine}]{(CH_3CO)_2O} \underset{NH-COCH_3}{\bigcirc} \xrightarrow[CH_3COOH]{Br_2}$$

$$\underset{\underset{Br}{NH-COCH_3}}{\bigcirc} \xrightarrow{H^+/OH^-} \underset{\underset{Br}{NH}}{\bigcirc}$$
(Major)

OR

(b) **(i)** The given reaction is an electrophilic substitution reaction that involves replacement of N_2^+ by H^+.

$$\overset{+}{N_2}Cl^- \xrightarrow{CH_3CH_2OH} \underset{\text{(Major)}}{\overset{H}{\bigcirc}} + N_2 + CH_3CHO + HCl$$
                                (1 Mark)

(ii) The conversion requires one extra carbon atom and the replacement of bromo group by amino group.

$$\underset{\text{Bromo ethane}}{CH_3CH_2-Br} \xrightarrow[\text{(aq.)}]{KCN} CH_3CH_2-CN \xrightarrow{LiAlH_4}$$

$$\underset{\text{Propanamine}}{CH_3CH_2-CH_2-NH_2}$$
                                (1 Mark)

22. **(a)** Oxidation of chloroform by air and light:

$$\underset{\text{Chloroform}}{2CHCl_3\ (l)} + O_2(g) \xrightarrow{h\nu} \underset{\text{Phosgene}}{2COCl_2(g)} + 2HCl\ (aq.)$$
                                (1 Mark)

(b) Electrophilic substitution of chlorobenzene with CH_3Cl in anhydrous $AlCl_3$:

$$\underset{Cl}{\bigcirc} \xrightarrow[AlCl_3]{CH_3Cl} \underset{\underset{\text{(Minor)}}{Cl}}{\bigcirc}CH_3 + \underset{\underset{\underset{\text{(Major)}}{CH_3}}{Cl}}{\bigcirc}$$
                                (1 Mark)

23. An increase in the temperature of a reaction mixture increases the thermal energy of the molecules that increases the kinetic energy of the molecules.

This leads to an increase in the number of collisions between the reactant molecules that increases the rate of the chemical reaction and therefore the **rate constant K**.

Since the thermal energy increases, the average energy possessed by the molecules increases and therefore the energy required to cross the energy barrier decreases.   **(1 Mark)**

Therefore, increase in the temperature decreases the activation Energy (E_a).   **(1 Mark)**

24. **(a)** **(i)** For a spontaneous reaction, the change in the standard Gibbs free energy is negative.

Thus, $\Delta G° < 0$ for a spontaneous reaction **(Negative)**

Since, $\Delta G° = -nFE°_{cell}$, $E°_{cell}$ should be **positive**.   **(1 Mark)**

(ii) **Faraday's First Law of Electrolysis:**

The amount of chemical reaction occurring at an electrode because of electrolysis, is directly proportional to the amount of current passed in the electrolytic solution.   **(1 Mark)**

OR

(b) From the cell representation:

Anode: $Fe\,(S) \longrightarrow Fe^{2+}\,(0.01\,M) + 2e^-$

Cathode: $2H^+\,(1\,M) + 2e^- \longrightarrow H_2\,(g)\,(1\,bar)$

$E^\circ_{cell} = +0.44\,V$

Thus, $E_{cell} = E^\circ_{cell} - \dfrac{0.059}{n}\log\dfrac{[Fe^{2+}]}{[H^+]^2}$ **(1 Mark)**

$$= (+0.44\,V) - \left[\dfrac{0.059}{2}\log\dfrac{(0.01\,M)}{1^2}\right]$$

$$= +0.44\,V - [0.0295 \times \log(0.01)]$$

$$= +0.44\,V - [0.0295 \times (-2)]$$

$$= 0.50\,V \qquad \textbf{(1 Mark)}$$

25. Glucose reacts with acetic anhydride and undergoes acetylation and gives pentaacetate.

$$\begin{array}{c} CHO \\ | \\ (CHOH)_4 \\ | \\ CH_2OH \end{array} \xrightarrow{\text{Acetic anhydride}} \begin{array}{c} CHO \quad\ O \\ | \qquad\ \parallel \\ (CH - O - C - CH_3)_4 \\ | \qquad\ O \\ | \qquad\ \parallel \\ CH_2 - O - C - CH_3 \end{array}$$

(1 Mark)

The formation of pentaacetate confirms the presence of five –OH groups.   **(1 Mark)**

SECTION - C

26. (a) (i) The C – O bond length in phenols is less than that in methanol because the carbon atom in phenol that is bonded to the oxygen atom is sp^2 - hybridized while that in methanol is sp^3 - hybridized.   **(1 Mark)**

The C–O bond in phenol has partial double bond character and therefore it is stronger and shorter.

(ii) n-butane has the lowest boiling point due to the weakest inter molecular forces (Van der Waals forces).

Butanol has the highest boiling point due to strongest inter molecular forces (Hydrogen - bonding) of attraction.

Among Ethoxyethane and butanal, butanal has a higher boiling point due to dipole-dipole interactions.   **(½ Mark)**

Thus, the increasing order of boiling point will be:

n-butane < ethoxy ethane < Butanal < Butanol

   (½ Mark)

(iii) Preparation of phenol from anisole:

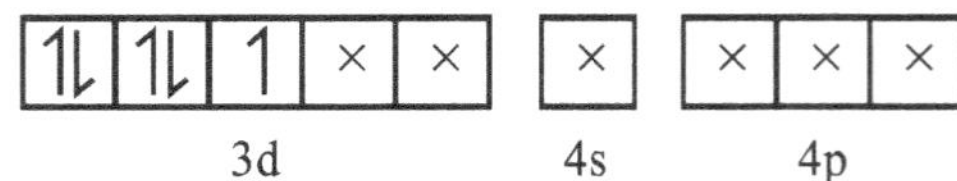

OR

(b) (i) The given reaction is the acid-catalysed nucleophilic substitution reaction (S_N2):

$$CH_3 - CH_2 - \overset{..}{\underset{..}{O}} - H + H^+ \longrightarrow CH_3 - CH_2 - \overset{..}{\underset{..}{O}}{}^+ - H$$

$$CH_3 - CH_2 - \overset{..}{\underset{..}{O}}H + CH_3 - CH_2 - \overset{+}{O} - H \longrightarrow$$

$$CH_3CH_2 - \overset{+}{\underset{H}{O}} - CH_2CH_3 + H_2O$$

(1 Mark)

$$CH_3CH_2 - \overset{+}{\underset{H}{O}} - CH_2CH_3 \longrightarrow$$

$$CH_3CH_2 - O - CH_2CH_3 + H^+$$

Ether

(1 Mark)

(ii) Hydroboration-oxidation:

$$CH_3 - CH = CH_2 + (H - BH_2)_2 \longrightarrow$$
$$(CH_3 - CH_2 - CH_2)_3 B$$

$$(CH_3 - CH_2 - CH_2)_3 B \xrightarrow[3H_2O_2,\ OH^-]{H_2O}$$

$$3CH_3 - CH_2 - CH_2 - OH + B(OH)_3 \text{ (1 Mark)}$$

27. (a) According to crystal field theory (CFT), when the ligands approach the central metal atom or ion, the five degenerate d-orbitals split into two different sets; e_g and t_{2g} according to the number of ligands present around the central atom/ion.

The e_g set has two orbitals and t_{2g} has three orbitals. For the d^5-configuration with a weak field ligand:

$$d^5 = e_g{}^2 t_{2g}{}^3 \quad \text{or} \quad t_{2g}{}^3 e_g{}^2 \qquad \textbf{(1 Mark)}$$

(b) $[Fe(CN)_6]^{3-}$ is an inner orbital complex because it has CN^- ligands that are strong field ligands that pair up the electrons in the Fe^{3+} ion and donate an electron pair in the inner d-orbital (3d-orbital).   **(1 Mark)**

1↿⇂	1↿⇂	1	×	×		×	×	×	×

     3d   4s   4p

$[FeF_6]^{3-}$ is an outer orbital complex because it has F^- ligands that are weak field ligands that are unable to pair the electrons in the Fe^{3+} ion and therefore donate their electron-pairs to the outer d-orbitals (4d).

   (1 Mark)

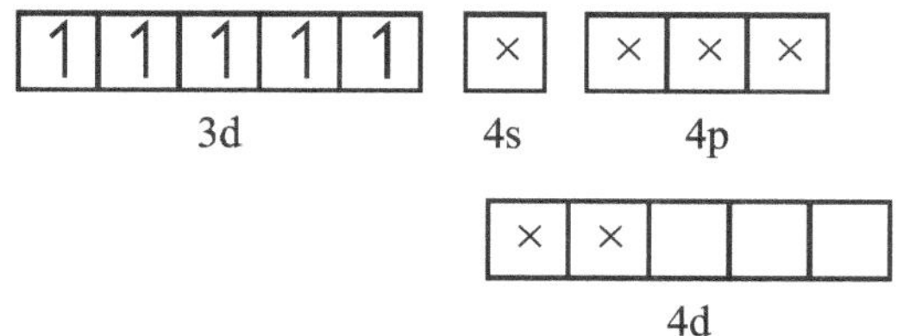

28. **(a)** Pentaacetate of glucose does not react with hydroxylamine because of the absence of a free – CHO group in the cyclic structure of glucose. **(1 Mark)**

The cyclic structure of glucose is :

$$CH_2OH$$

(b) Amino acids behave like salts because they have both, an acidic – COOH group and basic – NH_2 group due to which it forms a dipolar zwitter ion. **(1 Mark)**

$$H_3N - \overset{\overset{\displaystyle R}{|}}{\underset{\underset{\displaystyle H}{|}}{C}} - COOH \rightleftharpoons H_4\overset{+}{N} - \overset{\overset{\displaystyle R}{|}}{\underset{\underset{\displaystyle H}{|}}{C}} - COO^-$$

Zwitter-ion

(c) Water - soluble vitamins must be taken regularly in diet because they are excreted out of our body through urine.

These vitamins include vitamin B and C. **(1 Mark)**

(d) The two strands in DNA are complimentary to each other because the purines and pyrimidines of one strand bond to their counterparts in the second strand according to the rule A $\rightarrow$ T and G $\rightarrow$ C through Hydrogen bonds. **(1 Mark)**

29. **(a)** For the given reaction:

$$\text{Rate of reaction} = -\frac{1}{2}\frac{d[N_2O_5]}{dt} \qquad \textbf{(½ Mark)}$$

$$= -\frac{1}{2} \times (1.4 \times 10^{-3}\ Ms^{-1})$$

$$= -7.0 \times 10^{-4}\ Ms^{-1}$$

or $\qquad 7.0 \times 10^{-4}\ Ms^{-1}$ **(½ Mark)**

(b) For a first order reaction:

$$t = \frac{2.303}{k} \log \frac{a_0}{a} \qquad \textbf{(½ Mark)}$$

Now, $\qquad t_{99\%} \Rightarrow a = \dfrac{1}{100} a_0$

$$t_{90\%} \Rightarrow a = \frac{10}{100} a_0 = \frac{1}{10} a_0 \qquad \textbf{(½ Mark)}$$

Thus, $t_{99\%} = \dfrac{2.303}{k} \log \dfrac{a_0}{\dfrac{1}{100} a_0} = \dfrac{2.303}{k} \log 100$

$$= \frac{2.303}{k} \times 2$$

$$t_{90\%} = \frac{2.303}{k} \log \frac{a_0}{\frac{1}{10} a_0} = \frac{2.303}{k} \log 10 = \frac{2.303}{k}$$

(½ Mark)

Therefore, $t_{99\%} = 2 \times t_{90\%}$ **(½ Mark)**

30. **(a)** **Sandmeyer's reaction:**

$$\langle O \rangle - \overset{+}{N} \equiv N\ \overset{-}{Cl} + Cu/HCl \longrightarrow$$

$$\langle O \rangle - Cl + N_2 + CuCl$$

(1 Mark)

(b) In aqueous solutions, factors like hydrogen bonding and stabilization of the conjugate acid determine the strength of the amine. **(1 Mark)**

$(CH_3)_2 NH$ is a secondary amine while $(CH_3)_3 N$ is a tertiary amine.

Due to the absence of a hydrogen atom on nitrogen for hydrogen bonding in $(CH_3)_3 N$, which is available in $(CH_3)_2 NH$, and steric factors along with the effect of Inductive effect, the secondary amine $(CH_3)_2 NH$ is more basic than primary and tertiary amine $(CH_3)_3 N$.

(1 Mark)

SECTION - D

31. **(a)** Conductivity (k) of an electrolytic solution decreases with dilution because the number of ions per unit volume of the solution decreases upon dilution.

(1 Mark)

(b) Since, $\dfrac{\Lambda_m}{\Lambda_m^0} = \alpha$

We need to calculate and determine the value of Λ_m.

Now, $\Lambda_m = 141.0\ S\ cm^2\ mol^{-1}$ (from table)

$$\Rightarrow \quad \alpha = \frac{141.0}{150.0} = 0.94 \qquad \textbf{(1 Mark)}$$

(c) The value of molar conductivity Λ_m of HCl would be **higher** than that of KCl for the same concentration. This is due to the higher value of conductivity of the H^+ ions. **(1 Mark)**

OR

(c) Amit is using a weak electrolyte CH_3COOH instead of a strong electrolyte KCl.

Similarity: Conductivity would decrease upon dilution. **(½ Mark)**

Difference: Molar conductivity would increase steeply on dilution instead of a slow increase. **(½ Mark)**

32. (a) In S_N1 reactions, the first step involves the formation of a carbocation which is planar in structure. The second step involves the attack of the nucleophile on the planar carbocation which can occur from either side of the plane.

This results in the formation of an equimolar mixture of the two enantiomers that is **racemic** in nature. **(1 Mark)**

(b) Ethanol is less polar than water due to the presence of an alkyl group instead of a hydrogen atom. In water, the bond dipole moments add up that result in the greater polarity while this is not the case with ethanol that has a very small contribution to the bond dipole. **(1 Mark)**

(c) The reactivity in the case of an S_N2 reaction depends on the nature of the substrate, nucleophilicity and the nature of the solvent.

(i) $CH_3CH_2 - I$ will be more reactive than $CH_3CH_2 - Cl$ due to the weaker $C - I$ bond. **(1 Mark)**

(ii)  $CH_2 - Cl$ will be more reactive than

Cl as there is less crowding in

$CH_2 - Cl$ at the α-carbon. **(1 Mark)**

OR

(c) (i) Among the given compounds, 2-Bromo-2-methylbutane has the highest reactivity as it forms the most stable tertiary carbocation.

1-Bromopentane is least reactive as it forms a primary carbocation which is least stable.

Thus, order will be:

1-Bromopentane < 2-bromopentane < 2-bromo-2-methylbutane **(1 Mark)**

(ii) Among the given compounds, 2-bromo-2-methylbutane has the highest reactivity as it forms a tertiary carbocation while 1-bromo-3-methylbutane is least reactive as it forms a primary carbocation.

Thus, the order will be:

1-Bromo-3-methylbutane < 2-bromo-3-methylbutane < 2-bromo-2-methylbutane **(1 Mark)**

Note

Substitution Nucleophilic unimolecular (S_N1) reactions are two-step reactions in which the slowest or rate-determining step is the formation of a carbocation from the cleavage of C–X bond.

SECTION - E

33. (a) (i) **Cannizaro's reaction:**

$$2R - CHO \xrightarrow[\text{conc.}]{OH^-} R - COO^- + R - CH_2 - OH$$

(1 Mark)

where, R = H or ph.

Note

Cannizaro reaction is an organic redox reaction that involves disproportionation of a carbonyl compound to a corresponding alcohol and carboxylic acid.
It takes place in carbonyl compounds that do not have α-hydrogens.

(ii) Boiling points of aldehydes and ketones are lower than that of corresponding carboxylic acids due to the absence of hydrogen bonding in aldehydes and ketones. Weaker dipole-dipole forces are present in the carbonyl compounds. **(1 Mark)**

(iii) The given compound is an oxygen containing compound and since it gives a positive Iodoform and Tollen's test, it must have an α-methyl group attached to the carbonyl group, and an aldehydic group.

Since these are five carbon atoms in the compound the structure of the compound 'A' will be:

$$CH_3 - \overset{O}{\overset{\|}{C}} - CH_2 - CH_2 - \overset{O}{\overset{\|}{C}} - H \quad (A)$$

(1 Mark)

'A' reacts in the iodoform and Tollen's reaction as follows:

$$CH_3 - \overset{\overset{\displaystyle O}{\|}}{C} - CH_2 - CH_2 - \overset{\overset{\displaystyle O}{\|}}{C} - H \xrightarrow{NaOH/I_2}$$
(A)

$$NaOOC - CH_2 - CH_2 - \overset{\overset{\displaystyle O}{\|}}{C} - H$$
$$+ CHI_3 \text{ (yellow)}$$

$$\xrightarrow[\text{Tollen's reagent}]{(Ag_2O)} CH_3 - \overset{\overset{\displaystyle O}{\|}}{C} - CH_2 - CH_2 - \overset{\overset{\displaystyle O}{\|}}{C} - OH +$$
$$2Ag\downarrow$$

(2 Marks)

OR

(b) (i) Ethanal is an aldehyde that can be detected by **Tollen's test** that will give a silver mirror.

$$CH_3 - CHO \xrightarrow{Ag_2O} CH_3 - COOH \text{ (½ Mark)}$$
$$+ 2Ag\downarrow \text{ (silver)}$$

Ethanoic acid is a carboxylic acid that can be identified by **ester test** that will give a fruity smell.

$$CH_3 - COOH + CH_3CH_2OH \xrightarrow{H^+}$$
$$CH_3 - COOCH_2CH_3 + H_2O$$
Fruity smell

(½ Mark)

(ii) The α-hydrogens of aldehydes and ketones are bonded to the carbon atom that is bonded to the carbonyl group.

The conjugate base is called enolate ion which is stabilized by resonance and the strong electron - withdrawing nature of the carbonyl group makes the α-hydrogens acidic. **(1 Mark)**

(iii) The given compound contains oxygen so it can be an alcohol ether, aldehyde or ketone or a carboxylic acid/derivative. Since it is hydrolysed, it can be an ether or an ester. Since one of the products of hydrolysis can be oxidized to give the other product, the compound 'A' has to be an **ester**.

(1) So, $A = CH_3 - \overset{\overset{\displaystyle O}{\|}}{C} - OCH_2CH_3$ **(1 Mark)**

$$CH_3 - \overset{\overset{\displaystyle O}{\|}}{C} - OCH_2CH_3 \xrightarrow{H_2O/H^+}$$
$$CH_3 - \overset{\overset{\displaystyle O}{\|}}{C} - OH + CH_3CH_2OH$$
(B)   (C)

$$CH_3CH_2OH \xrightarrow[{[O]}]{KMnO_4/H+} CH_3COOH$$
(C)   (B)

$$CH_3COONa \xrightarrow[\Delta]{CaO/NaOH} CH_4 + CO_2 \uparrow$$

(1 Mark)

(2) Compound (B) CH_3COOH will have a higher boiling point as the extent of hydrogen bonding is greater in (B) than in (C). **(1 Mark)**

34. (a) (i) The boiling point of 1 M NaCl solution more than that of 1 M glucose solution because NaCl is an ionic compound that dissociates into ions Na^+ and Cl^- in aqueous solutions while glucose does not.

Boiling point is a colligative property that increases with an increase in the number of particles. **(1 Mark)**

(ii) The vapour pressure is reduced to 90% when certain mass of 'X' is dissolved in 78 g of benzene.

If $P^\circ_{benzene} = 1$ atm,

$$P^\circ_{Benzene} - P_{Benzene} = 0.1 \text{ atm} \quad \text{(½ Mark)}$$
$$M_{Benzene} = 78.11 \text{ g/mol} \approx 78 \text{ g/mol}$$
$$M_X = 50 \text{ g/mol}, W_{Benzene} = 78 \text{ g}$$

$$\Rightarrow x_X = \frac{\dfrac{W_X}{M_X}}{\dfrac{W_X}{M_X} + \dfrac{W_{Benzene}}{M_{Benzene}}} = 0.2 \quad \text{(½ Mark)}$$

$$= \frac{\dfrac{W_X}{50}}{\dfrac{W_X}{50} + 1} = 0.2$$

$$= \frac{W_X}{W_X + 50} = 0.2 \quad \text{(½ Mark)}$$

$$\Rightarrow 0.2W_X + 10 = W_X$$
$$\Rightarrow W_X - 0.2W_X = 10$$
$$\Rightarrow \quad 0.8W_X = 10$$

$$\Rightarrow \quad W_X = \frac{10}{0.8} = \textbf{12.5 g} \quad \text{(½ Mark)}$$

(iii) $\Delta T_b = iK_b m$

$$= iK_b \left[\frac{1000 \times W_2}{M_2 \times W_1} \right] \quad \text{(1 Mark)}$$

i for $MgCl_2 = 3 \times 0.512 \times \left[\dfrac{1000 \times 10}{95 \times 200} \right]$

$$= \textbf{0.808 K} \quad \text{(1 Mark)}$$

OR

(b) **(i)** The value of Van't Hoff factor for ethanoic acid in benzene is determined by its association in benzene.

It forms a dimer in benzene so:

$$i = \frac{\text{no. of particles present}}{\text{Theoretical no. of particles}} = \frac{1}{2} = 0.5$$

(1 Mark)

(ii) Osmotic pressure $(\pi) = \dfrac{i \times n_2 \times R \times T}{V}$

(½ Mark)

i for $K_2SO_4 = 3$ **(½ Mark)**

$$n_2 = \frac{m_2}{M_2} = \frac{2.32 \times 10^{-2}\ g}{174\ g/mol} = 1.33 \times 10^{-4}\ \text{moles}$$

$$\Rightarrow \pi = \frac{3 \times (1.33 \times 10^{-4}) \times (0.082) \times (298)}{2}$$

(½ Mark)

$= 0.00487$ atm or 4.87×10^{-3} atm.   **(½ Mark)**

(iii) $\Delta T_f = K_f \cdot m = K_f \left[\dfrac{1000 \times W_2}{M_2 \times W_1} \right]$ **(½ Mark)**

$$\Rightarrow \quad M_2 = \frac{K_f \times W_2 \times 1000}{\Delta T_f \times W_1}$$

$$= \frac{(5.12)\,(25.6)\,(\cancel{1000})}{0.512 \times \cancel{1000}} = 256\ g$$

(½ Mark)

$\Rightarrow$ Molecular formula of Sulphur

$$= \frac{M_{sulphur}}{At.\ mass} = \frac{256\ g}{32\ g/mol} = 8\ \text{(½ Mark)}$$

$\Rightarrow$ Molecular formula $= S_8$.   **(½ Mark)**

Note

Relative lowering of vapour pressure, osmotic pressure, elevation in boiling point and depression in freezing point are all colligative properties that are determined by the number of particles of the solute only. Further association or dissociation is determined by the Vant Hoff Factor (i) that gives the actual value of the property.

35. **(a)** The given electronic configuration has two electrons in 4s and three electrons in 3d subshell.

So, it can lose two 4s-electrons to exhibit +2 and also one or two electrons from the 3d-subshell to exhibit +3 and +4 states.

So, the species X = V (Vanadium) can exhibit V^{2+}, V^{3+} and V^{4+} states.   **(1 Mark)**

(b) Heating of $KMnO_4$ at 513 K causes it to decompose into potassium manganate, manganese oxide and dioxygen.

$$2KMnO_4 \xrightarrow{\ \Delta\ } K_2MnO_4 + MnO_2 + O_2 \quad \textbf{(1 Mark)}$$

(c) **(i)** Zinc has the lowest enthalpy of atomization due to the absence of unpaired electrons that results in weak interatomic forces.   **(1 Mark)**

(ii) Cu^+ ion is unstable in aqueous solution because its hydration enthalpy is smaller than that of Cu^{2+} ion which is smaller than Cu^+.   **(1 Mark)**

(iii) Actinoids show more number of oxidation states than lanthanoids because of the participation of the electrons of the 5f, 6d and 7s - subshells.

This is due to the poor shielding of these electrons and small energy gap between them.   **(1 Mark)**

All India *2022*

CBSE Board Solved Paper Term-II

Time Allowed : 2 Hours   ***Maximum Marks : 35***

General Instructions:

Read the following instructions carefully and strictly follow them.

(i) This question paper contains **12** questions. All questions are compulsory.

(ii) This question paper is divided into **three** Sections – Section **A**, **B** and **C**.

(iii) Section-A, Q. Nos. **1** to **3** are very short answer type questions carrying **2** marks each.

(iv) Section-B, Q. Nos. **4** to **11** are short answer type questions carrying **3** marks each.

(v) Section-C, Q. No. **12** is case based question carrying **5** marks.

(vi) Log tables and calculators are NOT allowed.

SECTION - A

1. An organic compound (A) with molecular formula C_3H_7NO on heating with Br_2 and KOH forms a compound (B). compound (B) on heating with $CHCl_3$ and alcoholic KOH produces a foul smelling compound (C) and on reacting with $C_6H_5SO_2Cl$ forms a compound (D) which is soluble in alkali. Write the structures of (A), (B), (C) and (D).

2. Write the products formed when benzaldehyde reacts with the following reagents (Any two) :

(i) CH_3CHO in presence of dilute NaOH

(ii) $H_2N - OH$ in presence of weak acid

(iii) Tollen's reagent

3. The conductivity of 0.001M acetic acid is 7.8×10^{-5} S cm^{-1}. Calculate its degree of dissociation if $\Lambda^°_m$ for acetic acid is 390 S cm^2 mol^{-1}.

SECTION - B

4. (i) Why are melting points of transition metals high?

(ii) Why the transition metals generally form coloured compounds?

(iii) Why E° value for Mn^{3+}/Mn^{2+} couple is highly positive?

5. (a) (i) Which acid of the following pair would you expect to be stronger?

$F - CH_2 - COOH$ or $CH_3 - COOH$

(ii) Arrange the following compounds in increasing order of their boiling points :

$CH_3CH_2OH, CH_3 - CHO, CH_3 - COOH$

(iii) Give simple chemical test to distinguish between Benzaldehyde and Acetophanone.

OR

(b) (i) Which will undergo faster nucleophilic addition reaction?

Acetaldehyde or Propanone

(ii) What is the composition of Fehling's reagent?

(iii) Draw structure of the semicarbazone of Ethanal.

6. Give reasons :

(i) Ammonolysis of alkyl halides is not a good method to prepare pure primary amines.

(ii) Aniline does not give Friedel-Crafts reaction.

(iii) Although $- NH_2$ group is o/p directing in electrophilic substitution reactions, yet aniline on nitration gives good yield of *m*-nitroaniline.

7. (a) What happens when

(i) Propanone is treated with CH_3MgBr and then hydrolysed?

(ii) Ethanal is treated with excess ethanol and acid?

(iii) Methanal undergoes Cannizzaro reaction?

OR

(b) Write the main product in the following reactions:

(i) $2CH_3COCl + (CH_3)_2Cd \rightarrow$

(ii) $CH_3CH_2CHO \xrightarrow{Zn(Hg)/conc.\ HCl}$

(iii) $\langle\!\bigcirc\!\rangle\!- COONa + NaOH \xrightarrow{CaO}{\Delta}$

8. (a) Differentiate between the following :

    (i) Adsorption and Absorption

    (ii) Lyophobic Sol and Lyophilic Sol

    (iii) Multimolecular Colloid and Macromolecular colloid

OR

(b) (I) Define the following terms :

    (i) Zeta Potential

    (ii) Coagulation

  (II) Why a negatively charged sol is obtained when $AgNO_3$ solution is added to KI solution?

9. Define transition metals. Why Zn, Cd and Hg are not called transition metals ? How is the variability in oxidation states of transition metals different from that of p-block elements?

10. (a) Using valence bond theory, predict the hybridization and magnetic character of the complex : $[Ni(CO)_4]$ (Atomic number : Ni = 28)

(b) Write IUPAC name of $[Pt(NH_3)_2\,Cl(NO_2)]$

(c) Why $[Co(en)_3]^{3+}$ is a more stable complex than $[Co(NH_3)_6]^{3+}$?

11. (a) Calculate $\Delta_r G°$ and $\log K_c$ for the following cell :

$$Ni(s) + 2\,Ag^+(aq) \rightarrow Ni^{2+}(aq) + 2Ag(s)$$

Given that $E°_{cell} = 1.05V$, $F = 96,500\ Cmol^{-1}$.

OR

(b) Calculate the e.m.f. of the following cell at 298K :

$$Fe(s)\,|\,Fe^{2+}\,(0.001\ M)\,\|\,H^+\,(0.01M)\,|\,H_2(g)\,(1\ bar)\,|\,Pt(s)$$

Given that $E°_{cell} = +0.44\ V$

$[\log 2 = 0.3010 \quad \log 3 = 0.4771 \quad \log 10 = 1]$

12. Read the following passage and answer the questions that follow :

The rate of reaction is concerned with decrease in concentration of reactants or increase in the concentration of products per unit time. It can be expressed as instantaneous rate at a particular instant of time and average rate over a large interval of time. A number of factors such as temperature, concentration of reactants, catalyst affect the rate of reaction. Mathematical representation of rate of a reaction is given by rate law :

$$Rate = k[A]^x\,[B]^y$$

x and y indicate how sensitive the rate is to the change in concentration of A and B. Sum of $x + y$ gives the overall order of a reaction.

When a seqeuence of elementary reactions gives us the products, the reactions are called complex reactions. Molecularity and order of an elementary, reaction are same. Zero order reactions are relatively uncommon but they occur under special conditions. All natural and artificial radioactive decay of unstable nuclei take place by first order kinetics.

(a) What is the effect of temperature on the rate constant of a reaction?

(b) For a reaction $A + B \rightarrow$ Product, the rate law is given by, Rate $= k[A]^2\,[B]^{1/2}$. What is the order of the raction?

(c) How order and molecularity are different for complex reactions ?

(d) A first order reaction has a rate constant $2 \times 10^{-3}s^{-1}$. How long will 6g of this reactant take to reduce to 2g ?

OR

The half life for radioactive decay of ^{14}C is 6930 years. An archaeological artifact containing wood had only 75% of the ^{14}C found in a living tree. Find the age of the sample. $[\log 4 = 0.6021 \quad \log 3 = 0.4771 \quad \log 2 = 0.3010 \quad \log 10 = 1]$

Solutions

1. 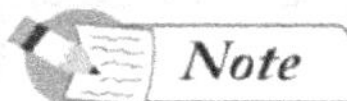

(2 Marks)

2. (i) Reaction of benzaldehyde with CH_3CHO in presence of NaOH (Aldol condensation)

$$\text{C}_6\text{H}_5\text{—CHO} + CH_3CHO \xrightarrow{\text{dil. NaOH}}$$

$$\text{C}_6\text{H}_5\text{—}\underset{\underset{\text{H}}{|}}{\overset{\overset{\text{OH}}{|}}{\text{C}}}\text{—CH}_2\text{—}\overset{\overset{\text{O}}{\|}}{\text{C}}\text{—H} \qquad \textbf{(1 Mark)}$$

3-Hydroxy-3-phenyl propanal
(Aldol)

> **Note**
>
> *Aldols readily lose water on heating and give α, β unsaturated carbonyl compounds.*

$$\text{C}_6\text{H}_5\text{—}\underset{\underset{\text{H}}{|}}{\overset{\overset{\text{OH}}{|}}{\text{C}}}\text{—CH}_2\text{—}\underset{\underset{\text{H}}{|}}{\overset{\overset{\text{O}}{\|}}{\text{C}}} \xrightarrow[-H_2O]{\Delta} \text{C}_6\text{H}_5\text{—}\underset{\underset{\text{H}}{|}}{\text{C}}\text{=CH—CHO}$$

(ii) Reaction of benzaldehyde with H_2N—OH in presence of weak acid

$$\text{C}_6\text{H}_5\text{—CHO} + H_2N\text{—OH} \xrightarrow{H^+}$$

$$\text{C}_6\text{H}_5\text{—}\underset{\underset{\text{H}}{|}}{\text{C}}\text{=N—OH} + H_2O \qquad \textbf{(1 Mark)}$$

(iii) Reaction of benzaldehyde with Tollen's reagent

$$\text{C}_6\text{H}_5\text{—CHO} + 2[Ag(NH_3)_2]^+ + 3OH^- \longrightarrow$$

$$\text{C}_6\text{H}_5\text{—COO}^- + 2Ag + 2H_2O + 4NH_3 \qquad \textbf{(1 Mark)}$$

3. $$\lambda_m = \frac{K}{c} = \frac{7.8 \times 10^{-5} \text{Scm}^{-1}}{0.001 \text{mol L}^{-1}} \times \frac{1000 \text{cm}^3}{L} = 78.05 \text{ cm}^2 \text{mol}^{-1}$$

$$\alpha = \frac{\lambda_m}{\lambda_m^\circ} = \frac{78.0 \text{ Scm}^2\text{mol}^{-1}}{390 \text{ Scm}^2\text{mol}^{-1}} = 0.2 \qquad \textbf{(2 Marks)}$$

4. (i) Transition metals have high melting point due to presence of unpaired electrons which are responsible for high strength of metallic bond. **(1 Mark)**

(ii) Transition metals generally form coloured compounds due to absorption of radiation from visible light region to excite the electrons from its one position to another position in *d*-orbitals. (d-d transition) **(1 Mark)**

(iii) The outer electronic configuration in case of Mn^{3+} is $3d^4$ while in case of Mn^{2+} is $3d^5$ which is more stable as compare to $3d^4$ due to which it shows highly positive E° value for Mn^{3+}/Mn^{2+}. **(1 Mark)**

5. (a) (i) Acidity is directly proportional to the –I effect which means electron withdrawing group increases the acidic character. **(1 Mark)**

In case of $F–CH_2–COOH$, flourine shows–I effect due to which acidic character of this compound increases.

(ii) The compounds which have strongest hydrogen bonding between the molecules will show higher boiling point. **(1 Mark)**

CH_3COOH will have highest boiling point due to strong hydrogen bonding while CH_3CHO have lowest boiling point due to absence of hydrogen bonding.

Therefore; increasing order of boiling point is:

$CH_3CHO < CH_3CH_2OH < CH_3COOH$

(iii) Benzaldehyde contains aldehydic functional group while Acetophenone contains ketonic functional group. Tollen's test is used to distinguish between benzaldehyde and acetophenone as it only respond in case of Aldehydes. Benzaldehyde reduces Tollen's reagent to give a silver mirror of Ag. **(1 Mark)**

OR

(b) (i) 

propanone contains two CH_3 groups (i.e. +I effect) which makes carbonyl group less electron deficient due to which acetaldehyde show faster nucleophilic addition reaction.

(1 Mark)

(ii) Fehling's reagent is composed of Fehling A and Fehling B. Fehling A is a blue-coloured aqueous solution of $CuSO_4$. Fehling B is colorless aqueous solution of potassium sodium tartrate ($KNaC_4H_4O_6.4H_2O$). **(1 Mark)**

> **Note**
>
> *Fehling reagent is used to test aldehydes. Ketones and aromatic aldehyde do not respond to Fehling's test.*

(iii) Structure of semicarbazone of ethanal

$$CH_3 \diagdown C = O + H_2N - NH - \overset{\overset{O}{\|}}{C} - NH_2 \longrightarrow NH - \overset{\overset{O}{\|}}{C} - NH_2$$

$$H_3C - \overset{\overset{H}{|}}{C} = N - NH - \overset{\overset{O}{\|}}{C} - NH_2 \qquad \textbf{(1 Mark)}$$
Semicarbazone

6. **(i)** Ammonolysis yields a mixture of primary, secondary, tertiary and quaternary salts. The separation of pure primary amines from ammonolysis of alkyl halide is a difficult process. **(1 Mark)**

(ii) Aniline does not give friedel-crafts reaction as it forms anilinium chloride salt which deactivates the ring for further acylation and alkylation reaction. **(1 Mark)**

(iii) $-NH_2$ group is electron donating group which activates the ring and gives ortho, para product but in case of nitration it will form anilinium ion in presence of acid and gives meta directing product. **(1 Mark)**

7. **(a)** **(i)** The reaction of propanone with Grignard reagent

$$CH_3 - \overset{\overset{O}{\|}}{C} - CH_3 + CH_3MgBr \xrightarrow{H_2O}$$
propanone

$$CH_3 - \overset{\overset{OH}{|}}{\underset{\underset{CH_3}{|}}{C}} - CH_3 \quad \textbf{(1 Mark)}$$
2-methylpropan-2-ol

(ii) When ethanal is reacted with excess ethanol and acid then acetal will form as a product.

$$CH_3 \diagdown C = O + C_2H_5OH \xrightarrow[-H_2O]{HCl} CH_3 \diagdown \overset{OH}{\underset{OC_2H_5}{C}}$$
Ethanal   Hemiacetal

$$\xrightarrow[-H_2O]{HCl, \ C_2H_5OH} H_3C \diagdown \overset{OC_2H_5}{\underset{OC_2H_5}{C}}$$
Acetal
(1 Mark)

(iii) Methanal undergoes cannizzaro reaction

$$2 \ \overset{H}{\underset{H}{\diagdown}} C = O + conc.KOH \longrightarrow$$
Methanal

$$H - \overset{\overset{H}{|}}{\underset{\underset{H}{|}}{C}} - OH + H - \overset{\overset{O}{\|}}{C} - OK$$
Methanol   Potassium
                 methanoate
(1 Mark)

> **Note**
>
> *Cannizzaro reaction involves disproportionation i.e., self oxidation and self reduction of aldehydes which do not have alpha hydrogen. One molecule of aldehyde is reduced to alcohol and another is oxidised to carboxylic acid.*

OR

(b) **(i)** $2CH_3COCl + (CH_3)_2Cd \longrightarrow CH_3 - \overset{\overset{O}{\|}}{C} - CH_3$ **(1 Mark)**

(ii) $CH_3CH_2CHO \xrightarrow[\text{Clemmensen Reduction}]{Zn(Hg)/Conc.HCl} CH_3CH_2CH_3$ **(1 Mark)**

(iii)

$$\bigcirc - COONa + NaOH \xrightarrow[\Delta]{CaO} \bigcirc - H + Na_2CO_3$$
(1 Mark)

8. **(a)**

(i)	**Adsorption**		**Absorption**
(a)	The substance is only concentrated at the surface not in the bulk.	(a)	The substance is uniformly distributed throughout the bulk of solid.
(b)	It is surface phenomenon.	(b)	It is bulk phenomenon.
(c)	It is exothermic process.	(c)	It is endothermic process.
(d)	It is temperature dependent.	(d)	It does not depend on the temperature. **(1 Mark)**

(ii)	**Lyophobic sol**		**Lyophilic sol**
(a)	Dispersed phase has no affinity for dispersion medium.	(a)	Dispersed phase has got affinity for dispersion medium.
(b)	It is irreversible process.	(b)	It is reversible process.
(c)	It is unstable.	(c)	It is stable.
(d)	Colloidal particles are electrically charged.	(d)	Colloidal particles may or may not be charged. **(1 Mark)**

(iii)	**Multimolecular colloid**		**Macromolecular colloid.**
(a)	They are formed by the aggregation of a large number of atoms or molecules which generally have diameters less than 1nm.	(a)	They are molecules of large size.
(b)	Examples-sols of gold and sulphur.	(b)	Examples-polymer like rubber, nylon, starch.
(c)	They usually have lyophobic character.	(c)	They usually have lyophilic character.
(d)	These are held by weak vander waals force.	(d)	They are held by stronger intermolecular forces. **(1 Mark)**

OR

(b) (I) (i) Zeta potential: The potential difference between the fixed layer and the diffused layer of opposite charges is called the electrokinetic potential or zeta potential.

(1 Mark)

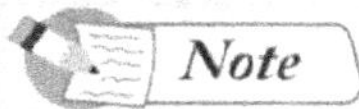

Note

The combination of the two layers of opposite charges around the colloidal particle is called Helmholtz double layer. The first layer of ions is firmly, held and is termed fixed layer while the second layer is mobile which is termed as diffused layer.

(ii) Coagulation: The process of settling of colloidal particles is called coagulation or precipitation of the Sol.

(1 Mark)

(II) When $AgNO_3$ solution is added to KI solution, negatively charged Sol of AgI is formed due to selective adsorption of I^- ion from the dispersion medium. **(1 Mark)**

9. Those elements which have d subshell, partially filled with electrons and has ability to form cations with an incompletely filled d orbitals are known as Transition Metals.

Zn, Hg and Cd have completely filled orbitals in their ground state due to which they are not called as transition metals.

In case of p-block the lower oxidation states are favoured by the heavier members due to inert pair effect while in case of d-block the higher oxidation states are favoured by the heavier members. **(3 Marks)**

10. (a) Electronic configuration of Ni in ground state

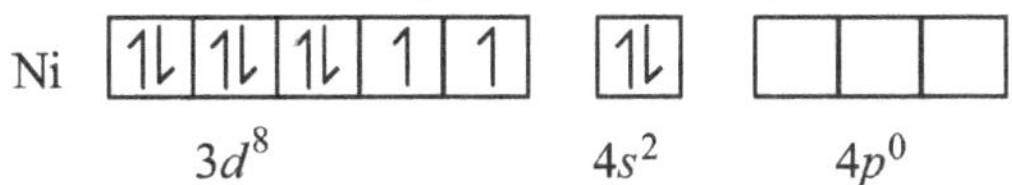

Electronic configuration of Ni atom in Ni (CO)$_4$

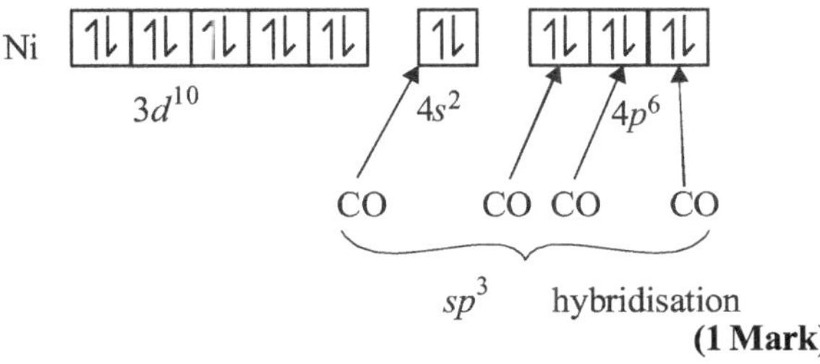

(1 Mark)

∴ Hybridisation of Ni (CO)$_4$ is sp^3 and diamagnetic in nature.

(b) IUPAC name of $[Pt(NH_3)_2Cl(NO_2)]$ is diamminechloridonitrito-N-platinum (II). **(1 Mark)**

(c) Ethylene diammine is a bidentate ligand and forms a stable chelate i.e. $[Co(en)_3]^{3+}$ chelating ligands form more stable complexes as compared to non-chelating ligands. Therefore; $[Co(en)_3]^{3+}$ is more stable complex than $[Co(NH_3)_6]^{3+}$. **(1 Mark)**

11. (a) $Ni(s) + 2Ag^+(aq) \longrightarrow Ni^{2+}(aq) + 2Ag(s)$

$\Delta G° = -n\,FE°_{cell}$

$\qquad = -2 \times 96500 \times 1.05$

$\qquad = -202,650\ J\,mol^{-1}$ **(1 Mark)**

$\Delta G° = -RT\ lnK_c = -2.303\ RT\ log\ K_c$

$-202.650 = -8.314 \times 298 \times 2.303\ log\ K_c$ **(1 Mark)**

$log\ K_c = 35.52$ **(1 Mark)**

OR

(b) $Fe(s) | Fe^{2+}(0.001M) || H^+(0.01M) | H_2(g)\,(1\ bar) | Pt(s)$

$E_{cell} = E°_{cell} - \dfrac{2.303\ RT}{nF} log \dfrac{[P]}{[R]}$

$= 0.44 - \dfrac{2.303 \times 8.314 \times 298}{2 \times 96500} log \dfrac{[0.001]}{[0.01]}$ **(1 Mark)**

$= 0.44 + \dfrac{5705.85}{193000} log\,[10]$ **(1 Mark)**

$= 0.44 + 0.0296$

$E_{cell} = 0.469\ V$ **(1 Mark)**

12. (a) Rate constant depends on the temperature and directly proportional to each other. On increasing the temperature, the rate constant of reaction increases according to Arrhenius Equation.

$$K = Ae^{-E_a/RT}$$

As temperature increases, the exponential part of the equation becomes less negative and value of rate constant increases. **(1 Mark)**

(b) $A + B \longrightarrow Product$

$Rate = k[A]^2\,[B]^{1/2}$

$Order = 2 + \dfrac{1}{2} = \dfrac{5}{2}$ **(1 Mark)**

(c) For complex reaction, order is given by the slowest step and molecularity of the slowest step is same as the order of the overall reaction. **(1 Mark)**

(d) For first order reaction;

$t = \dfrac{2.303}{k} log \dfrac{[R]_0}{[R]}$ **(1 Mark)**

$= \dfrac{2.303}{2 \times 10^{-3}} log \dfrac{[6]}{[2]}$

$= 550\ s$ **(1 Mark)**

OR

For first order reaction;

$k = \dfrac{0.693}{t_{1/2}} = \dfrac{0.693}{6930} = 0.0001\ years^{-1}$ **(1 Mark)**

It is known that,

$t = \dfrac{2.303}{k} log \dfrac{[R]_0}{[R]}$

$= \dfrac{2.303}{0.0001} log \dfrac{100}{75}$

$= 2875\ years$ **(1 Mark)**

All India *2022*

CBSE Board Solved Paper Term-I

Time Allowed : 90 Minutes Maximum Marks : 35*

General Instructions:
Read the following instructions very carefully and strictly follow them :
 (i) This question paper contains **55** questions out of which **45** questions are to be attempted. **All** questions carry equal marks.
 (ii) This question paper contains three Sections – Section A, B and C.
 (iii) Section-A contains **25** questions. Attempt any **20** questions from Q. No. **01** to **25**.
 (iv) Section-B contains **24** questions. Attempt any **20** questions from Q. No. **26** to **49**.
 (v) Section-C contains **6** questions. Attempt any **5** questions from Q. No. **50** to **55**.
 (vi) The first **20** questions attempted in **Section-A** & **Section-B** and first **5** questions attempted in **Section-C** by a candidate will be evaluated.
 (vii) There is only one correct option for every multiple choice question (MCQ). Marks will not be awarded for answering more than one option.
 (viii) There is no negative marking.

SECTION - A

*This section consists of **25** multiple choice questions with overall choice to attempt any **20** questions. In case more than desirable number of questions are attempted. ONLY first 20 questions will be considered for evaluation.*

1. Which one of the following pairs will form an ideal solution?
 (a) Chloroform and acetone
 (b) Ethanol and acetone
 (c) *n*-hexane and *n*-heptane
 (d) Phenol and aniline

2. Which of the following is known as amorphous solid ?
 (a) Glass (b) Plastic
 (c) Rubber (d) All of the above

3. The structure of pyrosulphuric acid is

(a) $HO-\overset{\overset{\textstyle O}{\|}}{\underset{\underset{\textstyle O}{\|}}{S}}-O-OH$

(b) $HO-\overset{\overset{\textstyle O}{\|}}{\underset{\underset{\textstyle O}{\|}}{S}}-OH$

(c) $HO-\overset{\overset{\textstyle O}{\|}}{\underset{\underset{\textstyle O}{\|}}{S}}-O-\overset{\overset{\textstyle O}{\|}}{\underset{\underset{\textstyle O}{\|}}{S}}-OH$

(d) $HO-\overset{\overset{\textstyle O}{\|}}{\underset{\underset{\textstyle O}{\|}}{S}}-O-O-\overset{\overset{\textstyle O}{\|}}{\underset{\underset{\textstyle O}{\|}}{S}}-OH$

4. The C – O – H bond angle in alcohol is
 (a) slightly greater than 109°28′.
 (b) slightly less than 109°28′.
 (c) slightly greater than 120°.
 (d) slightly less than 120°.

5. Consider the following reaction :

$$CH_3-CH=CH_2 \xrightarrow[\text{2. aq. KOH}]{\text{1. HBr}}$$

The major end product is

(a) $CH_3-\underset{\underset{\textstyle OH}{|}}{CH}-CH_3$ (b) $CH_3-\underset{\underset{\textstyle Br}{|}}{CH}-CH_3$

(c) $CH_3–CH_2–CH_2–OH$ (d) $CH_3–CH_2–CH_2–Br$

6. Nucleosides are composed of
(a) a pentose sugar and phosphoric acid
(b) a nitrogenous base and phosphoric acid
(c) a nitrogenous base and a pentose sugar
(d) a nitrogenous base, a pentose sugar and phosphoric acid

7. The oxidation state of -2 is most stable in :
(a) O (b) S
(c) Se (d) Te

8. Which of the following is not a characteristic of a crystalline solid ?
(a) A true solid
(b) A regular arangement of constituent particles
(c) Sharp melting point
(d) Isotropic in nature

9. Which of the following formula represents Raoult's law for a solution containing non-volatile solute ?
(a) $p_{solute} = p^\circ_{solute} \cdot x_{solute}$
(b) $p = K_H.X$
(c) $p_{total} = p_{solvent}$
(d) $p_{solvent} = p^\circ_{solvent} \cdot x_{solvent}$

10. An azeotropic solution of two liquids has a boiling point lower than either of the two when it
(a) shows a positive deviation from Raoult's law.
(b) shows a negative deviation from Raoult's law.
(c) shows no deviation from Raoult's law.
(d) is saturated.

11. Which of the following crystal will show metal excess defect due to extra cation ?
(a) AgCl (b) NaCl
(c) FeO (d) ZnO

12. Which of the following acids reacts with acetic anhydride to form a compound Aspirin ?
(a) Benzoic acid (b) Salicylic acid
(c) Phthalic acid (d) Acetic acid

13. Which of the following statements is wrong ?
(a) Oxygen shows $p\pi - p\pi$ bonding.
(b) Sulphur shows little tendency of catenation.
(c) Oxygen is diatomic whereas sulphur is polyatomic.
(d) O – O bond is stronger than S – S bond.

14. Amino acids which cannot be synthesized in the body and must be obtained through diet are known as
(a) Acidic amino acids (b) Essential amino acids
(c) Basic amino acids (d) Non-essential amino acids

15. Which one of the following halides contains $C_{sp^2} - X$ bond ?
(a) Allyl halide (b) Alkyl halide
(c) Benzyl halide (d) Vinyl halide

16. On mixing 20 mL of acetone with 30 mL of chloroform, the total volume of the solution is
(a) < 50 mL (b) $= 50$ mL
(c) > 50 mL (d) $= 10$ mL

17. Consider the following compounds :

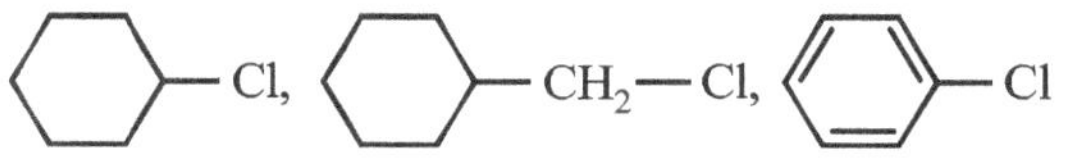

I $\quad$ II $\quad$ III

The correct order of reactivity towards S_N2 reaction
(a) I > III > II (b) II > III > I
(c) II > I > III (d) III > I > II

18. Which of the following forms strong $p\pi$–$p\pi$ bonding ?
(a) S_2 (b) Se_2
(c) Te_2 (d) O_2

19. F_2 acts as a strong oxidising agent due to
(a) low $\Delta_{bond} H^\circ$ and low $\Delta_{hyd} H^\circ$
(b) low $\Delta_{bond} H^\circ$ and high $\Delta_{hyd} H^\circ$
(c) high $\Delta_{bond} H^\circ$ and high $\Delta_{eg} H^\circ$
(d) low $\Delta_{hyd} H^\circ$ and low $\Delta_{eg} H^\circ$

20. Which of the following sugar is known as dextrose ?
(a) Glucose (b) Fructose
(c) Ribose (d) Sucrose

21. Cu reacts with dilute HNO_3 to evolve which gas ?
(a) N_2O (b) NO_2
(c) NO (d) N_2

22. Which of the following is a network solid ?
(a) SO_2 (b) SiO_2
(c) CO_2 (d) H_2O

23. Major product formed in the following reaction

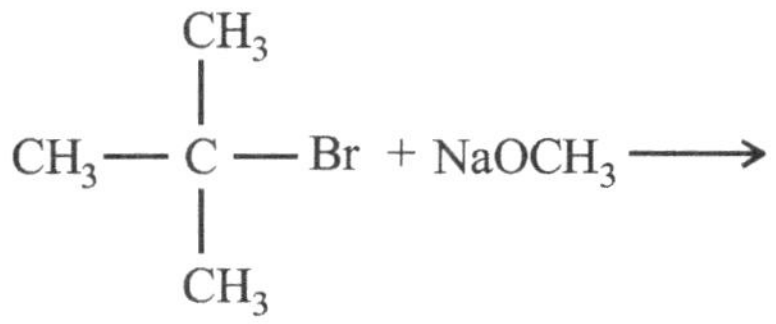

$$CH_3 - \underset{\underset{CH_3}{|}}{\overset{\overset{CH_3}{|}}{C}} - Br + NaOCH_3 \longrightarrow$$

(a) $CH_3 - \underset{\underset{CH_3}{|}}{\overset{\overset{CH_3}{|}}{C}} - ONa$ (b) $CH_3 - \underset{\underset{CH_3}{|}}{\overset{\overset{CH_3}{|}}{C}} - OCH_3$

(c) $CH_3 - \underset{\underset{CH_3}{|}}{\overset{\overset{CH_3}{|}}{C}} - O - \underset{\underset{CH_3}{|}}{\overset{\overset{CH_3}{|}}{C}} - CH_3$

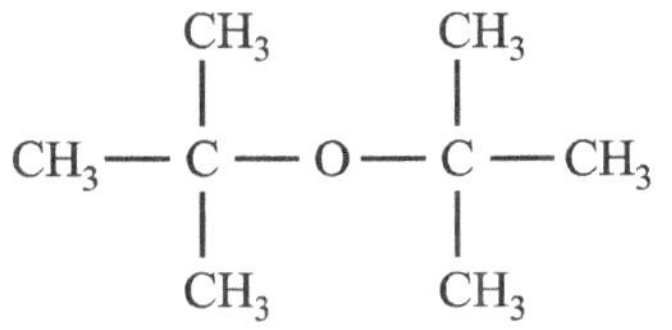

(d) 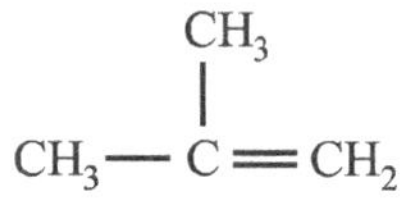 $CH_3 - \underset{\underset{CH_3}{|}}{\overset{\overset{CH_3}{|}}{C}} = CH_2$

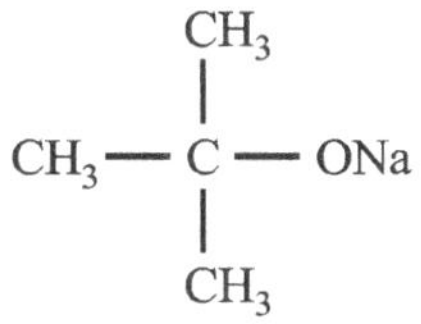

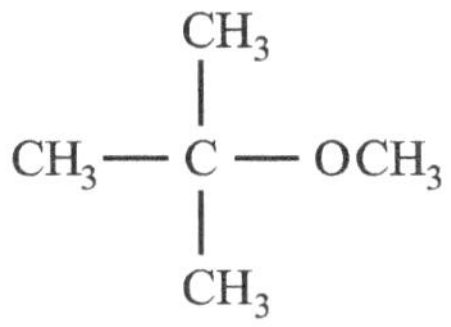

24. Chlorine reacts with cold and dilute NaOH to give
(a) NaCl and $NaClO_3$ (b) NaCl and NaClO
(c) NaCl and $NaClO_4$ (d) NaClO and $NaClO_3$

25. Elevation of boiling point is inversely proportional to
(a) molal elevation constant (K_b)
(b) molality (m)
(c) molar mass of solute (M)
(d) weight of solute (W)

SECTION - B

*This sections consists of **24** multiple choice questions with overall choice to attempt any **20** questions. In case more than desirable number of questions are attempted, ONLY first 20 questions will be considered for evaluation.*

26. An unknown gas 'X' is dissolved in water at 2.5 bar pressure and has mole fraction 0.04 in solution. The mole fraction of 'X' gas when the pressure of gas is doubled at the same temperature is
    (a) 0.08 (b) 0.04
    (c) 0.02 (d) 0.92

27. The base which is present in DNA but not in RNA, is
    (a) Cytosine (b) Guanine
    (c) Adenine (d) Thymine

28. In the following reaction

    $$CH_3 - CH = CH - CH_2 - OH \xrightarrow{\text{PCC}}$$
    the product formed is
    (a) $CH_3 - CHO$ and CH_3CH_2OH
    (b) $CH_3 - CH = CH - COOH$
    (c) $CH_3 - CH = CH - CHO$
    (d) $CH_3 - CH_2 - CH_2 - CHO$

29. Enantiomers differ only in
    (a) boiling point
    (b) rotation of polarised light
    (c) melting point
    (d) solubility

30. The number of lone pairs of electrons in XeF_4 is
    (a) zero (b) one
    (c) two (d) three

31. Sulphuric acid is used to prepare more volatile acids from their corresponding salts due to its
    (a) strong acidic nature
    (b) low volatility
    (c) strong affinity for water
    (d) ability to act as a dehydrating agent

32. An element with density 6 g cm^{-3} forms a *fcc* lattice with edge length of 4×10^{-8} cm. The molar mass of the element is ($N_A = 6 \times 10^{23} \text{ mol}^{-1}$)
    (a) 57.6 g mol^{-1} (b) 28.8 g mol^{-1}
    (c) 82.6 g mol^{-1} (d) 62 g mol^{-1}

33. In the reaction 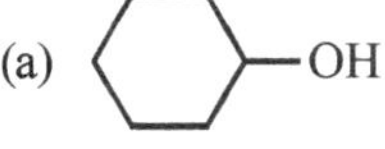 compound 'Y' is

    (a) 

34. Which of the following is the weakest reducing agent in group 15 ?
    (a) NH_3 (b) PH_3
    (c) AsH_3 (d) BiH_3

35. The boiling point of a 0.2 m solution of a non-electrolyte in water is (K_b for water $= 0.52 \text{ K kg mol}^{-1}$)
    (a) $100\,°C$ (b) $100.52\,°C$
    (c) $100.104\,°C$ (d) $100.26\,°C$

36. Nucleic acids are polymer of
    (a) amino acids (b) nucleosides
    (c) nucleotides (d) glucose

37. Which of the following gas dimerises to become stable ?
    (a) $CO_2(g)$ (b) $NO_2(g)$
    (c) $SO_2(g)$ (d) $N_2O(g)$

38. In the following diagram point, 'X' represents

    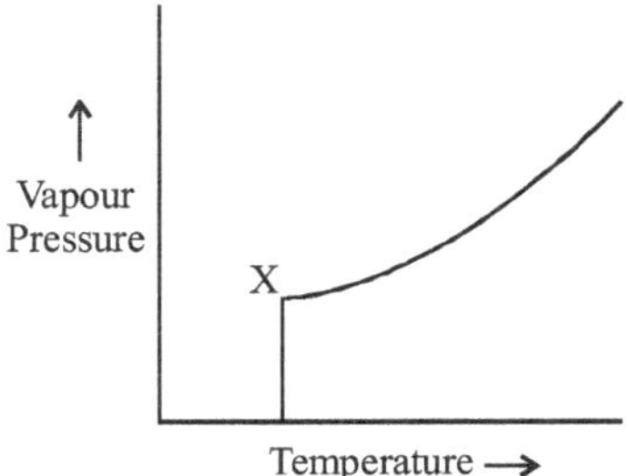

    (a) Boiling point of solution
    (b) Freezing point of solvent
    (c) Boiling point of solvent
    (d) Freezing point of solution

39. XeF_6 on reaction with NaF gives
    (a) $Na^+[XeF_7]^-$ (b) $[NaF_2]^-[XeF_5]^+$
    (c) $Na^+[XeF_6]^-$ (d) $[NaF_2]^+[XeF_5]^-$

40. Glucose on reaction with Br_2 water gives :
    (a) Saccharic acid (b) Hexanoic acid
    (c) Gluconic acid (d) Salicyclic acid

41. Which of the following is optically inactive ?
    (a) $(+)-$ Butan–2–ol (b) $(-)-$ Butan–2–ol
    (c) $(\pm)-$ Butan–2–ol (d) $(+)-$ 2 – Bromobutane

42. Which of the following is not a correct statement ?
    (a) Halogens are strong oxidising agents.
    (b) Halogens are more reactive than interhalogens.
    (c) All halogens are coloured.
    (d) Halogens have maximum negative electron gain enthalpy.

43. Which of the following has highest boiling point ?
    (a) $C_2H_5 - F$ (b) $C_2H_5 - Cl$
    (c) $C_2H_5 - Br$ (d) $C_2H_5 - I$

44. Which of the following isomer of pentane (C_5H_{12}) will give three isomeric monochlorides on photochemical chlorination ?

    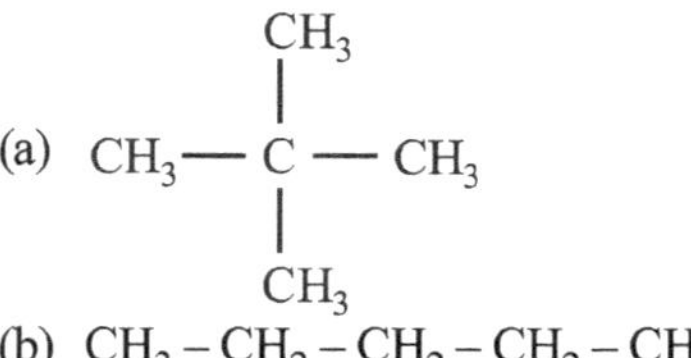
    (a) $CH_3 - \overset{\overset{\displaystyle CH_3}{|}}{\underset{\underset{\displaystyle CH_3}{|}}{C}} - CH_3$
    (b) $CH_3 - CH_2 - CH_2 - CH_2 - CH_3$
    (c) $CH_3 - \overset{}{\underset{\underset{\displaystyle CH_3}{|}}{CH}} - CH_2 - CH_3$
    (d) All of the above

DIRECTIONS (Qs. 45-49) : *Given below are the questions labelled as **Assertion (A)** and **Reason (R)**. Select the most appropriate answer from the options given below :*
(a)   Both A and R are true and R is the correct explanation of A.
(b)   Both A and R are true but R is not the correct explanation of A.
(c)   A is true but R is false.
(d)   A is false but R is true.

45.   **Assertion (A) :** A raw mango placed in a saline solution loses water and shrivel into pickle.
   Reason (R) : Through the process of reverse osmosis, raw mango shrivel into pickle.

46.   **Assertion (A) :** H_2S is less acidic than H_2Te.
   Reason (R) : H – S bond has more $\Delta_{bond} H°$ than H–Te bond.

47.   **Assertion (A) :** Chlorobenzene is less reactive towards nucleophilic substitution reaction.
   Reason (R) : Nitro group in chlorobenene increases its reactivity towards nucleophilic substi-tution reaction.

48.   **Assertion (A) :** Due to Schottky defect, there is no effect on the density of a solid.
   Reason (R) : Equal number of cations and anions are missing from their normal sites in Schottky defect.

49.   **Assertion (A) :** Fluorine forms only one oxoacid HOF.
   Reason (R) : Fluorine atom is highly electronegative.

SECTION - C

*This section consists of **6** multiple choice questions with an overall choice to attempt any **5** questions. In case more than desirable number of questions are attempted, ONLY first 5 questions will be considered for evaluation.*

50.   Match the following :

Column-I		Column-II	
(i)	Stoichiometric defects	(A)	Crystalline solids
(ii)	long range order	(B)	F-centres
(iii)	...ABC ABC ABC ...	(C)	Schottky and Frenkel defects
(iv)	Number of atoms per unit cell = 2	(D)	fcc structure
(v)	Metal excess defect due to anionic vacancies		

   Which of the following is the best matched options ?
(a)   (i) – (D), (ii) – (A), (iii) – (B), (iv) – (C)
(b)   (i) – (C), (ii) – (A), (iii) – (D), (v) – (B)
(c)   (i) – (C), (ii) – (A), (iii) – (D), (iv) – (B)
(d)   (i) – (A), (ii) – (B), (v) – (C), (iv) – (D)

51.   Which of the following analogies is correct ?
(a) XeF_2 : linear :: XeF_6 : square planar
(b)   moist SO_2 : Reducing agent :: Cl_2 : bleaching agent
(c) N_2 : Highly reactive gas :: F_2 : inert at room temperature
(d) NH_3 : strong base :: HI : weak acid.

52.   Complete the following analogy :
   Curdling of milk : A :: α-helix : B

(a)   A : Primary structure   B : Secondary structure
(b)   A : Denatured protein   B : Primary structure
(c)   A : Secondary structure   B : Denatured protein
(d)   A : Denatured protein   B : Secondary structure

Case Study : (Qs. 53-55)
Alcohols and Phenols are acidic in nature. Electron withdrawing groups in phenol increase its acidic strength and electron donating groups decrease it. Alcohols undergo nucleophilic substitution with hydrogen halides to give alkyl halides. On oxidation primary alcohols yield aldehydes with mild oxidising agents and carboxylic acids with strong oxidising agents while secondary alcohols yields ketones. The presence of – OH groups in phenols activates the ring towards electrophilic substitution. Various important products are obtained from pheonol like salicylaldehyde, salicylic acid, picric acid etc.

53.   Which of the following alcohols is resistant to oxidation ?

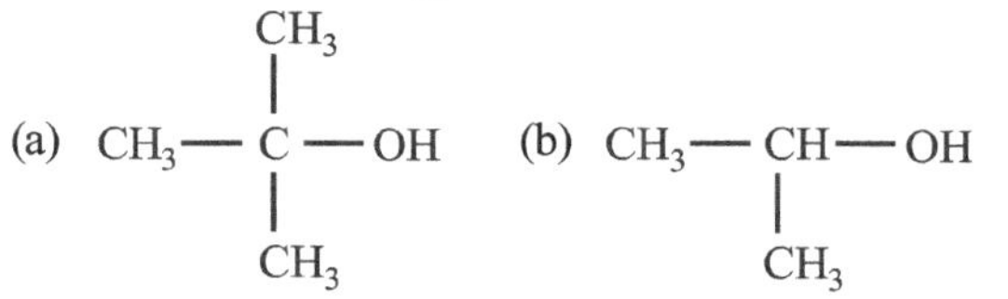

(a) $CH_3 - \overset{\overset{\displaystyle CH_3}{|}}{\underset{\underset{\displaystyle CH_3}{|}}{C}} - OH$ (b) $CH_3 - \overset{}{\underset{\underset{\displaystyle CH_3}{|}}{CH}} - OH$

(c) $CH_3 - CH_2 - OH$ (d) $CH_3 - OH$

54.   Which of the following group increases the acidic character of phenol ?
(a) $CH_3O -$ (b) $CH_3 -$
(c) $NO_2 -$ (d)   All of these

55.   Consider the following reaction :

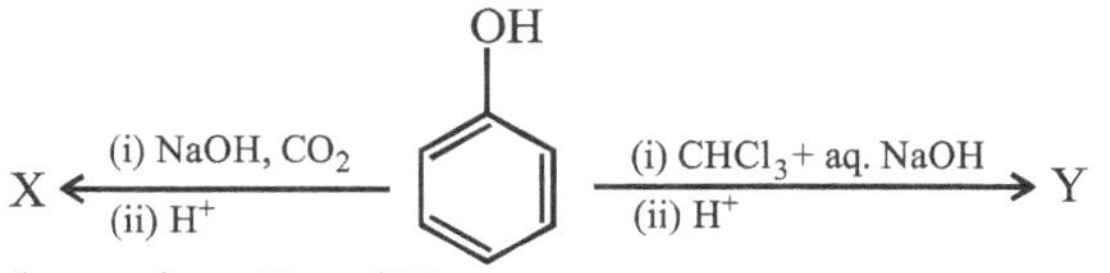

$$X \xleftarrow[\text{(ii) } H^+]{\text{(i) NaOH, } CO_2} \quad \text{[phenol]} \quad \xrightarrow[\text{(ii) } H^+]{\text{(i) } CHCl_3 + \text{ aq. NaOH}} Y$$

the products X and Y are

(a)   X = [2-hydroxybenzoic acid]   Y = [3-hydroxybenzaldehyde]

(b)   X = [2-hydroxybenzaldehyde]   Y = [2-hydroxybenzoic acid]

(c)   X = [3-hydroxybenzoic acid]   Y = [4-hydroxybenzaldehyde]

(d)   X = [2-hydroxybenzoic acid]   Y = [2-hydroxybenzaldehyde]

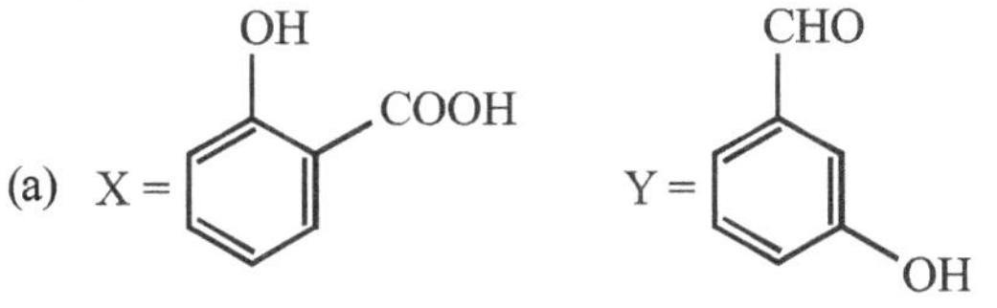

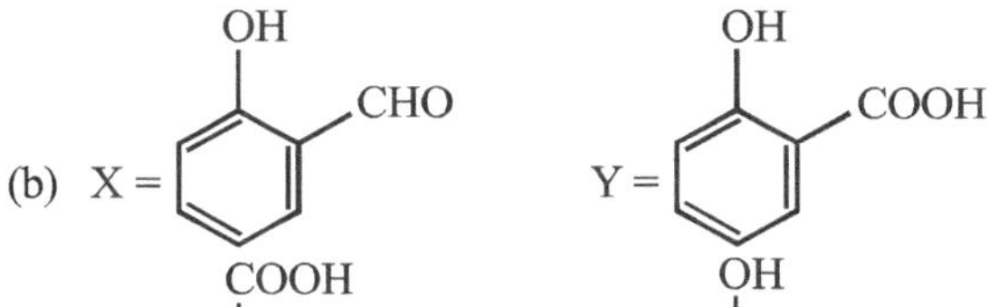

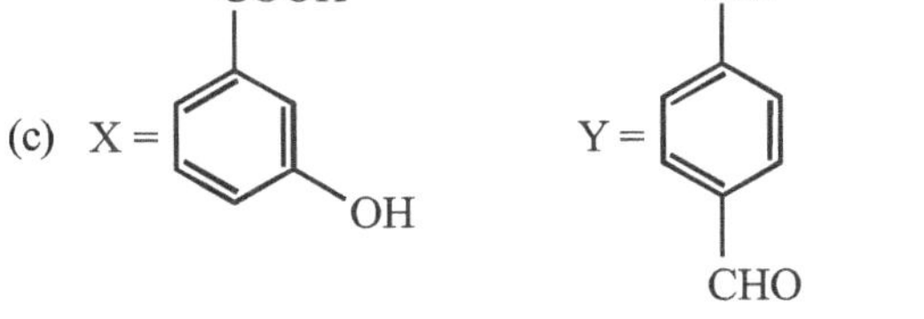

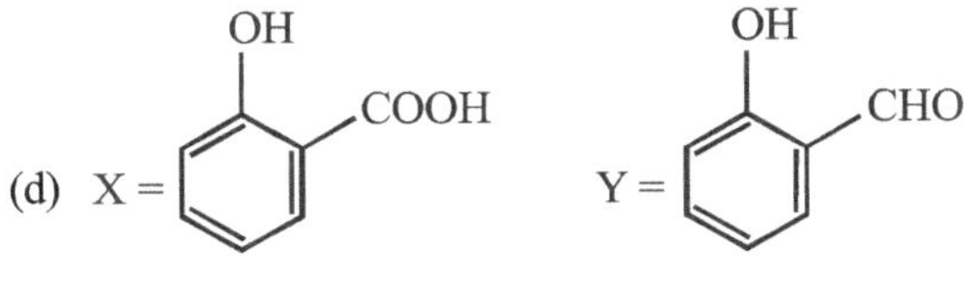

Solutions

1. **(c)** n-heptane and n-hexane obeys Raoult's law at all temperature and concentration. Hence; they will form an ideal solution.

2. **(d)** In amorphous solid, the constituent particles are not possess a regular three-dimensional arrangement. for example: Glass, Plastic, Rubber etc.

Note

Like liquids, amorphous solids have a tendency to flow, though very slowly, therefore sometimes these are called pseudo solids or super cooled liquids.

3. **(c)** The formula of pyrosulphuric acid is $H_2S_2O_7$ and the structure is:

$$HO—\overset{\overset{O}{\|}}{\underset{\underset{O}{\|}}{S}}—O—\overset{\overset{O}{\|}}{\underset{\underset{O}{\|}}{S}}—OH$$

Note

Both $H_2S_2O_8$ and $H_2S_2O_7$ contain same number of $S = O$ bonds i.e., 4 and $S – OH$ bond i.e., 2 but $H_2S_2O_8$ has peroxy linkage between two $S(S – O – O – S)$.

4. **(b)** The shape of alcohol is tetrahedral but due to presence of lone pair on oxygen atom, C—O—H bond angle decreases i.e. it will become less than $109°28'$.

5. **(a)** **Step I:** Addition of HBr

$$CH_3—CH=CH_2 \xrightarrow{HBr} CH_3—\underset{\underset{Br}{|}}{CH}—CH_3$$
$$\text{2-bromopropane}$$

The product is formed according to markovnikov rule.

Step II: Reaction with aq. KOH

$$CH_3—\underset{\underset{Br}{|}}{CH}—CH_3 \xrightarrow{aq.\,KOH} CH_3—\underset{\underset{OH}{|}}{CH}—CH_3$$

The final product is formed by S_N2 reaction.

6. **(c)** Nucleosides are composed of a nitrogenous base, and a pentose sugar.

7. **(a)** The most stable oxidation state of O is –2, S is +2, Se is +4 and Te is +4 and +6.

8. **(d)** Crystalline solids are anisotropic in nature, regular arrangement of constituent particles and have sharp melting point.

9. **(d)** Formula of Raoult's law for a non-volatile solute is:
$$P_{solvent} = P^°_{solvent} \cdot \chi_{solvent}$$

10. **(a)** Azeotropes are of two types:

(i) The solution which shows large positive deviation from Raoult's law form minimum boiling azeotrope at a specific composition.

(ii) The solution which shows large negative deviation from Raoult's law form maximum boiling azeotrope at a specific composition.

11. **(d)** ZnO will show metal excess defect due to extra cation i.e. Zn^{2+} ion which will move to interstitial sites and the electrons to neighbouring interstitial sites.

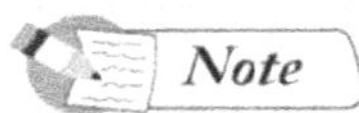

Note

When ZnO exhibits metal excess defect, its formula becomes $Zn_{1+x}O$.

12. **(b)**

Salicylic acid + Acetic anhydride $\xrightarrow{H^+}$

Aspirin + Acetic acid

When salicylic acid reacts with acetic anhydride then aspirin will form as a final product.

13. **(b)** Sulphur has greater tendency for catenation as it exists in S_8 form. On heating these rings break and link jointly into long chains.

14. **(b)** The amino acids which are not synthesized in our body and obtained through diet are essential amino acids. For example: histidine, lysine, leucine etc.

15. **(d)** The vinyl halide contains (C_{sp^2} – X bond)

$$H_2C=CH—X$$
$$\downarrow$$
$$sp^2$$
$$\text{Vinyl halide}$$

16. **(a)** The mixture of acetone and chloroform show negative deviation due to which the total volume of the solution will be less than 50.

17. **(c)** The order of reactivity towards S_N2 reaction is $1° > 2° > 3°$. Therefore, the correct order is II > I > III.

18. **(d)** Oxygen, being smaller in size can effectively form $p\pi – p\pi$ bonds with other atoms of itself. The other elements do not form $p\pi – p\pi$ bonds because of their relatively larger size.

19. **(b)** F_2 acts as a strong oxidising agent because of its low enthalpy of dissociation as F – F bond is weak due to electronic repulsion and high enthalpy of hydration.

20. **(a)** Glucose is a carbohydrate and act as a reducing sugar. It is also known as dextrose as it rotates the plane polarised light to the right.

21. **(c)** When copper reacts with dil. HNO_3, then nitric oxide gas is evolved.

$$3Cu + 8HNO_3 \longrightarrow 3Cu(NO_3)_2 + 4H_2O + \underset{\text{(Nitric oxide)}}{2NO\uparrow}$$
$$\underset{\text{(dilute)}}{} \qquad \underset{\substack{\text{Copper}\\\text{nitrate}}}{}$$

22. **(b)** In SiO_2 molecule, each silicon atom is surrounded with the four bonds of oxygen atom and makes four $Si - O$ bonds due to which it will form network solid like structure.

23. **(d)**
$$CH_3 - \underset{\underset{CH_3}{|}}{\overset{\overset{CH_3}{|}}{C}} - Br + NaOCH_3 \longrightarrow CH_3 - \underset{\underset{}{|}}{\overset{\overset{CH_3}{|}}{C}} = CH_2$$

The tertiary alkyl halides undergo elimination reaction to give alkenes.

Note

A primary alkyl halide will prefer an S_N2 reaction, a secondary halide prefers S_N2 or elimination depending upon the strength of base/nucleophile. A tertiary alkyl halide prefers S_N1 or elimination depending upon the stability of carbocation or the more substituted alkene.

24. **(b)** When chlorine reacts with cold and dilute $NaOH$, then it will form sodium chloride and sodium chlorate as a product and it is a type of disproportionation reaction.
$$2NaOH + Cl_2 \longrightarrow NaCl + NaOCl + H_2O$$

25. **(c)** The formula of elevation in boiling point is:
$$\Delta T_b = K_b \times m$$
$$\Delta T_b = \frac{K_b \times W_A}{M_B \times W_B(Kg)}$$

$\therefore$ Elevation in boiling point is inversely proportional to molar mass of solute (M_B).

26. **(a)** We know that;
$$\frac{P_1}{P_2} = \frac{\chi_1}{\chi_2}$$

Here;

$P_1 = $ initial pressure; $P_2 = $ final pressure; $\chi = $ mole fraction

$$\frac{2.5}{5} = \frac{0.04}{\chi_2}$$

$\chi_2 = 0.08$

27. **(d)** The bases which are present in RNA are adenine, uracil, guanine and cytosine.

28. **(c)** PCC act as a mild oxidising agent which converts $1°$ alcohol to aldehyde.
$$CH_3CH = CHCH_2OH \xrightarrow{\text{PCC}} CH_3CH = CH - CHO$$

29. **(b)** The compounds which are non-superimposable but have mirror images are known as enantiomers. They differ only in optical activity i.e. rotation of polarised light.

30. **(c)** The structure of XeF_4 is

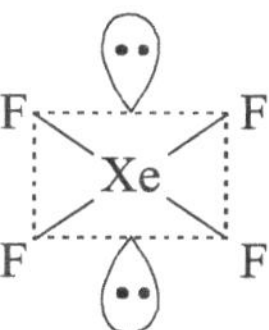

Therefore; the number of lone pairs of electrons in XeF_4 is two.

31. **(b)** Sulphuric acid is used to prepare more volatile acids from their corresponding salts due to its low volatility.

32. **(a)** As we know;
$$d = \frac{ZM}{N_A \times a^3}$$

for fcc, $Z = 4$

$$6 \text{ g cm}^{-3} = \frac{4 \times M}{6 \times 10^{23} \text{ mol}^{-1} \times (4 \times 10^{-8} \text{ cm})^3}$$

$M = 57.6 \text{g mol}^{-1}$

33. **(c)**

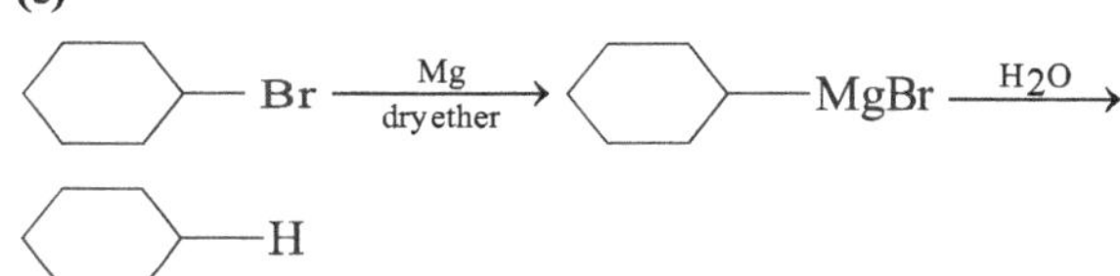

34. **(a)** The reducing property of the hydrides increases down the group due to decrease in bond dissociation enthalpy. Therefore; NH_3 is the weakest reducing agent in group 15.

35. **(c)** $\Delta T_b = K_b \times m$
$$= 0.52 \times 0.2$$
$$\Delta T_b = 0.104$$
$$T_b = T_b° + \Delta T_b$$
$$= 100 + 0.104$$
$$= 100.104°C$$

36. **(c)** Nucleic acids are biological macromolecules which are polymers of repeating monomeric units called nucleotides.

37. **(b)** NO_2 is an odd electron species which contains one unpaired electron and tend to form a dimer by pairing the unpaired electrons. Therefore, NO_2 gas dimerises to become stable.

38. **(b)** The point 'X' represents the freezing point of solvent. The freezing point of a substance may be defined as the temperature at which the vapour pressure of the substance in its liquid phase is equal to the vapour pressure in the solid phase.

39. **(a)** The reaction between XeF_6 and NaF is

$$XeF_6 + NaF \longrightarrow Na^+ [XeF_7]^-$$

40. **(c)**

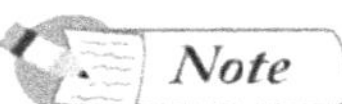

$$\underset{\text{Glucose}}{\underset{\displaystyle \overset{CHO}{\underset{\displaystyle CH_2OH}{|\atop (CHOH)_4 \atop |}}}{}} + [O] \xrightarrow{Br_2/water} \underset{\substack{\text{Gluconic} \\ \text{acid}}}{\underset{\displaystyle \overset{COOH}{\underset{\displaystyle CH_2OH}{|\atop (CHOH)_4 \atop |}}}{}}$$

41. **(c)** $(\pm)$ – butane-2-ol is a racemic mixture and behave as optically inactive.

42. **(b)** Interhalogens are more reactive than halogens as interhalogens are more likely to show hydrolysis and ionizes to give rise to polyatomic ions.

43. **(d)** On moving down the group, the size of halogen atoms and vander waals force of attraction increases due to which boiling point also increases. Therefore; $C_2H_5 – I$ has the highest boiling point.

Note

B. pt $\propto$ Strength of intermolecular forces

$\propto$ Molar mass of compound

$\propto$ Surface area

44. **(b)** *n*-Pentane will form three isomeric monochlorides on photochemical chlorination.

$$\overset{a}{CH_3}-\overset{b}{CH_2}-\overset{c}{CH_2}-\overset{b}{CH_2}-\overset{a}{CH_3}$$

$$\xrightarrow[hv]{Cl_2}$$

$$\longrightarrow CH_3-CH_2-CH_2-CH_2-Cl$$

$$\longrightarrow CH_3-CH_2-CH_2-\underset{\underset{Cl}{|}}{CH}-CH_3$$

$$\longrightarrow CH_3-CH_2-\underset{\underset{Cl}{|}}{CH}-CH_2-CH_3$$

45. **(c)** A is true but R is false. When raw mango is placed in a saline solution to prepare pickle the mango looses water due to osmosis and get shrivel. This event does not occur due to reverse osmosis.

Note

In reverse osmosis the direction of osmosis is reversed by making pressure larger than the osmotic pressure and is applied to the solution side. In this, pure solvent flows outside of the conc. solution through a semipermeable membrane.

46. **(a)** H_2S is less acidic than H_2Te as the bond dissociation enthalpy of $H – Te$ is lesser than $H – S$ bond.

47. **(b)** Chlorobenzene is less reactive towards nucleophilic substitution reaction because the carbon atom on which halogen is attached is sp^2 hybridised and decreases the nucleophilic substitution whereas NO_2 group in chlorobenzene increases the reactivity by withdrawing or by making the ring deficient.

48. **(d)** In Schottky defect, the density of solid decreases and equal number of cations and anions are missing from their normal sites in Schottky defect.

49. **(a)** Fluorine forms only one oxoacid i.e. HOF due to small size of fluorine and highly electronegative atom.

50. **(b)**

(i) Schottky and Frenkel defects are the type of stoichiometric defects.

(ii) Crystalline solids have long range order which means there is a regular pattern of arrangement of particles which repeats itself over the entire crystals.

(iii) *fcc* structure show ...... ABC ABC ABC ...... type pattern.

(iv) Metal excess defect due to anionic vacancies is known as F-centres.

51. **(b)** Moist SO_2 act as a reducing agent due to evolution of nascent hydrogen. Cl_2 act as a bleaching agent due to its oxidising properties as it produce nascent oxygen.

52. **(d)** A : Denatured protein

B : Secondary protein

• Curdling of milk is due to denaturation of proteins.

• α-helix is an element of secondary structure in which the amino acid chain is arranged in a spiral.

53. **(a)** Tertiary alcohols, i.e., $CH_3 - \underset{\underset{CH_3}{|}}{\overset{\overset{CH_3}{|}}{C}} - OH$ does not show oxidation.

Note

In tertiary alcohols, tertiary C does not have hydrogen and it is bonded to another carbon. It is difficult to break C – C bond for the oxidation of C bonded to OH. Therefore it does not undergo oxidation.

54. **(c)** Electron withdrawing group increases the acidic character of alcohol. Therefore; $(-NO_2)$ group will increases the acidic character.

55. **(d)**

CBSE Board Sample Paper Term-II

Time Allowed : 2 Hours   *Maximum Marks : 35*

General Instructions:

Read the following instructions carefully.

(i) There are **12** questions in this question paper with internal choice.

(ii) SECTION A - Q. No. **1** to **3** are very short answer questions carrying **2** marks each.

(iii) SECTION B - Q. No. **4** to **11** are short answer questions carrying **3** marks each.

(iv) SECTION C- Q. No. **12** is case based question carrying **5** marks.

(v) All questions are compulsory.

(vi) Use of log tables and calculators is not allowed.

SECTION - A

1. Arrange the following in the increasing order of their property indicated (any 2):

a. Benzoic acid, Phenol, Picric acid, Salicylic acid (pK_a values).

b. Acetaldehyde, Acetone, Methyl-tert-butyl ketone (reactivity towards NH_2OH).

c. ethanol, ethanoic acid, benzoic acid (boiling point)

$(1 \times 2 = 2 \text{ Marks})$

2. Solutions of two electrolytes 'A' and 'B' are diluted. The Λ_m of 'B' increases 1.5 times while that of A increases 25 times. Which of the two is a strong electrolyte? Justify your answer. Graphically show the behavior of 'A' and 'B'.

(2 Marks)

3. Give reasons to support the answer:

a. Presence of Alpha hydrogen in aldehydes and ketones is essential for aldol condensation.

b. 3 –Hydroxy pentan-2-one shows positive Tollen's test.

$(1 \times 2 = 2 \text{ Marks})$

SECTION - B

4. Account for the following:

a. Aniline cannot be prepared by the ammonolysis of chlorobenzene under normal conditions.

b. N-ethylethanamine boils at 329.3K and butanamine boils at 350.8K, although both are isomeric in nature.

c. Acylation of aniline is carried out in the presence of pyridine.

$(1 \times 3 = 3 \text{ Marks})$

OR

4. Convert the following:

a. Phenol to N-phenylethanamide.

b. Chloroethane to methanamine.

c. Propanenitrile to ethanal. $(1 \times 3 = 3 \text{ Marks})$

5. Answer the following questions:

a. $[Ni(H_2O)_6]^{2+}$ (aq) is green in colour whereas $[Ni(H_2O)_4 \, (en)]^{2+}$(aq)is blue in colour, give reason in support of your answer.

b. Write the formula and hybridization of the following compound: tris(ethane-1,2–diamine) cobalt(III) sulphate $(1 + 2 \text{ Marks})$

OR

5. In a coordination entity, the electronic configuration of the central metal ion is $t_{2g}^3 e_g^1$

a. Is the coordination compound a high spin or low spin complex?

b. Draw the crystal field splitting diagram for the above complex. $(1 + 2 \text{ Marks})$

6. Account for the following:

a. Ti(IV) is more stable than the Ti (II) or Ti(III).

b. In case of transition elements, ions of the same charge in a given series show progressive decrease in radius with increasing atomic number.

c. Zinc is a comparatively a soft metal, iron and chromium are typically hard. $(1 \times 3 = 3 \text{ Marks})$

7. An alkene 'A' (Mol. formula C_5H_{10}) on ozonolysis gives a mixture of two compounds 'B' and 'C'. Compound 'B' gives positive Fehling's test and also forms iodoform on treatment with I_2 and NaOH. Compound 'C' does not give Fehling's test but forms iodoform. Identify the compounds A, B and C. Write the reaction for ozonolysis and formation of iodoform from B and C. **(3 Marks)**

8. Observe the figure given below and answer the questions that follow:

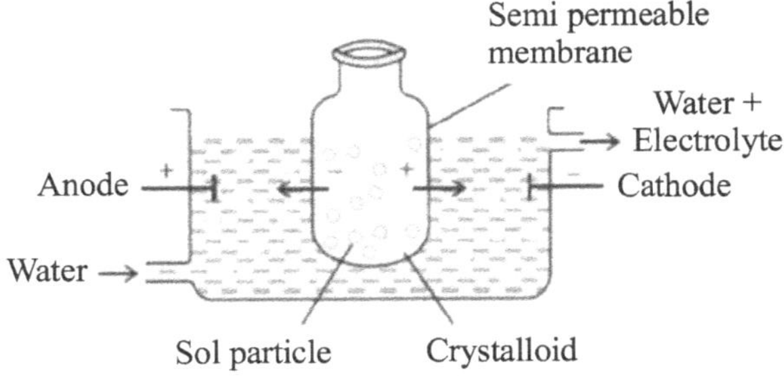

   a. Which process is represented in the figure?
   b. What is the application of this process?
   c. Can the same process occur without applying electric field? Why is the electric field applied?

9. What happens when reactions:
   a. N-ethylethanamine reacts with benzenesulphonyl chloride.
   b. Benzylchloride is treated with ammonia followed by the reaction with Chloromethane.
   c. Aniline reacts with chloroform in the presence of alcoholic potassium hydroxide. **(1 × 3 = 3 Marks)**

OR

9. a. Write the IUPAC name for the following organic compound:

$$CH_3 - N - CH_2CH_3$$

   b. Complete the following:

   $$C_6H_5NO_2 \xrightarrow{Sn/HCl} A \xrightarrow{Br_2/H_2O}$$

   $$B \xrightarrow[273-278K]{NaNO_2/HCl} C \xrightarrow[\Delta]{HBF_4} D$$

   (1 × 3 = 3 Marks)

10. Represent the cell in which the following reaction takes place. The value of $E°$ for the cell is 1.260 V. What is the value of E_{cell} ?

    $$2Al(s) + 3Cd^{2+}(0.1M) \rightarrow 3Cd(s) + 2Al^{3+}(0.01M)$$

    (3 Marks)

11. a. Why are fluorides of transition metals more stable in their higher oxidation state as compared to the lower oxidation state?
   b. Which one of the following would feel attraction when placed in magnetic field: $Co^{2+}, Ag^+, Ti^{4+}, Zn^{2+}$
   c. It has been observed that first ionization energy of 5 d series of transition elements are higher than that of 3d and 4d series, explain why? **(1 × 3 = 3 Marks)**

OR

11. On the basis of the figure given below, answer the following questions:

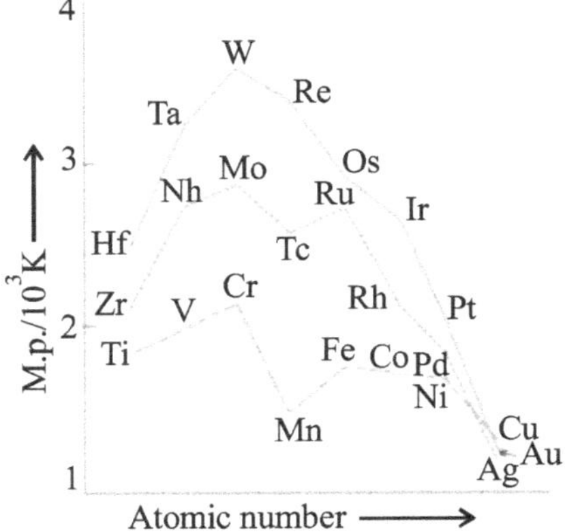

   a. Why Manganese has lower melting point than Chromium?
   b. Why do transition metals of $3d$ series have lower melting points as compared to $4d$ series?
   c. In the third transition series, identify and name the metal with the highest melting point.

   (1 × 3 = 3 Marks)

SECTION - C

12. Read the passage given below and answer the questions that follow.

Are there nuclear reactions going on in our bodies?

There are nuclear reactions constantly occurring in our bodies, but there are very few of them compared to the chemical reactions, and they do not affect our bodies much. All of the physical processes that take place to keep a human body running are chemical processes. Nuclear reactions can lead to chemical damage, which the body may notice and try to fix. The nuclear reaction occurring in our bodies is radioactive decay. This is the change of a less stable nucleus to a more stable nucleus. Every atom has either a stable nucleus or an unstable nucleus, depending on how big it is and on the ratio of protons to neutrons. The ratio of neutrons to protons in a stable nucleus is thus **around 1:1** for small nuclei ($Z < 20$). Nuclei with too many neutrons, too few neutrons, or that are simply too big are unstable. They eventually transform to a stable form through radioactive decay. Wherever there are atoms with unstable nuclei (radioactive atoms), there are nuclear reactions occurring naturally. The interesting thing is that there are small amounts of radioactive atoms everywhere: in your chair, in the ground, in the food you eat, and yes, in your body.

The most common natural radioactive isotopes in humans are carbon-14 and potassium-40. Chemically, these isotopes behave exactly like stable carbon and potassium. For this reason, the body uses carbon-14 and potassium-40 just like it does normal carbon and potassium; building them into the different parts of the cells, without knowing that they are radioactive. In time, carbon-14 atoms decay to stable nitrogen atoms and potassium-40 atoms decay to stable calcium atoms. Chemicals in the body that relied on having a carbon-14 atom or potassium-40 atom in a certain spot will suddenly have a nitrogen or calcium atom. Such a change damages the chemical. Normally, such changes are so rare, that the body can repair the damage or filter away the damaged chemicals.

The natural occurrence of carbon-14 decay in the body is the core principle behind carbon dating. As long as a person is alive and still eating, every carbon-14 atom that decays into a nitrogen atom is replaced on average with a new carbon-14 atom. But once a person dies, he stops replacing the decaying carbon-14 atoms. Slowly the carbon-14 atoms decay to nitrogen without being replaced, so that there is less and less carbon-14 in a dead body. The rate at which carbon-14 decays is constant and follows first order kinetics. It has a half - life of nearly 6000 years, so by measuring the relative amount of carbon-14 in a bone, archeologists can calculate when the person died. All living organisms consume carbon, so carbon dating can be used to date any living organism, and any object made from a living organism. Bones, wood, leather, and even paper can be accurately dated, as long as they first existed within the last 60,000 years. This is all because of the fact that nuclear reactions naturally occur in living organisms.

(source: The textbook Chemistry: The Practical Science by Paul B. Kelter, Michael D. Mosher and Andrew Scott states)

a. Why is Carbon -14 radioactive while Carbon -12 not? (Atomic number of Carbon: 6)

b. Researchers have uncovered the youngest known dinosaur bone, dating around 65 million years ago. How was the age of this fossil estimated?

c. Which are the two most common radioactive decays happening in human body?

d. Suppose an organism has 20 g of Carbon -14 at its time of death. Approximately how much Carbon -14 remains after 10,320 years? (Given antilog 0.517 = 3.289)

OR

d. Approximately how old is a fossil with 12 g of Carbon -14 if it initially possessed 32 g of Carbon -14? (Given log 2.667 = 0.4260)   **(1+1+1+2 Marks)**

Solutions

1.   (a)   Picric acid < salicylic acid < benzoic acid < phenol

(1 Mark)

    (b)   Methyl tert – butyl ketone < acetone < Acetaldehyde

(1 Mark)

    (c)   ethanol < ethanoic acid < benzoic acid (boiling point of carboxylic acids is higher than alcohols due to extensive hydrogen bonding, boiling point increases with increase in molar mass) **(1 Mark)**

2.   B is a strong electrolyte. The molar conductivity increases slowly with dilution as there is no increase in number of ions on dilution as strong electrolytes are completely dissociated. **(½ + ½ = 1 Mark)**

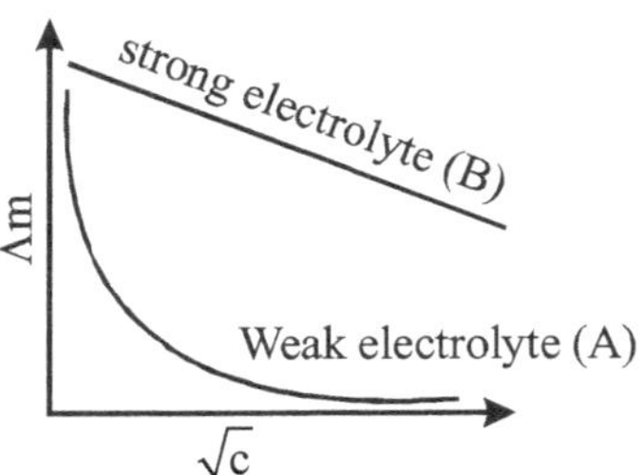

(1 Mark)

3.   (a)   The alpha hydrogen atoms are acidic in nature due to presence of electron withdrawing carbonyl group. These can be easily removed by a base and the carbanion formed is resonance stabilized. **(1 Mark)**

    (b)   Tollen's reagent is a weak oxidizing agent not capable of breaking the C-C bond in ketones . Thus ketones cannot be oxidized using Tollen's reagent itself gets reduced to Ag. But, 3-Hydroxypentan-2-one shows positive Tollen's test because it is an α-hydroxyketone that tautomerizes to an α-hydroxyenal that has an α-hydrogen atom. **(1 Mark)**

4.   (a)   In case of chlorobenzene, the C—Cl bond is quite difficult to break as it acquires a partial double bond character due to conjugation.

So Under the normal conditions, ammonolysis of chlorobenzene does not yield aniline. **(1 Mark)**

    (b)   Primary and secondary amines are engaged in intermolecular association due to hydrogen bonding between nitrogen of one and hydrogen of another molecule. Due to the presence of three hydrogen atoms, the intermolecular association is more in primary amines than in secondary amines as there are two hydrogen atoms available for hydrogen bond formation in it. **(1 Mark)**

    (c)   During the acylation of aniline, stronger base pyridine is added. This done in order to remove the HCl so formed during the reaction and to shift the equilibrium to the right hand side. **(1 Mark)**

OR

(a)   Phenol into N-phenylethanamide   **(1 Mark)**

$$\text{C}_6\text{H}_5\text{-OH} \xrightarrow{\text{Zinc dust}} \text{C}_6\text{H}_6 \xrightarrow{\text{conc HNO}_3/\text{H}_2\text{SO}_4} \text{C}_6\text{H}_5\text{-NO}_2 \xrightarrow{\text{Sn/HCl}} \text{C}_6\text{H}_5\text{-NH}_2 \xrightarrow[\text{Pyridine}]{\text{CH}_3\text{COCl}} \text{C}_6\text{H}_5\text{-NHCOCH}_3$$

(b)　Chloroethane to methanamine　　　　　　**(1 Mark)**

$$C_2H_5Cl \xrightarrow{\text{Aq NaOH}} C_2H_5OH \xrightarrow{\text{KMnO}_4} CH_3COOH$$

$$CH_3COOH \xrightarrow{\text{NH}_3/\text{heat}} CH_3CONH_2 \xrightarrow{\text{Br}_2/\text{KOH}} CH_3NH_2$$

(c)　Propanenitrile to ethanal　　　　　　**(1 Mark)**

$$CH_3CH_2CN \xrightarrow{\text{H}_3\text{O}^+} CH_3CH_2CONH_2 \xrightarrow{\text{Br}_2/\text{NaOH}} CH_3CH_2NH_2$$

$$CH_3CH_2NH_2 \xrightarrow{\text{HNO}_2} CH_3CH_2OH \xrightarrow{\text{PCC}} CH_3CHO$$

5.　(a)　The colour of coordination compound depends upon the type of ligand and dd transition taking place .

H_2O is weak field ligand, which causes small splitting, leading to the *d-d* transition corresponding green colour, however due to the presence of (en) which ia strong field ligand , the splitting is increased. Due to the change in $t_{2g\text{-}e_g}$ splitting the colouration of the compound changes from green to blue.　　　　**(1 Mark)**

(b)

(b)　Formula of the compound is

$[Co(H_2NCH_2CH_2NH_2)_3]_2(SO_4)_3$

The hybridisation of the compound is: d^2sp^3

(1 Mark)

OR

(a)　As the fourth electron enters one of the e_g orbitals giving the configuration $t_{2g}{}^3 e_g{}^1$, which indicates $\Delta_o < P$ hence forms high spin complex.

(b)

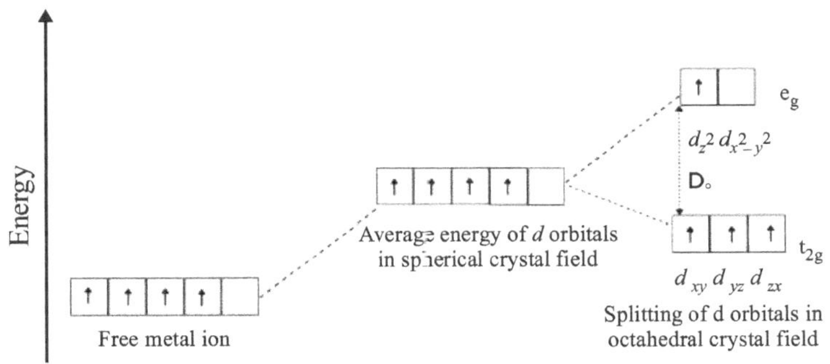

6. (a) Ti is having electronic configuration [Ar] $3d^2\,4s^2$. Ti (IV) is more stable as Ti^{4+} acquires nearest noble gas configuration on loss of 4 e⁻. **(1 Mark)**

(b) In case of transition elements, ions of the same charge in a given series show progressive decrease in radius with increasing atomic number. **(1 Mark)**

As the new electron enters a d-orbital each time the nuclear charge increases by unity. The shielding effect of a d-electron is not that effective, hence the net electrostatic attraction between the nuclear charge and the outermost electron increases and the ionic radius decreases.

(c) Iron and Chromium are having high enthalpy of atomization due to the presence of unpaired electrons, which accounts for their hardness. However, Zinc has low enthalpy of atomization as it has no unpaired electron. Hence zinc is comparatively a soft metal. **(1 Mark)**

7. Compound A is an alkene, on ozonolysis it will give carbonyl compounds. As both B and C have >C=O group,

B gives positive Fehling's test so it is an aldehyde and it gives iodoform test so it is so it has $CH_3C=O$ group. This means the aldehyde is acetaldehyde

C does not give Fehling's test, so it is a ketone. It gives positive iodoform test so it is a methyl ketone means it has $CH_3C=O$ group

Compound A (C_5H_{10}) on ozonlysis gives B (CH_3CHO)

$$+\,C\,(CH_3COR)$$

So "C" is CH_3COCH_3

$$CH_3CH{=}C(CH_3)_2 \xrightarrow{\text{(i) O}_3\text{(ii) Zn/H}_3O^+} $$
$$CH_3CHO + CH_3COCH_3$$
$$CH_3CHO + 2Cu^{2+} + 5OH^- \longrightarrow CH_3COO^-$$
$$+\,Cu_2O\,(\text{red ppt}) + 3H_2O$$
$$CH_3COCH_3 + 2Cu^{2+} + 5OH^- \longrightarrow \text{No reaction}$$
$$CH_3CHO + 3I_2 + 3\,NaOH \longrightarrow CHI_3\,(\text{yellow ppt})$$
$$+\,3HI + HCOONa$$
$$CH_3COCH_3 + 3I_2 + 3\,NaOH \longrightarrow CHI_3\,(\text{yellow ppt})$$
$$+\,3HI + CH_3COONa$$

$A = CH_3CH{=}C(CH_3)_2$

$B = CH_3CHO$

$C = CH_3COCH_3$ **(3 Marks)**

8. (a) electrodialysis **(1 Mark)**

(b) purification of colloidal solution **(1 Mark)**

(c) Yes. Dialysis is a very slow process to increase its speed electric field is applied **(1 Mark)**

9. (a) When N-ethylethanamine reacts with benzenesulphonyl chloride, N, N-diethylbenzenesulphonamide is formed. Which is insoluble in alkali.

(b) When benzylchloride is treated with ammonia, Benzylamine is formed which on reaction with chloromethane yields a secondary amine, N-methylbenzylamine.

(c) When aniline reacts with chloroform in the presence of alcoholic potassium hydroxide, phenyl isocyanides or phenyl isonitrile is formed that has foul small.

OR

(a) N-Ethyl-N-methylbenzenamine or N-Ethyl-N-ethylaniline

(b) NO₂ — Sn/HCl → NH₂ (A) — Br₂/H₂O → NH₂, Br, Br, Br (B) — NaNO₂/HCl, 273-278K → N₂Cl, Br, Br, Br (C) — HBF₄, Δ → F, Br, Br, Br (D)

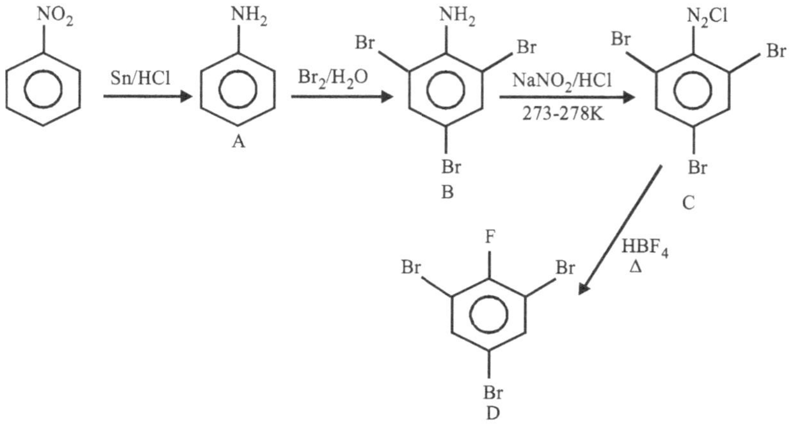

10. $Al(s) \mid Cd^{2+} (0.1M) \mid\mid Al^{3+} (0.01M) \mid Cd(s)$ **(½ Mark)**

$2Al(s) + 3Cd^{2+} (0.1M) \rightarrow 3Cd\,(s) + 2Al^{3+} (0.01M)$
(½ Mark)

$$E_{cell} = E^{\circ}_{cell} - \frac{0.059}{n} \, \log \frac{\left[Al^{3+}\right]^2}{\left[Cd^{2+}\right]^3}$$

$$E_{cell} = 1.26 - \frac{0.059}{6} \, \log \frac{(0.01)^2}{(0.1)^3} \qquad \textbf{(½ Mark)}$$

$$= 1.26 - \frac{0.059}{6} \, (-1) \qquad \textbf{(1 Mark)}$$

$$= 1.26 + 0.009 \qquad \textbf{(½ Mark)}$$

$$= 1.269\, V$$

11. (a)   The ability of fluorine to stabilize the highest oxidation state is attributed to the higher lattice energy or high bond enthalpy.   **(1 Mark)**

(b) Co^{2+} has three unpaired electrons so it would be paramagnetic in nature, hence Co^{2+} ion would be attracted to magnetic field.   **(1 Mark)**

(c)   The transition elements of $5d$ series have intervening $4f$ orbitals. There is greater effective nuclear charge acting on outer valence electrons due to the weak shielding by $4f$ electrons. Hence first ionisation energy of $5d$ series of transition elements are higher than that of $3d$ and $4d$ series.

(1 Mark)

OR

(a)   Manganese is having lower melting point as compared to chromium, as it has highest number of unpaired electrons, strong interatomic metal bonding, hence no delocalisation of electrons.   **(1 Mark)**

(b)   There is much more frequent metal – metal bonding in compounds of the heavy transition metals i.e $4d$ and $5d$ series, whixh accounts for lower melting point of $3d$ series.
(1 Mark)

(c)   Tungsten   **(1 Mark)**

12. (a)   Ratio cf neutrons to protons is 2.3 which is not the stable ratio of $1:1$ **(1 Mark)**

(b)   Age of fossils can be estimated by C-14 decay. All living organisms have C-14 which decays without being replaced back once the organism dies.   **(1 Mark)**

(c)   carbon-14 atoms decay to stable nitrogen atoms and potassium-40 atoms decay to stable calcium   **(1 Mark)**

(d) $t = \dfrac{2.303}{k} \, \log (C_0/C_t)$ **(½ Mark)**

$C_o = 20\, g,\ C_t = ?$

$t = 10320$ years, $k = \dfrac{0.693}{6000}$ (half-life given in passage)

substituting in equation:

$$10320 = \left[\frac{2.303}{(0.693/6000)}\right] \log \frac{20}{C_t} \qquad \textbf{(½ Mark)}$$

$$0.517 = \frac{\log 20}{C_t} \quad \text{antilog}\,(0.517) = \frac{20}{C_t}$$

$$3.289 = \frac{20}{C_t} \qquad \textbf{(½ Mark)}$$

$$C_t = 6.17\, g \qquad \textbf{(½ Mark)}$$

OR

$$t = \frac{2.303}{k} \, \log (C_0/C_t) \qquad \textbf{(½ Mark)}$$

$C_o = 32\, g;\ C_t = 12g$

$t = ?,\ k = \dfrac{0.693}{6000}$ (half life given in passage)

substituting in equation:

$$t = \left[\frac{2.303}{(0.693/6000)}\right] \log \frac{32}{12} \qquad \textbf{(½ Mark)}$$

$$t = \left[\frac{2.303 \times 60000}{0.693}\right] \log 2.667 \qquad \textbf{(½ Mark)}$$

$$t = \left[\frac{2.303 \times 6000 \times 0.4260}{0.693}\right]$$

$$= 8494 \text{ years} \qquad \textbf{(½ Mark)}$$

All India *2021-22*

CBSE Board Sample Paper Term-I

Time Allowed : 90 Minutes　　　　　　　　　　　　　　　　*Maximum Marks : 35*

General Instructions:
 (i) The Question Paper contains three sections.
 (ii) Section A has **25** questions. Attempt any **20** questions.
 (iii) Section B has **24** questions. Attempt any **20** questions.
 (iv) Section C has **6** questions. Attempt any **5** questions.
 (v) All questions carry equal marks.
 (vi) There is no negative marking.

*This section consists of 25 multiple choice questions with overall choice to attempt **any 20** questions. In case more than desirable number of questions are attempted, ONLY first 20 will be considered for evaluation.*

1. Which of the following statements is true:
 (a) Melting point of Phosphorous is less than that of Nitrogen
 (b) N_2 is highly reactive while P_4 is inert
 (c) Nitrogen shows higher tendency of catenation than P
 (d) N-N is weaker than P-P

2. Which of the following is a non-stoichiometric defect?
 (a) Frenkel defect
 (b) Schottky defect
 (c) metal deficiency defect
 (d) interstitial defect

3. Identify the law which is stated as:
 "For any solution, the partial vapour pressure of each volatile component in the solution is directly proportional to its mole fraction."
 (a) Henry's law
 (b) Raoult's law
 (c) Dalton's law
 (d) Gay-Lussac's Law

4. Pink colour of LiCl crystals is due to:
 (a) Schottky defect
 (b) Frenkel defect
 (c) Metal excess defect
 (d) Metal deficiency defect

5. Which of the following isomer has the highest melting point:
 (a) 1,2-dichlorobenzene
 (b) 1,3 -dichlorobenzene
 (c) 1,4-dichlorobenzene
 (d) all isomers have same melting points

6. Which one of the following reactions is not explained by the open chain structure of glucose:
 (a) Formation of pentaacetate of glucose with acetic anhydride.
 (b) formation of addition product with 2,4 DNP reagent.
 (c) Silver mirror formation with Tollen's reagent.
 (d) existence of alpha and beta forms of glucose.

7. Williamson's synthesis of preparing dimethyl ether is an:
 (a) S_N1 reaction
 (b) Elimination reaction
 (c) S_N2 reaction
 (d) Nucleophilic addition reaction

8. Chlorine water loses its yellow colour on standing because:
 (a) HCl gas is produced, due to the action of sunlight.
 (b) a mixture of HOCl and HCl is produced in the presence of light.
 (c) HOCl and hydrogen gas is produced.
 (d) a mixture of HCl and ClO_3 is produced, due to the action of sunlight.

9. During dehydration of alcohols to alkenes by heating with concentrated H_2SO_4, the initiation step is:
 (a) protonation of alcohol molecule
 (b) formation of carbocation
 (c) elimination of water
 (d) formation of an ester

10. Amorphous solids are:
    (a) isotropic   (b) anisotropic
    (c) isotopic   (d) isomeric

11. Which of the following reactions is used to prepare salicylaldehyde?
    (a) Kolbe's reaction
    (b) Etard reaction
    (c) Reimer-Tiemann reaction
    (d) Stephen's reduction.

12. Which of the following is an example of a solid solution?
    (a) sea water   (b) sugar solution
    (c) smoke   (d) 22 carat gold

13. The boiling points of alcohols are higher than those of hydrocarbons of comparable masses due to:
    (a) Hydrogen bonding
    (b) Ion – dipole interaction
    (c) Dipole-dipole interaction
    (d) Van der Waal's forces.

14. Which of the following has the lowest boiling point:
    (a) H_2O (b) H_2S
    (c) H_2Se (d) H_2Te

15. Which of the following statement is correct:
    (a) Fibrous proteins are generally soluble in water
    (b) Albumin is an example of fibrous proteins
    (c) In fibrous proteins, the structure is stabilised by hydrogen bonds and disulphide bonds
    (d) pH does not affect the primary structure of protein.

16. Major product obtained on reaction of 3-Phenyl propene with HBr in presence of organic peroxide :
    (a) 3- Phenyl 1-bromopropane
    (b) 1-Phenyl-3-bromopropane
    (c) 1-Phenyl-2-bromopropane
    (d) 3-Phenyl-2-bromopropane

17. Which of the following is a correct statement for C_2H_5Br?
    (a) It reacts with metallic Na to give ethane.
    (b) It gives nitroethane on heating with aqueous solution of $AgNO_2$
    (c) It gives C_2H_5OH on boiling with alcoholic potash.
    (d) It forms diethylthioether on heating with alcoholic KSH.

18. Covalency of nitrogen is restricted to:
    (a) 2   (b) 3
    (c) 4   (d) 5

19. Solubility of gases in liquids decreases with rise in temperature because dissolution is an:
    (a) endothermic and reversible process
    (b) exothermic and reversible process
    (c) endothermic and irreversible process
    (d) exothermic and irreversible process

20. All elements of Group 15 show allotropy except:
    (a) Nitrogen   (b) Arsenic
    (c) Antimony   (d) Bismuth

21. Which of the following is a polysaccharide?
    (a) glucose   (b) maltose
    (c) glycogen   (d) lactose

22. Substance having the lowest boiling point:
    (a) Hydrogen   (b) Oxygen
    (c) Nitrogen   (d) Helium

23. Lower molecular mass alcohols are:
    (a) miscible in limited amount of water
    (b) miscible in excess of water
    (c) miscible in water in all proportions
    (d) immiscible in water

24. Maximum oxidation state exhibited by Chlorine is:
    (a) +1   (b) +3
    (c) +5   (d) +7

25. In which of the following cases blood cells will shrink:
    (a) when placed in water containing more than 0.9% (mass/volume) NaCl solution.
    (b) when placed in water containing less than 0.9% (mass /volume) NaCl solution.
    (c) when placed in water containing 0.9% (mass/volume) NaCl solution.
    (d) when placed in distilled water.

SECTION - B

*This section consists of 24 multiple choice questions with overall choice to attempt **any 20** questions. In case more than desirable number of questions are attempted, ONLY first 20 will be considered for evaluation.*

26. How much ethyl alcohol must be added to 1 litre of water so that the solution will freeze at $-14°C$?
    (K_f for water = 1.86°C/mol)
    (a) 7.5 mol   (b) 8.5 mol
    (c) 9.5 mol   (d) 10.5 mol

27. Which reagents are required for one step conversion of chlorobenzene to toluene?
    (a) $CH_3Cl / AlCl_3$
    (b) CH_3Cl, Na, Dry ether
    (c) CH_3Cl / Fe dark
    (d) $NaNO_2 / HCl / 0\text{-}5°C$

28. On partial hydrolysis, XeF_6 gives:
    (a) $XeO_3 + 4HF$ (b) $XeO_2F + HF$
    (c) $XeOF_4 + H_2$ (d) $XeO_2F_2 + 4HF$

29. Which one of the following statement is correct about sucrose:
  (a) It can reduce tollen's reagent however cannot reduce fehling's reagent
  (b) It undergoes mutarotation like glucose and fructose
  (c) It undergoes inversion in the configuration on hydrolysis
  (d) It is laevorotatory in nature .

30. Phenol does not undergo nucleophilic substitution reaction easily due to:
  (a) acidic nature of phenol
  (b) partial double bond character of C-OH bond
  (c) partial double bond character of C-C bond
  (d) instability of phenoxide ion

31. Which of the following has highest ionisation enthalpy?
  (a) Nitrogen   (b) Phosphorus
  (c) Oxygen   (d) Sulphur

32. Metal M ions form a ccp structure. Oxide ions occupy $\frac{1}{2}$ octahedral and $\frac{1}{2}$ tetrahedral voids. What is the formula of the oxide?
  (a) MO (b) MO_2
  (c) MO_3 (d) M_2O_3

33. The reaction of toluene with Cl_2 in presence of $FeCl_3$ gives 'X' while that of toluene with Cl_2 in presence of light gives 'Y'. Thus 'X' and 'Y' are:
  (a) X = benzyl chloride Y = o and p – chlorotoluene
  (b) X = m – chlorotoluene Y = p – chlorotoluene
  (c) X = o and p–chlorotoluene Y = trichloromethylbenzene
  (d) X= benzyl chloride, Y = m-chlorotoluene

34. Ozone is a/ an __________ molecule and the two O-O bond lengths in ozone are (i)_______ and (ii) ________
  (a) linear ,110pm; 148pm
  (b) angular, 110pm; 148pm
  (c) linear, 128pm; 128pm
  (d) angular, 128pm; 128pm

35. Water retention or puffiness due to high salt intake occurs due to:
  (a) diffusion
  (b) vapour pressure difference
  (c) osmosis
  (d) reverse osmosis

36. In the following reaction, identify A and B:

$$C_6H_{12}O_6 \xrightarrow{\text{Acetic anhydride}} A$$
$$\Big\downarrow \text{Conc.nitric acid}$$
$$B$$

  (a) $A = COOH-(CH_2)_4-COOH, B = OHC-(CHOCOCH_3)_4-CH_2OCOCH_3$
  (b) $A = COOH-(CH_2)_4-CHO, B = OHC-(CHOCOCH_3)_4-CH_2OCOCH_3$
  (c) $A = OHC-(CHOCOCH_3)_3-CH_2OCOCH_3, B = COOH-(CH_2)_4-CHO$
  (d) $A = OHC-(CHOCOCH_3)_4-CH_2OCOCH_3, B = COOH-(CH_2)_4-COOH$

37. In lake test for Al^{3+} ions, there is the formation of coloured 'floating lake'. It is due to:
  (a) Absorption of litmus by $[Al(OH)_4]^-$
  (b) Absorption of litmus by $Al(OH)_3$
  (c) Adsorption of litmus by $[Al(OH)_4]^-$
  (d) Adsorption of litmus by $Al(OH)_3$

38. A unit cell of NaCl has 4 formula units. Its edge length is 0.50 nm. Calculate the density if molar mass of NaCl = 58.5 g/mol.
  (a) $1\ g/cm^3$ (b) $2\ g/cm^3$
  (c) $3\ g/cm^3$ (d) $4g/cm^3$

39. Which one of the following are correctly arranged on the basis of the property indicated:
  (a) $I_2 < Br_2 < F_2 < Cl_2$ [increasing bond dissociation enthalpy]
  (b) $H_2O > H_2S < H_2Te < H_2Se$ [increasing acidic strength]
  (c) $NH_3 < N_2O < NH_2OH < N_2O_5$ [increasing oxidation state]
  (d) $BiH_3 < SbH_3 < AsH_3 < PH_3 < NH_3$ [increasing bondangle]

40. What would be the reactant and reagent used to obtain 2, 4-dimethyl pentan-3-ol?
  (a) Propanal and propyl magnesium bromide
  (b) 3-methylbutanal and 2-methyl magnesium iodide
  (c) 2-dimethylpropanone and methyl magnesium iodide
  (d) 2-methylpropanal and isopropyl magnesium iodide

41. o-hydroxy benzyl alcohol when reacted with PCl_3 gives the product as (IUPAC name)
  (a) o- hydroxy benzyl chloride
  (b) 2-chloromethylphenol
  (c) o-chloromethylchlorobenzene
  (d) 4-hydroxymethylphenol

42. Which of the following statements is true:
  (a) Ammonia is the weakest reducing agent and the strongest base among Group 15 hydrides.
  (b) Ammonia is the strongest reducing agent as well as the strongest base among Group 15 hydrides.
  (c) Ammonia is the weakest reducing agent as well as the weakest base among Group 15 hydrides.
  (d) Ammonia is the strongest reducing agent and the weakest base among Group 15 hydrides.

43. Identify the secondary alcohols from the following set:
    (i) $CH_3CH_2CH(OH)CH_3$　(ii) $(C_2H_5)_3COH$

    (iii) [benzene ring with OH]　(iv) [benzene ring with CH(OH)CH₃]

    (a) (i) and (iv)　　　　(b) (i) and (iii)
    (c) (i) and (ii)　　　　(d) (i), (iii) and (iv)

44. Alkenes decolourise bromine water in presence of CCl_4 due to formation of :
    (a) allyl bromide　　　(b) vinyl bromide
    (c) bromoform　　　　(d) vicinal dibromide

DIRECTIONS (Qs. 45-49) : *Given below are the questions labelled as **Assertion (A)** and **Reason (R)**. Select the most appropriate answer from the options given below :*

(a) Both A and R are true and R is the correct explanation of A.
(b) Both A and R are true but R is not the correct explanation of A.
(c) A is true but R is false.
(d) A is false but R is true.

45. **Assertion (A):** Electron gain enthalpy of oxygen is less than that of Flourine but greater than Nitrogen.
    Reason (R): Ionisation enthalpies of the elements follow the order Nitrogen > Oxygen > Fluorine

46. **Assertion (A):** Alkyl halides are insoluble in water.
    Reason (R): Alkyl halides have halogen attached to sp^3 hybrid carbon.

47. **Assertion (A):** Molarity of a solution changes with temperature.
    Reason (R): Molarity is a colligative property.

48. **Assertion (A):** SO_2 is reducing while TeO_2 is an oxidising agent.
    Reason (R): Reducing property of dioxide decreases from SO_2 to TeO_2.

49. **Assertion (A):** Cryoscopic constant depends on nature of solvent.
    Reason (R): Cryoscopic constant is a universal constant.

SECTION - C

*This section consists of 6 multiple choice questions with an overall choice to attempt **any 5**. In case more than desirable number of questions are attempted, ONLY first 5 will be considered for evaluation.*

50. Match the following:

	I		II
(i)	Amino acids	(A)	Protein
(ii)	Thymine	(B)	Nucleic acid
(iii)	Insulin	(C)	DNA
(iv)	Phosphodiester linkage	(D)	Zwitter ion
(v)	Uracil		

Which of the following is the best matched options?
(a) (i) – (A); (v) – (D); (iii) – (C); (iv) – (B)
(b) (i) – (D); (ii) – (C); (iii) – (A); (iv) – (B)
(c) (i) – (D); (v) – (D); (iii) – (A); (iv) – (B)
(d) (i) – (A); (ii) – (C); (iii) – (D); (iv) – (B)

51. Which of the following analogies is correct:
    (a) Nitrogen: $1s^2 2s^2 2p^3$: : Argon: $1s^2 2s^2 2p^6$
    (b) Carbon: maximum compounds :: Xenon: no compounds
    (c) XeF_2: Linear : : ClF_3: Trigonal planar
    (d) Helium: meteorological observations : : Argon: metallurgical processes

52. Complete the following analogy:
    Same molecular formula but different structures: A : : Non superimposable mirror images: B
    (a) A : Isomers : : B : Enantiomer
    (b) A : Enantiomers : : B : Racemic mixture
    (c) A : Stereoisomers : : B : Retention
    (d) A : Isomers : : B : Sterioisomers

Case Study : *Read the following paragraph and answers the questions.*

Early crystallographers had trouble solving the structures of inorganic solids using X-ray diffraction because some of the mathematical tools for analyzing the data had not yet been developed. Once a trial structure was proposed, it was relatively easy to calculate the diffraction pattern, but it was difficult to go the other way (from the diffraction pattern to the structure) if nothing was known *a priori* about the arrangement of atoms in the unit cell. It was important to develop some guidelines for guessing the coordination numbers and bonding geometries of atoms in crystals. The first such rules were proposed by Linus Pauling, who considered how one might pack together oppositely charged spheres of different radii. Pauling proposed from geometric considerations that the quality of the "fit" depended on the **radius ratio** of the anion and the cation.

If the anion is considered as the packing atom in the crystal, then the smaller cation fills interstitial sites ("holes"). Cations will find arrangements in which they can contact the largest number of anions. If the cation can touch all of its nearest neighbour anions then the fit is good. If the cation is too small for a given site, that coordination number will be unstable and it will prefer a lower coordination structure. The table below gives the ranges of cation/anion radius ratios that give the best fit for a given coordination geometry.

Coordination number	Geometry	$\rho = r_{cation}/r_{anion}$
2	linear	0-0.155
3	triangular	0.155-0.225
4	tetrahedral	0.225-0.414
4	square planar	0.414-0.732
6	octahedral	0.414-0.732
8	cubic	0.732-1.0
12	cuboctahedral	1.0

(**Source:** Ionic Radii and Radius Ratios. (2021, June 8). Retrieved June 29, 2021, from https://chem.libretexts.org/@go/page/183346)

53. The radius of Ag^+ ion is 126pm and of I^- ion is 216pm. The coordination number of Ag^+ ion is:
    - (a) 2
    - (b) 3
    - (c) 6
    - (d) 8

54. A solid AB has square planar structure. If the radius of cation A^+ is 120pm, calculate the maximum possible value of anion B^-
    - (a) 240 pm   (b) 270 pm   (c) 280 pm   (d) 290 pm

55. A "good fit" is considered to be one where the cation can touch:
    - (a) all of its nearest neighbour anions.
    - (b) most of its nearest neighbour anions.
    - (c) some of its nearest neighbour anions.
    - (d) none of its nearest neighbour anions.

Solutions

1. **(d)** N-N is weaker than P-P;

  (a) Phosphorus has a higher melting point due to bigger size than Nitrogen.

  (b) Nitrogen is inert due to formation of triple bonds and has a lower covalence due to non-availability of d-orbitals.

  (c) Since nitrogen atom is smaller there is greater repulsion of electron density between two nitrogen atoms, thereby weakening the N-N bond. Hence, Nitrogen shows lesser tendency of catenation than phosphorus.

2. **(c)** Metal deficiency defect (cation is missing from lattice site); in Frenkel defect the smaller ion occupies the interstitial sites and Schottky defect equal number of cations and anions are missing. Interstitial defect an atom or molecule occupies interstitial sites so in these three defects the ratio of positive and negative ions (Stoichiometry) of a solid is not disturbed.

3. **(b)**

4. **(c)** Pink colour of LiCl crystal is due to metal excess defect and formation of anionic vacancies (F-Centre).

5. **(c)** 1,4-dicholorbenzene (para isomers are more symmetric than ortho and meta isomers)

6. **(d)** Glucose is found to exist in two different crystalline forms which are named as α and β which can not be explained by open chain structure of glucose.

7. **(c)** Reaction since alkoxide ion reacts with primary alkyl halide in a single step to form ether. Hence, it is S_N2 reaction.

8. **(b)** Chlorine water loses its yellow colour on standing because in the presence of light a mixture of hypochlorous acid (HOCl) and hydrochloric acid are fomed.

$$H_2O + Cl_2 \longrightarrow HOCl + HCl$$

9. **(a)** Protonation of alcohol molecule

  Step 1: Formation of protonated alcohol

Ethanol $+ H^+ \xrightleftharpoons{\text{Fast}}$ Protonated alcohol (Ethyl oxonium ion)

Step 2: Formation of carbocation: It is the slowest step and hence, the rate determining step of the reaction.

Protonated alcohol $\xrightleftharpoons{\text{Slow}}$ carbocation $+ H_2O$

Step 3: Formation of ethene by elimination of a proton.

carbocation $\rightleftharpoons$ Ethene $+ H^+$

10. **(a)** The value of any physical property of amorphous solids is same along any direction. Hence, amorphous solids are isotropic.

11. **(c)** Kolbe's reaction is used to prepare salicylic acid, Etard reaction for benzaldehyde, Reimer-Tiemann reaction for salicylaldehyde and Stephen's reduction for aldehyde.

12. **(d)** 22 carat gold (it is an alloy so solid in solid solution)

13. **(a)** Alcohols form intermolecular hydrogen bonds due to which their b.pt. is high.

14. **(b)** Boiling point increases down the group but water forms strong hydrogen bonds so it has higher boiling point than H_2S.

15. **(d)** pH does not affect the primary structure of protein while pH affects the tertiary structure.

16. **(a)** $C_6H_5CH_2CH = CH_2 + HBr \xrightarrow[\substack{\text{Anti Markovnikov's} \\ \text{Addition}}]{\text{Organic peroxide}}$

$C_6H_5CH_2CH_2CH_2Br$
1-bromo-3-phenylpropane

17. **(b)** It gives nitroethane on heating with aqueous solution of $AgNO_2$.

(C_2H_5Br reacts with metallic Na to give butane, gives ethene on boiling with alcoholic potash and forms C_2H_5SH (thiol) on heating with alcoholic KSH)

18. **(c)** Covalency of nitrogen is restricted to 4 due to non availability of d-orbitals.

19. **(b)** Exothermic and reversible process (according to Le - Chatlier principle solubility of gases in liquids decreases with rise in temperature)

20. **(a)** Nitrogen does not show allotropy due to small size and high electronegativity as N-N is weak.

21. **(c)** Glycogen (It is a polymer of glucose)

22. **(d)** Helium is monoatomic and has low atomic mass.

23. **(c)** Miscible in water in all proportions. Lower molecular mass alcohols are able to form hydrogen bonds with water

24. **(d)** ($Cl : 1s^2 2s^2 2p^6 3s^2 3p^5$)

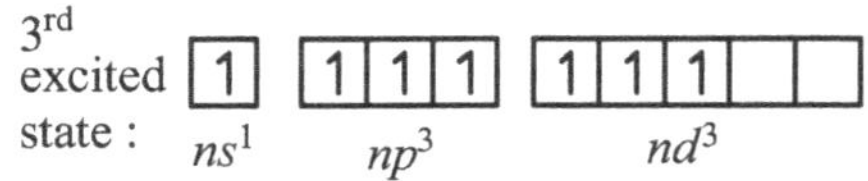

3rd excited state :

(7 unpaired electrons account for +7 oxidation state)

25. **(a)** When placed in water containing more than 0.9% (mass/volume) NaCl solution because fluid inside blood cells is isotonic with 0.9% NaCl solution.

26. **(a)** $7.5\,mol$

$$\Delta T_f = K_f m$$

$$\Delta T_f = K_f \frac{n_2 \times 1000}{w_1}$$

$$14 = 1.86 \times \frac{n_2 \times 1000}{1000}$$

$$n_2 = 7.5\,mol$$

27. **(b)**

Chlorobenzene + Na + CH_3Cl $\xrightarrow[\text{fittig rxn}]{\text{Ether}\atop\text{Wurtz}}$ Toluene

28. **(d)** $XeF_4 + H_2O \rightarrow XeO_2F_2 + 4HF$

29. **(c)** It undergoes inversion in the configuration on hydrolysis.

30. **(b)** Due to partial double bond character of C–OH bond.

31. **(a)** High IE of N is because of smallest size in the group and have stable half - filled p subshell.

32. **(d)** Metal M ions form ccp structure. Let number of ions of M be : X

No. of tetrahedral voids = 2x

No. of octahedral voids = x

Number of oxide ions will be $\frac{1}{2}x + \frac{1}{2}(2x) = \frac{3}{2x}$

Formula of oxide $= \dfrac{M_x O_3}{2x} = M_2 O_3$

33. **(c)** The reaction of toluene with Cl_2 in presence of $FeCl_3$ gives 'X' due to electrophilic substitution reaction taking place at ortho and para positions and reaction in the presence of light gives 'Y', due to substitution reaction occurring via free radical mechanism.

Thus X = o and p–chlorotoluene Y = trichloromethylbenzene

34. **(d)** angular, 128pm; 128pm (Ozone is a resonance hybrid of two equivalent structures)

35. **(c)** Osmosis

36. **(d)** $A = OHC - (CHOCOCH_3)_4 - CH_2OCOCH_3$

$B = COOH - (CH_2)_4 - COOH$

$$CHO$$
$$|$$
$$(CHOCOCH_3)_4 + 5CH_3COOH$$
$$\qquad |\qquad\quad O$$
$$\qquad\qquad\qquad\quad ||$$
$$CH_2O - C - CH_3$$

Glucose penta acetate

37. **(d)** In lake test for Al^{3+} ions, there is the formation of coloured 'floating lake' due to adsorption of litmus by $Al(OH)_3$.

38. **(c)** $3\ g/cm^3$

Using formula

$$\text{Density} = \frac{(Z \times M)}{(a^3 \times N_A)}$$

$$D = \frac{4 \times 58.5}{(0.5 \times 10^{-7})^3 \times 6.023 \times 10^{23}} = 3.1\ g/cm^3$$

39. **(d)** $BiH_3 < SbH_3 < AsH_3 < PH_3 < NH_3$ [increasing bond angle] correct order

(a) $I_2 < Br_2 < F_2 < Cl_2$ [increasing bond dissociation enthalpy]: incorrect order , correct order is $Cl_2 > Br_2 > F_2 > I_2$.

(b) $H_2O > H_2S < H_2Te < H_2Se$ [increasing acidic strength]: incorrect order , correct order is

$H_2O < H_2S < H_2Se < H_2Te$

(c) $NH_3 < N_2O < NH_2OH < N_2O_5$ [increasing oxidation state]: incorrect order NH_3 (Oxidation state-3) N_2O (Oxidation state +1) NH_2OH(Oxidation state-1) N_2O_5 (Oxidation state + 5)

40. **(d)**
$$\qquad\qquad\qquad H$$
$$\qquad\qquad\qquad |$$
$$CH_3 - CH - C = O + (CH_3)_2CHMgI \longrightarrow$$
$$\qquad\qquad |\qquad\qquad\quad \text{Isopropyl magnesium iodide}$$
$$\qquad\qquad CH_3$$

2-Methylpropanal

$$\qquad\quad H\qquad\qquad\qquad\qquad\qquad H$$
$$\qquad\quad |\qquad\qquad\qquad\qquad\qquad\quad |$$
$$(CH_3)_2CH - C - OMgI \xrightarrow{H_2O} (CH_3)_2CH - C - OH$$
$$\qquad\quad |\qquad\qquad\qquad\qquad\qquad\quad |$$
$$\qquad\quad CH(CH_3)_2\qquad\qquad\qquad CH(CH_3)_2$$

2, 4-Dimethylpentan-3-ol

41. **(b)**

2-chloromethylphenol

42. **(a)** Ammonia is the weakest reducing agent and the strongest base among Group 15 hydrides.

The reducing character of hydrides increases down the group due to decrease in bond dissociation enthalpy.

43. **(a)**

(i) $CH_3CH_2CH(OH)CH_3$ (secondary)

(ii) $(C_2H_5)_3COH$ (tertiary)

(iii) (Phenol not an alcohol)

(iv) CH_3 (secondary)

44. **(d)** $CH_2 = CH_2 + Br_2 \rightarrow BrCH_2 - CH_2Br$
$$\qquad\qquad\qquad\qquad\qquad\qquad \text{vicinal dibromide}$$

45. **(c)** Electron gain enthalpy of oxygen is less than that of Flourine but greater than Nitrogen.

Ionisation enthalpies of the elements follow the order: Fluorine > Nitrogen > Oxygen

46. **(b)** Alkyl halides are insoluble in water.

Alkyl halides have halogen attached to sp^3 hybrid carbon. Alkyl halides are insoluble in water because they are unable to form hydrogen bonds with water or break pre-existing hydrogen bonds.

47. **(c)** Molarity of a solution changes with temperature.

Molarity is not a colligative property.

Molarity is a means to express concentration. It is not a physical property.

48. **(a)** SO_2 is reducing while TeO_2 is an oxidising agent and reducing property of dioxide decreases from SO_2 to TeO_2.

49. **(c)** Cryoscopic constant depends on nature of solvent.

Cryoscopic constant is not a universal constant.

Cryoscopic constant varies with type of solvent.

50. (b) (i) – (D); (ii) – (C); (iii) – (A); (iv) – (B)

Amino acids form proteins and exist as zwitter ion, Thymine is a nitrogenous base in DNA, Insulin is a protein, phosphodiester linkage is found in nucleic acids so also in DNA and Uracil is nitrogenous base found in RNA which is a nucleic acid.

51. (d) Helium: meteorological observations :: Argon: metallurgical processes

(a) Nitrogen: $1s^2 2s^2 2p^3$: : Argon: $1s^2 2s^2 2p^6$ is configuration of Neon not Argon

(b) Carbon: maximum compounds : : Xenon: no compounds , Xenon forms compounds

(c) XeF_2: Linear : : ClF_3: Trigonal planar , ClF_3 is T shaped not trigonal planar

52. (a) A : Isomers : : B: Enantiomer

Isomers have Same molecular formula but different structure

Enantiomers are Non superimposable mirror images

53. (c) The radius of Ag^+ ion is 126 pm and of I^- ion is 216 pm. The coordination number of Ag^+ ion is:

$$\rho = \frac{r_{cation}}{r_{anion}} = \frac{126}{216} = 0.58$$

Radius ratio lies in the range $0.414 - 0.732$, so has coordination number 6 or 4 according to the table. Since none of the options is 4, so the answer is 6.

54. (d) 290 pm

Square planar means radius, ratio is between $0.414 - 0.732$ If radius of cation is 120 pm then anion should be in the

range $\rho = \dfrac{r_{cation}}{r_{anion}}$

$0.414 = \dfrac{120}{x}$ so x = 289.8 = 290 pm

$0.732 = \dfrac{120}{x}$ so x = 163.9 = 164 pm

55. (a) All of its nearest neighbour anions.

All India *2020*
CBSE Board Solved Paper

Time Allowed : 3 Hours   *Maximum Marks : 70*

General Instructions:

Read the following instructions very carefully and strictly follow them:

  (i)   This question paper comprises **four** Sections A, B, C and D. There are **37** questions in the questions paper. **All** questions are compulsory.

  (ii) **Section A:** Questions no. **1** to **20** are very short answer type questions, carrying **1** mark each. Answer these questions in one word or one sentence.

 (iii) **Section B:** Questions no. **21** to **27** are short answer type questions, carrying **2** mark each.

 (iv) **Section C:** Questions no. **28** to **34** are long answer type-I questions, carrying **3** mark each.

  (v) **Section D:** Questions no. **35** to **37** are long answer type-II questions, carrying **5** mark each.

 (vi) There is no overall choice in the question paper. However, an internal choice has been provided in 2 questions of two marks, 2 questions of three marks and all the 3 questions of five marks. You have to attempt only one of the choices in such questions.

 (vii) In addition to this, separate instructions are given with each section and question, wherever necessary.

(viii) Use of calculators and log tables is not permitted.

SECTION - A

Read the given passage and answer the questions number 1 to 5 that follow:

The substitution reaction of alkyl halide mainly occurs by S_N1 or S_N2 mechanism. Whatever mechanism alkyl halides follow for the substitution reaction to occur, the polarity of the carbon halogen bond is responsible for these substitution reactions. The rate of S_N1 reactions are governed by the stability of carbocation whereas for S_N2 reactions steric factor is the deciding factor. If the starting material is a chiral compound, we may end up with an inverted product or racemic mixture depending upon the type of mechanism followed by alkyl halide. Cleavage of ethers with HI is also governed by steric factor and stability of carbocation, which indicates that in organic chemistry, these two major factors help us in deciding the kind of product formed.

1. Predict the stereochemistry of the product formed if an optically active alkyl halide undergoes substitution reaction by S_N1 mechanism.

2. Name the instrument used for measuring the angle by which the plane polarised light is rotated.

3. Predict the major product formed when 2-bromopentane reacts with alcoholic KOH.

4. Give one use of CHI_3.

5. Write the structures of the products formed when anisole is treated with HI.

Questions number 6 to 10 are one word answers:

6. Identify which liquid will have a higher vapour pressure at 90°C if the boiling points of two liquids A and B are 140°C and 180°, respectively.

7. Out of zinc and tin, whose coating is better to protect iron objects?

8. Will the rate constant of the reaction depend upon T if the E_{act} (activating energy) of the reaction is zero?

9. Give the structure of the monomer of PVC.

10. Which structural unit present in a detergent makes it non-biodegradable?

Questions number 11 to 15 are multiple choice questions:

11. Out of the following, the strongest base in aqueous solution is

  (a) Methylamine

  (b) Dimethylamine

  (c) Trimethylamine

  (d) Aniline

12. Iodoform test is not given by

(a) Ethanol

(b) Ethanal

(c) Pentan-2-one

(d) Pentan-3-one

13. Out of the following transition elements, the maximum number of oxidation states are shown by

(a) $Sc(Z = 21)$ (b) $Cr(Z = 24)$

(c) $Mn(Z = 25)$ (d) $Fe(Z = 26)$

14. Hardening of leather in tanning industry is based on

(a) Electrophoresis

(b) Electro-osmosis

(c) Mutual coagulation

(d) Tyndall effect

15. What is the correct IUPAC name of the given compound?

$$CH_3-\underset{\underset{COOH}{|}}{\overset{\overset{CH_3}{|}}{C}}-CH_2-CH_3$$

(a) 2, 2-Dimethylbutanoic acid

(b) 2-Carboxyl-2-methylbutane

(c) 2-Ethyl-2-methylpropanoic acid

(d) 3-Methylbutane carboxylic acid

For questions number 16 to 20, two statements are given – one labelled Assertion (A) and the other labelled Reason (R). Select the correct answer to these questions from the codes (i), (ii), (iii) and (iv) as given below:

(i) Both Assertion (A) and Reason (R) are correct statements, and Reason (R) is the correct explanation of the Assertion (A).

(ii) Both Assertion (A) and Reason (R) are correct statements, but Reason (R) is not the correct explanation of the Assertion (A).

(iii) Assertion (A) is correct, but Reason (R) is incorrect statement.

(iv) Assertion (A) is incorrect, but Reason (R) is correct statement.

16. **Assertion (A) :** Au and Ag are extracted by leaching their ores with a dil. solution of NaCN.

    Reason (R) : Impurities associated with these ores dissolve in NaCN.

17. **Assertion (A) :** F – F bond in F_2 molecule is weak.

    Reason (R) : F atom is small in size.

18. **Assertion (A) :** Linkage isomerism arises in coordination compounds because of ambidentate ligand.

    Reason (R) : Ambidentate ligand like NO_2 has two different donor atoms i.e., N and O.

19. **Assertion (A) :** Sucrose is a non-reducing sugar.

    Reason (R) : Sucrose has glycosidic linkage.

20. **Assertion (A) :** The molecularity of the reaction $H_2 + Br_2 \rightarrow 2HBr$ appears to be 2.

    Reason (R) : Two molecules of the reactants are involved in the given elementary reaction.

SECTION B

21. Define the following terms:

(a) Tranquilizers

(b) Antiseptic

OR

Explain the cleansing action of soaps.

22. For a 5% solution of urea (Molar mass = 60 g/mol), calculate the osmotic pressure at 300 K. [R = 0.0821 L atm K^{-1} mol^{-1}]

OR

Visha took two aqueous solutions – one containing 7.5 g of urea (Molar mass = 60 g/mol) and the other containing 42.75 g of substance Z in 100 g water, respectively. It was observed that both the solutions froze at the same temperature. Calculate the molar mass of Z.

23. Analyse the given graph, drawn between concentration of reactant vs. time.

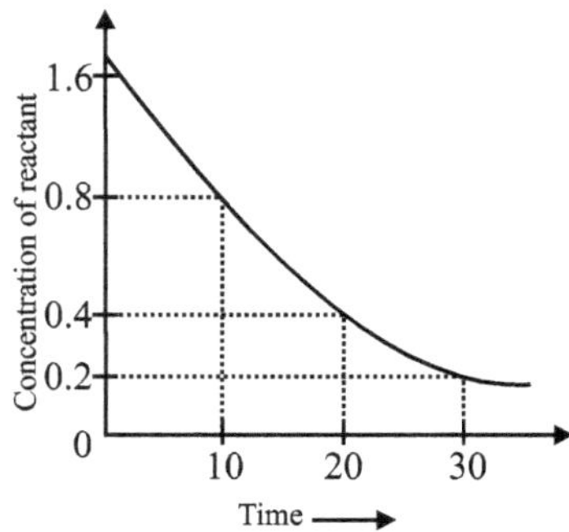

(a) Predict the order of reaction.

(b) Theoretically, can the concentration of the reactant reduce to zero after infinite time? Explain

24. Draw the shape of the following molecules:

(a) $XeOF_4$

(b) BrF_3

25. Give the formulae of the following compounds:

   (a) Potassium tetrahydroxidozincate (II)

   (b) Hexaammineplatinum (IV) chloride

26. What happens when

   (a) Propanone is treated with methylmagnesium iodide and then hydrolysed, and

   (b) Benzene is treated with CH_3COCl in presence of anhydrous $AlCl_3$?

27. Write the names and structures of monomers in the following polymers:

   (a) Bakelite   (b) Neoprene

SECTION - C

28. Give the structures of A and B in the following sequence of reactions:

   (a) $CH_3COOH \xrightarrow[\Delta]{NH_3} A \xrightarrow{NaOBr} B$

   (b) $C_6H_5NO_2 \xrightarrow{Fe/HCl} A \xrightarrow[0° - 5°C]{NaNO_2 + HCl} B$

   (c) $C_6H_5N_2^+ Cl^- \xrightarrow[\Delta]{CuCN} A \xrightarrow{H_2O/H^+} B$

OR

   (a) How will you distinguish between the following pairs of compounds:

     (i) Aniline and Ethanamine

     (ii) Aniline and N-Methylaniline

   (b) Arrange the following compounds in decreasing order of their boiling points:

     Butanol, Butanamine, Butane

29. Give the plausible explanation for the following:

   (a) Glucose doesn't give 2,4-DNP test.

   (b) The two strands in DNA are not identical but are complementary.

   (c) Starch and cellulose both contain glucose unit as monomer, yet they are structurally different.

30. Account for the following:

   (a) Sulphurous acid is a reducing agent.

   (b) Fluorine forms only one oxoacid.

   (c) Boiling point of noble gases increases from He to Rn.

OR

Complete the following chemical reactions:

   (a) $MnO_2 + 4HCl \longrightarrow$

   (b) $XeF_6 + KF \longrightarrow$

   (c) $I^-(aq) + H^+(aq) + O_2(g) \longrightarrow$

31. Explain the role of the following:

   (a) NaCN in the separation of ZnS and PbS.

   (b) SiO_2 in the metallurgy of Cu containing Fe as impurity.

   (c) Iodine in the refining of Ti.

32. Give three points of difference between physisorption and chemisorption.

33. How will the rate of the reaction be affected when

   (a) Surface area of the reactant is reduced,

   (b) Catalyst is added in a reversible reaction, and

   (c) Temperature of the reaction is increased?

34. Calculate the mass of ascorbic acid (Molar mass = 176 g mol^{-1}) to be dissolved in 75 g of acetic acid, to lower its freezing point by 1.5°C. (k_f = 3.9 K kg mol^{-1})

SECTION - D

35. (a) Calculate $\Delta G°$ for the reaction

     $Zn(s) + Cu^{2+}(aq) \longrightarrow Zn^{2+}(aq) + Cu(s)$

     Given: E° for Zn^{2+}/Zn = –0.76 V and

            E° for Cu^{2+}/Cu = + 0.34 V

            R = 8.314 JK^{-1} mol^{-1}

            F = 96500 C mol^{-1}

   (b) Give two advantages of fuel cells.

OR

   (a) Out of the following pairs, predict with reason which pair will allow greater conduction of electricity:

     (i) Silver wire at 30°C or silver wire at 60°C.

     (ii) 0.1 M CH_3COOH solution or 1 M CH_3COOH solution.

     (iii) KCl solution at 20°C or KCl solution at 50°C.

   (b) Give two points of differences between electro chemical and electrolytic cells.

36. (a) Account for the following:

     (i) Copper (I) compounds are white whereas copper (II) compounds are coloured.

     (ii) Chromates change their colour when kept in an acidic solution.

     (iii) Zn, Cd, Hg are considered as *d*-block elements but not as transition elements.

   (b) Calculate the spin-only moment of Co^{2+} (Z = 27) by writing the electronic configuration of Co and Co^{2+}.

OR

(a) Give three points of difference between lanthanoids and actinoids.

(b) Give reason and select one atom/ion which will exhibit asked property:

    (i) Sc^{3+} or Cr^{3+} (Exhibit diamagnetic behaviour)

    (ii) Cr or Cu (High melting and boiling point)

37. (a) Out of *t*-butyl alcohol and *n*-butanol, which one will undergo acid catalyzed dehydration faster and why?

    (b) Carry out the following conversions:

(i) Phenol to salicylaldehyde

(ii) *t*-Butylchloride to *t*-butyl ethyl ether

(iii) Propene to propanol

OR

(a) Give the mechanism for the formation of ethanol from ethene.

(b) Predict the reagent for carrying out the following conversions:

    (i) Phenol to benzoquinone

    (ii) Anisole to *p*-bromoanisole

    (iii) Phenol to 2,4,6-tribromophenol

Solutions

SECTION - A

1. Inversion occurs more than retention, leading to partial racemization.

2. Polarimeter

3. 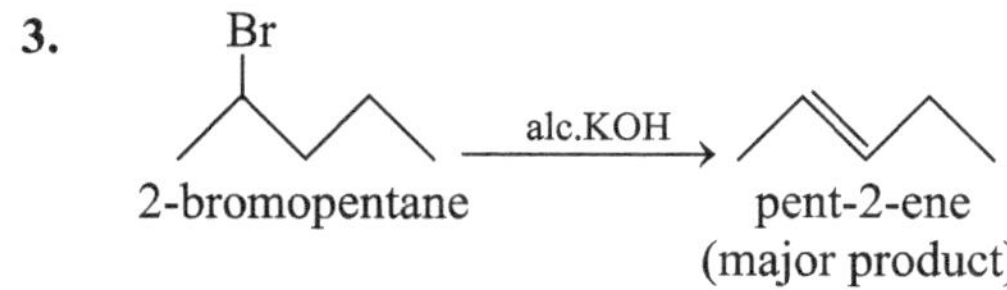

2-bromopentane $\xrightarrow{\text{alc.KOH}}$ pent-2-ene (major product)

4. Iodoform (CHI_3) is used as a disinfectant.

5. 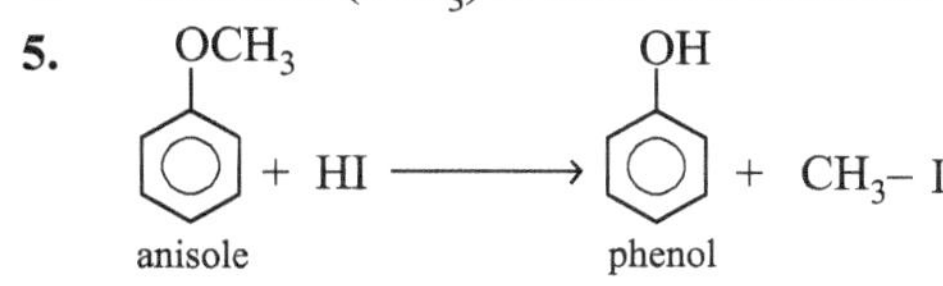

anisole + HI ⟶ phenol + $CH_3- I$

6. Liquid A has higher vapour pressure.

7. Zn coating is better to protect iron objects.

8. No

9. $CH_2 = CHCl$
   vinyl chloride

10. Branched hydrocarbon chains.

11. (b) Order of basicity in aqueous solution for amines :
    $2° > 1° > 3° > NH_3$

12. (d) The iodoform test is a test for the presence of carbonyl compounds with the structure $RCOCH_3$ and CH_3CHO; and alcohols with the structure $R - CH(OH)CH_3$.

13. (c) $Mn(25) = 1s^2\ 2s^2\ 2p^6\ 3s^2\ 3p^6\ 3d^5\ 4s^2$
    Mn has maximum number of oxidation states from +1 to +7 due to $3d^5 4s^2$.

14. (c) Tannin contains a negatively charged colloidal particle whereas leather has a positively charged colloidal particle. Thus, coagulation occurs when leather is soaked in tannin.

15. (a) 2, 2-Dimethylbutanoic acid

$$\overset{1}{\underset{}{}}H_3C - \overset{2}{\underset{|}{C}} - \overset{3}{CH_2} - \overset{4}{CH_3}$$

with CH_3 above position 2 and $COOH$ below position 1.

16. (iii) Au and Ag are extracted by leaching their ores with a dil. solution of NaCN because Au and Ag form a soluble complex compound with CN^- and can be separated from their ores. Hence, assertion is correct but reason is incorrect.

17. (i) Because of small size of F atoms, there is repulsion of electrons in F_2 molecule. Thus, F-F bond in F_2 molecule is weak.
    Hence, reason is the correct explanation of given assertion.

18. (i) Ambidentate ligand like NO_2 has two different donor atoms *i.e.* N and O. Thus, it can form coordinate bonds through N and O both or we can say that it can form linkage isomers.

19. (ii) Sucrose is a non-reducing sugar because the two monosaccharide units are held together by a glycosidic linkage between C_1 of α-glucose and C_2 of β-fructose. The reducing groups are involved in glycosidic bond formation.

20. (i) The molecularity of a reaction depends only on the stoichiometry of the reaction. Hence, molecularity of the reaction $H_2 + Br_2 \rightarrow 2HBr$ is two.
    Hence, reason is the correct explanation of given assertion.

SECTION - B

21. (a) **Tranquilizers:** These are the chemical compounds which are used for the treatment of stress and mental diseases.   **(1 Mark)**

    (b) **Antiseptic:** These are the chemical compounds which prevent the growth of micro-organism or may even kill them.   **(1 Mark)**

OR

Cleansing action of soaps: A molecule of soap is sodium or potassium salts of long-chain carboxylic acids. Dirt or oil does not dissolve in water. But the carbon chain of soap dissolves in oil and the ionic end dissolves in water. Soap molecules form micelle around the dirt particle in such a way that hydrophobic part of soap is in dirt particle and hydrophilic part is in water. Therefore, soap forms an emulsion in water and helps in dissolving dirt.

(2 Marks)

22. 5% urea solution means. 5g urea is present in 100 mL of solution.

Molarity of solution

$$C = \frac{5g}{60\ \text{g/mol}} \times \frac{1000}{100L}$$

$$C = \frac{10}{12}\ \text{mol/L} \qquad \textbf{(1 Mark)}$$

Osmotic pressure, $\pi = CRT$

$$\pi = \frac{10}{12} \times 0.0821 \times 300$$

$$= 20.525\ \text{atm} \qquad \textbf{(1 Mark)}$$

OR

It is given that the depression in freezing points of the two given aqueous solution are same.

$$(\Delta T_f)_{urea} = (\Delta T_f)_z \qquad \textbf{(½ Mark)}$$

$$m_{urea} \times (k_f)_{water} = m_z \times (k_f)_{water}$$

$$\Rightarrow \quad \dfrac{\dfrac{7.5}{60}}{\dfrac{100}{1000}} = \dfrac{\dfrac{42.75}{M_z}}{\dfrac{100}{1000}} \qquad \textbf{(½ Mark)}$$

$$\Rightarrow \quad M_z = 3\,342 \text{ g/mol} \qquad \textbf{(1 Mark)}$$

23. (a) Half-life calculation from the given graph: Concentration of reactant reduces from 0.8 to 0.4 in $(20 - 10) = 10$ seconds.

Again the concentration reduces to half (0.4 to 0.2) in $(30 - 20) = 10$ seconds.

Thus, the half-life of reaction remains constant or we can say that order of reaction is one. **(1 Mark)**

(b) For a first order reaction, concentration never reduces to zero. For first order reaction $\ln \dfrac{[A]}{[A]_0} = -kt$

$[A] = [A]_0\, e^{-kt}$

where $[A]_0$ is the initial concentration of the reactant. Mathematically, $[A] > 0$ for all $t < \infty$ **(1 Mark)**

24. (a)

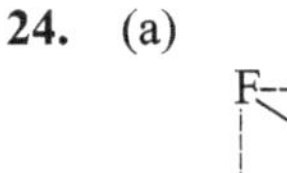

Shape: Square pyramidal
No. of sigma bonds = 5
No. of lone pair of electrons with Xe = 1 **(1 Mark)**

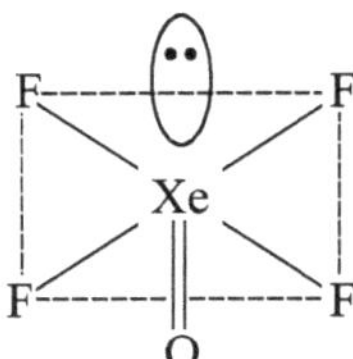

Note

The molecular geometry of XeOF$_4$ will be octahedral with 5 bond pairs of electrons and one lone pair of electrons. To reduce the lp-bp repulsions, the electron pair will occupy one of the axial position.

(b)

T-Shape
No. of sigma bonds = 3
No. of lone pairs of electrons = 2 **(1 Mark)**

Note

3 bond pairs and 2 lone pairs of electrons take the geometry of trigonal bipyramidal. To reduce the lp-bp repulsions, BrF$_3$ forms T-shape molecule.

25. (a) Potassium tetrahydroxidozincate(II), $K_2[Zn(OH)_4]$ **(1 Mark)**

(b) Hexaammineplatinum(IV) chloride, $[Pt(NH_3)_6]Cl_4$ **(1 Mark)**

26. (a)

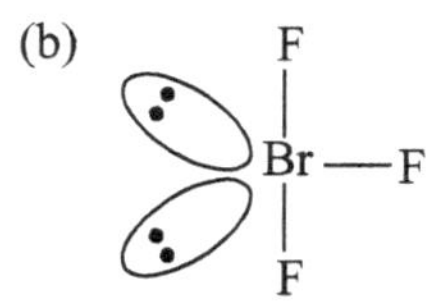

(1 Mark)

(b)

(1 Mark)

27. (a)

(1 Mark)

(b) $CH_2 = C - CH = CH_2$ with Cl substituent
chloroprene **(1 Mark)**

SECTION - C

28. (a) $CH_3{-}COOH + NH_3 \longrightarrow CH_3COO^-NH_4^+ \xrightarrow[-H_2O]{\Delta}$

$\underset{(A)}{CH_3 - CO - NH_2} \xrightarrow{NaOBr} \underset{(B)}{CH_3 - NH_2}$

(½ + ½ = 1 Mark)

Note

Conversion of A to B is Hofmann Degradation reaction.

Step 1:

$$R-N=C=O$$
Isocyanate

Step 3:

$$R-N=C=O \xrightarrow{OH^-} R-\ddot{N}-\underset{OH}{\overset{OH}{C}}-O^- \rightleftharpoons$$

$$R-N-\overset{O^-}{\underset{H}{C}}-O \xrightarrow{H^+} R-NH_2 + CO_2$$

(b)
$$\underset{(NO_2)}{\bigcirc} \xrightarrow{Fe/HCl} \underset{(A)}{\underset{(NH_2)}{\bigcirc}} \xrightarrow[0°-5°C]{NaNO_2 + HCl} \underset{(B)}{\overset{N\equiv NCl^-}{\bigcirc}}$$

(½ + ½ = 1 Mark)

(c)
$$\underset{(A)}{\overset{N_2^+Cl^-}{\bigcirc}} \xrightarrow[\Delta]{CuCN} \underset{(A)}{\overset{CN}{\bigcirc}} \xrightarrow{H_2O/H^+} \underset{(B)}{\overset{COOH}{\bigcirc}}$$

(½ + ½ = 1 Mark)

OR

(a) (i) Aniline and ethanamine can be distinguished by the azo-dye test.

An orange dye is obtained when aniline reacts with $(NaNO_2 + $ dil. HCl$)$ at $0°-5°C$ followed by a reaction with alkaline solution of 2-naphthol.

Ethanamine gives a brisk effervescences with the same solution due to evolution of N_2 gas.

(ii)

$$\underset{\substack{\text{Aniline}\\(1° \text{ Amine})}}{\overset{NH_2}{\bigcirc}} \qquad \underset{\substack{\text{N-Methylaniline}\\(2° \text{ Amine})}}{\overset{NHCH_3}{\bigcirc}}$$

Only primary amines react with $(CHCl_3 + KOH)$ to give a foul odour of isocyanide (carbylamine reaction). Hence, aniline will give this test but N-methylaniline will not. Also, aniline will form azo dye as in (i), but N-methylaniline will not form dye.

(1 + 1 = 2 Marks)

(b) $CH_3 - CH_2 - CH_2 - CH_2 - OH$ (butanol)
$CH_3 - CH_2 - CH_2 - CH_2 - NH_2$ (butanamine)
$CH_3 - CH_2 - CH_2 - CH_3$ (butane)
Due to hydrogen bonding, the decreasing order of boiling point is:
Butanol > Butanamine > Butane   **(1 Mark)**

29. (a) Aldehyde group is not free in glucose, it is involved in the formation of cyclic structure in glucose. Thus, it does not react with 2, 4-dinitrophenylhydrazine.

(1 Mark)

(b) The two strands in DNA are held together by hydrogen bonds between specific pair of bases (cytosine with guanine and adenine with thymine). Thus, the two strands are complementary to each other. **(1 Mark)**

(c) Starch contains α-D-glucose, while cellulose contains β-D-glucose as their monomers. **(1 Mark)**

30. (a) Sulphurous acid can be oxidized to sulphuric acid, therefore it can act as a reducing agent. **(1 Mark)**

(b) Due to small size and high electronegativity, fluorine cannot remain in higher oxidation state and therefore, cannot act as a central atom in higher oxoacids. It forms only one oxoacid, HOF. **(1 Mark)**

(c) Only weak vander Waals forces act as interatomic attraction in noble gases. Thus, as the atomic mass increases, boiling point increases from He to Rn.

(1 Mark)

OR

(a) $MnO_2 + 4HCl \longrightarrow MnCl_2 + Cl_2 + 2H_2O$

(b) $XeF_6 + KF \longrightarrow K^+ [XeF_7]^-$

(c) $4I^-(aq) + 4H^+(aq) + O_2(g) \longrightarrow 2I_2 + 2H_2O$

(1 + 1 + 1 = 3 Marks)

31. (a) Sulphide ores are concentrated by froth floatation method in which NaCN is used as depressant. NaCN reacts with ZnS to form $Na_2[Zn(CN)_4]$ but does not react with PbS and allow PbS to come with the froth.

(1 Mark)

(b) If the sulphide ore of Cu contains impurity of FeO, then SiO_2 (acidic flux) can remove the impurity FeO (basic gangue) as $FeSiO_3$ (slag). **(1 Mark)**

(c) $$\underset{(impure)}{Ti} + 2I_2 \xrightarrow{\Delta} Ti\,I_4$$

$$Ti\,I_4 \xrightarrow[1800K]{W,\ wire} \underset{(pure)}{Ti} + 2I_2\uparrow$$

(1 Mark)

32.

	Physisorption		Chemisorption
(a)	It arises because of van der Waals' forces.	(a)	It is caused by chemical bond formation.
(b)	It is reversible in nature.	(b)	It is irreversible.
(c)	Low temperature is favourable for adsorption.	(c)	High temperature is favourable for adsorption.

(1 + 1 + 1 = 3 Marks)

33. (a) When surface area of the reactant is reduced, the rate of reaction will also reduce. **(1 Mark)**

(b) A catalyst increases the rate of both forward and backward reactions of a reversible reaction to the same extent. **(1 Mark)**

(c) Increase in temperature reduces the activation energy and thus increases the rate of reaction. **(1 Mark)**

34. Let 'w' be the required mass of ascorbic acid.

Molality of ascorbic and

$$m = \frac{(w/176)}{(75/1000)} \implies m = \frac{w}{176} \times \frac{1000}{75} \quad \textbf{(½ Mark)}$$

$(k_f)_{acetic} = 3.9 \text{ K kg mol}^{-1}$ **(1 Mark)**

$\Delta T_f = 1.5 \,^{\circ}\text{C} \implies \Delta T_f = 1.5 \text{ K}$

$$\Delta T_f = m.k_f \quad \textbf{(½ Mark)}$$

$$\implies 1.5 = \frac{w}{176} \times \frac{1000}{75} \times 3.9$$

$$\implies w = 5.08 \text{ g} \approx 5\text{g} \quad \textbf{(1 Mark)}$$

SECTION - D

35. (a) $\text{Zn(s)} + \text{Cu}^{2+}(\text{aq}) \longrightarrow \text{Zn}^{2+}(\text{aq}) + \text{Cu(s)}$

$$E^{\circ}_{Cu^{2+}/Cu} = E^{\circ}_{cathode} = +0.34 \text{ V}$$

$$E^{\circ}_{Zn^{2+}/Zn} = E^{\circ}_{anode} = -0.76 \text{ V}$$

$$E^{\circ}_{cell} = E^{\circ}_{cathode} - E^{\circ}_{anode}$$
$$= 0.34 - (-0.76) = 1.1 \text{ V} \quad \textbf{(1 Mark)}$$

$$n = 2 \quad \textbf{(½ Mark)}$$

$$F = 96500 \text{ C mol}^{-1}$$

$$\Delta G^{\circ} = -nF \, E^{\circ}_{cell} \quad \textbf{(½ Mark)}$$
$$= -2 \times 96500 \times 1.1$$
$$= -212.27 \text{ kJ mol}^{-1} \quad \textbf{(1 Mark)}$$

(b) (i) Fuel cells produce electricity with an efficiency of about 70% as compared to thermal plants whose efficiency is about 40%.

(ii) Fuel cells are pollution free because the by-product of H_2–O_2 fuel cell is H_2O. **(1 + 1 = 2 Marks)**

OR

(a) (i) Electrical conduction of metals decreases with increase in temperature. Thus, silver wire at 30°C will show greater conduction of electricity. **(1 Mark)**

(ii) Conductance of solution increases on increase in dilution. Hence, 0.1 M CH_3COOH solution will allow greater conduction of electricity. **(1 Mark)**

As the number of ions per litre of electrolyte increases with dilution, conductance also increases with dilution which implies less concentrated solution has greater conductance.

(iii) Increase in temperature increases the dissociation of an ionic compound. Thus, KCl solution at 50°C will show greater conduction of electricity. **(1 Mark)**

(b)

	Electrochemical cell		Electrolytic cell
(i)	It generates electricity by chemical reactions.	(i)	Chemical reactions takes place by consuming electricity.
(ii)	Anode has negative and cathode has positive potential with respect to solution.	(ii)	Anode has positive and cathode has negative potential with respect to solution.

(1 + 1 = 2 Marks)

36. (a) (i) $_{29}\text{Cu} = 1s^2\, 2s^2\, 2p^6\, 3s^2 3p^6 3d^{10}\, 4s^1$

$\text{Cu}^+ = 1s^2\, 2s^2\, 2p^6\, 3s^2 3p^6 3d^{10}$

$\text{Cu}^{2+} = 1s^2\, 2s^2\, 2p^6\, 3s^2 3p^6 3d^9$

Due to unpaired electron, Cu^{2+} is coloured and due to all paired electrons, Cu^+ is white. **(1 Mark)**

d–d transition impart colouration to certain compounds which have unpaired electrons.

(ii) In acidic solution, yellow coloured chromate ions change to orange coloured dichromate ions. $2\text{CrO}_4^{2-} + 2\text{H}^+ \longrightarrow \text{Cr}_2\text{O}_7^{2-} + \text{H}_2\text{O}$ **(1 Mark)**

(iii) Zn, Cd and Hg are in d-block of modern periodic table but they have fully filled (d^{10}) d-orbitals, hence they are not considered as transition elements. **(1 Mark)**

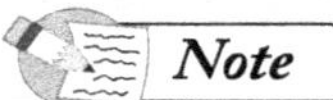

General electronic configuration of transition elements is $(n{-}1)d^{1-9}ns^2$. Elements which have partially filled d-orbital are considered as transition elements.

(b) $_{27}\text{Co} = 1s^2\, 2s^2\, 2p^6\, 3s^2\, 3p^6\, 3d^7\, 4s^2$

$\text{Co}^{2+} = 1s^2\, 2s^2\, 2p^6\, 3s^2\, 3p^6\, 3d^7$ **(1 Mark)**

$3d$

$\uparrow\downarrow$	$\uparrow\downarrow$	$\uparrow$	$\uparrow$	$\uparrow$

Unpaired electrons, $n = 3$

Spin only magnetic moment $= \sqrt{n(n+2)}$ B.M.

$= \sqrt{3(3+2)}$ B.M. $= \sqrt{15}$ B.M. $= 3.87$ B.M. **(1 Mark)**

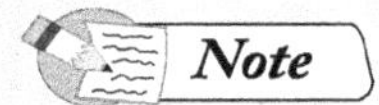

Spin only magnetic moment is given by unpaired electrons only.

OR

(a)

	Lanthanoids		**Actinoids**
(i)	Lanthanoid contraction is the consequence of poor shielding by $4f$-electrons.	(i)	Actinoid contraction is greater from element to element resulting from poorer shielding by $5f$-electrons.
(ii)	Most common oxidation state in lanthanoids is +3.	(ii)	There is a greater range of oxidation states because $5f$, $6d$ and $7s$ levels are of comparable energies.
(iii)	Less tendency of complex formation. Lanthanoids are non-radioactive, except promethium.	(iii)	These are more reactive metals. Actinoids are radioactive.

(1 + 1 + 1 = 3 Marks)

(b) (i) $_{21}Sc = 1s^2\ 2s^2\ 2p^6\ 3s^2 3p^6 3d^1\ 4s^2$

$Sc^{3+} = 1s^2\ 2s^2 2p^6\ 3s^2 3p^6$

Because of no unpaired electrons, Sc^{3+} is diamagnetic. **(1 Mark)**

When a magnetic field is applied to substance, diamagnetic substances are repelled by the applied field.

$Cr^{3+} = 1s^2\ 2s^2\ 2p^6\ 3s^2\ 3p^6\ 3d^3$

It has 3 unpaired electrons, hence paramagnetic.

(ii) $_{24}Cr = 1s^2\ 2s^2\ 2p^6\ 3s^2 3p^6 3d^5\ 4s^1$

$\begin{array}{cc} 3d & 4s \\ \boxed{\uparrow}\boxed{\uparrow}\boxed{\uparrow}\boxed{\uparrow}\boxed{\uparrow} & \boxed{\uparrow} \end{array}$

$_{29}Cu = 1s^2\ 2s^2\ 2p^6\ 3s^2\ 3p^6\ 3d^{10}\ 4s^1$

$\begin{array}{cc} 3d & 4s \\ \boxed{\uparrow\downarrow}\boxed{\uparrow\downarrow}\boxed{\uparrow\downarrow}\boxed{\uparrow\downarrow}\boxed{\uparrow\downarrow} & \boxed{\uparrow} \end{array}$

Due to greater number of unpaired electrons which lead to metallic bonding, Cr has high melting point than Cu.

Due to high enthalpy of atomisation, Cr has high boiling point than that of Cu. **(1 Mark)**

Greater number of unpaired electrons leads to stronger interatomic interaction resulting in higher enthalpy of atomisation.

37. (a) In the acid catalysed dehydration of alcohols, the slowest step or the rate determining step is the formation of carbocation. Thus dehydration of tertiary alcohols will be fastest because tertiary carbocation is most stable. **(1 + 1 = 2 Marks)**

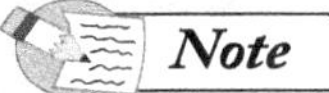

(b) (i)

(1 Mark)

It is an example of Reimer-Tiemann reaction. Reimer-Tiemann reaction is an electrophillic substitution reaction in which dichlorocarbene is generated in the first step and act as strong electrophile.

(ii)

(1 Mark)

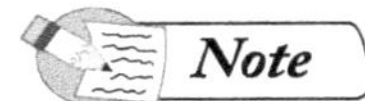

Note

It is an example of Williamson Synthesis. Williamson synthesis is S_N2 reaction. Nucleophile attacks from the back side which results in inversion of configuration at the site of the leaving group.

(iii)

$$6CH_3 - CH = CH_2 + B_2H_6 \longrightarrow 2(CH_3 - CH_2 - CH_2)_3B$$

propene   diborane

$$(CH_3 - CH_2 - CH_2)_3B \xrightarrow{H_2O_2}$$

$$CH_3 - CH_2 - CH_2 - OH + B(OH)_3$$

propanol   boric acid

(1 Mark)

OR

(a) **Step 1:**

$$H_2O + H_2SO_4 \longrightarrow H_3\overset{\oplus}{O} + HSO_4^{\ominus}$$

Step 2:

$$CH_2 = CH_2 + H_3O^+ \longrightarrow CH_3 - \overset{+}{C}H_2 + H_2O$$

Ethene

Step 3:

$$CH_3 - \overset{+}{C}H_2 + :\overset{..}{O}H_2 \longrightarrow CH_3 - CH_2 - \overset{+}{O}H_2$$

Step 4:

$$CH_3 - CH_2 - \overset{+}{O}H_2 \xrightarrow{H_2O} CH_3 - CH_2 + OH + H_3O^+$$

Ethanol

(2 Mark)

(b) (i)

phenol   benzoquinone   **(1 Mark)**

(ii) H_3CO —anisole— $\xrightarrow[\text{ethanoic acid}]{Br_2}$ H_3CO —Br (*p*-bromoanisole)

(1 Mark)

(iii) phenol $+ 3Br_2(aq.) \longrightarrow$ 2, 4, 6-tribromophenol $+ 3HBr$

(1 Mark)

Note

Solvent has great influence in the reaction; when water act as solvent in bromination of phenol tri-subsituted product is formed, while with CS_2 as solvent, mono-subsituted products are formed with p-isomer as major product.

Delhi *2020*

CBSE Board Solved Paper

Time Allowed : 3 Hours   *Maximum Marks : 70*

General Instructions:

Read the following instructions very carefully and strictly follow them:

  (i) This question paper comprises **four** Sections A, B, C and D. There are **37** questions in the questions paper. **All** questions are compulsory.

  (ii) **Section A:** Questions no. **1** to **20** are very short answer type questions, carrying **1** mark each. Answer these questions in one word or one sentence.

  (iii) **Section B:** Questions no. **21** to **27** are short answer type questions, carrying **2** mark each.

  (iv) **Section C:** Questions no. **28** to **34** are long answer type-I questions, carrying **3** mark each.

  (v) **Section D:** Questions no. **35** to **37** are long answer type-II questions, carrying **5** mark each.

  (vi) There is no overall choice in the question paper. However, an internal choice has been provided in 2 questions of two marks, 2 questions of three marks and all the 3 questions of five marks. You have to attempt only one of the choices in such questions.

  (vii) In addition to this, separate instructions are given with each section and question, wherever necessary.

  (viii) Use of calculators and log tables is not permitted.

SECTION - A

Read the given passage and answer the questions number 1 to 5 that follow:

The halogens have the smallest atomic radii in their respective periods. The atomic radius of fluorine is extremely small. All halogens exhibit –1 oxidation state. They are strong oxidising agents and have maximum negative electron gain enthalpy. Among halogens, fluorine shows anomalous behaviour in many properties. For example, electronegativity and ionisation enthalpy are higher for fluorine than expected whereas bond dissociation enthalpy, m.p. and b.p and electron gain enthalpy are quite lower than expected. Halogens react with hydrogen to give hydrogen halides (HX) and combine amongst themselves to form a number of compounds of the type XX', XX'_3, XX'_5 and XX'_7, called inter-halogens.

1. Why halogens have maximum negative electron gain enthalpy?

2. Why fluorine shows anomalous behaviour as compared to other halogens?

3. Arrange the hydrogen halides (HF to HI) in the decreasing order of their reducing character.

4. Why fluorine is a stronger oxidizing agent than chlorine?

5. What are the sizes of X and X′ in the interhalogen compounds?

Questions number 6 to 10 are one word answers:

6. Out of ![Cl-benzene] and ![CH2-Cl benzene] , which will undergo S_N1 reaction faster with OH^-?

7. Write the IUPAC name of $CH_3-N(CH_3)-C_6H_5$

8. What type of linkage is present in polysaccharides?

9. Name an artificial sweetener whose use is limited to cold drinks.

10. Name the polymer which is used for making non-stick utensils.

Questions number 11 to 15 are multiple choice questions:

11. Kohlrausch gave the following relation for strong electrolytes:

$$\wedge = \wedge_0 - A\sqrt{C}$$

Which of the following equality holds?

(a) $\wedge = \wedge_0$ as $C \rightarrow \sqrt{A}$

(b) $\wedge = \wedge_0$ as $C \rightarrow \infty$

(c) $\wedge = \wedge_0$ as $C \rightarrow 0$

(d) $\wedge = \wedge_0$ as $C \rightarrow 1$

12. In an electrochemical process, a salt bridge is used

(a) as a reducing agent

(b) as an oxidizing agent

(c) to complete the circuit so that current can flow

(d) none of these

13. In a chemical reaction $X \rightarrow Y$, it is found that the rate of reaction doubles when the concentration of X is increased four times. The order of the reaction with respect to X is

(a) 1   (b) 0

(c) 2   (d) $\dfrac{1}{2}$

14. Which of the following will give a white precipitate upon reacting with $AgNO_3$?

(a) $K_2[Pt(en)_2Cl_2]$ (b) $[Co(NH_3)_3Cl_3]$

(c) $[Cr(H_2O)_6]Cl_3$ (d) $[Fe(H_2O)_3Cl_3]$

15. Copper matte contains

(a) Cu_2S, Cu_2O and silica

(b) Cu_2S, CuO and silica

(c) Cu_2S, FeO and silica

(d) Cu_2S, FeS and silica

For questions number 16 to 20, two statements are given – one labelled Assertion (A) and the other labelled Reason (R). Select the correct answer to these questions from the codes (i), (ii), (iii) and (iv) as given below:

(i) Both Assertion (A) and Reason (R) are correct statements, and Reason (R) is the correct explanation of the Assertion (A).

(ii) Both Assertion (A) and Reason (R) are correct statements, but Reason (R) is *not* the correct explanation of the Assertion (A).

(iii) Assertion (A) is correct, but Reason (R) is wrong statement.

(iv) Assertion (A) is wrong, but Reason (R) is correct statement.

16. Assertion (A) : 0.1 M solution of KCl has greater osmotic pressure than 0.1 M solution of glucose at same temperature.

Reason (R) : In solution, KCl dissociates to produce more number of particles.

17. Assertion (A) : Conductivity of an electrolyte increases with decrease in concentration.

Reason (R) : Number of ions per unit volume decreases on dilution.

18. Assertion (A) : Ortho and para-nitrophenols can be separated by steam distillation.

Reason (R) : Ortho isomer associates through intermolecular hydrogen bonding while para isomer associates through intramolecular hydrogen bonding.

19. Assertion (A) : Oxidation of ketones is easier than aldehydes.

Reason (R) : C–C bond of ketones is stronger than C–H bond of aldehydes.

20. Assertion (A) : Low spin tetrahedral complexes are rarely observed.

Reason (R) : Crystal field splitting energy is less than pairing energy for tetrahedral complexes.

21. Write the role of

(a) Dilute NaCN in the extraction of gold.

(b) CO in the extraction of iron.

OR

How is leaching carried out in the case of low grade copper ores? Name the method used for refining of copper metal.

22. State Raoult's law for a solution containing volatile components. What is the similarity between Raoult's law and Henry's law?

23. Draw the structures of the following:

(i) $H_2S_2O_7$

(ii) BrF_5

24. Define adsorption with an example. What is the role of adsorption in heterogeneous catalysis?

OR

Define Brownian movement. What is the cause of Brownian movement in colloidal particles? How is it responsible for the stability of colloidal sol?

25. Identify the monomers in the following polymers:

(i)
$$\left[\!\!\begin{array}{c} \underset{\textstyle OH}{}\text{—}CH_2\text{—}\underset{\textstyle OH}{}\text{—}CH_2\text{—} \end{array}\!\!\right]_n$$

(ii) $\left[NH-(CH_2)_6-NH-\underset{\displaystyle O}{\overset{\displaystyle \|}{C}}-(CH_2)_4-\underset{\displaystyle O}{\overset{\displaystyle \|}{C}} \right]_n$

26. Discuss the nature of bonding in metal carbonyls.

27. How do antiseptics differ from disinfectants? Name a substance which can be used as a disinfectant as well as an antiseptic.

SECTION - C

28. Identify A, B, C, D, E and F in the following:

$$E \xleftarrow{H_2O} D \xleftarrow[\text{dry ether}]{Mg} CH_3 - \overset{\overset{\displaystyle CH_3}{|}}{C}H - CH_2 - Br \xrightarrow{\text{alcoholic KOH}} A$$

$$\xrightarrow{NaOC_2H_5} F \qquad \downarrow HBr$$

$$C \xleftarrow{\text{Na/dry ether}} B$$

29. A 0.01 m aqueous solution of $AlCl_3$ freezes at –0.068 °C. Calculate the percentage of dissociation.

[Given: K_f for water = 1.86 K kg mol^{-1}]

30. Define the following terms with a suitable example in each:

(a) Polysaccharides   (b) Denatured protein

(c) Fibrous protein

31. When a steady current of 2A was passed through two electrolytic cells A and B containing electrolytes $ZnSO_4$ and $CuSO_4$ connected in series, 2 g of Cu were deposited at the cathode of cell B. How long did the current flow? What mass of Zn was deposited at cathode of cell A?

[Atomic mass: Cu = 63.5 g mol^{-1}, Zn = 65 g mol^{-1}; 1F = 96500 C mol^{-1}]

32. Write three differences between lyophobic sol and lyophilic sol.

OR

Define the following terms:

(a) Protective colloid

(b) Zeta potential

(c) Emulsifying agent

33. Give the structures of final products expected from the following reactions:

(a) Hydroboration of propene followed by oxidation with H_2O_2 in alkaline medium.

(b) Dehydration of $(CH_3)_3C–OH$ by heating it with 20% H_3PO_4 at 358 K.

(c) heating of ⟨benzene⟩–CH_2–O–⟨benzene⟩ with HI.

OR

How can you convert the following?

(a) Phenol to o-hydroxybenzaldehyde.

(b) Methanal to ethanol

(c) Phenol to phenyl ethanoate.

34. Give reasons:

(a) Aniline does not undergo Friedal-Craft's reaction.

(b) Aromatic primary amines cannot be prepared by Gabriel phthalimide synthesis.

(c) Aliphatic amines are stronger bases than ammonia.

SECTION - D

35. (a) A first order reaction is 25% complete in 40 minutes. Calculate the value of rate constant. In what time will the reaction be 80% completed?

(b) Define order of reaction. Write the condition under which a bimolecular reaction follows first order kinetics.

OR

(a) A first order reaction is 50% complete in 30 minutes at 300 K and in 10 minutes at 320 K. Calculate activation energy (E_a) for the reaction.

[R = 8.314 J K^{-1} mol^{-1}] [Given: log 2 = 0.3010, log 3 = 0.4771, log 4 = 0.6021, log 5 = 0.6991]

(b) Write the two conditions for collisions to be effective collisions.

(c) How order of reaction and molecularity differ towards a complex reaction?

36. (a) Give reasons:

(i) Transition metals and their compounds show catalytic activities.

(ii) Separation of a mixture of lanthanoid elements is difficult.

(iii) Zn, Cd and Hg are soft and have low melting point.

(b) Write the preparation of the following:

(i) $Na_2Cr_2O_7$ from Na_2CrO_4

(ii) K_2MnO_4 from MnO_2

OR

(a) Account for the following:

(i) Ti^{3+} is coloured, whereas Sc^{3+} is colourless in aqueous solution.

(ii) Cr^{2+} is a strong reducing agent.

(b) Write two similarities between chemistry of lanthanoids and actinoids.

(c) Complete the following ionic equation:

$$3MnO_4^{2-} + 4H^+ \longrightarrow$$

37. (a) Write the products formed when benzaldehyde reacts with the following reagents:

(i) CH_3CHO in presence of dilute NaOH

(ii) $H_2N - NH -$⟨phenyl⟩

(iii) Conc. NaOH

(b) Distinguish between the following:

    (i) $CH_3 - CH = CH - CO - CH_3$ and
       $CH_3 - CH_2 - CO - CH = CH_2$

    (ii) Benzaldehyde and benzoic acid.

OR

(a) Write the final products in the following:

    (i) $\begin{array}{c} CH_3 \\ CH_3 \end{array}\!\!> C = O \xrightarrow[\text{Conc. HCl}]{\text{Zn/Hg}}$

(ii) ⟨phenyl⟩$- COONa \xrightarrow[\Delta]{\text{NaOH/CaO}}$

(iii) $CH_2 = CH - CH_2 - CN \xrightarrow[\text{(b)}\,H_3O^+]{\text{(a)}\,\text{DIBAL-H}}$

(b) Arrange the following in the increasing order of their reactivity towards nucleophilic addition reaction:

CH_3COCH_3, $HCHO$, CH_3CHO, ⟨phenyl⟩$- COCH_3$

(c) Draw the structure of 2, 4-DNP derivative of acetaldehyde.

Solutions

SECTION - A

1. Halogens have maximum negative electron gain enthalpy because of highest nuclear charge in their respective periods.

2. Fluorine shows anomalous behaviour as compared to other halogens due to small size and high electronegativity.

3. HI > HBr > HCl > HF

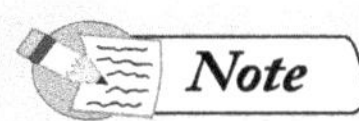

Note

Reducing character is determined by bond strength. As the bond strength increases reducing character decreases.

4. The electron affinity of fluorine is less than that of chlorine but still it is the stronger oxidising agent than chlorine. This is because of its low bond dissociation energy and high hydration enthalpy.

5. In the interhalogen compounds, XX′, X is larger sized halogen whereas X′ is smaller sized halogen.

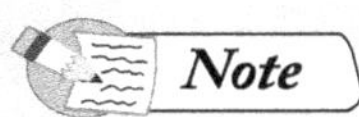

Note

$X^{\oplus}$ *is cation while* $X'^{\ominus}$ *is anion. Thus X must be more electropositive than X′ or we can say that X must be below to X′ in halogen group.*

6. Benzyl chloride will undergo reaction faster as compared to chlorobenzene due to the formation of more stable benzyl cation in the rate determining step.

7. N, N – Dimethylaniline

8. Glycosidic linkage is present in polysaccharides.

9. Use of aspartame is limited because it is unstable at cooking temperature.

10. Polytetrafluoroethylene (PTFE), commonly known as teflon, is used for making non-stick utensils.

11. (c) $\wedge = \wedge_0$ as $C \to 0$

$$\wedge = \wedge_0 - A\sqrt{C}$$

when $C = 0$, $\wedge = \wedge_0$

12. (c)   Salt bridge is used to complete the circuit so that current can flow.

13. (d) $\dfrac{1}{2}$

$$X \longrightarrow Y$$

$$r_1 = R \propto [X]^n$$

$$r_2 = 2R \propto [4X]^n$$

$$\Rightarrow \quad \frac{2R}{R} = \frac{[4X]^n}{[X]^n}$$

$$\Rightarrow \quad 2 = 4^n$$

$$\Rightarrow \quad n = \frac{1}{2}$$

14. (c) $[Cr(H_2O)_6]Cl_3$

This compound dissociates to $[Cr(H_2O)_6]^{3+}$ and $3Cl^-$ ions. Thus, it will give white precipitate of AgCl on reacting with $AgNO_3$.

15. (d)   Copper matte contains Cu_2S, FeS and silica

16. (i)   KCl is an electrolyte, thus in solution it produces more number of particles than glucose. Hence, solution of KCl has greater osmotic pressure than glucose.

17. (iv)   Conductivity of an electrolyte decreases with decrease in concentration because number of ions per unit volume decreases on dilution.

18. (iii)   *Ortho* and *para*-nitrophenols can be separated by steam distillation because *para* isomer associates through intermolecular hydrogen bonding, while *ortho* isomer has intramoleculer H-bonding. Thus the boiling point of ortho isomer is low because of less inter-molecular forces acting between their molecules.

19. (iv)   Oxidation of ketones is difficult than aldehydes because C–C bond of ketones is stronger than C–H bond of aldehydes.

20. (i)   For tetrahedral complexes, the orbital splitting energy is not sufficiently large for forcing pairing of electrons. Therefore, low spin tetrahedral configurations are rarely observed.

SECTION - B

21. (a)   In the extraction of gold, NaCN is used for leaching process.

It oxidises Au to Au^+ in the presence of atmospheric oxygen. Gold dissolves due to the formation of an aurocyanide complex.

$$4Au + 8NaCN + 2H_2O + O_2 \longrightarrow$$
$$4Na[Au(CN)_2] + 4NaOH$$

(1 Mark)

(b) Carbon monoxide acts as a reducing agent in the extraction of iron. It reduces iron oxides to Fe.

(1 Mark)

OR

Copper is leached out by hydrometallurgy (using acid or bacteria) from low grade ores.

Copper is refined using electrolytic method.

(2 Marks)

22. **Raoult's law:** For a solution of volatile liquids, the partial vapour pressure of each component of the solution is directly proportional to its mole fraction in solution, $P \propto x$; $P = x\,P°$.

by Henry's law,

$$P = x.K_H$$

Here, P is the partial pressure of gas, x is mole fraction of it in the solution and K_H is the Henry's law constant.

In both Henry's law and Raoult's law, partial pressure of volatile component is directly proportional to mole fraction of it in the solution. **(1 + 1 = 2 Marks)**

23. (i)

$$H_2S_2O_7$$

(1 Mark)

(ii)

$$BrF_5$$

(1 Mark)

24. **Adsorption:** The accumulation of molecular species at the surface rather than in the bulk of a solid or liquid is termed adsorption. For example, adsorption of H_2 gas on charcoal in a closed vessel.

Role of adsorption in heterogeneous catalysis: In heterogeneous catalysis, reactants and catalyst are in different phase. The reactants in gaseous state or in solutions are adsorbed on the surface of the solid catalyst to start the reaction. **(1 + ½ + ½ = 2 Marks)**

OR

Brownian movement: Colloidal particles are always in a state of continuous zig-zag motion. This motion is known as Brownian movement. The Brownian movement is due to the unbalanced bombardment on the particles by the molecules of the dispersion medium. The Brownian movement has a stirring effect which does not permit the particles to settle and thus it is responsible for the stability of colloidal sol.

(1 + 1 = 2 Marks)

25. (i) Phenol and Formaldehyde (H—C—H) **(1 Mark)**

(ii) $H_2N(CH_2)_6\,NH_2$ (hexamethylenediamine) and $HOOC(CH_2)_4COOH$ (adipic acid) **(1 Mark)**

26. The metal-carbon bond in metal carbonyls possess both σ and π character. The M–C σ bond is formed by the donation of lone pair of electrons from the carbonyl carbon into a vacant orbital of metal. The M–C π bond is formed by the donation of a pair of electrons from a filled d-orbital of metal into the vacant antibonding π* orbital of carbon monoxide.

This type of metal to ligand bonding creates a synergic effect which strengthens the metal-carbon bond.

(1 + 1 = 2 Marks)

27. Antiseptics and disinfectants are the chemicals which either kill or prevent the growth of microrganisms.

Antiseptics are applied to the living tissues whereas disinfectants are applied to inanimate objects such as floors, drainage system, instruments etc.

0.2% solution of phenol is an antiseptic, while its 1% solution can be used as a disinfectant. **(2 Marks)**

SECTION - C

28.

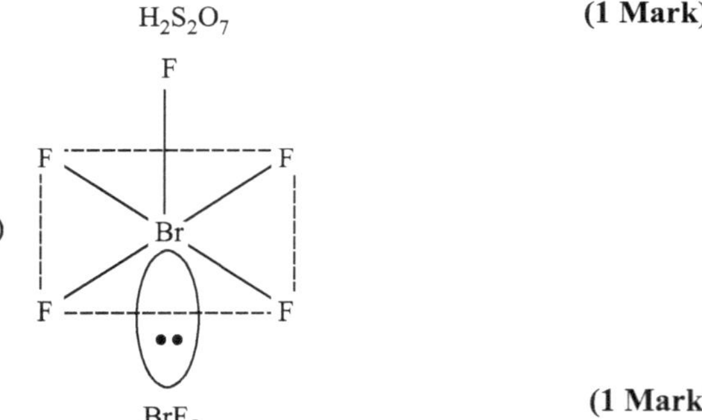

$$CH_3-CH-CH_2-Br \xrightarrow[\text{dry ether}]{Mg} CH_3-CH-CH_2MgBr$$
$$\quad\quad\quad |\quad\quad\quad\quad\quad\quad\quad\quad\quad\quad\quad\quad |$$
$$\quad\quad CH_3 \quad\quad\quad\quad\quad\quad\quad\quad\quad\quad CH_3$$
$$\text{(D)}$$

$$\xrightarrow{H_2O} CH_3-CH-CH_3 + Mg\,(OH)\,Br$$
$$\quad\quad\quad\quad\quad |$$
$$\quad\quad\quad\quad CH_3$$
$$\text{(E)}$$

$$(\tfrac{1}{2}+\tfrac{1}{2}+\tfrac{1}{2}+\tfrac{1}{2}+\tfrac{1}{2}+\tfrac{1}{2} = \textbf{3 Marks})$$

29. $m = 0.01;\ \Delta T_f = 0.068°C;\ K_f = 1.86\ \text{K kg mol}^{-1}$

If i is the van't Hoff factor for the aqueous solution of $AlCl_3$, then

$$\Delta T_f = i.K_f.m \qquad\qquad \textbf{(½ Mark)}$$

$$\Rightarrow\qquad i = \frac{\Delta T_f}{K_f.m}$$

$$= \frac{0.068}{1.86\times0.01} \qquad\qquad \textbf{(½ Mark)}$$

$$= 3.66 \qquad\qquad \textbf{(½ Mark)}$$

$$AlCl_3 \rightleftharpoons Al^{3+} + 3Cl^- \quad \textbf{(½ Mark)}$$

initial	1	0	0
at equilibrium	$1-x$	x	$3x$

$$i = \frac{(1-x)+x+3x}{1} \qquad\qquad \textbf{(½ Mark)}$$

$$\Rightarrow\qquad 3.66 = 1 + 3x$$
$$\Rightarrow\qquad x = 0.89$$

x is degree of dissociation.

$\therefore$ Percentage of dissociation = 89%. $\qquad$ **(½ Mark)**

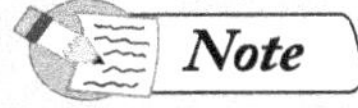

Note

$$i = \frac{\textit{Total number of moles after dissociation/association}}{\textit{Total number of moles before dissociation/association}}$$

30. (a) Polysaccharides: Carbohydrates which yield a large number of monosaccharide units on hydrolysis are called polysaccharides. *Example:* Starch **(1 Mark)**

(b) Denatured protein: When a protein is subjected to physical change like change in pH, the hydrogen bonds are disturbed. Due to this, globules unfold and helix get uncoiled and protein loses its biological activity. This form is called 'denatured protein'. *Example:* Coagulation of egg white on boiling

(1 Mark)

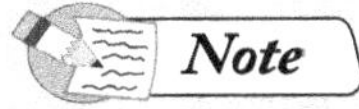

Note

Denaturation destroys secondary and tertiary structures of protein, but primary structure remains intact.

(c) Fibrous protein: When the polypeptide chains run parallel and are held together by hydrogen and disulphide bonds, then fibre like structure is formed. Such type of proteins are called 'fibrous proteins' *Example:* Keratin **(1 Mark)**

31. $i = 2A,\ W_{Cu} = 2g$

$$E_{Cu} = \frac{63.5}{2},\ E_{Zn} = \frac{65}{2} \qquad\qquad \textbf{(½ Mark)}$$

$$E = F \times Z \qquad\qquad \textbf{(½ Mark)}$$

$$Z_{Cu} = \frac{E_{Cu}}{F}$$

$$Z_{Cu} = \frac{63.5}{2}\times\frac{1}{96500} \qquad\qquad \textbf{(½ Mark)}$$

$$W_{Cu} = Z_{Cu}.\,i\,.\,t \qquad\qquad \textbf{(½ Mark)}$$

$$t = \frac{W_{Cu}}{Z_{Cu}.i}$$

$$= \frac{2\times2\times96500}{63.5\times2} = \textbf{3039 seconds} \qquad \textbf{(½ Mark)}$$

$$\frac{W_{Zn}}{W_{Cu}} = \frac{E_{Zn}}{E_{Cu}}$$

$$W_{Zn} = \frac{E_{Zn}\times W_{Cu}}{E_{Cu}} = \frac{65}{2}\times2\times\frac{2}{63.5} = \textbf{2.05 g}\ \textbf{(½ Mark)}$$

32. Differences between lyophilic and lyophobic sols.

Property	Lyophilic sol	Lyophobic sol
Visibility	The particles can not be detected even under ultramicroscope.	The particles can be detected under ultramicroscope.
Viscosity	Much higher than that of medium.	Same as that of medium.
Reversibility	Reversible i.e. if the dispersion medium is separated from the dispersed phase, the sol can be reconstituted by simply remixing.	Irreversible i.e. once precipitated, they do not give back the colloidal sol by simple addition of dispersion medium.

(1 + 1 + 1 = 3 Marks)

OR

(i) Protective colloid: When a lyophilic sol is added to a lyophobic sol, the lyophilic particles form a layer around lyophobic particles and thus protect the latter from electrolytes. Lyophilic colloids used for this purpose are called protective colloids. **(1 Mark)**

(ii) Zeta potential: Colloidal particles always carry an electric charge. The charges of opposite signs on the fixed and diffused parts of the double layer results in a potential difference between these layers. This potential difference is called the zeta potential.

(1 Mark)

(iii) **Emulsifying agent:** For stabilisation of an emulsion, emulsifying agent is usually added. The emulsifying agent forms an interfacial film between suspended particles and the medium. **(1 Mark)**

Note

For oil/water emulsions, proteins, gum and soaps are used as emulsifying agents, while for water/oil emulsions, heavy metal salts of fatty acids and alcohols are used as emulsifying agents.

33. (a) $CH_3 - CH = CH_2 \xrightarrow{B_2H_6} (CH_3 - CH_2 - CH_2)_3B$

$\xrightarrow[OH^-]{H_2O_2} CH_3 - CH_2 - CH_2 - OH + B(OH)_3$

(1 Mark)

Note

Hydroboration-oxidation is an anti-Markonikov addition reaction in which hydroxyl group is attached to less substituted carbon.

(b) $H_3C - \underset{\underset{CH_3}{|}}{\overset{\overset{CH_3}{|}}{C}} - OH \xrightarrow[358\ K]{20\%\ H_3PO_4} H_3C - \underset{\underset{CH_3}{|}}{\overset{\overset{CH_2}{||}}{C}} + H_2O$ **(1 Mark)**

(c)   Ph$-CH_2 - O-$Ph $\xrightarrow[\Delta]{HI}$ Ph$-CH_2 - I + HO-$Ph

(1 Mark)

Note

In acidic cleavage of ethers, alkyl or aryl halides are formed from the more stable carbocation.

OR

(a)   Phenol $\xrightarrow[aq.\ NaOH]{CHCl_3}$ *o*-hydroxybenzaldehyde   **(1 Mark)**

Reimer – Tiemann reaction

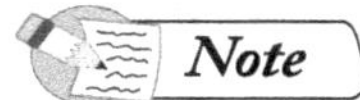

Note

Dichlorocarbene is the reactive intermediate which is formed in the first step of the reaction.

(b) $H - \underset{\underset{O}{||}}{C} - H + CH_3 - MgBr \longrightarrow$

Methanal

$H - \underset{\underset{O-MgBr}{|}}{\overset{\overset{CH_3}{|}}{C}} - H \xrightarrow{HOH} H - \underset{\underset{OH}{|}}{\overset{\overset{CH_3}{|}}{C}} - H + Mg(OH)Br$

Ethanol

(1 Mark)

(c)   Phenol $+ CH_3COOH \rightleftharpoons$ Phenyl ethanoate $+ H_2O$

(1 Mark)

34. (a)   Aniline is basic in nature. It does not undergo Friedal-Crafts reaction due to salt formation with aluminium chloride, the Lewis acid, which is used as a catalyst. Anilinium ion is formed in which nitrogen of aniline acquires positive charge and hence acts as a strong deactivating group for further reaction.   **(1 Mark)**

(b)   Aromatic primary amines cannot be prepared by Gabriel phthalimide synthesis because aryl halides do not undergo nucleophilic substitution with the anion formed by phthalimide.   **(1 Mark)**

(c)   Aliphatic amines are stronger bases than ammonia due to + I effect of alkyl groups leading to high electron density on the nitrogen atom.   **(1 Mark)**

SECTION - D

35. (a)   For a first order reaction,

$$k = \frac{2.303}{t}\log\left(\frac{a}{a-x}\right)$$ **(½ Mark)**

when $t = 40$ minutes, $x = 0.25a$

$$k = \frac{2.303}{40}\log\left(\frac{a}{a-0.25a}\right)$$ **(½ Mark)**

$$= \frac{2.303}{40}\log\left(\frac{1}{0.75}\right)$$

$$= 0.058 \times \log\left(\frac{4}{3}\right)$$ **(½ Mark)**

$$= 0.058(0.6021 - 0.4771)$$

$$= 7.25 \times 10^{-3}\ min^{-1}$$ **(½ Mark)**

Now, when reaction is 80% completed, $x = 0.8a$

$$t = \frac{2.303}{k}\log\left(\frac{a}{a-x}\right)$$

$$t = \frac{2.303}{7.25 \times 10^{-3}}\log\left(\frac{a}{a-0.8a}\right)$$ **(½ Mark)**

$$= \frac{2.303}{7.25 \times 10^{-3}} \log\left(\frac{1}{0.2}\right)$$

$$= 317.66 \log 5$$

$$= 317.66 \times 0.6991$$

$$= 222.08 \text{ min} \qquad \textbf{(½ Mark)}$$

(b) The sum of powers of the concentration of the reactants in the rate law expression is called the order of that chemical reaction.

In a bimolecular reaction, when one reactant is in large excess, the concentration of it does not alter, and the rate of reaction depends only on the other reactant. In these conditions, a bimolecular reaction follows first order kinetics. **(2 Marks)**

OR

(a) $k = \dfrac{0.693}{t_{1/2}}$ **(½ Mark)**

at $T_1 = 300$ K, $t_{1/2} = 30$ min
at $T_2 = 320$ K, $t_{1/2} = 10$ min

Thus, $k_1 = \dfrac{0.693}{30}$ and $k_2 = \dfrac{0.693}{10}$ **(½ Mark)**

$\Rightarrow \quad \dfrac{k_2}{k_1} = \dfrac{0.693}{10} \times \dfrac{30}{0.693} = 3$ **(½ Mark)**

$\log\dfrac{k_2}{k_1} = \dfrac{E_a}{2.303\text{R}}\left(\dfrac{1}{T_1} - \dfrac{1}{T_2}\right)$ **(½ Mark)**

$\Rightarrow \quad \log 3 = \dfrac{E_a}{2.303 \times 8.314}\left(\dfrac{1}{300} - \dfrac{1}{320}\right)$ **(½ Mark)**

$\Rightarrow \quad 0.4771 = \dfrac{E_a}{19.147} \times \dfrac{(320-300)}{300 \times 320}$

$\Rightarrow \quad E_a = 43848$ J/mol $= 43.848$ kJ/mol **(½ Mark)**

(b) Conditions for effective collisions are:

  (i) Molecules should collide with sufficient kinetic energy i.e. equal to or more than threshold energy.

  (ii) Molecules should collide with proper orientation. **(1 Mark)**

(c) Complex reactions are the reactions in which there is a sequence of reactions which leads to product. Order of the reaction is given by the slowest step of the mechanism. In a complex reaction, the order of reaction is equal to the molecularity of the slowest step. **(1 Mark)**

36. (a) (i) The catalytic activity of transition metals is due to their characteristic of multiple oxidation states and formation of complex compounds. **(1 Mark)**

Transition metals utilise vacant orbitals to form bond between reactant molecules and atoms on the surface of catalyst. This increases the concentration of reactants at the catalyst surface and also weakens the bonds in the reacting molecules.

  (ii) Lanthanoid elements have similar chemical properties, therefore separation of a mixture of lanthanoid elements is difficult. **(1 Mark)**

Note

Lanthanoid contraction in 4f series causes similarities in the properties of the elements.

  (iii) Zn, Cd and Hg are soft and have low melting point due to completely filled orbitals. Their electrons are not involved in the interatomic metallic bonding. **(1 Mark)**

(b) (i) $2Na_2CrO_4 + H_2SO_4 \longrightarrow$
$$Na_2Cr_2O_7 + Na_2SO_4 + H_2O \quad \textbf{(1 Mark)}$$

  (ii) $2MnO_2 + 4KOH + O_2 \xrightarrow{\Delta}$
$$2K_2MnO_4 + 2H_2O \quad \textbf{(1 Mark)}$$

OR

(a) (i) Ti^{3+} has an unpaired electron ($3d^1$), whereas Sc^{3+} has no unpaired electron, therefore d-d transition is possible in Ti^{3+}.

Hence, Ti^{3+} is coloured and Sc^{3+} is colourless. **(1 Mark)**

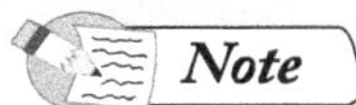

Note

When white light falls on the transition metal compounds, some wave length is absorbed and promotes electrons from t_{2g} to e_g within the same d-subshell. The remainder light is reflected which imparts, particular colour to the compound.

  (ii) Upon oxidation Cr^{2+} becomes Cr^{3+}

In Cr^{3+}, the t_{2g} level is half-filled which makes it very stable. Hence, Cr^{2+} can easily oxidise to Cr^{3+} or we can say that Cr^{2+} is a strong reducing agent. **(1 Mark)**

(b) (i) Both (lanthanoids and actinoids) show +3 as the most common oxidation state. **(1 Mark)**

  (ii) As the atomic number increases, both show a contraction of radii. **(1 Mark)**

(c) $3MnO_4^{2-} + 4H^+ \longrightarrow 2MnO_4^- + MnO_2 + 2H_2O$ **(1 Mark)**

37. (a) (i)

$$H-C=O$$

(benzaldehyde) $+ CH_3-C=O$ (with H) $\xrightarrow[\text{aldol condensation}]{\text{dil. NaOH}}$

$$H-C=CH-\overset{\overset{\displaystyle O}{||}}{C}-H$$ (cinnamaldehyde)

(1 Mark)

(ii) $\underset{H}{C_6H_5-C}=O + H_2N-N(H)-C_6H_5 \xrightarrow{-H_2O} \underset{H}{C_6H_5-C}=N-\underset{H}{N}-C_6H_5$

(1 Mark)

(iii) $2\ (C_6H_5-C(H)=O) + \text{conc. NaOH} \xrightarrow[\text{Cannizzaro reaction}]{\Delta}$

$$CH_2-OH \ (C_6H_5) \quad + \quad COO^-Na^+ \ (C_6H_5)$$

(1 Mark)

(b) (i) $CH_3CH = CH - COCH_3$ and

$CH_3CH_2 - CO - CH = CH_2$

can be distinguished by the iodoform test as the first compound contains a methyl ketonic group $(-\overset{\overset{\displaystyle O}{||}}{C}-CH_3)$ and undergoes iodoform test, whereas the other compound does not.

(1 Mark)

(ii) Benzaldehyde does not react with sodium bicarbonate $(NaHCO_3)$ whereas benzoic acid evolves carbon dioxide upon reaction with $NaHCO_3$ because of its acidic character.

(1 Mark)

OR

(a) (i)

$$\underset{CH_3}{\overset{CH_3}{>}}C=O \xrightarrow[\text{Conc.HCl}]{\text{Zn/Hg}} \underset{CH_3}{\overset{CH_3}{>}}CH_2$$

(1 Mark)

(ii) $C_6H_5-COONa + NaOH \xrightarrow[\Delta]{CaO}$

$$C_6H_6 + Na_2CO_3$$

(1 Mark)

(iii) $CH_2 = CH - CH_2 - CN \xrightarrow[\text{(b) } H_3O^+]{\text{(a) DIBAL-H}}$

$$CH_2 = CH-CH_2-\overset{\overset{\displaystyle }{}}{C}-H \ (\text{with } O)$$

(1 Mark)

(b)

$$C_6H_5-\overset{\overset{\displaystyle }{}}{C}(O)-CH_3 < CH_3-\overset{\overset{\displaystyle }{}}{C}(O)-CH_3$$
$$< CH_3-\overset{\overset{\displaystyle }{}}{C}(O)-H < H-\overset{\overset{\displaystyle }{}}{C}(O)-H$$

(1 Mark)

(c) $CH_3-\underset{H}{C}=O + H_2N-\underset{H}{N}-(C_6H_3(O_2N)(NO_2)) \xrightarrow{-H_2O}$

Acetaldehyde $\qquad$ 2, 4 – DNP

$$CH_3-\underset{H}{C}=N-\underset{H}{N}-(C_6H_3(O_2N)(NO_2))$$

2, 4 – DNP derivative of acetaldehyde

(1 Mark)

All India *2019*

CBSE Board Solved Paper

Time Allowed : 3 Hours *Maximum Marks : 70*

General Instructions:
  (i)   All questions are compulsory.
  (ii) Section A : Questions number **1** to **5** are very short answer questions and carry **1** mark each.
  (iii) Section B : Questions number **6** to **12** are short answer questions and carry **2** marks each.
  (iv) Section C : Questions number **13** to **24** are also short answer questions and carry **3** marks each.
  (v)   Section D : Questions number **25** to **27** are long answer questions and carry **5** marks each.
  (vi) Use of log tables, if necessary. Use of calculators is not allcwed.

SECTION - A

1. What would be the nature of solid if there is no energy gap between valence band and conduction band?

2. Write the main reason for the stability of colloidal sols.

3. When a coordination compound $CrCl_3 \cdot 6H_2O$ is mixed with $AgNO_3$, two moles of $AgCl$ are precipitated per mole of the compound. What is the structural formula of the coordination compound?

OR

What is the difference between a complex and a double salt?

4. Write the IUPAC name of

$$\text{(benzene ring)} - CH_2 - CH_2 - Cl$$

5. Write the reaction involved in the Hoffmann bromamide degradation reaction.

OR

Propanamine and N, N-dimethylmethanamine contain the same number of carbon atoms, even though propanamine has higher boiling point than N, N-dimethylmethanamine. Why?

SECTION - B

6. When dilute ferrous sulphate solution is added to an aqueous solution containing nitrate ion followed by careful addition of concentrated sulphuric acid along the sides of the test tube, a brown ring is formed at the interface between the solution and sulphuric acid layers. Which anion is confirmed by the appearance of brown ring? What is the composition of the brown ring?

OR

How can you prepare Cl_2 from HCl and HCl from Cl_2? Write reactions only.

7. Using the E^0 values of X and Y, predict which is better for coating the surface of iron to prevent rust and why?

Given: $[E^°_{(Fe^{2+}/Fe)} = -0.44 \text{ V}$

$$E^°_{(X^{2+}/X)} = -2.36 \text{ V}$$

$$E^°_{(Y^{2+}/Y)} = -0.14 \text{ V}]$$

8. Give reasons for the following:
  (a) Aquatic species are more comfortable in cold water than warm water.
  (b) At higher altitudes, people suffer from anoxia resulting in inability to think.

OR

What type of azeotropic mixture will be formed by a solution of acetone and chloroform? Justify on the basis of strength of intermolecular interactions that develop in the solution.

9. Write the name of monomers and their structures for the following polymers:
  (a) Neoprene   (b) Nylon-6

10. Classify the following as addition and condensation polymers giving reason:
  (a) Teflon   (b) PHBV

11. Use the data to answer the following and also justify giving reason:

	Cr	Mn	Fe	Co
$E^0_{M^{2+}/M}$	-0.91	-1.18	-0.44	-0.28
$E^0_{M^{3+}/M^{2+}}$	-0.41	$+1.57$	$+0.77$	$+1.97$

(a) Which is a stronger reducing agent in aqueous medium, Cr^{2+} or Fe^{2+} and why?

(b) Which is the most stable ion in $+2$ oxidation state and why?

12. What happens when

(a) Phenol reacts with conc. HNO_3 ?

(b) Ethyl chloride reacts with $NaOC_2H_5$?

Write the chemical equations involved in the above reactions.

SECTION - C

13. At 300 K, 30 g of glucose present in a litre of its solution has an osmotic pressure of $4 \cdot 98$ bar. If the osmotic pressure of a glucose solution is $1 \cdot 52$ bar, at the same temperature what would be its concentration?

14. Chromium crystallises in *bcc* structure. If its edge length is 300 pm, find its density. Atomic mass of chromium is 52 u. $[N_A = 6 \cdot 022 \times 10^{23} \, mol^{-1}]$

15. Define the following terms with a suitable example of each;
(a) Sol   (b) Aerosol
(c) Hydrosol

16. Calculate $\Delta_r G^\circ$ and $\log K_c$ for the following reaction:
$$Cd^{2+}(aq) + Zn(s) \longrightarrow Zn^{2+}(aq) + Cd(s)$$

Given: $E^\circ_{Cd^{2+}/Cd} = -0.403 \, V$

$ E^\circ_{Zn^{2+}/Zn} = -0.763 \, V$

OR

Chromium metal is electroplated using an acidic solution containing CrO_3 according to the following equation:
$$CrO_3(aq) + 6H^+ + 6e^- \longrightarrow Cr(s) + 3H_2O$$
Calculate how many grams of chromium will be electroplated by 24,000 coulombs. How long will it take to electroplate 1.5 g chromium using 12.5 A current?
[Atomic mass of Cr = 52 g mol^{-1}, 1 F = 96500 C mol^{-1}]

17. Write the hybridisation and magnetic character of the following complexes:

(i) $[Fe(H_2O)_6]^{2+}$

(ii) $[Ni(CN)_4]^{2-}$

[Atomic number : Fe = 26, Ni = 28]

18. Explain the method, of preparation of sodium dichromate from chromite ore. Give the equation representing oxidation of ferrous salts by dichromate ion.

OR

Complete the following reactions:
(a) $MnO_2 + KOH + O_2 \longrightarrow$
(b) $I^- + MnO_4^- + H^+ \longrightarrow$
(c) $Cr_2O_7^{2-} + Sn^{2+} + H^+ \longrightarrow$

19. What is the role of
(a) Depressants in froth floatation ?
(b) Carbon monoxide in Mond's process?
(c) Concentrated sodium hydroxide in leaching of alumina from bauxite?

OR

Write chemical reactions taking place in the extraction of aluminium from bauxite ore.

20. (a) What are antidepressant drugs ? Give an example.

(b) Name the sweetening agent used in preparation of sweets for a diabetic patient.

(c) Why are detergents non-biodegradable?

21. (a) What is the difference between native protein and denatured protein?

(b) Which one of the following is a disaccharide :

Glucose, Lactose, Amylose, Fructose

(c) Write the name of the vitamin responsible for the coagulation of blood.

22. (a) Give one chemical test to distinguish between the compounds of the following pairs :

(i) CH_3NH_2 and $(CH_3)_2NH$

(ii) Aniline and Ethanamine

(b) Why aniline does not undergo Friedel-Crafts reaction?

23. (a) Butan-1-ol has a higher boiling point than diethyl ether. Why?

(b) Write the mechanism of the following reaction:

$$2CH_3CH_2OH \xrightarrow[413K]{H^+}$$
$$CH_3CH_2 - O - CH_2 - CH_3$$

24. Give reasons for the following :

(a) The presence of $- NO_2$ group at ortho or para position increases the reactivity of haloarenes towards nucleophilic substitution reactions.

(b) *p*-Dichlorobenzene has higher melting point than that of ortho or meta isomer.

(c) Thionyl chloride method is preferred for preparing alkyl chloride from alcohols.

OR

(a) Write equation for preparation of 1-iodobutane from 1-chlorobutane.

(b) Out of 2-bromopentane, 2-bromo-2-methylbutane and 1-bromopentane, which compound is most reactive towards elimination reaction and why?

(c) Give IUPAC name of

$$CH_3 - CH = CH - \underset{\underset{Br}{|}}{\overset{\overset{CH_3}{|}}{C}} - CH_3$$

SECTION - D

25. (a) Draw the structure of the following:

(i) $HClO_3$

(ii) $H_2S_2O_3$

(b) Give reasons for the following:

(i) Above 1000 K sulphur shows paramagnetism.

(ii) Although electron gain enthalpy of fluorine is less negative than that of chlorine, yet flourine is a better oxidising agent than chlorine.

(iii) In solid state PCl_5 exists as an ionic compound.

OR

(a) Complete the following reactions:

(i) $PbS(s) + O_3 \longrightarrow$

(ii) $XeF_6 + NaF \longrightarrow$

(b) Arrange the following in increasing order of property indicated, giving reason:

(i) Hydrides of group 15 – boiling points

(ii) Hydrides of group 17 – acidic strength

(iii) Hydrides of group 16 – reducing character

26. (a) Carry out the following conversions:

(i) *p*-Nitrotoluene to 2-bromobenzoic acid

(ii) Propanoic acid to acetic acid

(b) An alkene with molecular formula C_5H_{10} on ozonolysis gives a mixture of two compounds, B and C. Compound B gives positive Fehling test and also reacts with iodine

and NaOH solution. Compound C does not give Fehling solution test but forms iodoform. Identify the compounds A, B and C.

OR

(a) Carry out the following conversions:

(i) Benzoic acid to aniline

(ii) Bromomethane to ethanol

(b) Write the structure of major product(s) in the following:

(i) $CH_3 - CH_2 - \underset{\underset{O}{\|}}{C} - H \xrightarrow[\text{(b) KOH, Glycol/heat}]{\text{(a) } H_2N - NH_2}$

(ii) $CH_3 - \underset{\underset{CH_3}{|}}{\overset{\overset{CH_3}{|}}{C}} - CHO \xrightarrow{\text{conc. NaOH}}$

(iii) 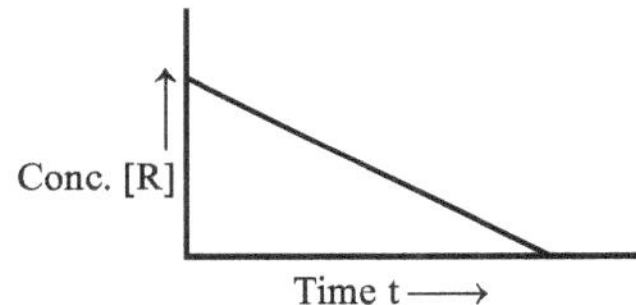 $\xrightarrow{\text{NaOH}}$

27. (a) Consider the reaction R → P for which the change in concentration of R with time is shown by the following graph:

(i) Predict the order of reaction.

(ii) What does the slope of the curve indicate?

(b) The rate of reaction quadruples when temperature changes from 293 K to 313 K. Calculate E_a assuming that it does not change with time.

$$[R = 8 \cdot 314 \, JK^{-1} \, mol^{-1}]$$

OR

(a) Draw the plot of *ln k* vs 1/T for a chemical reaction. What does the intercept represent? What is the relation between slope and E_a?

(b) A first order reaction takes 30 minutes for 20% decomposition. Calculate $t_{1/2}$ [log 2 = 0·3010]

Solutions

SECTION - A

1. If there is no energy gap between valence band and conduction band, the nature of solid will be conductor.
(1 Mark)

2. Electrostatic stabilisation and solvation are the two reasons for the stability of colloidal sols. **(1 Mark)**

3. Structural formula: $[Cr(H_2O)_5 Cl] Cl_2 . H_2O$ **(1 Mark)**

Note

Since 2 moles of AgCl get precipitated, two Cl^- ions are present outside the coordination sphere. While five H_2O molecules and one Cl^- ion are present in the coordination sphere, making the coordination number 6.

OR

The main difference between a double salt (like alums, Mohr's salt, etc.) and a complex (like ferrocyanide ion) is that the former dissociates completely into ions in aqueous solution and gives tests of the constituent ions, while latter does not dissociate into ions and thus do not give positive test of the constituent ions. **(1 Mark)**

4.
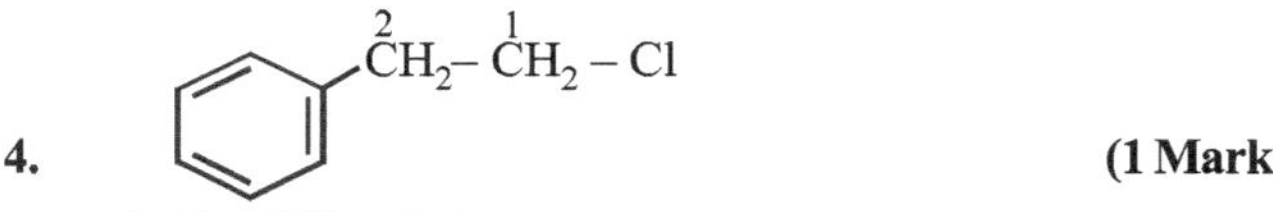
1-chloro-2-Phenylethane
(1 Mark)

5.
$$CH_3 - \overset{\overset{O}{\|}}{C} - NH_2 + Br_2 + 4NaOH \longrightarrow$$
Ethanamide (2C)
(Acetamide)
$$CH_3NH_2 + Na_2CO_3 + 2NaBr + 2H_2O$$
Methylamine (1C)
(1 Mark)

Note

Hoffmann bromamide reaction: Reaction of an acid amide with bromine in an aqueous or ethanolic solution of sodium hydroxide to form a primary amine, with one carbon atom less, is known as Hoffmann bromamide reaction.

OR

$CH_3CH_2CH_2NH_2$ (1° amine)
Propanamine

and $CH_3 - \overset{\overset{CH_3}{|}}{N} - CH_3$ (3° amine)
N,N-Dimethylmethanamine

Due to the presence of two H-atoms on N-atom of primary amines, they undergo extensive intermolecular H-bonding while tertiary amines due to the absence of H-atom on the N-atom do not undergo H-bonding. As a result, primary amines (*e.g.* propanamine) have higher boiling points than tertiary amines (*e.g.* N, N-dimethyl methanamine) of comparable molecular mass. **(1 Mark)**

SECTION - B

6. Nitrate ion is confirmed by the appearence of brown ring.
$$NO_3^- + Fe^{2+} + H^+ \longrightarrow Fe^{3+} + NO + H_2O \quad \textbf{(1 Mark)}$$
$$\left[Fe(H_2O)_6\right]^{2+} + NO \longrightarrow \left[Fe(H_2O)_5 NO\right]^{2+} + H_2O$$
(brown ring)
(1 Mark)

OR

$$4HCl + O_2 \xrightarrow{CuCl_2} 2Cl_2 + 2H_2O \quad \textbf{(1 Mark)}$$
$$2Cl_2 + 2H_2O \longrightarrow 4HCl + O_2 \quad \textbf{(1 Mark)}$$

Note

The ring test fails when nitrite is present even in traces. This happens because nitrite forms a black solution when ferrous sulphate solution is added. The ring test also fails in the presence of bromide or iodide on both when present along with nitrate in the mixture.

7. Corrosion is basically a process of oxidation, so oxidation potential is considered here.
Oxidation potential of Fe = 0.44 V
Oxidation potential of X = 2.36 V
Oxidation potential of Y = 0.14 V
Since, X has a higher oxidation potential than that of iron, so it will oxidise faster than Fe. Therefore, X is better for coating. **(2 Marks)**

8. (a) Solubility of gases in liquid is inversly proportional to temperature. As temperature increases, solubility of dissolved gases in water decreases. Hence, aquatic species find difficult to breath in warm water due to decreased availability of oxygen. **(1 Mark)**

(b) Henry's Law states that the solubility of a gas in a liquid at a given temperature is directly proportional to the partial pressure of the gas.
At higher altitude, partial pressure of oxygen is less than that at ground level, so low O_2 in blood causes climbers to become weak and makes them unable to think clearly.
(1 Mark)

OR

Maximum boiling azeotropes mixture will be formed by mixing of acetone and chloroform. In these solutions, the A—B interactions are stronger than the A—A and B—B molecular interactions present in the two liquids forming the solution. Hydrogen bonding will decrease the escaping tendency of the molecules.   **(1 + 1 = 2 Marks)**

9. (a) Monomer of neoprene is :

$$CH_2 = \overset{\overset{\displaystyle Cl}{|}}{C} - CH = CH_2$$ **(½ + ½ = 1 Mark)**

Chloroprene or 2-Chloro-1,3-butadiene

(b) The repeating unit of nylon-6 is

which is derived from the monomer caprolactam.

$$\text{(caprolactam structure)}$$ **(½ + ½ = 1 Mark)**

10. (a) Teflon is an addition polymer because it is obtained by the addition of infinite number of tetrafluoroethene, $F_2C = CF_2$, by addition reaction in the presence of persulphate catalyst at high pressure.
                                   (½ + ½ = 1 Mark)

(b) PHBV (poly β-hydroxy butyrate-co-β-hydroxy valerate) is a condensation polymer because it is obtained by the condensation of 3-Hydroxybutanoic acid and 3 Hydroxy pentanoic acid molecules with the elimination of water molecule.   **(½ + ½ = 1 Mark)**

> *Note*
>
> *Usage of biodegradable polymers can lower the cost of labour used for the removal of conventional plastics from the environment since they degrade naturally. Teflon can also be used to coat dental filings, to prevent them from sticking to adjacent teeth.*

11. (a) Cr^{2+} is a stronger reducing agent because the more negative the electrode potential, greater is the reducing power of the electrode.

$$E^\circ_{Cr^{2+}/Cr} = -0.91 > E^\circ_{Fe^{2+}/Fe} = -0.44$$
                                   (½ + ½ = 1 Mark)

(b) Mn^{2+} is the most stable ion because it $(Mn^{2+} - d^5)$

| 1 | 1 | 1 | 1 | 1 |

has half filled electronic configuration and it has most negative reduction potential $E^\circ_{Mn^{2+}/Mn} = -1.18\,V$ **(½ + ½ = 1 Mark)**

12. (a) 

2, 4, 6 Tritritrophenol
(Picric acid)   **(1 Mark)**

(b) 

$$CH_3CH_2Cl + NaOC_2H_5 \xrightarrow{\,S_N2\,} CH_3CH_2OC_2H_5$$
Diethyl ether   **(1 Mark)**

> *Note*
>
> *When picric acid is hydrated then it is safe to handle, but it becomes a powerful explosive when dry (less than 10% H_2O). Dry picric acid is highly sensitive to heat, shock and friction. The moistened solid is classified as a flammable solid.*

SECTION - C

13. Osmotic pressure,

$$\pi = CRT$$
$$\pi_1 = C_1RT$$ **(1 Mark)**

$$4.98 = \frac{30/180}{1} RT \qquad \text{...(i)}$$

$$1.52 = C_2RT \qquad \text{...(ii)}$$

Divide equation (i) by (ii)

$$\frac{4.98}{1.52} = \frac{1}{6 \times C_2} \Rightarrow C_2 = 0.0508\,mol\,L^{-1} \quad \textbf{(1 Mark)}$$

> *Note*
>
> *The measurement of osmotic pressure can be used to determine molecular weight of compounds and is also used in the desalination and purification of sea water, which involves the process of reverse osmosis.*

14. $$d = \frac{ZM}{a^3 N_A}$$ **(½ Mark)**

Z = No. of lattice points per unit cell
M = Molar mass of metal
a^3 = Volume of the unit cell
N_A = Avagadro constant
For *bcc* $Z = 2$ **(½ Mark)**
$$M = 52\,u$$
$$a = 300\,pm = 300 \times 10^{-10}\,cm$$
$$N_A = 6.022 \times 10^{23}$$

$$d = \frac{2 \times 52}{(300 \times 10^{-10})^3 \times 6.022 \times 10^{23}} \quad \textbf{(1 Mark)}$$

$$= \frac{104}{16.259}$$

$$= 6.396 \text{ g cm}^{-3} \quad \textbf{(1 Mark)}$$

15. (a) **Sol :** Sols are the colloidal system in which solid is dispersed phase and liquid is dispersion medium.

eg. ink $(½ + ½ = \textbf{1 Mark})$

(b) **Aerosol:** It is a colloidal dispersion of a liquid in a gas, *e.g.,* fog. $(½ + ½ = \textbf{1 Mark})$

(c) **Hydrosol:** It is a colloidal sol of a solid in water as the dispersion medium, *e.g.,* starch sol or gold sol.

$(½ + ½ = \textbf{1 Mark})$

16. $Cd^{2+}(aq) + Zn(s) \longrightarrow Zn^{2+} + Cd(s)$

$$E^{\circ}_{cell} = E^{\circ}_{Cd^{2+}/Cd} - E^{\circ}_{Zn^{2+}/Zn} \quad (½ \textbf{ Mark})$$

$$= -0.403 - (-0.763) = 0.36 \text{V} \quad (½ \textbf{ Mark})$$

$$\Delta G^{\circ} = -nFE^{\circ}_{cell}$$

$$n = 2$$

$$\Delta G^{\circ} = -2 \times 96500 \times 0.36 = -69480 \text{ J mol}^{-1}$$

$$= -69.480 \text{ kJ mol}^{-1} \quad \textbf{(1 Mark)}$$

$$\Delta G^{\circ} = -2.303 \text{ RT log K}_c \quad (½ \textbf{ Mark})$$

$$\frac{\Delta G^{\circ}}{-2.303 \text{ RT}} = \log K_c$$

$$\frac{-69480}{-2.303 \times 8.314 \times 298} = \log K_c$$

$$12.17 = \log K_c \quad (½ \textbf{ Mark})$$

Note

Relation between E°_{cell} and K_c might be calculated as given below which can used to determine the value of K_c directly from given value of E°_{cell}.

$$\because \quad \Delta G = -nF E^{\circ}_{cell}$$

$$\because \quad \Delta G = -2.303 \text{ RT log K}_c$$

Now, $nF E^{\circ}_{cell} = 2.303 \text{ RT log K}_c$

$$n E^{\circ}_{cell} = \frac{2.303 \text{ RT}}{F} . \log K_c$$

$$= \frac{2.303 \times 8.314 \times 298}{96500} \log K_c$$

$$= 0.059 \log K_c$$

$$n E^{\circ}_{cell} = 0.059 \log K_c$$

OR

$$m = \frac{\text{Atomic mass}}{n \times F} \times Q \quad (½ \textbf{ Mark})$$

where m = mass deposited

t = time

Atomic mass = 52 g mol^{-1}

$Q = 24000 \text{ C}$

$F = 96500 \text{ C mol}^{-1}$

$$\overset{+6}{CrO_3} \xrightarrow{n=6} \overset{0}{Cr} \quad (½ \textbf{ Mark})$$

$$m = \frac{52 \times 24000}{6 \times 96500} = \frac{12480}{5790} = 2.15 \text{ g}$$

$(½ \textbf{ Mark})$

2.15 g of Cr will be electroplated by 24000 C

$$Q = i \times t \quad (½ \textbf{ Mark})$$

$$m = \frac{\text{Atomic mass}}{n \times F} \times i \times t$$

$$m = 1.5 \text{ g}; i = 12.5 \text{ A}, t = ?$$

$$1.5 = \frac{52}{6 \times 96500} \times 12.5 \times t$$

$$t = \frac{1.5 \times 6 \times 96500}{52 \times 12.5} \quad (½ \textbf{ Mark})$$

$$= 1336.15 \text{ sec} \quad (½ \textbf{ Mark})$$

Note

$[Fe(H_2O)_6]^{2+}$ complex.

$Fe^{2+} = 3d^6$

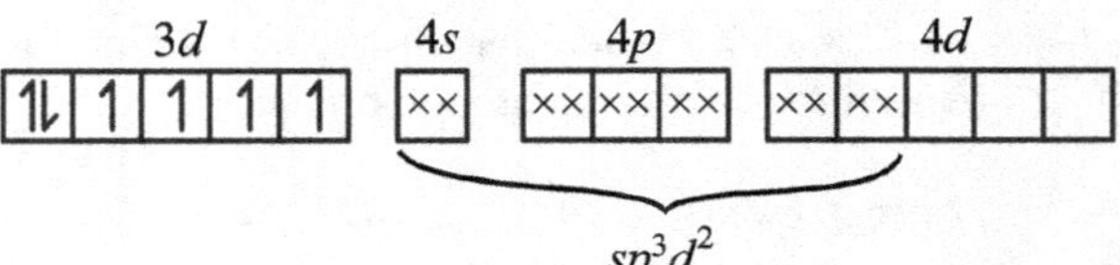

$$sp^3d^2$$

(H_2O is a weak ligand does not lead to pairing of electrons). It will be a outer orbital complex.

Magnetic character

$n = 4$ *(4 unpaired e^- s), paramagnetic due to unpaired e^- s*

$[Ni(CN)_4]^{2-}$ complex.

$Ni^{2+} - 3d^8$

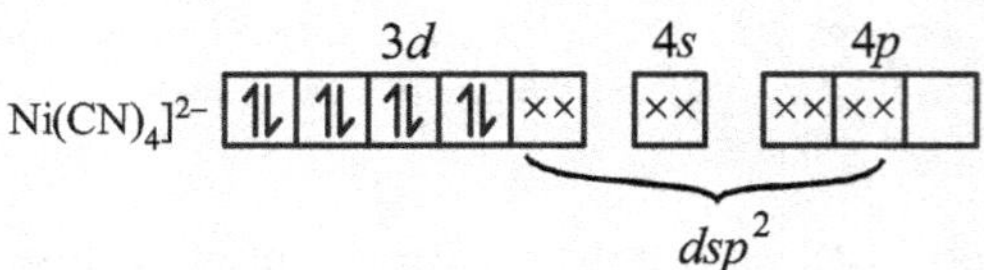

$$dsp^2$$

Pairing of electrons occurs due to strong CN^- ligand.

Magnetic nature

$n = 0$ *(no. unpaired electron). Diamagnetic*

17. (i) $[Fe(H_2O)_6]^{2+}$ complex is sp^3d^2 hybridised. **(1 Mark)**

Complex is paramagnetic due to presenc of unpaired electrons. $(½ \textbf{ Mark})$

(ii) $[Ni(CN)_4]^{2-}$ complex is dsp^2 hybridised. **(1 Mark)**

Complex is diamagnetic due to absence of unpaired electrons. $(½ \textbf{ Mark})$

18. Chromite ore $\longrightarrow$ sodium dichromate

STEPS

- Chromite ore is fused with sodium carbonate in excess of air to give yellow solution of Na_2CrO_4 (sodium chromate). **(1 Mark)**

$$4FeCr_2O_4 + 8Na_2CO_3 + 7O_2 \longrightarrow$$
Chromite ore

$$8Na_2CrO_4 + 2Fe_2O_3 + 8CO_2$$
Sod. chromate
(yellow)

- Yellow sodium chromate is filtered and acidified with sulphuric acid to give orange coloured sodium dichromate. **(1 Mark)**

$$2Na_2CrO_4 + 2H^+ \longrightarrow Na_2Cr_2O_7 + H_2O + 2Na^+$$
Sod. dichromate
(orange colour)

Ferrous salts (Fe^{2+}) are oxidised to ferric (Fe^{3+}) salts when they are treated with acidified $K_2Cr_2O_7$.

$$Cr_2O_7^{2-} + 6Fe^{2+} + 14H^+ \longrightarrow 2Cr^{3+} + 6Fe^{3+} + 7H_2O$$
(1 Mark)

OR

(a) $2MnO_2 + 4KOH + O_2 \rightarrow 2K_2MnO_4 + 2H_2O$
(1 Mark)

(b) $10I^- + 2MnO_4^- + 16H^+ \rightarrow 2Mn^{2+} + 8H_2O + 5I_2$
(1 Mark)

(c) $Cr_2O_7^{2-} + 3Sn^{2+} + 14H^+ \rightarrow 2Cr^{3+} + 3Sn^{4+} + 7H_2O$
(1 Mark)

19. (a) The role of depressant is to prevent one type of sulphide ore particles from forming the froth with air bubbles.

For example, NaCN is used as a depressant to separate lead sulphide (PbS) from zinc sulphide (ZnS). NaCN forms a zinc complex, $Na_2[Zn(CN)_4]$ thereby preventing it from the formation of froth.

$$4NaCN + ZnS \longrightarrow Na_2[Zn(CN)_4] + Na_2S$$
Sodium tetracyano zincate (II)

Thus, only lead sulphide forms froth and can be separated from zinc sulphide ore. **(1 Mark)**

(b) Carbon monoxide reacts with crude Ni to form nickel tetracarbonyl which on heating gives pure Ni.

$$\underset{\text{Crude}}{Ni} + 4CO \xrightarrow{330-350K} Ni(CO)_4$$

$$\xrightarrow[450-470K]{heat} \underset{\text{Pure}}{Ni} + 4CO \uparrow$$
(1 Mark)

(c) Bauxite ore is heated in a solution of NaOH. Sodium hydroxide dissolves bauxite forming a soluble complex of sodium meta-aluminate, while the impurities remain insoluble.

$$\underset{\text{Bauxite}}{Al_2O_3(s)} + 2NaOH(aq.) + 3H_2O(l) \longrightarrow$$

$$\underset{\substack{\text{Sod. meta–aluminate}\\\text{(soluble)}}}{2Na[Al(OH)_4](aq.)}$$
(1 Mark)

OR

(1) $Al_2O_3(s) + 2NaOH(aq) + 3H_2O \xrightarrow{473\text{-}523\text{ K}}$

$$\underset{\text{Sodium meta-aluminate}}{2Na[Al(OH)_4](aq)}$$

(2) $2Na[Al(OH)_4](aq) + 2CO_2(g) \longrightarrow$

$$Al_2O_3 \cdot nH_2O(s) + 2NaHCO_3(aq.)$$

(3) $Al_2O_3 \cdot xH_2O(s) \xrightarrow{1473K} Al_2O_3(s) + xH_2O(g)$

(4) $2Al_2O_3 + 3C \longrightarrow 4Al + 3CO_2$
(1 + ½ + ½ + 1 = 3 Marks)

 **Note**

Al_2O_3 has a very high melting point (over 2000°C), so Na_3AlF_6 is used which lowers the melting point of the Al_2O_3 and the process of electrolysis is widely known as Hall - Heroult process.

20. (a) **Antidepressants** are drugs that produce a feeling of well being and confidence in the person of depressed mood. Therefore, these are also called mood booster drugs. The common examples are vitalin, cocaine, methedrine etc. **(½ + ½ = 1 Mark)**

(b) Saccharin, aspartame or alitame may be used in the preparation of sweets for a diabetic patient. **(1 Mark)**

 **Note**

Aspartame is the most widely used artificial sweetener and is 100 times as sweet as cane sugar but use of it, is limited due to unstability at cooking temperature.

(c) Detergents are Non-biodegradable detergents because they contains branched hydrocarbon chains which are not easily degraded by the microorganisms. These accumulate in river and water ways and cannot be broken down into simple molecules by microbes.
(1 Mark)

21. (a) Proteins which are found in a biological system with unique 3D-structure and biological activity are called native proteins. When a native protein is subjected to physical and chemical change, it loses its biological activity and are called as denatured protein. **(1 Mark)**

(b) Lactose is a disaccharide. **(1 Mark)**

(c) Vitamin K is responsible for the coagulation of blood.
(1 Mark)

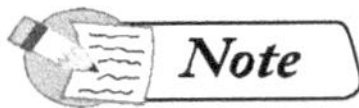

Note

Deficiency of vitamin K is rare, but, in severe cases, it can increase clotting time, leading to the hemorrhage and excessive bleeding.

22. (a)

(i) CH_3NH_2 and $(CH_3)_2NH$
      Methyl amine   Dimethyl amine

Methyl amine, being a primary amine, undergoes carbylamine reaction (carbylamines have foul smell).

$$CH_3NH_2 + CHCl_3 + 3KOH \longrightarrow$$

$$CH_3NC + 3KCl + 3H_2O$$
Methylisocyanide
(carbylamine)

Dimethyl amine, a secondary amine, does not respond carbylamine reaction.   **(1 Mark)**

(ii) $C_2H_5NH_2$ and $C_6H_5NH_2$
      Ethanamine   Aniline

Aniline, a primary aromatic amine, when treated with a solution of sodium nitrite in dil. HCl at 273–278 K followed by treatment with an alkaline solution of β-naphthol gives an orange coloured dye (**azo dye test**).

Benzene diazonium chloride

β-Naphthol

1-Phenylazo-2-naphthol
(**orange dye**)

Ethyl amine, a primary aliphatic amine, when treated with a solution of $NaNO_2$ in dil. HCl gives a primary alcohol along with a brisk evolution of N_2 gas.

$$C_2H_5NH_2 + HONO \xrightarrow{273-278K}$$

$$C_2H_5OH + N_2\uparrow + H_2O$$

(1 Mark)

(b)   Aniline, being a Lewis base, reacts with the Lewis acid ($AlCl_3$, catalyst for Friedel-Craft reaction) to form a salt. Thus the catalyst $AlCl_3$ is consumed. Moreover, the product has positive charge on N, which is deactivating for electrophilic substitution.

Aniline (Lewis base)
(having activating
$-\ddot{N}H_2$ group)

$AlCl_3$
Lewis acid

Salt
(having deactivting
$\overset{+}{N}H_2AlCl_3^-$ group)

(1 Mark)

23. (a)   Boiling point of butan-ol-1 is higher than diethyl ether because the former forms hydrogen bond among their molecules, while diethyl ether molecules do not form intermolecular hydrogen bond.

$$CH_3(CH_2)_2CH_2 - O - H \cdots OH_2C(CH_2)_2CH_3$$

$$C_2H_5 - O - C_2H_5$$
No H-bond because
it does not have H with O.

Thus, alcohol molecules, being polar, are associated through intermolecular hydrogen bonds and hence their boiling points are high.   **(1 Mark)**

Note

The hydrogen bond is an attractive interaction between a hydrogen atom from a molecule or a molecular fragment X – H in which X is more electronegative than hydrogen, and an atom on a group of atoms in the same or a different molecule.

If it takes place between different molecules then it is intermolecular hydrogen bonding.
If it takes place in same molecule than it is intermolecular hydrogen bonding.

(b) (i) $CH_3CH_2OH \xrightarrow{H^+} CH_3CH_2\overset{+}{O}H_2$

(ii) $CH_3CH_2 - \overset{..}{\underset{..}{O}} - H + CH_3 - CH_2 - \overset{+}{O}H_2 \xrightarrow{-H_2O}$

$$CH_3CH_2 - \overset{+}{O} - CH_2CH_3$$
$$H$$

(iii) $CH_3CH_2 - \overset{+}{O} - CH_2CH_3 \xrightarrow{(-H^+)}$
$$\underset{H}{|}$$

$$CH_3CH_2-O-CH_2CH_3$$
Diethyl ether

(½ + 1 + ½ = 2 Marks)

24. **(a)** The presence of electron-withdrawing groups such as $-NO_2$, $-CN$, etc. at o-and p-positions (but not at m-position) w.r.t. the halogen greatly activates the halogen towards nucleophilic displacemnt. The NO_2 group at o- and p- positions withdraws electrons from the benzene ring and thus makes the ring electron deficient and facilitates the attack of the nucleophile (OH^-) on haloarenes. **(1 Mark)**

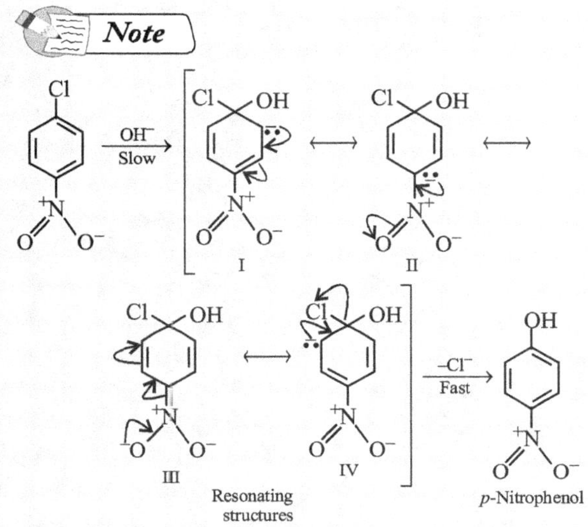

(b) p-Dichlorobenzene, being symmetrical, fits tightly in its crystal lattice. Thus the intermolecular forces of attraction in the p-isomer are stronger than those in the o-and m- isomers; which requires larger amount of energy to melt or dissolve the p-isomer than the o- and m-isomers. Consequently, the melting point of the p-isomer will be higher and its solubility lower than the corresponding o- and m-isomers. **(1 Mark)**

(c) Thionyl chloride method is preferred over hydrogen chloride or phosphorus pentachloride method since both the by-products (SO_2 and HCl) in this reaction being gases escape leaving the chloro alkanes in almost pure state.

$$R-OH + \underset{\text{Thionyl chloride}}{SOCl_2} \xrightarrow{\text{Pyidine}}$$

$$\underset{\text{Haloalkane}}{R-Cl} + SO_2\uparrow + HCl\uparrow$$

(1 Mark)

OR

(a) $\underset{\text{1−chlorobutane}}{CH_3CH_2CH_2CH_2Cl} + NaI \xrightarrow{\text{acetone}}$

$$\underset{\text{1−Iodobutane}}{CH_3CH_2CH_2CH_2I} + NaCl\downarrow$$

(1 Mark)

(b) 2-Bromo-2-methyl butane is most reactive towards elimination reaction.

$$\underset{\text{1-Bromopentane}}{CH_3-CH_2CH_2CH_2CH_2-Br} \qquad 1° \text{ alkyl halide}$$

$$\underset{\text{2-Bromopentane}}{CH_3-CH_2-CH_2-\overset{\overset{\displaystyle Br}{|}}{CH}-CH_3} \quad 2° \text{ alkyl halide}$$

$$\underset{\text{2-Bromo-2-methylbutane}}{CH_3CH_2-\overset{\overset{\displaystyle Br}{|}}{\underset{\underset{\displaystyle CH_3}{|}}{C}}-CH_3} \qquad 3° \text{ alkyl halide}$$

$3°$ Alkyl halide is most reactive towards elimination reaction (E_1) due to the formation of more stable $3°$ carbocation which loses proton to form alkene.

$$\underset{3° \text{ Carbocation}}{CH_3CH_2-\overset{+}{\underset{\underset{\displaystyle CH_3}{|}}{C}}-CH_3} \xrightarrow{-H^+} \underset{\text{Saytzeff's product}}{CH_3-CH=\overset{}{\underset{\underset{\displaystyle CH_3}{|}}{C}}-CH_3}$$

(1 Mark)

(c) 4-Bromo-4-methylpent-2-ene. **(1 Mark)**

25. **(a)** **(i)** Structure of $HClO_3$ (chloric acid)

(1 Mark)

Note

$HClO_3$ *decomposes if its concentrations exceeds above 30% on warming. Therefore it must be kept in cold all the time.*

(ii) Structure of $H_2S_2O_8$ (Marshall's acid).

(1 Mark)

Note

The key difference between caro's acid (H_2SO_5) and Marshall's acid ($H_2S_2O_8$) is that caro's acid contains one sulfate group whereas Marshall's acid contains two sulfate groups.

(b) **(i)** At room temperature, sulphur exists in solid state (S_8). Above 1000K, sulphur changes to the vapour state. In vapour state, S_2 is the dominant species which is paramagnetic due to presence of two unpaired e⁻ in antibonding orbital. **(1 Mark)**

(ii) F_2 is a better oxidising agent than chlorine. The oxidising power of a substance depends upon three factors:

- Bond dissociation energy
- Electron gain enthalpy
- Hydration enthalpy

Although the electron gain enthalpy of F_2 is less negative than of chlorine but

- bond dissociation energy of F_2 is much lower than that of Cl_2.
- hydration enthalpy of F^- ion is much higher than that of Cl^-.

These two energies compensate the effect of electron gain enthalpy. ∴ F_2 is a better oxidising agent. **(1 Mark)**

(iii) In gaseous state, PCl_5 exists as a covalent compound and has a trigonal bipyramidal structure.

The three equatorial bonds are shorter and stronger whereas the two axial bonds are longer and weaker. On heating it easily dissociates, therefore it is not much stable

$$PCl_5 \xrightarrow{\Delta} PCl_3 + Cl_2$$

But in solid state, it forms two ions $[PCl_4]^+ [PCl_6]^-$ As ions can be stabilized by lattice energy therefore in solid state it prefers to exist in the ionic form to gain stabilization. **(1 Mark)**

OR

(a) (i) $$PbS(s) + 2O_3 \longrightarrow PbSO_4 + O_2$$

(ii) $$XeF_6 + NaF \longrightarrow Na^+[XeF_7]^-$$ **(2 Marks)**

(b) (i) Group 15 members form MH_3 type of hydrides. As we move from N $\longrightarrow$ Bi, molecular mass increases, so van der Waal force also increases which in turn increases the boiling point so the order should be $NH_3 < PH_3 < AsH_3 < SbH_3 < BiH_3$ But N being an electronegative atom NH_3 can form intermolecular H-bond, therefore, has a higher boiling point than PH_3 and AsH_3. Thus the correct order is $PH_3 < AsH_3 < NH_3 < SbH_3 < BiH_3$ **(1 Mark)**

(ii) Group 17 members form H–X type of hydrides. As we move from F $\longrightarrow$ I, size of atom increases which in turn increases the bond length of H–X bond thereby strength of H–X bond decreases and its ability to release H^+ ion increases. Thus the order of acidity is HF < HCl < HBr < HI **(1 Mark)**

(iii) Group 16 members form H_2M type of hydrides. As we move from S $\longrightarrow$ Te, the size of the atom increases thereby the strength of M–H bond decreases.

Thus the reducing character $H_2O < H_2S < H_2Se < H_2Te$ **(1 Mark)**

26. (a) (i)

p-Nitrotoluene   2-Bromobenzoic acid

(1 Mark)

Note

In step (I), the trisubstitution is controlled by - o, - p directing group i.e., CH_3 group. Because -p position with respect to CH_3 is blocked then Br will substitute - o position with respect to CH_3.

(ii) 
$$CH_3CH_2COOH \xrightarrow[\Delta]{NH_3} CH_3CH_2CONH_2$$

$$\xrightarrow[\substack{\text{(Hofmann} \\ \text{bromamide} \\ \text{reaction)}}]{Br_2/KOH} CH_3CH_2NH_2 \xrightarrow{HONO} CH_3CH_2OH$$

$$CH_3COOH \xleftarrow[\text{(Oxidation)}]{(O)}$$
Acetic acid

(1 Mark)

(b) $$C_5H_{10} \xrightarrow{ozonolysis} B + C$$

Compound B gives +ve Fehling test and reacts with I_2, NaOH. This implies that compound B is an aliphatic aldehyde, it should be CH_3CHO.

Compound C does not give Fehling test, but forms iodoform. This implies compound C is a ketone and contains a methyl ketone group. Therefore, compound A is

$$CH_3 - CH = \underset{\underset{CH_3}{|}}{C} - CH_3$$

$$CH_3 - CH = \underset{\underset{CH_3}{|}}{C} - CH_3 \xrightarrow[\text{(ii) Zn/H}_2\text{O}]{\text{(i) O}_3}$$

(A) C_5H_{10}

$$\underset{\text{(B)}}{CH_3 - \overset{\overset{O}{||}}{C} - H} + \underset{\text{(C)}}{CH_3 - \overset{\overset{O}{||}}{C} - CH_3}$$

(1 + 1 + 1 = 3 Marks)

Note

Fehling test : In this test the presence of aldehyde but not ketones is detected by reduction of the deep blue solution of copper (II) to a red ppt. of insoluble copper oxide. It is commonly used for reducing sugars. Iodoform test is used to check the presence of carbonyl compounds with the structure $R-CO-CH_3$ or alcohols with the structure $RCH(OH)-CH_3$ in a given unknown substance.

OR

(a) (i)

Benzoic acid → Aniline

COOH $\xrightarrow[\Delta]{NH_3}$ CONH$_2$ $\xrightarrow{Br_2/KOH}$ NH$_2$

(1 Mark)

(ii) $CH_3Br \longrightarrow CH_3CH_2OH$
Bromomethane   Ethanol

$CH_3Br \xrightarrow{KCN \text{ (alc.)}} CH_3 - CN \xrightarrow{H_3O^+}$

$CH_3COOH \xrightarrow{LiAlH_4} CH_3CH_2OH$ **(1 Mark)**

(b) (i) $CH_3CH_2 - CH_3$ **(1 Mark)**

(ii) $(CH_3)_3CCH_2OH + (CH_3)_3CCOONa$ **(1 Mark)**

(iii) COONa (on benzene ring)   **(1 Mark)**

Note

Reaction (i) is an example of wolf-Kishner reduction. In this reaction carbonyl compounds are reduced to alkane. Reaction (ii) is on example of cannizzaro reaction in which one molecule of an alkehyde is reduced to produce a primary alcohol and another oxidised to carboxylic acid using a hydroxide base Reaction (iii) is an example of acid base reaction.

27. (a) (i) It is a zero order reaction   **(1 Mark)**

(ii) 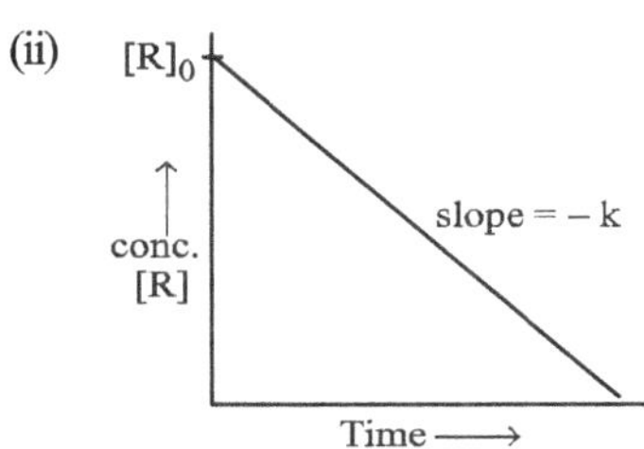

$R = -kt + [R]_0; \quad y = mx + c$

The slope of the curve is negative which means concentration of reactant is decreasing with time.

(1 Mark)

(b) $T_1 = 293\,K$; $k_1 = k$

$T_2 = 313\,K$; $k_2 = 4k$

$$\log\frac{k_1}{k_2} = \frac{E_a}{2.303R}\left[\frac{1}{T_2} - \frac{1}{T_1}\right]$$ **(1 Mark)**

$$\log\frac{1}{4} = \frac{E_a}{2.303 \times 8.314}\left[\frac{1}{313} - \frac{1}{293}\right]$$

$$-0.6020 = \frac{E_a}{2.303 \times 8.314}\left[\frac{293 - 313}{(313)(293)}\right]$$ **(1 Mark)**

$$E_a = \frac{-0.6020 \times 2.303 \times 8.314 \times 313 \times 293}{-20}$$

$E_a = 52854.55\,J\,mol^{-1} = 52.854\,kJ\,mol^{-1}$ **(1 Mark)**

OR

(a) $k = Ae^{-E_a/RT}$ (Arrhenius equation)

$$\ln k = \ln A - \frac{E_a}{RT}$$

$$y = c + mx$$
$$y = \ln k; \; x = 1/T$$
$$c = \ln A$$
$$m = -E_a/R$$

A plot of *lnk* v/s $\dfrac{1}{T}$ for a chemical reaction is as straight line.   **(1 Mark)**

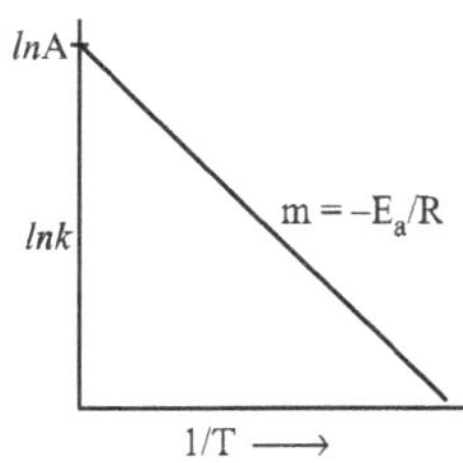

The intercept represents lnA, where A = frequency factor or pre-exponential factor.

$$\text{slope} = \frac{-E_a}{R}$$

$$E_a = -(\text{slope} \times R) \qquad \textbf{(1 Mark)}$$

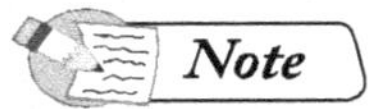

High temperature and low activation energy favour larger rate constant, and therefore speed up the reaction. Arrhenius equation is generally a combination of the concepts of activation energy and the Maxwell-Boltzmann distribution.

(b) For first order reaction

$$k = \frac{2.303}{t} \log \frac{a}{a-x} \qquad \textbf{(½ Mark)}$$

20% compound has been decomposed in 30 min. i.e. 80% compound is left.

$$k = \frac{2.303}{30} \log \frac{100}{100-20} \qquad \textbf{(½ Mark)}$$

$$= \frac{2.303}{30} \log 1.25$$

$$= \frac{2.303}{30} \times 0.0969 = 0.0074 \text{ min}^{-1} \textbf{(1 Mark)}$$

$$t_{1/2} = \frac{0.693}{k} = \frac{0.693}{0.0074} = 93.64 \text{ min } \textbf{(1 Mark)}$$

CBSE Board Solved Paper

Time Allowed : 3 Hours   *Maximum Marks : 70*

General Instructions:
(i) All questions are compulsory.
(ii) Section A : Q. no. **1** to **5** are very short-answer questions and carry **1** mark each.
(iii) Section B : Q. no. **6** to **12** are short-answer questions and carry **2** marks each.
(iv) Section C : Q. no. **13** to **24** are also short-answer questions and carry **3** marks each.
(v) Section D : Q. no. **25** to **27** are long answer questions and carry **5** marks each.
(vi) Use log tables if necessary. Use of calculators is **not** allowed.

SECTION - A

1. Out of NaCl and AgCl, which one shows Frenkel defect and why?
2. Arrange the following in increasing order of boiling points:
$(CH_3)_3N$, C_2H_5OH, $C_2H_5NH_2$
3. Why are medicines more effective in colloidal state?

OR

What is difference between an emulsion and a gel?

4. Define ambident nucleophile with an example.
5. What is the basic structural difference between glucose and fructose?

OR

Write the products obtained after hydrolysis of lactose.

SECTION - B

6. Write balanced chemical equations for the following processes:
(i) XeF_2 undergoes hydrolysis.
(ii) MnO_2 is heated with conc. HCl.

OR

Arrange the following in order of property indicated for each set
(i) H_2O, H_2S, H_2Se, H_2Te - increasing acidic character
(ii) HF, HCl, HBr, HI - decreasing bond enthalpy

7. State Raoult's law for a solution containing volatile components. Write two characteristics of the solution which obeys Raoult's law at all concentrations.

8. For a reaction
$$2H_2O_2 \xrightarrow[\text{alkaline medium}]{I^-} 2H_2O + O_2$$
the proposed mechanism is as given below:
(1) $H_2O_2 + I^- \rightarrow H_2O + IO^-$ (slow)
(2) $H_2O_2 + IO^- \rightarrow H_2O + I^- + O_2$ (fast)
(i) Write rate law for the reaction.
(ii) Write the overall order of reaction.
(iii) Out of steps (1) and (2), which one is rate determining step?

9. When MnO_2 is fused with KOH in the presence of KNO_3 as an oxidizing agent, it gives a dark green compound (A). Compound (A) disproportionates in acidic solution to give purple compound (B). An alkaline solution of compound (B) oxidises KI to compound (C) whereas an acidified solution of compound (B) oxidises KI to (D). Identify (A), (B), (C), and (D).

10. Write IUPAC name of the complex $[Pt(en)_2Cl_2]$. Draw structures of geometrical isomers for this complex.

OR

Using IUPAC norms write the formulae for the following:
(i) Hexaamminecobalt(III) sulphate
(ii) Potassium trioxalatochromate(III)

11. Out of $[CoF_6]^{3-}$ and $[Co(en)_3]^{3+}$, which one complex is
(i) paramagnetic
(ii) more stable
(iii) inner orbital complex and
(iv) high spin complex
(Atomic no. of Co = 27)

12. Write structures of compounds A and B in each of the following reactions:

(i) 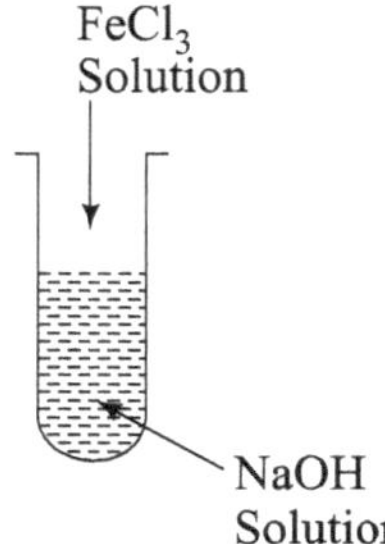

$$\text{(with CH}_2\text{CH}_3\text{ on benzene ring)} \xrightarrow{\text{KMnO}_4 + \text{KOH}} A \xrightarrow{\text{H}_3\text{O}^+} B$$

(ii) (cyclohexanol, OH group) $\xrightarrow{\text{CrO}_3} A \xrightarrow{\text{H}_2\text{N–NH–CONH}_2} B$

SECTION - C

13. The decomposition of NH_3 on platinum surface is zero order reaction. If rate constant (k) is 4×10^{-3} Ms^{-1}, how long will it take to reduce the initial concentration of NH_3 from 0.1 M to 0.064 M.

14. (i) What is the role of activated charcoal in gas mask?

FeCl$_3$ Solution

NaOH Solution

(ii) A colloidal sol is prepared by the given method in figure. What is the charge on hydrated ferric oxide colloidal particles formed in the test tube? How is the sol represented?

(iii) How does chemisorption vary with temperature?

15. An element crystallizes in fcc lattice with a cell edge of 300 pm. The density of the element is 10.8 g cm^{-3}. Calculate the number of atoms in 108 g of the element.

16. A 4% solution(w/w) of sucrose (M = 342 g mol^{-1}) in water has a freezing point of 271.15 K. Calculate the freezing point of 5% glucose (M = 180 g mol^{-1}) in water. (Given: Freezing point of pure water = 273.15 K)

17. (a) Name the method of refining which is
    (i) used to obtain semiconductor of high purity,
    (ii) used to obtain low boiling metal.
(b) Write chemical reactions taking place in the extraction of copper from Cu_2S.

18. Give reasons for the following:
(i) Transition elements and their compounds act as catalysts.
(ii) $E°$ value for (Mn^{2+}|Mn) is negative whereas for (Cu^{2+}|Cu) is positive.

(iii) Actinoids show irregularities in their electronic configuration.

19. Write the structures of monomers used for getting the following polymers:
(i) Nylon-6,6   (ii) Glyptal
(iii) Buna-S

OR

(i) Is $\text{–[CH}_2\text{–CH]}_n$ (with CH_3 substituent) homopolymer or copolymer? Give reason.

(ii) Write the monomers of the following polymer:

$$\text{–(HN–}C_3N_3\text{–NH–CH}_2\text{–)}_n \text{ (with NH group)}$$

(iii) What is the role of Sulphur in vulcanization of rubber?

20. (i) What type of drug is used in sleeping pills?
(ii) What type of detergents are used in toothpastes?
(iii) Why the use of alitame as artificial sweetener is not recommended?

OR

Define the following terms with a suitable example in each:
(i) Broad-spectrum antibiotics
(ii) Disinfectants
(iii) Cationic detergents

21. (i) Out of $(CH_3)_3C – Br$ and $(CH_3)_3C–I$, which one is more reactive towards S_N1 and why?
(ii) Write the product formed when p-nitrochlorobenzene is heated with aqueous NaOH at 443 K followed by acidification.
(iii) Why *dextro* and *laevo* – rotatory isomers of Butan-2-ol are difficult to separate by fractional distillation?

22. An aromatic compound 'A' on heating with Br_2 and KOH forms a compound 'B' of molecular formula C_6H_7N which on reacting with $CHCl_3$ and alcoholic KOH produces a foul smelling compound 'C'. Write the structures and IUPAC names of compounds A, B and C.

23. Complete the following reactions:

(i) (benzaldehyde, CHO group) $\xrightarrow{\text{NaCN/HCl}}$

(ii) $(C_6H_5CH_2)_2Cd + 2CH_3COCl \longrightarrow$

(iii) $CH_3– CH(CH_3) – COOH \xrightarrow[\text{(ii) H}_2\text{O}]{\text{(i) Br}_2/\text{Red P}_4}$

OR

Write chemical equations for the following reactions:
(i) Propanone is treated with dilute $Ba(OH)_2$.
(ii) Acetophenone is treated with Zn(Hg)/Conc. HCl
(iii) Benzoyl chloride is hydrogenated in presence of Pd/$BaSO_4$.

24. Differentiate between the following:
(i) Amylose and Amylopectin
(ii) Peptide linkage and Glycosidic linkage
(iii) Fibrous proteins and Globular proteins

OR

Write chemical reactions to show that open structure of D-glucose contains the following:
(i) Straight chain
(ii) Five alcohol groups
(iii) Aldehyde as carbonyl group

SECTION - D

25. $E°_{cell}$ for the given redox reaction is 2.71 V

$$Mg(s) + Cu^{2+}(0.01\ M) \longrightarrow Mg^{2+}(0.001\ M) + Cu(s)$$

Calculate E_{cell} for the reaction. Write the direction of flow of current when an external opposite potential applied is
(i) less than 2.71 V and
(ii) greater than 2.71 V

OR

(a) A steady current of 2 amperes was passed through two electrolytic cells X and Y connected in series containing electrolytes $FeSO_4$ and $ZnSO_4$ until 2.8 g of Fe deposited at the cathode of cell X. How long did the current flow? Calculate the mass of Zn deposited at the cathode of cell Y.
(Molar mass: Fe = 56 g mol^{-1} Zn = 65.3 g mol^{-1}, 1F = 96500 C mol^{-1})

(b) In the plot of molar conductivity ($\wedge_m$) vs square root of concentration ($c^{1/2}$), following curves are obtained for two electrolytes A and B:

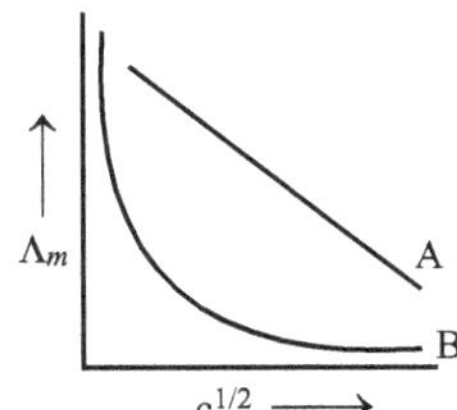

Answer the following:
(i) Predict the nature of electrolytes A and B.
(ii) What happens on extrapolation of $\wedge_m$ to concentration approaching zero for electrolytes A and B?

26. (a) How do you convert the following:
(i) Phenol to Anisole
(ii) Ethanol to Propan-2-ol

(b) Write mechanism of the following reaction:

$$C_2H_5OH \xrightarrow[443K]{H_2SO_4} CH_2 = CH_2 + H_2O$$

(c) Why phenol undergoes electrophilic substitution more easily than benzene?

OR

(a) Account for the following:
(i) o-nitrophenol is more steam volatile than p-nitrophenol.
(ii) t-butyl chloride on heating with sodium methoxide gives 2-methylpropene instead of t-butylmethylether.

(b) Write the reaction involved in the following:
(i) Reimer-Tiemann reaction
(ii) Friedal-Crafts Alkylation of Phenol

(c) Give simple chemical test to distinguish between Ethanol and Phenol.

27. (a) Give reasons for the following:
(i) Sulphur in vapour state shows paramagnetic behaviour.
(ii) N-N bond is weaker than P-P bond.
(iii) Ozone is thermodynamically less stable than oxygen.

(b) Write the name of gas released when Cu is added to
(i) dilute HNO_3 and
(ii) conc. HNO_3

OR

(a) (i) Write the disproportionation reaction of H_3PO_3.
(ii) Draw the structure of XeF_4.

(b) Account for the following:
(i) Although fluorine has less negative electron gain enthalpy yet F_2 is strong oxidizing agent.
(ii) Acidic character decreases from N_2O_3 to Bi_2O_3 in group 15.

(c) Write a chemical reaction to test sulphur dioxide gas. Write chemical equation involved.

Solutions

1. AgCl will show frenkel defect due to large difference in the size of cation and anions. **(1 Mark)**

2. $(CH_3)_3 N < C_2 H_5 NH_2 < C_2 H_5 OH$ **(1 Mark)**

Note

Alcohols have a higher boiling point as compared to that of amines because of strong hydrogen bonding. Oxygen being more electronegative forms strong hydrogen bond as compared to nitrogen. In tertiary amine, there is no hydrogen to form hydrogen bond. Hence it has lowest boiling point.

3. Medicines are more effective in colloidal state because colloids have a large surface area. Thus they get easily assimilated, absorbed and digested. **(1 Mark)**

OR

Emulsion	Gel
Emulsions are the colloidal sol in which both the dispersed phase and dispersion medium is a liquid.	Gel is a kind of colloid in which the dispersed phase is a liquid and the dispersion medium is a solid.

4. Ambident nucleophile are those nucleophile which have more than one binding site but bind to the central atom through any one site at a time. **(½ Mark)**

Example: NO_2^- ion is an ambident nucleophile

Nitrite ion can coordinate through oxygen or nitrogen to the central metal atom. **(½ Mark)**

5. *Glucose:*

   • It is a aldohexose and contains aldehyde functional group. **(½ Mark)**

   Fructose:

   • It is a ketohexose contains ketone functional group. **(½ Mark)**

OR

The products of hydrolysis of lactose are β-D-glucose and β-D-galactose. **(1 Mark)**

6. (i) XeF_2 undergoes hydrolysis when treated with water and evolves oxygen

   $$2XeF_2(s) + 2H_2O(l) \longrightarrow 2Xe(g) + 4HF(aq) + O_2(g)$$
   (1 Mark)

(ii) MnO_2 is heated conc. HCl forms $MnCl_2$, water and chlorine.

$$MnO_2 + 4HCl \xrightarrow{heat} MnCl_2 + Cl_2 + H_2O \text{ (1 Mark)}$$

OR

(i) The order of increasing acidic strength is

$H_2O < H_2S < H_2Se < H_2Te$ **(1 Mark)**

Note

Acidic strength is determined by availability of lone pair of electrons. As the size of the central atom increases lone pair is less readily available results into increase in the acidic strength of group 16 hydrides.

(ii) The decreasing order of bond enthalpy is

$HF > HCl > HBr > HI$ **(1 Mark)**

7. According to Raoult's law for a solution containing volatile components.

"The partial vapour pressure of each component of the solution is directly proportional to it's mole fraction present in solution"

The characteristics of the solution which obeys Raoult's law at all concentrations are as follows:

(i) In a binary solution of components, *A* and *B*, the enthalpy of mixing $\Delta H_{mix} = 0$, i.e., in prepration of an ideal solution no thermal change is observed.

(ii) In an ideal solution, the volume of mixing $\Delta V_{mix} = 0$, i.e., the final volume of the solution is equal to the sum of volumes of components being mixed.

(1 + 1 = 2 Marks)

8. (i) Rate law for the reaction **(1 Mark)**

   Rate = $k[H_2O_2] [I^-]$

(ii) Order of reaction is 2. **(½ Mark)**

(iii) Step 1 is rate determining step because it is the slowest step. **(½ Mark)**

9. $MnO_2 \xrightarrow[KNO_3]{KOH} K_2MnO_4 \xrightarrow{H^+} KMnO_4 + MnO_2$
   $\qquad\qquad\qquad$ Green $\qquad\qquad$ Purple
   $\qquad\qquad\qquad$ (A) $\qquad\qquad\quad$ (B)

$KMnO_4 \xrightarrow[H^+]{KI} Mn^{2+} + I_2,$
$\quad$ (B) $\qquad\qquad\qquad$ (D)

$KMnO_4 \xrightarrow[OH]{KI} MnO_2 + IO_3 + OH^-$
$\quad$ (B) $\qquad\qquad\qquad$ (C)

(½ + ½ + ½ + ½ = 2 Marks)

10. Bis(ethylene diamine) dichloro platinum (II)

Geometrical isomers

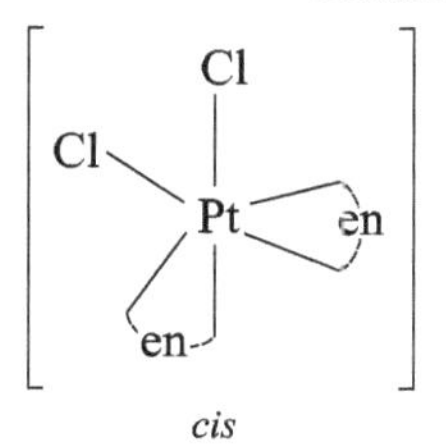 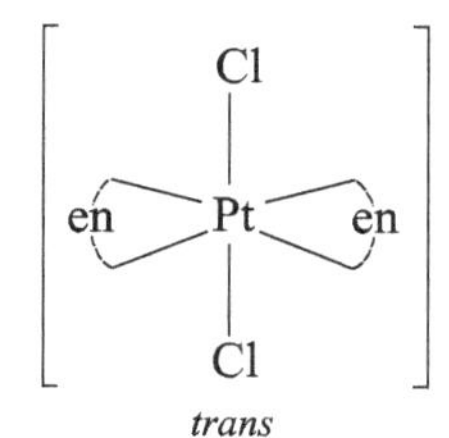

cis   trans

(1 + 1 = 2 Marks)

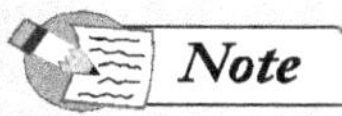 **Note**

cis-isomer of [Pt(en)$_2$Cl$_2$] has enantiomer pair i.e., d and l form while trans-isomer is optically inactive due to plane of symmetry in the molecule.

OR

(i) Hexaamminecobalt (III) sulphate   **(1 Mark)**

$$[Co(NH_3)_6]_2 (SO_4)_3$$

(ii) Potassium trioxalatochromate (III)   **(1 Mark)**

$$K_3[Cr(C_2O_4)_3]$$

11. (a) $[CoF_6]^{3-}$ is paramagnetic   **(½ Mark)**

(b) $[Co(en)_3]^{3+}$ is more stable than $[CoF_6]^{3-}$ **(½ Mark)**

(c) $[Co(en)_3]^{3+}$ forms inner orbital complex   **(½ Mark)**

(d) $[CoF_6]^{3-}$ forms high spin complex.   **(½ Mark)**

 **Note**

$[CoF_6]^{3-}$

$Co (27) \Rightarrow 1s^2\, 2s^2\, 2p^6\, 3s^2\, 3p^6\, 4s^2\, 3d^7$

$Co^{3+} = 3d^6\, 4s^0$

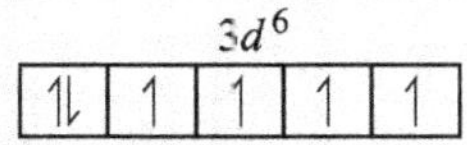

F$^-$ is a weak field ligand, therefore pairing of electron will not take place

$[CoF_6]^{3-}$

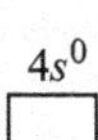 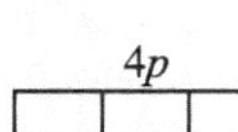

This complex has four unpaired electron.

For $[Co(en)_3]^{3-}$

$Co^{3+} = 3d^6\, 4s^0$

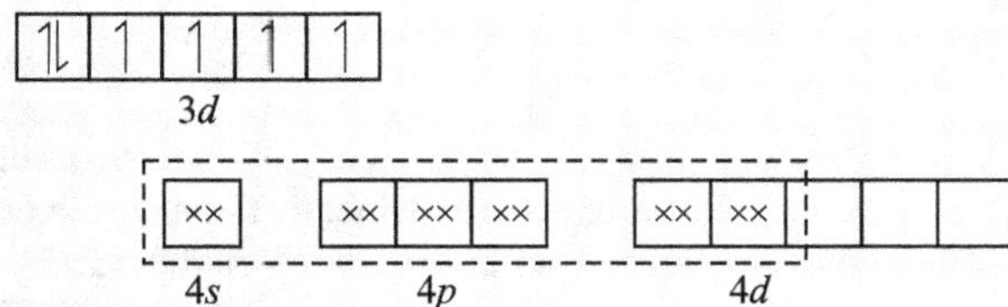

12. (i)

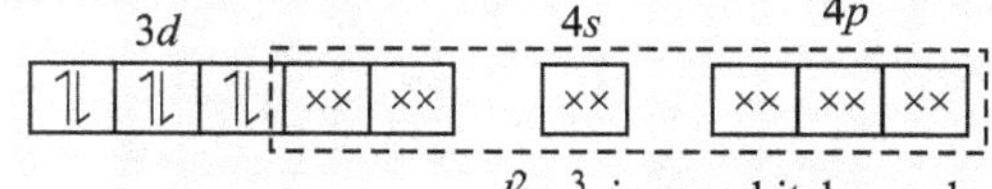

A   **(½ + ½ = 1 Mark)**   B

(ii)

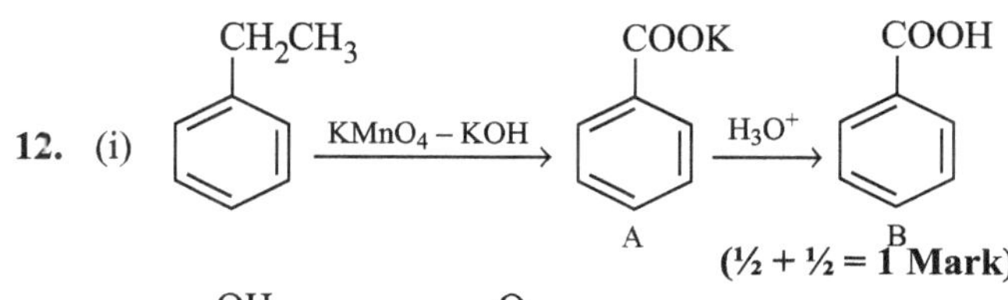

A

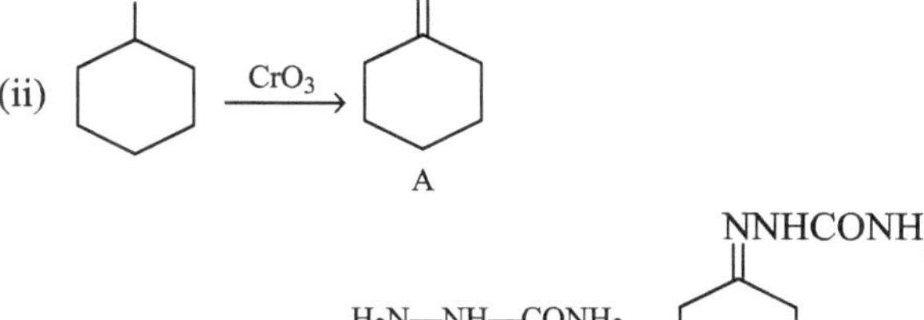

B

(½ + ½ = 1 Mark)

Right column top:

$[Co(en)_3]^{3+}$

(en) is strong field ligand, therefore pairing of electron takes place

$[Co(en)_3]^{3+}$

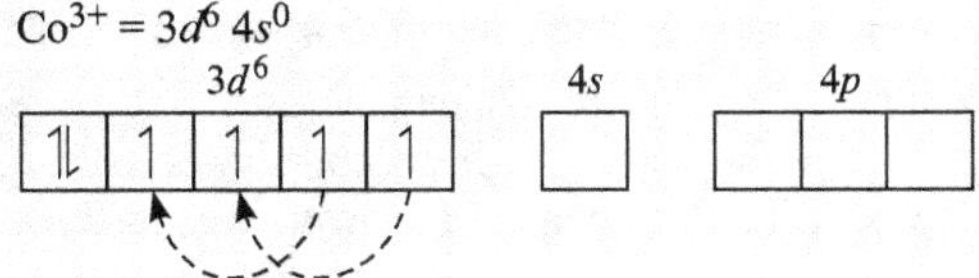

d^2sp^3, inner orbital complex

This complex does not have any unpaired electron.

SECTION - C

13. Initial concentration of $NH_3 = [A]_0 = 0.1$ M

Final concentration $[A] = 0.064$ M

$$k = 4 \times 10^{-3}\ Ms^{-1}$$

For zero order reaction

$$kt = [A]_0 - [A] \qquad \textbf{(1 Mark)}$$

$$4 \times 10^{-3} \times t = 0.1 - 0.064$$

$$t = \frac{0.036}{4 \times 10^{-3}} \qquad \textbf{(1 Mark)}$$

$$= 0.009 \times 10^{-3} = 9\ sec \qquad \textbf{(1 Mark)}$$

14. (i) Activated charcoal is an extremely porous carbon that has a very large surface area available for adsorption or chemical reactions. It is the most widely used adsorbent for preparing gas masks to selectively absorb toxic gases.   **(1 Mark)**

(ii) The coagulation will take place when $FeCl_3$ is added to NaOH solution. A negatively charged sol of hydrated ferric oxide is formed. The sol is represented as   **(1 Mark)**

$$Fe_2O_3 . x\, H_2O\, /\, OH^-$$

(iii) In chemisorption, the rate of adsorption increases with initial rise in temperature, but with further rise in temperature, after a certain limit, the rate of adsorption decreases.   **(1 Mark)**

15. Edge of cell (a) = 300 pm = 300×10^{-10} cm

    Density of element = 10.8 g cm^{-3}

In fcc lattice $Z = 4$

We know $d = \dfrac{Z \times M}{N_A \times a^3}$ **(1 Mark)**

$$M = \dfrac{10.8 \times N_A \times (3 \times 10^{-8})^3}{4}$$

$$= 72.9 \times 10^{-24} \times N_A = 43.9 \text{ g}$$ **(1 Mark)**

43.9 g of element = 6.02×10^{23} atoms

108 g of element = $\dfrac{6.023 \times 10^{23}}{43.9} \times 108$

$$= 14.8 \times 10^{23} \text{ atoms}$$ **(1 Mark)**

16. We know, $\Delta T_f = k_f m$

or $\Delta T_f = \dfrac{k_f \times w_{\text{sucrose}} \times 1000}{E_{\text{sucrose}} w_{\text{water}}}$ ...(i) **(1 Mark)**

$\Delta T_f = 273.15 - 271.15 = 2$ K

put the value in (i) for 4% solution of sucrose in water

$$2 = \dfrac{k_f \times 4 \times 1000}{342 \times 100} \Rightarrow k_f = 17.1 \text{ K kg mol}^{-1}$$

For 5% solution of glucose

$\Delta T_f = \dfrac{k_f \times w_{\text{glucose}} \times 1000}{M_{\text{glucose}} \times w_{\text{water}}}$ **(1 Mark)**

$$= \dfrac{17.1 \times 5 \times 1000}{180 \times 100} = 4.75 \text{ K}$$

$T_f = 273.15 - 4.75 = 268.4$ K   **(1 Mark)**

17. (a) (i) Zone refining is the method which is used to obtain semiconductor like germanium, silicon and gallium of high purity. **(½ Mark)**

    (ii) Distillation process is used to obtain metal which have low boiling point like zinc and mercury. **(½ Mark)**

(b) (1) Roasting of sulphide ore

$$2Cu_2S(s) + 3O_2(s) \rightarrow 2Cu_2O(s) + 2SO_2(g)\uparrow$$

    (2) Reduction of copper (I) oxide with copper (I) sulphide

$$2Cu_2O + Cu_2S \rightarrow 6Cu(s) + SO_2(g)\uparrow$$

(1 + 1 = 2 Marks)

18. (i) Transition elements and their compounds act as catalyst because

    (1) They have ability to show variable oxidation state and form complexes.

    (2) Transition metal also provide large surface area for the reaction to occur. **(1 Mark)**

(ii) $E^\circ_{(M^{2+}/M)}$ for any metal is related to the sum of ethalpy changes taking place in following steps :

$$M(s) + \Delta_a H \rightarrow M(g)$$
$$M(g) + \Delta_i H \rightarrow M^{2+}(g)$$
$$M^{2+}(g) + aq \rightarrow M^{2+}(aq) + \Delta_{\text{hyd.}} H$$

Cu has high enthalpy of atomisation $\Delta_a H$ and low enthalpy of hydration ($\Delta_{\text{hyd.}} H$). The high energy required to transform Cu(s) to Cu^{2+} (aq) is not balanced by its hydration enthalpy.

$\therefore$ E$^\circ$ value for Cu^{2+}/Cu is positive. **(1 Mark)**

(iii) Actinoids show irregularities in their electronic configuration because the energy difference between 5f, 6d, 7s subshell of the actinides is very small and hence electrons can be accommodated in any of them. **(1 Mark)**

Note

Actinoid contraction is more pronounced than lanthanoid contraction in the series due to poor sheilding effect of 5f electrons. Consequently energy of 5f, 6d, 7s subshells nearly become comparable.

19. (i) Hexamethylene diamine and adipic acid are the monomers of Nylon-6, 6 **(1 Mark)**

$$NH_2(CH_2)_6NH_2 \text{ and } HOOC(CH_2)_4COOH$$

(ii) Ethylene glycol and phthalic acid are the monomer of glyptal **(1 Mark)**

$$HO-(CH_2)_2-OH \text{ and } C_6H_4(COOH)_2$$

(iii) 1,-3-butadiene and styrene are the monomers of Buna-S. **(1 Mark)**

$$CH_2{=}CH-CH{=}CH_2 \text{ and } C_6H_5CH{=}CH_2$$

OR

(i) $\left[\!-CH_2-\overset{\overset{\textstyle CH_3}{|}}{CH}-\!\right]_n$ is a homopolymer Because it is formed from the same type of monomers. **(1 Mark)**

(ii) The monomers of the given polymer are melamine and formaldehyde

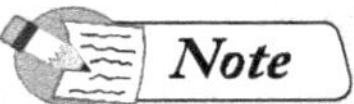

and   CH$_2$O **(1 Mark)**

(iii) Natural rubber is heated at 373 – 415 K with sulphur in vulcanisation, process which acts on active double bonds to form cross links making rubber hard which improve its properties. **(1 Mark)**

20. (i) Tranquilizers are used to treat mental disease and now used as sleeping pills. **(1 Mark)**

(ii) Anionic detergents are used in toothpastes. **(1 Mark)**

(iii) Alitame is not recommended as artificial sweetener because alitame is a high potency sweetener and it become difficult to control the sweetness of food. **(1 Mark)**

OR

(i) Broad spectrum antibiotics are the one which are used to treat a wide range of infections caused by both gram-positive and gram-negative bacteria. **(1 Mark)**

For example : ampicillin and amoxycillin.

(ii) Disinfectants are those chemical which kill microbes rapidly. They are harmful for living tissues, so they are used on non-living substances like floor, instruments, etc. They cannot be applied on skin and wounds. For example: Cl_2 (0.2 – 0.4 ppm). **(1 Mark)**

(iii) Cationic detergent are quaternary ammonium salts of amines with acetates, chlorides, bromide, etc. They contain long chain in their cationic part and have positive charge on nitrogen-atom.

Example: Cetyltrimethylammonium bromide. It is used in hair conditioners. **(1 Mark)**

21. (i) $(CH_3)_3\,C$—I is more reactive towards S_N1 than $(CH_3)_3\,C$—Br because I^- is a better leaving group than Br^-. **(1 Mark)**

(ii)

p-nitrochlorobenzene

p-nitrophenol

(1 Mark)

(iii) Dextro and laevo-rotatory isomers of butan-2-ol have identical boiling points, so they are difficult to separate by fractional distillation. **(1 Mark)**

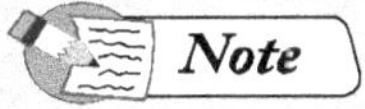

Note

Enantiomers have identical physical properties except the direction in which they rotate plane polarized light.

22.

(A) Benzamide

(B) Aniline or Phenylamine

(C) Phenylisocyanide

(1 + 1 + 1 = 3 Marks)

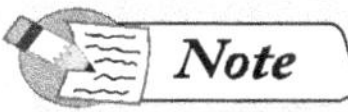

Note

Carbylamine reaction is given by aliphatic and aromatic primary amine only.

23. (i)

(1 Mark)

(ii) $(C_6H_5CH_2)_2Cd + 2CH_3COCl \longrightarrow$
$$2C_6H_5CH_2COCH_3 + CdCl_2$$
(1 Mark)

(iii)

(1 Mark)

OR

(i)

(1 Mark)

Note

Mechanism:

(ii) C_6H_5—CO—CH_3 + 4[H] $\xrightarrow[\Delta]{Zn-Hg+Conc.\ HCl}$

Acetophenone

$$C_6H_5CH_2CH_3 + H_2O$$

Ethyl benzene

(1 Mark)

(iii)
$$C_6H_5-\overset{\overset{\displaystyle O}{\parallel}}{C}-Cl + H_2 \xrightarrow{Pd/BaSO_4} C_6H_5-\overset{\overset{\displaystyle O}{\parallel}}{C}-H + HCl$$

Benzoyl chloride   Benzaldehyde

(1 Mark)

24. (i) Amylose and Amylopectin

Amylose: It is a linear polymer of α-D glucose having approximately 200 –1000 α-D-glucose units. C-1 of one α-D glucose is attached to C-4 of another α-D glucose with glycosidic bond. It is water soluble and it forms 15-20% part of starch and give blue colour with I_2.

Amylopectin: It is a branched chain polymer of α-D glucose which is constituted by hundreds of small chain having 20-30 α-D glucose unit. In it small chain are formed by glycosidic bonds between C-1 and C-4. These chain are joined by C_1— C_6 bonds. This fraction does not give blue colour with I_2. **(1 Mark)**

(ii) Peptide linkage and Glycosidic linkange

The bond conecting two or more similar or different amino acid in protein is commonly called *peptide bond* or *peptide linkage*. In the formation of peptide bond —NH_2 group of one amino acid is condensed with —COOH of adjacent amino acid to form —CONH linkage.

When —OH group of hemiacetal carbon of one monosaccharide is condensed with — OH group of another, glycosidic bond is formed, which links two monosacharide together. **(1 Mark)**

(iii)

Fibrous Proteins	Globular Proteins
(i) Proteins which are made up of linear, thread like molecules are called fibrous protein. In these molecules, poly-peptide chains are held together with H bonds.	(i) In these proteins poly-peptides attain spherical shape and poly-peptides are held together with relatively weaker-H-bonds.
(ii) They are insoluble in water but soluble in strong acid and bases. **Example:** Keratin, Myosin	(ii) They are soluble in water, alkalies, salt solutions and acid solutions. **Example:** Globulin, Pepsin

(1 Mark)

OR

(i) Glucose on heating with HI and red phosphorous at 100°C, it forms *n*-hexane. This proves the presence of straight chain of six carbon atom in glucose.

$$\overset{\displaystyle CHO}{\underset{\displaystyle CH_2OH}{\overset{\displaystyle |}{(CHOH)_4}}} \xrightarrow[\Delta]{HI,\ Red\ P}$$

$$CH_3-CH_2-CH_2-CH_2-CH_2-CH_3$$

n-hexane

(1 Mark)

(ii) Glucose forms pentaacetyl derivatives with acid chloride and acid anhydride in the presence of anhydrous zinc chloride. It proves that one molecule of glucose contains five —OH groups.

$$\overset{\displaystyle CHO}{\underset{\displaystyle CH_2OH}{\overset{\displaystyle |}{(CHOH)_4}}} + 5\ CH_3COCl \xrightarrow[acetylchloride]{ZnCl_2\ \ \Delta} \overset{\displaystyle CHO}{\underset{\displaystyle CH_2OCOCH_3}{\overset{\displaystyle |}{(CHOCOCH_3)_4}}} + 5\ HCl$$

Glucose pentaacetate

(1 Mark)

(iii) Glucose reacts with hydrogen cyanide to form, cyanohydrin. This reaction proves the presence of carbonyl group.

$$\overset{\displaystyle CHO}{\underset{\displaystyle CH_2OH}{\overset{\displaystyle |}{(CHOH)_4}}} \xrightarrow{HCN} \overset{\displaystyle CH{<}^{CN}_{OH}}{\underset{\displaystyle CH_2OH}{\overset{\displaystyle |}{(CHOH)_4}}}$$

Glucose cyanohydrin **(1 Mark)**

25. $Mg(s) + Cu^{2+}(0.01M) \longrightarrow Mg^{2+}(0.001M) + Cu(s)$

$$E_{cell} = E^{\circ}_{cell} - \frac{0.0591}{n} \log \frac{\left[Mg^{2+}\right]}{\left[Cu^{2+}\right]}$$ **(1 Mark)**

$$= 2.71 - \frac{0.0591}{2} \log \frac{[0.001]}{[0.01]}$$

$$= 2.71 - 0.0295 \log \frac{10^{-3}}{10^{-2}}$$ **(1 Mark)**

$$= 2.71 + 0.0295 = 2.7395\ V$$

$$E_{cell} = 2.7395\ V$$ **(1 Mark)**

(i) When an external opposite potential applied is less than 2.71 V, then current will flow from Cu to Mg, i.e., cathode to anode (same direction) **(1 Mark)**

(ii) When an external opposite potential applied is greater than 2.71 V, then current will flow from Mg to Cu, i.e., anode to cathode (opposite direction) **(1 Mark)**

OR

(a) According to Faraday's first law

$$w = z \times I \times t$$

$$w = \frac{E \times I \times t}{F} \quad \text{Where } (z = E/F)$$ **(1 Mark)**

For, Fe, $w = 2.8$ g, E of Fe $= 56/2 = 28$

$$w = \frac{28 \times 2 \times t}{96500} \quad \Rightarrow \quad 2.8 = \frac{28 \times 2 \times t}{96500}$$

$$t = 4825 \text{ sec} \qquad \textbf{(1 Mark)}$$

For, Zn, $w = ?$, E of Zn $= 65.3/2$

$$w = \frac{65.3 \times 2 \times 4825}{2 \times 96500} = 3.265 \text{ g} \quad \textbf{(1 Mark)}$$

The current flow for 4825 sec and weight of Zn deposited at cathode is 3.265 g

(b)

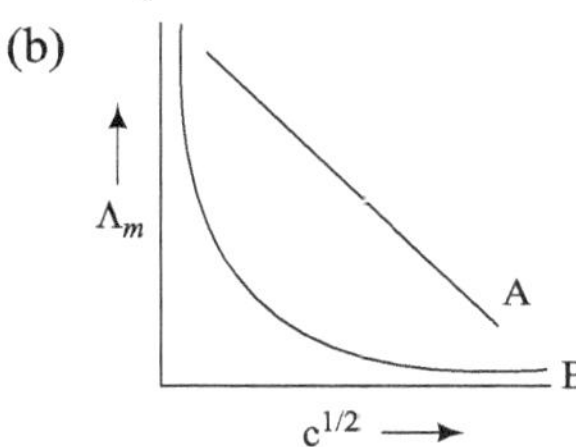

(i) A represents the strong electrolytes whereas B represents the weak electrolytes. **(½ Mark)**

(ii) It can be found from the graph that for a strong electrolyte A, as the concentration approaches the zero value, the molar conductance approaches a limiting value called molar conductance at infinite dilution.

The curve for a weak electrolyte B is a rectangular hyperbola and does not intercept the y-axis. Even though the concept of molar conductance at infinite dilution exists for a weak electrolyte, graphically the value cannot be evaluated. **(1½ Marks)**

26. (a) (i) Phenol to anisole

(1 Mark)

(ii) Ethanol to propan-2-ol

$$CH_3-CH_2OH \xrightarrow[\text{oxidation}]{PCC} CH_3-\overset{\displaystyle O}{\overset{\|}{C}}-H + CH_3MgI$$

$$\xrightarrow[\text{ether}]{\text{Dry}} \left[CH_3-\overset{\displaystyle OMgI}{\underset{\displaystyle}{CH}}-CH_3 \right] \xrightarrow{H^+/H_2O}$$

$$CH_3-\overset{\displaystyle OH}{\underset{\displaystyle}{CH}}-CH_3 + Mg\overset{\displaystyle I}{\underset{\displaystyle O}{\diagdown}}$$

(1 Mark)

(b) $C_2H_5OH \xrightarrow[443K]{H_2SO_4} CH_2=CH_2 + H_2O$

Mechanism is as follows:

Step I: $CH_3CH_2\ddot{O}H + H-O-\overset{\displaystyle O}{\underset{\displaystyle O}{\overset{\|}{S}}}-O-H$

$$\rightleftharpoons CH_3CH_2\overset{+}{O}H_2 + HSO_4^-$$

Step II: $CH_3CH_2-\overset{\displaystyle H}{\underset{\displaystyle +}{O}}-H \rightleftharpoons CH_3\overset{+}{C}H_2 + H_2O$

Step III: $H-\overset{\displaystyle H}{\underset{\displaystyle H}{C}}-\overset{+}{C}H_2 + {}^-O-\overset{\displaystyle O}{\underset{\displaystyle O}{\overset{\|}{S}}}-O-H \rightleftharpoons$

$$CH_2=CH_2 + H_2SO_4$$

(2 Marks)

(c) The rate of any electrophilic substitution reaction depends upon the electron density in the aromatic ring. Higher the electron density in the aromatic ring, higher is the rate of electrophilic substitution reaction. The presence of OH group in phenol, increases the electron density at ortho and para position by +R effect. Since the electron density is more in phenol than in benzene. Therefore phenol undergoes electrophilic substitution more easily than benzene. **(1 Mark)**

OR

(a) (i) Ortho nitrophenol is more steam volatile than para nitrophenol because o-Nitrophenol has intra molecular hydrogen bonding where as para nitrophenol has intermolecular H-bonding. Energy is required to overcome attractive forces in the molecules of *p*-nitrophenol. This means that boiling point of *o*-nitrophenol is less and is steam volatile while that of *p*-nitrophenol is more, and is non-volatile. **(1 Mark)**

(ii) Sodium methoxides is a strong nucleophile and a strong base. Thus elimination predominates substitution. In this reaction E_1 favored over S_N1. So t-butyl chloride on heating with sodium methoxide gives 2-methylpropene instead of t-butyl methyl ether. **(1 Mark)**

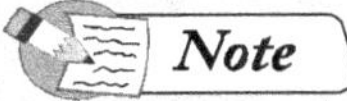

> **Note**
>
> *Elimination reaction is favored under strong base condition while substitution reaction is favored under weak nucleophile condition.*

(b) (i) 2 $+ CHCl_3 \xrightarrow{3 \text{ KOH}}$

$$+ 3 \text{ KCl} + 2H_2O$$

(1 Mark)

(ii) Friedel Craft alkylation of phenol

In this reaction phenol react with alkyl halide in the presence of anhydrous $AlCl_3$ & forms o-methyl phenol, p-methyl phenol.

(1 Mark)

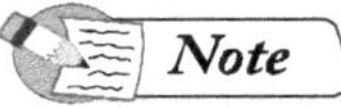

Note

Phenols undergoes Friedel craft alkylation with very low yield due to the formation of complex with $AlCl_3$.

(c) Ethanol and phenol can be distinguished by iodoform test.

$$CH_3CH_2OH + 4I_2 + 6NaOH \longrightarrow$$
ethanol

$$CH I_3\downarrow + HCOONa + 5H_2O$$
Iodoform (yellow)

$$\text{(phenol)} + I_2 + NaOH \longrightarrow \text{No reaction}$$

(1 Mark)

27. (a) (i) In vapour state sulphur partially exists as S_2 molecule, which has two unpaired electrons in antibinding π orbitals, just like O_2 molecule. Hence, it shows paramagnetic behaviour.

(1 Mark)

(ii) N–N bond is weaker than P–P bond because N–N bond has small bond length as comparison to P–P bond therefore it has high interelectronic repulsion of the non-bonding electrons. Another factor is the absence of d-orbitals in the valence shell of nitrogen. As a result nitrogen was not able to form $d\pi$-$p\pi$ bond. **(1 Mark)**

(iii) Ozone is thermodynamically less stable than oxygen because decomposition of ozone results into oxygen with the liberation of heat ($\Delta H = -$ve) and an increase in entropy ($\Delta S = +$ve). So decomposition is exothermic, resulting a large negative Gibb's energy change and make ozone thermodynamically unstable. **(1 Mark)**

(b) (i) $3Cu + 8HNO_3 \xrightarrow{\text{(dil.)}} 2NO + 3Cu(NO_3)_2 + 4H_2O$

when copper is added to dil.HNO_3, nitric oxide gas releases. **(1 Mark)**

(ii) $Cu + 3HNO_3 \xrightarrow{\text{(conc.)}} NO_2 + Cu(NO_3)_2 + H_2O$

when copper is added in conc. HNO_3, nitrogen dioxide gas releases. **(1 Mark)**

OR

(a) (i) $4H_3PO_3 \longrightarrow \underset{\text{Orthophospric acid}}{3H_3PO_4} + \underset{\text{Phosphine}}{PH_3}$

(1 Mark)

Note

Disproportionation is a type of redox reaction where a molecule is transformed into two or more dissimilar products.

(ii) 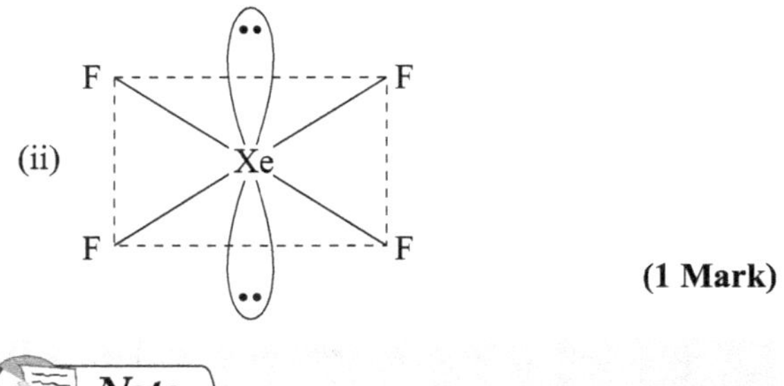

(1 Mark)

Note

According to VSEPR theory structure of XeF_4 is square planer. It has 2 lone pair of electrons.

(b) (i) Fluorine has the less negative electron gain enthalpy yet F_2 is strong oxidizing agent. There are two main reasons for this:

(a) F_2 has a low enthalpy of dissociation.

(b) F_2 has high free energy of hydration arising from smaller size of the F^- ion. **(1 mark)**

(ii) Electronegativity of central atom of oxides determine the acidic or basic character of the oxide. Acidic character of oxides increases with increase in electro negativity value of central atom of oxides. In group 15 on moving top to bottom, electronegativity decrease therefore acidic character of its oxides also decreases.

(1 Mark)

(c) SO_2 turns a filter paper moistened with acidified potassium dichromate solution green, due to formation of Cr^{3+} where SO_2 act as a reducing agent.

$$K_2Cr_2O_7 + 3SO_2 + H_2SO_4 \longrightarrow$$
$$Cr_2(SO_4)_3 + K_2SO_4 + H_2O$$

(1 Mark)

All India *2018*
CBSE Board Solved Paper

Time Allowed : 3 Hours   *Maximum Marks : 70*

General Instructions:
(i) All question are compulsory.
(ii) Section A : Question number **1 to 5** are very short answer questions and carry **1** mark each.
(iii) Section B : Question number **6 to 10** are short answer questions and carry **2** marks each.
(iv) Section C : Question number **11 to 22** are also short answer questions and carry **3** marks each.
(v) Section D : Question number **23** is a value based question and carry **4** marks.
(vi) Section E : Question number **24 to 26** are long answer questions and carry **5** marks each.
(vii) Use log tables, if necessary. Use of calculator is not allowed.

SECTION - A

1. Write the coordination number and oxidation state of Platinum in the complex $[Pt(en)_2Cl_2]$.

2. Analysis shows that FeO has a non-stoichiometric composition with formula $Fe_{0.95}O$. Give reason.

3. Out of chlorobenzene and benzyl chloride, which one gets easily hydrolysed by aqueous NaOH and why?

4. Write the IUPAC name of the following:

$$CH_3-\underset{\underset{C_2H_5OH}{|}}{\overset{\overset{CH_3}{|}}{C}}-\underset{|}{CH}-CH_3$$

5. $CO(g)$ and $H_2(g)$ react to give different products in the presence of different catalysts. Which ability of the catalyst is shown by these reactions?

SECTION - B

6. Among the hydrides of Group - 15 elements, which have the
   (a) lowest boiling point?
   (b) maximum basic character?
   (c) highest bond angle?
   (d) maximum reducing character?

7. Calculate the freezing point of a solution containing 60 g glucose (Molar mass = 180 g mol^{-1}) in 250 g of water. (k_f of water = 1.86 K kg mol^{-1})

8. How do you convert the following?
   (a) Ethanal to Propanone
   (b) Toluene to Benzoic acid

OR

Account for the following :
(a) Aromatic carboxylic acids do not undergo Friedel Crafts reaction.
(b) pK_a value of 4-nitrobenzoic acid is lower than that of benzoic acid.

9. Complete and balance the following chemical equations:
   (a) $Fe^{2+} + MnO_4^- + H^+ \longrightarrow$
   (b) $MnO_4^- + H_2O + I^- \longrightarrow$

10. For the reaction
$$2N_2O_5(g) \longrightarrow 4NO_2(g) + O_2(g),$$
the rate of formation of $NO_2(g)$ is 2.8×10^{-3} M s^{-1}. Calculate the rate of disappearance of $N_2O_5(g)$.

SECTION - C

11. (a) Identify the chiral molecule in the following pair :

OH (i)   &   OH (ii)

   (b) Write the structure of the product when chlorobenzene is treated with methyl chloride in the presence of sodium metal and dry ether.

   (c) Write the structure of the alkene formed by dehydrohalogenation of 1-bromo-1 methylcyclohexane with alcoholic KOH.

12. A first order reaction is 50% completed in 40 minutes at 300 K and in 20 minutes at 320 K. Calculate the activation energy of the reaction.

    (Given : $\log 2 = 0.3010$, $\log 4 = 0.6021$, $R = 8.314\ JK^{-1}\ mol^{-1}$)

13. An element 'X' (At mass = 40 g mol^{-1}) having f.c.c. structure, has unit cell edge length of 400 pm. Calculate the density of 'X' and the number of unit cells in 4 g 'X'. ($N_A = 6.022 \times 10^{23}\ mol^{-1}$)

14. Given reasons for the following :

    (a) Measurement of osmotic pressure method is preferred for the determination of molar masses of macromolecules such as proteins and polymers.

    (b) Aquatic animals are more comfortable in cold water than in warm water.

    (c) Elevation of boiling point of 1 M KCl solution is nearly double than of 1 M sugar solution.

15. What happens when

    (a) a freshly prepared precipitate of $Fe(OH)_3$ is shaken with a small amount of $FeCl_3$ solution?

    (b) persistent dialysis of a colloidal solution is carried out?

    (c) an emulsion is centrifuged?

16. Write the chemical reactions involved in the process of extraction of Gold. Explain the role of dilute NaCN and Zn in this process.

17. (A), (B) and (C) are three non-cyclic functional isomers of a carbonyl compound with molecular formula C_4H_8O. Isomers (A) and (C) give positive Tollens' test whereas isomer (B) does not give Tollens' test but give positive Iodoform test. Isomers (A) and (B) on reduction with Zn(Hg)/conc. HCl give the same product (D).

    (a) Write the structures of (A), (B), (C) and (D).

    (b) Out of (A), (B) and (C) isomers , which one is least reactive towards addition of HCN?

18. (a) Why is bithional added to soap?

    (b) What is tincture of iodine? Write its one use.

    (c) Among the following, which one acts as a food preservative?

    Aspartame, Aspirin, Sodium Benzoate, Paracetamol

19. (a) Write the formula of the following coordination compound:

    Iron (III) hexacyanoferrate (II)

    (b) What type of isomerism is exhibited by the complex $[Co(NH_3)_5Cl]SO_4$?

    (c) Write the hybridisation and number of unpaired electrons in the complex $[CoF_6]^{3-}$.

    (Atomic No. of Co = 27)

20. Define the following with an example of each :

    (a) Polysaccharides

    (b) Denatured protein

    (c) Essential amino acids

    OR

    (a) Write the product when D-glucose react with conc. HNO_3.

    (b) Amino acids show amphoteric behaviour. Why?

    (c) Write one difference between α-helix and β-pleated structures of proteins.

21. Write the structures of the main products in the following reactions:

    (i) [cyclohexanone with substituent $CH_2-\underset{\underset{O}{\|}}{C}-OCH_3$] $\xrightarrow{NaBH_4}$

    (ii) [phenyl]$CH=CH_2 + H_2O \xrightarrow{H^+}$

    (iii) [phenyl with OC_2H_2] $+ HI \longrightarrow$

22. Give reasons :

    (a) $E°$ value for Mn^{3+}/Mn^{2+} couple is much more positive than that for Fe^{3+}/Fe^{2+}.

    (b) Iron has higher enthalpy of atomization than that of copper.

    (c) Sc^{3+} is colourless in aqueous solution whereas Ti^{3+} is coloured.

SECTION - D

23. Shyam went to a grocery shop to purchase some food items. The shopkeeper packed all the items in polythene bags and gave them to Shyam. But Shyam refused to accept the polythene bags and asked the shopkeeper to pack the items in paper bags. He informed the shopkeeper about the heavy penalty imposed by the government for using polythene bags. The shopkeeper promised that he would use paper bags in future in place of polythene bags.

    Answer the following :

    (a) Write the values (at least two) shown by Shyam.

    (b) Write one structural difference between low-density polythene and high-density polythene.

    (c) Why did shyam refuse to accept the items in polythene bags?

    (d) What is a biodergradable polymer? Give an example.

SECTION - E

24. (a) Write the reactions involved in the following :

    (i) Hoffmann bromamide degradation reaction

    (ii) Diazotisation

    (iii) Gabriel phthalimide synthesis

(b) Give reasons :

    (i) $(CH_3)_2NH$ is more basic than $(CH_3)_3N$ in an aqueous solution.

    (ii) Aromatic diazonium salts are more stable than aliphatic diazonium salts.

OR

(a) Write the structures of the main products of the following reactions :

    (i) $C_6H_5NH_2 \xrightarrow[\text{Pyridine}]{(CH_3CO)_2O}$

    (ii) $C_6H_5{-}SO_2Cl \xrightarrow{(CH_3)_2NH}$

    (iii) $C_6H_5N_2^+Cl^- \xrightarrow{CH_3CH_2OH}$

(b) Give a simple chemical test to distinguish between aniline and N, N- dimethylaniline.

(c) Arrange the following in the increasing order of their pK_b values :

$C_6H_5NH_2, C_2H_5NH_2, C_6H_5NHCH_3$

25. (a) Give reasons :

    (i) H_3PO_3 undergoes disproportionation reaction but H_3PO_4 does not.

    (ii) When Cl_2 reacts with excess of F_2, ClF_3 is formed and not FCl_3.

    (iii) Dioxygen is a gas while sulphur is a solid at room temperature.

(b) Draw the structures of the following :

    (i) XeF_4 (ii) $HClO_3$

OR

(a) When concentrated sulphuric acid was added to an unknown salt present in a test tube a brown gas (A) was evolved. This gas intensified when copper turnings were added to this test tube. On cooling, the gas (A) changed into a colourless solid (B).

    (i) Identify (A) and (B).

    (ii) Write the structures of (A) and (B).

    (iii) Why does gas (A) change to solid on cooling?

(b) Arrange the following in the decreasing order of their reducing character :

    HF, HCl, HBr, HI

(c) Complete the following reaction :

    $XeF_4 + SbF_5 \longrightarrow$

26. (a) Write the cell reaction and calculate the e.m.f. of the following cell at 298 K :

    $Sn\,(s)\,|\,Sn^{2+}\,(0.004\,M)\,\|\,H^+\,(0.020\,M)\,|\,H_2\,(g)\,(1\,bar)\,|\,Pt(s)$

    $\left(\text{Given} : E^\circ_{Sn^{2+}/Sn} = -0.14V\right)$

(b) Give reasons :

    (i) On the basis of E° values, O_2 gas should be liberated at anode but it is Cl_2 gas which is liberated in the electrolysis of aqueous NaCl.

    (ii) Conductivity of CH_3COOH decreases on dilution.

OR

(a) For the reaction

    $2AgCl\,(s) + H_2\,(g)\,(1\,atm) \longrightarrow$

    $2Ag\,(s) + 2H^+\,(0.1\,M) + 2Cl^-\,(0.1\,M), \Delta G^\circ = -43600\,J$ at $25°C$

    Calculate the e.m.f of the cell.

    $[\log 10^{-n} = -n]$

(b) Define fuel cell and write its two advantages.

Solutions

SECTION - A

1. $[Pt(en)_2Cl_2]$

   Co-ordination number = 6

   Oxidation number = +2   **(1 Mark)**

2. FeO has non-stoichiometric composition with formula $Fe_{0.95}O$. This is due to metal deficiency defect.

         (1 Mark)

3. Out of chlorobenzene and benzyl chloride, benzyl chloride gets easily hydrolysed, because Cl attached to sp^3 hybridised carbon in benzyl chloride is easier to break as compared to chlorobenzene where Cl is attached to sp^2 hybridised carbon which has a partial double bond character due to resonance.   **(1 Mark)**

4.
$$^5CH_3 - {}^4CH_2 - \overset{\overset{\displaystyle CH_3}{|}}{\underset{\underset{\displaystyle CH_3}{|}}{{}^3C}} - \overset{}{\underset{\underset{\displaystyle OH}{|}}{{}^2CH}} - {}^1CH_3$$

   3, 3 – Dimethylpentan-2-ol.   **(1 Mark)**

5. It is the selectivity of the catalyst which direct a given reaction to give different products.   **(1 Mark)**

SECTION - B

6. The Hydrides of group 15 elements are:

   NH_3, PH_3, AsH_3, SbH_3, BiH_3

   (i) **PH_3** has the lowest boiling point.   **(½ Mark)**

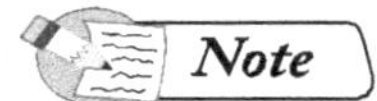

   Note

   Boiling point depends on mass. Down the group, atomic mass of central atom increases, so boiling point increases. However, NH_3 has higher boiling point than PH_3 due to hydrogen bonding.

   (ii) **NH_3** has the maximum basic character.   **(½ Mark)**

   Note

   Basic character depends on the ease of release of lone pair on the central atom (lewis base), which is turn depends upon the charge density on the central atom. Smaller the size of the central atom, more is the charge density, easier is the availability of lone pair and hence more is the basicity.

(iii) **NH_3** has the highest bond angle.   **(½ Mark)**

Note

In NH_3, N being small in size and highly electronegative, pulls the electron pair of the N–H bond towards itself. As a result, the bond pairs get closer resulting in increased repulsions between them. So, to minimize the repulsion, the bond pairs move away from each other giving a bond angle of 107.8°.

(iv) **BiH_3** has the maximum reducing character.   **(½ Mark)**

Note

Reducing character depends on the ease of release of H which in turn depends on the strength of the bond between central atom and hydrogen. Down the group, size of the central atom increases, bond length increases and hence, bond strength decreases. Thus, it becomes easier to release H. Hence, reducing character increases.

7. Given : Mass of glucose $(C_6H_{12}O_6)$, $w_2 = 60$ g

   Mass of water, $w_1 = 250$ g

   Molecular mass of (glucose) $(M_2) = 180$ g mol^{-1}

   $k_f = 1.86$ K kg mol^{-1}

   Freezing point of solution, $T_f = ?$

   We know,

   $$\Delta T_f = ik_f m$$

   for glucose, $i = 1$

   $$\therefore \quad \Delta T_f = k_f m$$

   $$= k_f \times \frac{w_2}{M_2} \times \frac{1000}{w_1} \qquad \textbf{(1 Mark)}$$

   $$\Delta T_f = 1.86 \times \frac{60}{180} \times \frac{1000}{250} = 2.48 \text{ K}$$

   Now,

   $$\Delta T_f = T_f^0 - T_f$$

   $$2.48 = 0\,°C - T_f$$

   $$\therefore \quad T_f = -2.48\,°C$$

   $$= 270.67 \text{ K} \qquad \textbf{(1 Mark)}$$

8. (a) **Ethanal to propanone:** CH_3CHO to CH_3COCH_3

   $$CH_3CHO \xrightarrow{CH_3MgBr} \underset{\underset{\displaystyle OH}{|}}{CH_3CHCH_3} \xrightarrow{CrO_3} CH_3COCH_3$$

   Ethanal   Propanone

         (1 Mark)

(b) Toluene to Benzoic acid:

CH$_3$ $\xrightarrow[\Delta]{\text{alk. KMnO}_4}$ COO$^-$K$^+$ $\xrightarrow{\text{H}^+}$ COOH

Toluene   Benzoic acid

(1 Mark)

OR

(a) Aromatic carboxylic acids do not undergo Friedel crafts reaction. This is because the carboxyl group is an electron withdrawing group and hence deactivates the benzene ring towards Friedel crafts reaction. The catalyst (anhydrous AlCl$_3$) gets bonded to the carboxyl group thus preventing the desired reaction.

(1 Mark)

> **Note**
>
> *The Friedel-crafts alkylation may give polyalkylated products, so the Friedel-crafts acylation is a valuable alternative. The acylated products may easily be converted to the corresponding alkanes via clemmensen reduction or wolff-kishner reduction.*

(b) pK$_a$ value of 4–nitrobenzoic acid is lower than that of benzoic acid. This is because in 4-nitrobenzoic acid, nitro group being electron withdrawing in nature, makes the O–H bond in –COOH more polar, thus facilitating the release of H$^+$. Thus, 4-nitrobenzoic acid is more acidic. More is the acidity, lesser is the pK$_a$ value. **(1 Mark)**

> **Note**
>
> *Acid strength increases as we move to the right along a row of the periodic table, and as we move down a column.*

9. (a) $MnO_4^- + 8H^+ + 5e^- \rightarrow Mn^{2+} + 4H_2O$

$$\underline{\qquad Fe^{2+} \rightarrow Fe^{3+} + 1e^- \times 5 \qquad}$$

$$MnO_4^- + 5Fe^{2+} + 8H^+ \rightarrow Mn^{2+} + 5Fe^{3+} + 4H_2O$$

(1 Mark)

(b) $[MnO_4^- + 2H_2O + 3e^- \rightarrow MnO_2 + 4OH^-] \times 2$

$$\underline{\qquad I^- + 6OH^- \rightarrow IO_3^- + 3H_2O + 6e^- \qquad}$$

$$2MnO_4^- + I^- + H_2O \rightarrow 2MnO_2 + IO_3^- + 2OH^-$$

(1 Mark)

10. Given : $2N_2O_5(g) \rightarrow 4NO_2(g) + O_2(g)$

Rate of formation of $NO_2(g) = 2.8 \times 10^{-3}$ Ms^{-1}

Rate of reaction $= -\dfrac{1}{2}\dfrac{d[N_2O_5]}{dt} = +\dfrac{1}{4}\dfrac{d[NO_2]}{dt}$ **(1 Mark)**

$\therefore \quad -\dfrac{d[N_2O_5]}{dt} = \dfrac{2}{4}\dfrac{d[NO_2]}{dt} = \dfrac{1}{2} \times 2.8 \times 10^{-3}\,\text{Ms}^{-1}$

$\Rightarrow \quad -\dfrac{d[N_2O_5]}{dt} = 1.4 \times 10^{-3}\,\text{Ms}^{-1}$ **(1 Mark)**

SECTION - C

11. (a)

(structure of 2-methyl-2-butanol type with chiral centre *, OH)

(1 Mark)

> **Note**
>
> *Chirality depends upon the pressence of asymmetric carbon atoms.*

(b)

C$_6$H$_5$Cl + CH$_3$Cl $\xrightarrow[\substack{\text{dry ether} \\ \text{Wurtz-Fitting} \\ \text{reaction}}]{2\text{Na}}$ C$_6$H$_5$—CH$_3$ + 2NaCl

(1 Mark)

(c)

(1-bromo-1-methylcyclohexane) $\xrightarrow[\text{KOH}]{\text{alc.}}$ (1-methylcyclohexene, major) + (methylenecyclohexane, minor)

(major)   (minor)

(This is in accordance with the Saytzeff's rule) **(1 Mark)**

12. Given : $T_1 = 300$ K, $T_2 = 320$ K

        $(t_{1/2})_1 = 40$ min $(t_{1/2})_2 = 20$ min

To find : activation energy, E$_a$ = ?

Solution :

$$k_1 = \frac{0.693}{(t_{1/2})_1} \quad ; \qquad k_2 = \frac{0.693}{(t_{1/2})_2}$$ **(1 Mark)**

$$k_1 = \frac{0.693}{40} \quad ; \qquad k_2 = \frac{0.693}{20}$$

we know, $\log\dfrac{k_2}{k_1} = \dfrac{E_a}{2.303R}\left(\dfrac{1}{T_1} - \dfrac{1}{T_2}\right)$ **(1 Mark)**

$$\therefore \quad \log\frac{(0.693/20)}{(0.693/40)} = \frac{E_a}{2.303R}\left(\frac{1}{300} - \frac{1}{320}\right)$$

$$\log\frac{40}{20} = \log 2 = \frac{E_a}{2.303 \times 8.314} \times \left(\frac{320-300}{320 \times 300}\right)$$

$$\Rightarrow \quad E_a = \frac{\log 2 \times 2.303 \times 8.314}{\left(\dfrac{20}{320 \times 300}\right)}$$

$$= 27663.79 \text{ J mol}^{-1} \approx 27.66 \text{ kJ mol}^{-1} \qquad \textbf{(1 Mark)}$$

13. Given: *fcc* structure, Z = 4

edge length, a = 400 pm = 4̸0̸0̸ × 10⁻⁸ cm

$N_A = 6.022 \times 10^{23} \text{ mol}^{-1}$

atomic mass, M = 40 g mol⁻¹

To find : Density, d = ?

Number of unit cells = ?

Solution: $d = \dfrac{Z.M}{a^3 N_A} = \dfrac{4 \times 40}{(4̸0̸0̸ \times 10^{-8})^3 \times 6.022 \times 10^{23}}$

$$d = 4.15 \text{ g cm}^{-3} \qquad \text{1 Mark)}$$

Volume of one unit cell = a^3

$$= (4 \times 10^{-8})^3 \text{ cm}^3$$

$$= 64 \times 10^{-24} \text{ cm}^3$$

Volume 4 g of 'x' = $\dfrac{\text{Mass}}{\text{Density}} = \dfrac{4 \text{ g}}{4.5 \text{ g cm}^{-3}}$

(1 Mark)

0.9636 cm³ number of unit cell = $\dfrac{\text{Vol. of 4 g}}{\text{Vol. of unit cell}}$

$$= \frac{0.9636 \text{ cm}^3}{64 \times 10^{-24} \text{ cm}^{-3}} = 1.505 \times 10^{22} \text{ unit cells}$$

(1 Mark)

14. (a) Osmotic pressure method is preferred for the determination of molar masses of macromolecules. This is because it is done around room temperature and molarity of solution is used instead of molality. As compared to other colligative properties, its magnitude is large even for very dilute solutions. This method is preferred for biomolecules as they are not stable at higher temperatures and polymers have poor solubility. **(1 Mark)**

(b) Aquatic animals are more comfortable in cold water than in warm water. This is because as temperature increase, solubility of gases in water decreases (from Le-chatelier's principle). Thus, in warm water the amount of oxygen available decreases. As a result, aquatic animals are more comfortable in cold water.

(1 Mark)

(c) Elevation of boiling point for 1M KCl solution is nearly double than that of 1 M sugar solution. This is because elevation of boiling point depends on the value of '*i*'. KCl being a strong electrolyte completely dissociates in water to give K^+ and Cl^- ions. Thus, $i = 2$ for KCl. On the other hand, sugar does not dissociate/associate in water so $i = 1$ for sugar solution. Hence ΔT_b (KCl) = $2\Delta T_b$ (sugar)

(1 Mark)

15. (a) When a freshly prepared precipitate of $Fe(OH)_3$ is shaken with a small amount of $FeCl_3$ solutions peptization takes place.

(In peptization, the precipitate adsorbs one common ion of the electrolyte, which then breaks into smaller particles of colloidal size). **(1 Mark)**

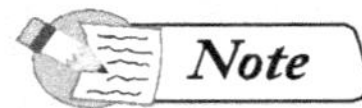

Where do we see peptization in everyday life? The clay that you use to do things like make pottery is produced through peptization.

(b) When persistent dialysis of a colloidal solution is carried out, coagulation takes place.

(On persistent dialysis, the electrolyte present in the sol is removed completely, the colloid becomes unstable and coagulates). **(1 Mark)**

(c) When an emulsion is centrifuged, demulsification takes place, i.e. the emulsion is broken down into constituent liquids. **(1 Mark)**

There are two basic types of emulsions oil in water e.g., milk and vanishing cream. In milk, liquid is dispersed in water and second is water in oil e.g., butter and cream. Emulsions can also be broken into constituent parts by heating, freezing etc.

16. The chemical reactions involved in the process of extraction of gold are:

$$4Au(s) + 8CN^- (aq) + 2H_2O (aq) + O_2(g) \rightarrow$$
$$\text{(Impure)}$$
$$4[Au (CN)_2]^- + 4OH^- (aq)$$
$$2[Au(CN)_2]^- + Zn(s) \rightarrow 2Au(s) + [Zn(CN)_4]^{2-} (aq)$$
$$\text{(pure)}$$

(2 Marks)

The role of NaCN is to leach out gold by forming a complex, leaving the impurities behind. Zn acts as a reducing agent. (Zn being more reactive than Au displaces it from the complex to give pure Au) **(1 Mark)**

17. Given : A, B, C → molecular formula C_4H_8O

(A) and (C) → positive Tollen's test

(B) → does not give tollen's test but gives iodoform test

(A) and (B) $\xrightarrow[\substack{\text{Zn–Hg} \\ \text{conc HCl}}]{\text{reduction}}$ (D)

(a) According to the given information, as A and C give positive Tollen's test, they have an aldehydic group. Moreover, as they have 4 carbon atoms, one of them is butanal and other must be 2–methylpropanal.

Further, as B does not give positive test but gives iodoform test, so B is a ketone. It should be Butanone. Aldehydes and ketones on reduction with Zn(Hg) in presence of conc. HCl give alkanes (Clemmensen reduction). So, D is butane.

Thus, the structures of A, B, C and D are:

(A) : $CH_3 CH_2 CH_2 CHO$
Butanal

O
$\parallel$
(B) : $CH_3 CCH_2 CH_3$
Butanone

(C) : $CH_3 CHCHO$
            $|$
            CH_3
2-Methylpropanal

(D) : $CH_3 CH_2 CH_2 CH_3$
Butane   (½ + ½ + ½ + ½ = **2 Marks**)

(b) Ketones are less reactive towards HCN than aldehydes due to steric and electronic factors. Thus, 'B' is least reactive towards HCN. **(1 Mark)**

18. (a) Bithional acts as an antiseptic agent and reduces odours produced by bacterial decomposition of organic matter on skin. **(1 Mark)**

(b) Tincture of iodine is a 2–3 percent solution of iodine in alcohol- water mixture. It is applied on wounds.
(1 Mark)

(c) Sodium benzoate acts as a food preservative.
(1 Mark)

19. (a) Iron (III) hexacyanoferrate (II)

The formula is $Fe_4[Fe(CN)_6]_3$ **(1 Mark)**

(b) The complex $[Co(NH_3)_5Cl]SO_4$ exhibits ionization isomerism.

(the isomers are $[Co(NH_3)_5Cl]SO_4$ and $[Co(NH_3)_5(SO_4)]Cl$ **(1 Mark)**

(c) $[CoF_6]^{3-}$ hybridisation : sp^3d^2

number of unpaired e⁻s : 4 **(1 Mark)**

$[Co(27)]$: $[Ar]\, 3d^7\, 4s^2$

Co^{3+} : $[Ar]\, 3d^6\, 4s^0$

$[Co\,F_6]^{3-}$:

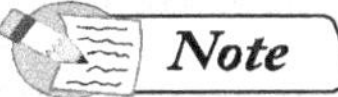

Note

Such type of problems might be asked in several wayes and are very important from compitative point of view. So in order to determine the hybridisation and no. of unpaired electrons in any complexes spectrochemical series plays a very important role. So you should memorised it always.

20. (a) **Polysaccharides :** These carbohydrates yield a large number of monosaccharide units on hydrolysis.

For ex : starch, cellulose, gums (any one)

(1 Mark)

(b) **Denatured protein :** When a protein in its native form is subjected to a physical change like change in temperature or chemical change like change in pH, the H-bonds break, globules unfold, the helix gets uncoiled and the protein loses its biological activity. This is denatured protein.

For ex : coagulation of egg white on boiling, curdling of milk (any one) **(1 Mark)**

Note

Food, especially meat is cooked in order to denature the proteins within and make them easier to digest.

(c) **Essential amino acids** : These amino acids cannot be synthesised in the body and must be obtained through diet.

For ex : Valine, leucine, lysine **(1 Mark)**

Note

The nine essential amino acids are histidine, isoleucine, leucine, lysin, methionine, phenylalanine, threonine, tryptophan and valine.

OR

(a) When glucose reacts with conc HNO_3, saccharic acid is formed.

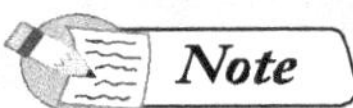

(1 Mark)

(b) Amino acids show amphoteric behaviour in zwitter ionic form as they react both with acids and bases. Due to presence of both acidic (carboxyl group) and basic (amino group) in same molecule, amino acids exist as zwitter ion form and can react with acids as well bases. **(1 Mark)**

(c) **α-Helix:** The polypeptide chains twist into a right handed screw with –NH group of amino acid hydrogen bonded with $\geq$C = O group of an adjacent turn of the helix.

β-pleated: The polypeptide chains stretch to maximum extension and lay side by side in a zig-zag manner to form a flat sheet. Each chain is held to two neighbouring chains by hydrogen bond. **(1 Mark)**

21. (i) 

(NaBH$_4$ does not reduce the ester group, so only ketonic group gets reduced to alcohol) **(1 Mark)**

(ii)

(This is in accordance with Markovnikov's rule) **(1 Mark)**

(iii)

(The O – C$_2$H$_5$ bond breaks to give C$_2$H$_5$I. C$_6$H$_5$– O does not break due to partial double bond character) **(1 Mark)**

22. (a) E° value for Mn^{3+} | Mn^{2+} couple is much more positive than that of Fe^{3+} | Fe^{2+}. This is explained as below : **(1 Mark)**

$$Mn(Z = 25) \longrightarrow Mn^{2+} \longrightarrow Mn^{3+}$$
$$[Ar]\,3d^5\,4s^2 \qquad [Ar]\,3d^5 \qquad [Ar]\,3d^4$$

$$Fe(Z = 26) \longrightarrow Fe^{2+} \longrightarrow Fe^{3+}$$
$$[Ar]\,3d^6\,4s^2 \qquad [Ar]\,3d^6 \qquad [Ar]\,3d^5$$

We see that Mn is more stable in Mn^{2+} state due to extra stable half-filled configuration of the d-orbital. In Mn^{3+}, the stability is less. As a results, Mn^{3+} readily gets reduced to Mn^{2+}.

On the other hand, Fe is more stable in +3 state due to stable d^5 configuration. Thus it does not reduce to Fe^{2+} easily.

(1 Mark)

(b) Iron has higher enthalpy of atomization than copper. Enthalpy of atomisation depends on the number of metallic bonds which in turn depends on the number of unpaired electrons. Iron ([Ar] $3d^6 4s^2$) has 4 unpaired e$^-$s while copper ([Ar] $3d^{10}4s^1$) has only one unpaired electron. Thus, iron forms stronger metallic bonds and thus has higher enthalphy of atomisation. **(1 Mark)**

(c) Sc^{3+} is colourless in aqueous solution whereas Ti^{3+} is coloured. The colour of transition metal ions is due to d-d transitions. Sc^{3+} is [Ar] $3d^0$ i.e., a stable noble gas configuration thus no d-d transition and hence, no colour. Ti^{3+} has one unpaired e$^-$ which results in d-d transition and hence colour. **(1 Mark)**

> **Note**
>
> *Color in octahedral complexes:*
>
> | *Weak field ligand* | *Strong field ligand* |
> |---|---|
> | • Δ_0 *small* | • Δ_0 *large* |
> | • *High spin complex* | • *Low spin complex* |
> | • *Absorb yellow / orange / red end of spectra* | • *Absorb violet / blue / green end of spectra* |
> | • *Transmit violet / blue / green end of spectra* | • *Transmit yellow / orange / red end of spectra* |

SECTION - D

23. (a) Shyam is a well awared boy. He is considerate, responsible and cares for the environment. **(1 Mark)**

(b) LDPE is a highly branched structure, whereas HDPE has a linear structure. **(1 Mark)**

(c) Shyam refused to accept items in polythene bags because polythene is non-biodegradable. **(1 Mark)**

(d) A biodegrable polymer is a one which can degrade in the environment over a period of time. For ex: PHBV, Nylon - 2 - nylon - 6 **(1 Mark)**

SECTION - E

24. (a) The reaction involed in :

    (i) Hoffmann bromamide degradation reaction :

$$R-\overset{\overset{\displaystyle O}{\|}}{C}-NH_2 + Br_2 + 4NaOH \longrightarrow$$

$$R-NH_2 + Na_2CO_3 + 2NaBr + 2H_2O$$

(1 Mark)

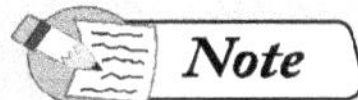

Mechanism :

Isocyanate

1° amine

(ii) Diazotisation :

$$\text{(aniline)} + NaNO_2 + 2HCl \xrightarrow{273\text{-}278K}$$

$$N_2^+Cl^- + NaCl + 2H_2O$$

(1 Mark)

(iii) Gabriel phthalimide synthesis :

$$\text{Phthalimide} \xrightarrow{KOH\,(alc)}$$

$$\xrightarrow[S_N2]{R-X}$$

$$\xrightarrow{NaOH(aq)}$$

(Phthalimide sodium salt) + R — NH$_2$ (1° amine)

(1 Mark)

(b) (i) In aqueous solution, the factors controlling basicity of amines are inductive effect, solvation effect and steric hindrance of the alkyl group. Based on these, $(CH_3)_2NH$ is found to be more basic than $(CH_3)_3N$.   **(1 Mark)**

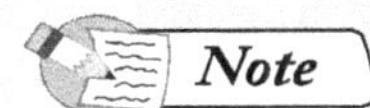

In gaseous state the basicity order of given amines is reverse because in the gaseous state the basicity can simply be compared on the basis of availability of lone pair. In tertiary amine, the availability of electron density is higher compared to other amine (secondary) due to +I effect of –CH₃ groups. So, in secondary amine its lone pair is not readily available as of tertiary amines.

(ii) Aromatic diazonium salts are more stable than aliphatic diazonium salts. The stability of aromatic diazonium salts is due to resonance which is absent in aliphatic diazonium salts.   **(1 Mark)**

OR

(a) (i)

$$\text{(aniline, }NH_2) \xrightarrow[\text{pyridine}]{(CH_3CO)_2O} \text{(}NHCOCH_3\text{)}$$

(1 Mark)

(ii) 

(1 Mark)

(iii)    **(1 mark)**

(b)   Aniline and N, N-dimethylaniline can be distinguished using the **carbylamine** test :

Aniline being primary aromatic amine give a positive carbylamine test whereas N, N-dimethylaniline does not.

Phenyl isocyanide (foul smell)

(1 mark)

(c) $C_2H_5NH_2 < C_6H_5NHCH_3 < C_6H_5NH_2$ **(1 mark)**

Increasing order of pK_b : pK_b tells the strength of a base. Lower is pK_b value, stronger is the base. Now $C_6H_5NH_2$ is a weak base because the lone pair is involved in resonance with the benzene and is thus not available for donation while in $C_2H_5NH_2$, C_2H_5 is an electron donating group, which increases the e– density on N thus facilitating the release of lone pair. Hence, $C_2H_5NH_2$ is a strong base.

25. (a) (i) H_3PO_3 undergoes disproportionation reaction but H_3PO_4 does not. This is because in H_3PO_3, P is in +3 oxidation state which can get oxidised as well as reduced. Thus, H_3PO_3 gives disproportionation, reaction as :

$$H_3PO_3 \longrightarrow H_3PO_4 + PH_3$$

On the other hand, in H_3PO_4, P is in its maximum oxidation state of +5, which can only be reduced but not oxidised further. So, H_3PO_4 does not show disproportionation.   **(1 Mark)**

H_3PO_4 has basicity of 3 while H_3PO_3 acid has basicity of 2. Why is H_3PO_3 more acidic than H_3PO_4?

It is because H_3PO_3 is more polar than H_3PO_4. In H_3PO_4, there are three OH and an oxygen, so it kind of balances out more towards the centre. In H_3PO_3, there is a H on the phosphorus atom which doesn't pull as much on electron as oxygen do and hence that part of the molecule becomes more positive causing a stronger dipole moment than that in H_3PO_4.

(ii) When Cl_2 reacts with excess of F_2, ClF_3 is formed and not FCl_3. This is because of small size and high electronegativity of F due to which it cannot show positive oxidation state. Also, due to small size and non-availability of vacant d-orbitals, F is not able to accomodate three big Cl atoms around itself. Thus, FCl_3 is not formed. On the other hand, Cl being larger in size and due to availability of vacant d-orbitals, can accomodate 3F atoms around itself thus forming ClF_3.

(1 Mark)

(iii) Dioxygen is a gas while sulphur is a solid at room temperature. This is due to formations of $p\pi$-$p\pi$ multiple bonds in oxygen, it exists as O_2 and the O_2 molecules are held together by weak vander waals forces of attraction. In contrast, S cannot form $p\pi$-$p\pi$ bonds and exists as S_8. The forces of attraction in S_8 molecules are stronger and so it exists as a solid.   **(1 Mark)**

(b) (i) XeF_4

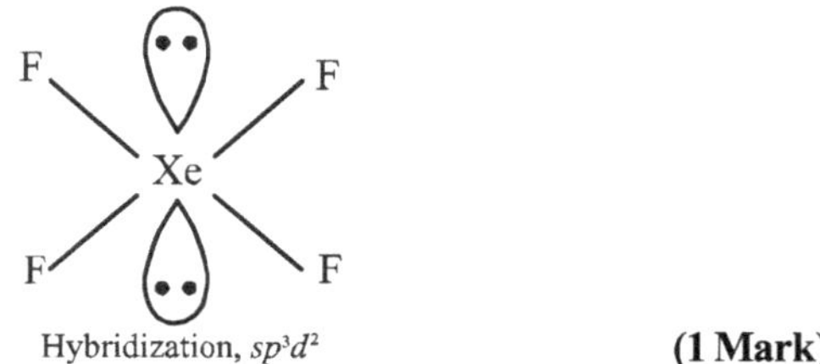

Hybridization, sp^3d^2 **(1 Mark)**

(ii) $HClO_3$

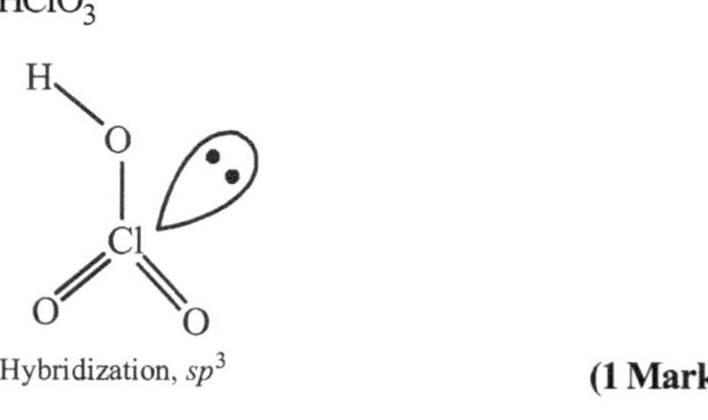

Hybridization, sp^3 **(1 Mark)**

OR

(a) According to question,

$$\text{Unknown salt} \xrightarrow[\text{H}_2\text{SO}_4]{\text{Conc}} \text{gas 'A' (brown)} \xrightarrow{\text{Cu turnings}}$$

$$\text{intensifies}$$

$$\text{gas 'A'} \xrightarrow{\text{Cooling}} \text{'B' (colourless solid)}$$

(i) (A) is NO_2 gas (because NO_3^- salt reacts with conc H_2SO_4 to give NO_2 gas which is brown). (B) is N_2O_4. **(1 Mark)**

(ii) (A) NO_2

(B) N_2O_4 **(1 Mark)**

(iii) NO_2 (A) is an odd electron species, so on cooling it dimerises to from (B) which is a solid.

$$2NO_2 \underset{\text{heat}}{\overset{\text{cool}}{\rightleftharpoons}} N_2O_4 \qquad \textbf{(1 Mark)}$$

 **Note**

Knowledge about the nature of different oxides of nitrogen might be helpful to distinguish in analytical problems. For example,

$N_2O \rightarrow$ Non flammable gaseous compound
$NO \rightarrow$ Colourless gaseous compound
$N_2O_3 \rightarrow$ Deep blue solid
$N_2O_5 \rightarrow$ Colourless solid

(b) $HF > HCl > HBr > HI$ **(1 Mark)**

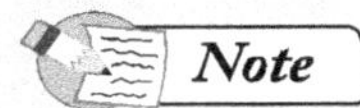 **Note**

Reducing character depends on the ease of release of hydrogen. Down the group, atomic size of halogen increases, bond length increases, bond strength decreases, thus it becomes easier to release Hydrogen.

(c) $XeF_4 + SbF_5 \rightarrow [XeF_3]^+ [SbF_6]^-$ **(1 Mark)**

26. (a) Given : $E^\circ_{Sn^{2+}|Sn} = -0.14$ V

To find : cell emf. $E_{cell} = ?$
Solution :
The cell reaction is:

$$2Sn(s) + 2H^+(aq) \rightarrow Sn^{2+}(aq) + H_2(g)$$

Number of electrons n = 2

$$E^\circ_{cell} = E^\circ_{cathode} - E^\circ_{Anode}$$
$$= 0 - (-0.14) = 0.14 \text{ V}$$

From Nernst rquation,

$$E_{cell} = \dfrac{E^\circ_{cell} - \dfrac{RT}{nF}\ln\dfrac{\left[Sn^{2+}\right]}{[H^+]^2}}{} \qquad \textbf{(1 Mark)}$$

$$E_{cell} = E^\circ_{cell} - \dfrac{0.059}{2}\log\dfrac{[Sn^{2+}]}{[H^+]^2}$$

$$= 0.14 - \dfrac{0.059}{n}\log\dfrac{[Sn^{2+}]}{[H^+]^2}$$

$$= 0.14 - \dfrac{0.059}{2}\log\dfrac{0.004}{(0.02)^2} \qquad \textbf{(1 Mark)}$$

$$= 0.14 - \dfrac{0.059}{2}\log\dfrac{0.004}{0.02 \times 0.02}$$

$$E_{cell} = 0.1105 \text{ V} \qquad \textbf{(1 Mark)}$$

Thus the emf of the cell is 0.1105 V.

(b) (i) On the basis of E° values, O_2 gas should be liberated at anode but Cl_2 gas is liberated. This is because of over-potential required for O_2 which makes the process difficult to occur. **(1 Mark)**

(ii) Conductivity depends on the number of ions per unit volume. On dilution, the number of ions per unit volume decreases and hence conductivity of CH_3COOH decreases with dilution. **(1 Mark)**

OR

(a) Given :

$$2AgCl(s) + H_2(g)\,(1\text{ atm}) \rightarrow 2Ag(s) + 2H^+ + 2Cl^-$$

$$\Delta G^\circ = -43600 \text{ J}$$

$$T = 25°C = 298 \text{ K}$$

To find : $E_{cell} = ?$

Solution : $\Delta G^\circ = -nFE^\circ_{cell}$

$$n = 2$$

$$\therefore \quad E^\circ_{cell} = \dfrac{-\Delta G^\circ}{nF}$$

$$= \dfrac{-(-43600)}{2 \times 96500} = 0.226 \text{ V} \qquad \textbf{(1 Mark)}$$

$$E_{cell} = E^\circ_{cell} - \dfrac{0.059}{n}\log$$

$$\frac{[H^+]^2[Cl^-]^2[Ag]}{[AgCl]^2[H_2]} = 0.226 - \frac{0.059}{2}\log[H^+]^2[Cl^-]^2$$

(1 Mark)

$$= 0.226 - \frac{0.059}{2}\log(0.1)^2(0.1)^2$$

$$= 0.226 - \frac{0.059}{2}\log 10^{-4}$$

$$= 0.226 - \frac{0.059}{2}(-4)$$

$$= 0.226 + 0.118$$

$$E_{cell} = 0.344\,V \qquad \textbf{(1 Mark)}$$

(b) Fuels cells are the cells which convert energy of combustion of fuels like hydrogen, methane, methanol, etc directly into electrical energy.

Advantages of fuel cell :

1. They have a high efficiency of about 70%.
2. They are pollution free and run continuously as long as reactants are supplied. **(2 Marks)**

All India *2017*
CBSE Board Solved Paper

Time Allowed : 3 Hours   *Maximum Marks : 70*

General Instructions:

(i)   All question are compulsory.

(ii)   Section A : Question number **1 to 5** are very short answer questions and carry **1** mark each.

(iii) Section B : Question number **6 to 10** are short answer questions and carry **2** marks each.

(iv) Section C : Question number **11 to 22** are also short answer questions and carry **3** marks each.

(v)   Section D : Question number **23** is a value based question and carry **4** marks.

(vi) Section E : Question number **24 to 26** are long answer questions and carry **5** marks each.

(vii) Use log tables, if necessary. Use of calculator is not allowed.

SECTION - A

1. Out of

$CHCl_2$ and CH_2CH_2Cl (on benzene rings)

which is an example of benzylic halide?

2. What is the effect of adding a catalyst on

(a)   Activation energy (E_a), and

(b)   Gibbs energy (ΔG) of a reaction?

3. Write the formula of the compound of iodine which is obtained when conc. HNO_3 oxidises I_2.

4. What type of colloid is formed when a gas is dispersed in a liquid? Give an example.

5. Write the IUPAC name of the following compound:

$$CH_3 - O - \underset{\underset{CH_3}{|}}{\overset{\overset{CH_3}{|}}{C}} - CH_3$$

SECTION - B

6. Draw the structures of the following

(a) XeF_4

(b) BrF_5

7. Write the name of the cell which is generally used in transistors. Write the reactions taking place at the anode and the cathode of this cell.

8. (a)   Arrange the following compounds in the increasing order of their acid strength:

      p-cresol, *p*-nitrophenol, phenol

(b)   Write the mechanism (using curved arrow notation) of the following reaction:

$$CH_2 = CH_2 \xrightarrow{H_3O^+} CH_3 - CH_2^+ + H_2O$$

OR

Write the structures of the products when Butan–2 – ol reacts with the following

(a) CrO_3

(b) $SOCl_2$

9. Using IUPAC norms write the formula for the following:

(a)   Potassium trioxalatoaluminate (III)

(b)   Dichloridobis (ethane-1, 2-diamine) cobalt (III)

10. Calculate the number of unit cells in 8.1 g of aluminium if it crystallizes in a face-centred cubic (f.c.c) structure. (Atomic mass of Al = 27 g mol^{-1})

SECTION - C

11. (a)   What type of isomerism is shown by the complex $[Co(NH_3)_5(SCN)]^{2+}$?

(b)   Why is $[NiCl_4]^{2-}$ paramagnetic while $[Ni(CN)_4]^{2-}$ is diamagnetic? (Atomic number of Ni = 28)

(c)   Why are low spin tetrahedral complexes rarely observed?

12. Write one difference in each of the following:

(a)   Multimolecular colloid and Associated colloid

(b)   Coagulation and Peptization

(c)   Homogeneous catalysis and Heterogeneous catalysis

OR

(a) Write the dispersed phase and dispersion medium of milk.

(b) Write one similarity between physisorption and chemisorption

(c) Write the chemical method by which $Fe(OH)_3$ sol is prepared from $FeCl_3$.

13. (a) The cell in which the following reaction occurs:

$$2Fe^{3+}(aq) + 2I^-(aq) \longrightarrow 2Fe^{2+}(aq) + I_2(s)$$

has $E^{\circ}_{cell} = 0.236$ V at 298 K. Calculate the standard Gibbs energy of the cell reaction

(Given: 1 F = 96,500 C mol^{-1})

(b) How many electrons flow through a metallic wire if a current of 0.5 A is passed for 2 hours ?

(Given: 1F = 96,500 C mol^{-1})

14. (a) Based on the nature of intermolecular forces, classify the following solids:

Sodium sulphate, Hydrogen

(b) What happens when $CdCl_2$ is doped with AgCl?

(c) Why do ferrimagnetic substances show better magnetism than antiferromagnetic substances?

15. (a) Write the principle of electrolytic refining.

(b) Why does copper obtained in the extraction from copper pyrites have a blistered appearance?

(c) What is the role of depressants in the froth floatation process?

16. Write the structures of compounds A, B and C in the following reactions.

(a) $CH_3 - COOH \xrightarrow{NH_3/\Delta} A \xrightarrow{Br_2/KOH(aq)} B$

$\xrightarrow{CHCl_3 + alc.KOH} C$

(b) $C_6H_5N_2^+BF_4^- \xrightarrow[\Delta]{NaNO_2/Cu} A \xrightarrow{Fe/HCl} B$

$\xrightarrow{CH_3COCl/pyridine} C$

17. Give reasons for the following :

(a) Acetylation of aniline reduces its activation effect.

(b) CH_3NH_2 is more basic than $C_6H_5NH_2$.

(c) Although $-NH_2$ is o/p directing group, yet aniline on nitration gives a significant amount of m-nitroaniline.

18. Give reasons for the following:

(a) Red phoshorus is less reactive than white phosphorus.

(b) Electron gain enthalpies of halogens are largely negative.

(c) N_2O_5 is more acidic than N_2O_3.

19. Define the following :

(a) Cationic detergents

(b) Broad spectrum antibiotics

(c) Tranquilizers

20. Write the structures of the monomers used for getting the following polymers:

(a) Teflon

(b) Melamine-formaldehyde polymer

(c) Neoprene

21. The following compounds are given to you:

2-Bromopentane, 2-Bromo-2-methylbutane,

1-Bromopentane

(a) Write the compound which is most reactive towards S_N2 reaction.

(b) Write the compound which is optically active.

(c) Write the compound which is most reactive towards β-elimination reaction.

22. A first order reaction takes 20 minutes for 25% decomposition. Calculate the time when 75% of the reaction will be completed. (Given : $\log 2 = 0.3010$, $\log 3 = 0.4771$, $\log 4 = 0.6021$)

SECTION - D

23. After watching a programme on TV about the presence of carcinogens (cancer causing agents) potassium bromate and potassium iodate in bread and other bakery products, Rupali a class XII student decided to make others aware about the adverse effects of these carcinogens in foods. She consulted the school principal and requested him to instruct the canteen contractor to stop selling sandwiches pizzas, burgers and other bakery products to the students. The principal took an immediate action and instructed the canteen contractor to replace the bakery products with some protein and vitamin rich food like fruits, salads, sprouts, etc. The decision was welcomed by the parents and the students.

After reading the above passage, answer the following question:

(a) What are the values (atleast two) dispalyed by Rupali?

(b) Which polysaccharide component of carbohydrates is commonly present in bread?

(c) Write the two type of secondary structures of proteins.

(d) Give two examples of water soluble vitamins.

SECTION - E

24. (a) Write the products(s) in the following reactions:

(i)   [cyclohexanone] $+ HCN \longrightarrow$?

(ii)   [benzene ring]—COONa $+ NaOH \xrightarrow[\Delta]{CaO}$?

(iii) $CH_3 - CH = CH - CN \xrightarrow[\text{(b) } H_2O/HCl]{\text{(a) DIBAL} - H}$?

(b) Give simple chemical tests to distinguish between the following pairs of compounds

(i)   Butanal and butan-2-one

(ii)   Benzoic acid and phenol

OR

(a) Write the reaction involved in the following:

(i)   Etard reaction

(ii)   Stephen reduction

(b) How will you convert the following in not more than two steps:

(i)   Benzoic acid to benzaldehyde

(ii)   Acetophenone to benzoic acid

(iii)   Ethanoic acid to 2-Hydroxyethanoic acid

25. (a) Account for the following:

(i)   Transition metals show variable oxidation states.

(ii)   Zn, Cd and Hg are soft metals.

(iii) $E°$ value for the Mn^{3+}/Mn^{2+} couple is highly positive (+1.57 V) as compared to Cr^{3+}/Cr^{2+}

(b) Write one similarity and one difference between the chemistry of lanthanoid and actinoid elements.

OR

(a) Following are the transition metal ions of $3d$ series:
$Ti^{4+}, V^{2+}, Mn^{3+}, Cr^{3+}$

(Atomic numbers: Ti = 22, V = 23, Mn = 25, Cr = 24)

Answer the following:

(i)   Which ion is most stable in an aqueous solutions and why?

(ii)   Which ion is a strong oxidising agent and why?

(iii)   Which ion is colourless and why?

(b) Complete the following equations:

(i) $2MnO_4^- + 16\,H^+ + 5S^{2-} \longrightarrow$

(ii) $KMnO_4 \xrightarrow{\text{heat}}$

26. (a) A 10% solution (by mass) of sucrose in water has a freezing point of 269.15K. Calculate the freezing point of 10% glucose in water if the freezing point of pure water is 273.15K

Given:

(Molar mass of sucrose = 342 g mol^{-1})

(Molar mass of glucose = 180 g mol^{-1})

(b) Define the following terms:

(i)   Molality (m)

(ii)   Abnormal molar mass

OR

(a) 30 g of urea (M = 60 g mol^{-1}) is dissolved in 846 g of water. Calculate the vapour pressure of water for this solutions if vapour pressure of pure water at 298 K is 23.8 mm Hg.

(b) Write two difference between ideal solutions and non-ideal solutions.

Solutions

SECTION - A

1. The example of benzylic halide is

(1 Mark)

> **Note**
>
> *In benzylic halides the halogen atom is bonded to an sp^3-hybridised carbon atom which is directly attached with an aromatic ring.*

2. (a) Catalyst lowers the activation energy.

(b) There is no effect on Gibbs free energy.

(½ + ½ = 1 Mark)

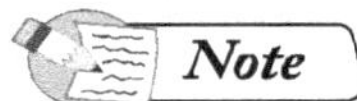

> **Note**
>
> *The catalyst provides an alternate pathway for the reaction by lowering the activation energy (E_a) between reactants and products.*

Since the energy of reactants or products are not affected by the catalyst, so there will be no effect of catalyst on Gibbs energy.

3. Iodine is oxidised to iodic acid when it reacts with conc. HNO_3.

$$I_2 + 10\,HNO_3 \rightarrow 2\,HIO_3 + 10\,NO_2 + 4\,H_2O$$ **(1 Mark)**

4. When a gas is disperesed in a liquid then foam type of colloid is formed. Example : Froth and shaving cream.

(½ + ½ = 1 Mark)

5. IUPAC name of the given compound is 2-Methoxy-2-methylpropane.   **(1 Mark)**

SECTION - B

6. (a) XeF_4

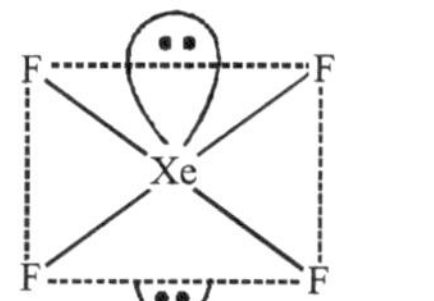

(1 Mark)

(b) BrF_5

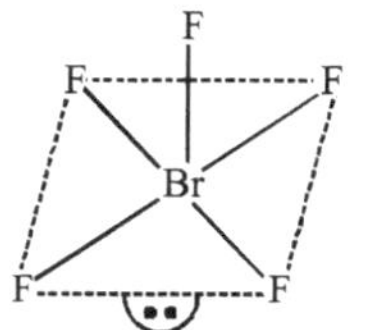

(1 Mark)

7. The dry cell also known as Leclanche cell is used in transistors.

The reactions taking place at the anode and cathode are given below.

Cathode Reaction :

$$MnO_2 + NH_4^+ + e^- \longrightarrow MnO(OH) + NH_3$$

Anode Reaction:

$$\frac{Zn - 2e^- \longrightarrow Zn^{2+}}{Zn^{2+} + 2NH_3 \longrightarrow [Zn(NH_3)_2]^{2+}}$$

(1 + 1 = 2 Marks)

8. (a) Increasing order of acid strength is p-cresol < phenol < p-nitrophenol   **(1 Mark)**

(b) Reaction :

$$CH_2 = CH_2 \xrightarrow{H_3O^+} CH_3 - CH_2^+ + H_2O$$

Mechanism :

$$\underset{H}{\overset{H}{>}}C = C\underset{H}{\overset{H}{<}} + H\!-\!\overset{+}{\underset{\cdot\cdot}{O}} - H$$

$$\rightleftharpoons H - \overset{\overset{\displaystyle H}{|}}{\underset{\underset{\displaystyle H}{|}}{C}} - \overset{+}{C}\underset{H}{\overset{H}{<}} + H_2\ddot{O}$$

(1 Mark)

OR

(a) Secondary alcohol (butan-2-ol) on reaction with chromic anhydride (CrO_3) oxidises to ketone (butan-2-one).

$$\underset{\text{Butan-2-ol}}{CH_3 - CH_2 - \overset{\overset{\displaystyle OH}{|}}{CH} - CH_3}$$

$$\xrightarrow{CrO_3} \underset{\text{Butan-2-one}}{CH_3 - CH_2 - \overset{\overset{\displaystyle O}{||}}{C} - CH_3}$$

(1 Mark)

(b) Butan-2-ol on treating with $SOCl_2$ forms 2-chlorobutane

$$\underset{\text{Butan-2-ol}}{CH_3 - CH_2 - \overset{\overset{\displaystyle OH}{|}}{CH} - CH_3}$$

$$\xrightarrow{SOCl_2} \underset{\text{2-Chlorobutane}}{CH_3 - CH_2 - \overset{\overset{\displaystyle Cl}{|}}{CH} - CH_3 R}$$

(1 Mark)

9. (a) $K_3[Al(C_2O_4)_3]$

(b) $[CoCl_2(en)_2]^+$ **(1 + 1 = 2 Marks)**

Note

Bis, tris, tetrakis etc. should not be used when ligands are arranged in alphabetical order to write the IUPAC name of the complexes or draw the formula.

10. Number of Al atoms present in 27 g (1 mol) of Al
$$= 6.023 \times 10^{23}$$
Number of Al atoms present in 8.1 g of Al
$$= \frac{6.023 \times 10^{23}}{27} \times 8.1$$ **(½ Mark)**

Since, aluminium crystallizes in a face-centred cubic (f.c.c.) structure, the number of atoms per unit cell is 4. **(½ Mark)**
So, number of unit cells in 8.1 g of aluminimum
$$= \frac{1}{4} \times \frac{6.023 \times 10^{23}}{27} \times 8.1 = 4.5 \times 10^{22}$$

Hence, the number of unit cells in 8.1 g of aluminium if it crystallizes in a face-centred cubic (f.c.c.) structure is 4.5×10^{22}.   **(1 Mark)**

SECTION - C

11. (a) Linkage isomerism is shown by the given complex.
$$[CO(NH_3)_5(SCN)]^{2+}$$
$$[CO(NH_3)_5(NCS)^{2+}$$
Therefore, it has Co-SCN and Co-NCS linkages.

                 (1 Mark)

(b) $[Ni(CN)_4]^{2-}$, Ni is in +2 state
$$\therefore \quad Ni^{2+} : 3d^8 \, 4s^0$$

CN^- ligand being a strong field ligand pairs up the electrons, thus

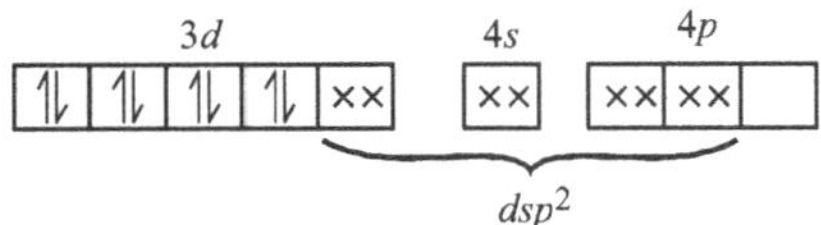

Since no unpaired electron is present, so $[Ni(CN)_4]^{2-}$ is diamagnetic.
$[NiCl_4]^{2-}$: Ni is in +2 state, thus Ni^{2+} : $3d^8$
Cl^- ligand being a weak field ligand cannot pair up the electrons

$$\therefore \quad [NiCl_4]^{2-} :$$

Since it has unpaired electrons, so $[NiCl_4]^{2-}$ is paramagnetic.   **(1 Mark)**

(c) In a tetrahedral complex, Δ_t is relatively small even with strong field ligands as there are fewer ligands to with. It is rare for the Δ_t of tetrahedral complexes to exceed the pairing energy. Usually, electrons will be more up to the higher energy orbitals rather than pair. Because of this low spin complexes are rarely observed.
                 (1 Mark)

12. (a)

	Multimolecular Colloids	Associated Colloids
(i)	They are formed by the aggregation of large number of atoms or molecules which generally have diameters less than 1 nm.	They are formed by the aggregation of large number of ions in concentrated solution.
(ii)	Examples – sols of gold and sulphur.	Examples – soap sol.

                 (1 Mark)

(b) Coagulation and peptization :

Coagulation	Peptization
Settling of colloidal particles is called coagulation or precipitation of the sol	Conversion of precipitate into colloidal sol by shaking it with dispersion medium in presence of small amount of electrolyte (peptising agent) is known as peptization.

                 (1 Mark)

(c) Homogeneous catalysis and heterogeneous catalysis:

Homogeneous Catalysis	Heterogeneous Catalysis
The catalysts and the reactants are in same phases.	The catalysts and the reactants are in different phases.
The catalyst dissolves in the reaction medium.	The catalyst does not dissolve in the reaction medium.

                 (1 Mark)

OR

(a) Liquid fat is dispersed phase and water is dispersion medium in milk.   **(1 Mark)**

(b) Both physical adsorption and chemisorption increases with increase of surface area of the adsorbent.

                 (1 Mark)

(c) Fe(OH) sol is prepared from $FeCl_3$ by hydrolysis method.   **(1 Mark)**

$$FeCl_3 + 3H_2O \xrightarrow{\text{Hydrolysis}} \underset{\text{(sol)}}{Fe(OH)_3} + 3HCl$$

13. (a) Here $n = 2$, $E^0_{cell} = 0.236\,V$, $T = 298\,K$

We know that

$$\Delta G^0 = -n F E^0_{cell} = -2 \times 96500 \times 0.236$$
$$= -45548\,J\,mol^{-1}$$
$$= -45.548\,kJ\,mol^{-1} \quad \textbf{(1 Mark)}$$

(b) $i = 0.5\,A$

$t = 2\,hours = 2 \times 60 \times 60\,s = 7200\,s$

Thus $Q = i \times t = 0.5\,A \times 7200\,s = 3600\,C$ **(1 Mark)**

We know that 96500 C

$= 6.023 \times 10^{23}$ number of electrons

Then, no. of electrons in 3600 C

$$= \frac{6.023 \times 10^{23} \times 3600}{96500} = 2.25 \times 10^{22}$$

Hence, 2.25×10^{22} number of electrons will flow through the wire. **(1 Mark)**

14. (a) Sodium sulphate is ionic solid.

Hydrogen is molecular solid (non-polar molecular solid). **(1 Mark)**

(b) When $CdCl_2$ is doped with AgCl impurity defect arises. Cd^{2+} is divalent and Ag^+ is univalent, so there will be cationic vacancies. **(1 Mark)**

Note

In a p-type semiconductor, the III group elements like Al, Ga and In element, whereas in n-type the V group elements like P, As, Sb, Bi etc. is the doping element moreover, in a p-type semiconductor, the majority carrier are holes while in n-type semi-conductor, electrons are majority carriers.

(c) In antiferromagnetic substances equal number of magnetic moments are aligned in opposite directions, so as to give zero net magnetic moment, whereas in ferrimagnetic substances unequal number of magnetic moments are aligned in opposite directions, so the net magnetic moment is not zero. Hence, ferrimagnetic substance show better magnetism than antiferromagnetic substance. **(1 Mark)**

15. (a) **Electrolytic refining:** Many metals, such as Cu, Ag, Au, Al, Pb, etc., are purified by this method. The impure metal is made the anode while a thin sheet of pure metal acts as a cathode. The electrolytic solution consists of a salt or a complex of the metal. On passing the current, the pure metal is deposited on the cathode while the impurities fall down as anode mud.

Anode: $M \rightarrow M^{n+} + ne^-$

Cathode: $M^{n+} + ne^- \rightarrow M$ **(1 Mark)**

(b) Solidified copper obtained from copper pyrites has blistered appearance due to the evolution of SO_2. **(1 Mark)**

(c) In the froth floatation process, the role of the depressants is to separate two sulphide ores by selectively preventing one ore from forming froth. For example to separate two sulphide ores (ZnS and PbS), NaCN is used as a depressant which selectively allows PbS to come with froth but prevents ZnS from coming to froth. This happens because NaCN reacts with ZnS to form $Na_2[Zn(CN)_4]$. **(1 Mark)**

16. (a) $CH_3COOH \xrightarrow{NH_3/\Delta} \underset{(A)}{CH_3CONH_2} \xrightarrow{Br_2/KOH(eq)}$

$\underset{(B)}{CH_3NH_2} \xrightarrow{CHCl_3 + \text{alc. KOH}} \underset{(C)}{CH_3NC}$

$(\frac{1}{2} + \frac{1}{2} + \frac{1}{2} = 1\frac{1}{2}\,\textbf{Marks})$

(b) $C_6H_5N_2BF_4^+ \xrightarrow[\Delta]{NaNO_2/Cu} \underset{(A)}{C_6H_5NO_2}$

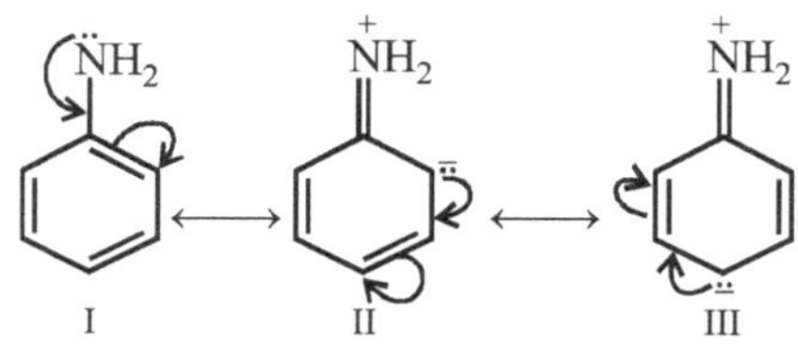

$\xrightarrow{Fe/HCl} \underset{(B)}{C_6H_5NH_2} \xrightarrow[\text{pyridine}]{CH_3COCl} \underset{(C)}{C_6H_5 - NH - \overset{\overset{O}{\|}}{C} - CH_3}$

$(\frac{1}{2} + \frac{1}{2} + \frac{1}{2} = 1\frac{1}{2}\,\textbf{Marks})$

17. (a) The lone pair present on nitrogen will get involved in resonance with the carbonyl group. Thus it will reduce the activation effect in aniline. The resonance is shown below. **(1 Mark)**

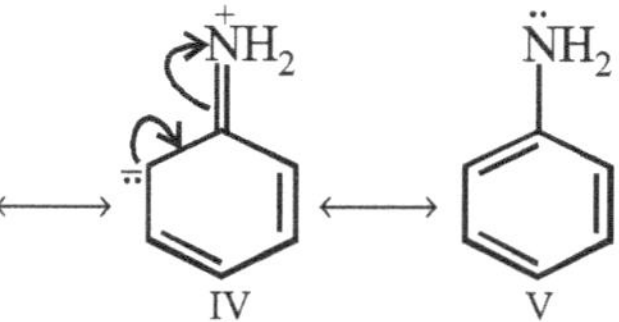

(b) Aniline may be regarded as a resonance hybrid of the following structures:

As a result of resonance, the lone pair of electrons on the nitrogen atom gets delocalized over the benzene ring and thus is less easily available for protonation. Therefore, aromatic amines are weaker bases than primary amine. **(1 Mark)**

(c) Nitration is carried out with a mixture of concentrated HNO_3 and concentrated H_2SO_4. Aniline gets protonated to form anilinium ion. Therefore, in presence of acids, the reaction mixture consists of aniline and anilinium ion. Nitration of aniline due to steric hindrance at ortho position mainly gives para nitroaniline and the nitration of anilinium ion gives *m*-nitroaniline as it is meta directing.

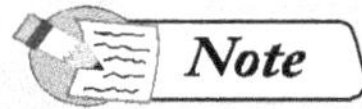

Thus due to protonation of the amino group nitration of aniline gives a substantial amount of *m*-nitroaniline. **(1 Mark)**

Note

m-directing groups deactivate the -o and -p position but not affected the -m position. So electron density is enhanced at m-position, hence preferably electrophilic substitution reaction occurs at m-position, results substantial amount of m-derivative.

18. (a) Presence of angular strain in any molecule make it reactive. Such angular strain is found in the white phosphorus, P_4 molecule where the angles are only $60°$ making it more reactive. White phosphorous is made of discrete tetrahedral P_4 molecules while red phosphorus is consist of chains of P_4 tetrahedra linked together. Due to these facts it can be concluded that red phosphorus is less reactive than white phosphorus. **(1 Mark)**

(b) Halogens have high effective nuclear charge due to smallest size consequently they readily accept one electron to acquire noble gas electronic configuration. **(1 Mark)**

(c) Oxidation state of N in $N_2O_5 = +5$
Oxidation state of N in $N_2O_3 = +3$

In N_2O_5 nitrogen is present in highest oxidation state of $+5$. The oxide of an element in it's highest oxidation state is more strongly acidic. Thus N_2O_5 is more acidic than N_2O_3. **(1 Mark)**

19. (a) **Cationic detergents :** Cationic detergent are quarternary ammounium salts of amines with acetates,

chlorides or bromides as anions. Cationic part consist of a long hydrocarbon chain and a positive charge on nitrogen atom. Therefore, these are called cationic detergents. Example, Cetyltrimethyl ammonium bromide **(1 Mark)**

(b) **Broad spectrum antibiotics :** These are the antibiotics which are effective against a variety of diseases. The common examples are *Tetracycline*, *Chloromycetin* and *Chloramphenicol* which are effective against a variety of diseases. Therefore, these can be used for curing typhoid, acute fever, dysentery, whooping cough, pneumonia, eye infection, certain urine infection. The structure of chloramphenicol is :

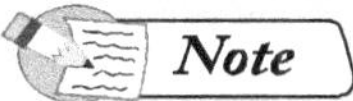

Chloramphenicol **(1 Mark)**

Note

Antibiotics which kill or inhibit a wide range of gram positive and Gram-negative bacteria are also called broad spectrum antibiotics, while those affective against Gram-positive or Gram-negative bacteria are said to be narrow spectrum antibiotics.

(c) The chemical substances used to cure mental diseases are called **tranquilizers**. These are used to release mental tension and reduce anxiety. These are the constituents of sleeping pills. Examples of tranquilizers are iproniazid, phenelzine, equanil, valium etc. **(1 Mark)**

20. (a) Teflon
Polymer-Teflon
Monomer-Tetrafluroethene
Structure :
$CF_2 = CF_2$ **(1 Mark)**

(b) **Monomers**, melamine and formaldehyde are used in the synthesis of melamine-formaldehyde polymer. **(1 Mark)**

(c) **Neoprene :** Monomeric unit is chloroprene. **(1 Mark)**

$$CH_2 = C - CH = CH_2$$
$$\quad\quad\;\; |$$
$$\quad\quad\;\; Cl$$
Chloroprene

21. Structure of the given compounds are :

$$H_3C - CH_2 - CH_2 - CH_2 - CH_2 - Br$$

1-Bromopentane
(A)

$$H_3C - CH_2 - CH_2 - \overset{\overset{\displaystyle Br}{|}}{CH} - CH_3$$

2-Bromopentane
(B)

$$H_3C - CH_2 - \overset{\overset{\displaystyle Br}{|}}{\underset{\underset{\displaystyle CH_3}{|}}{C}} - CH_3$$

2-Bromo-2-methylbutane
(C)

(a) As we can see in the above figures, (A), contains the least steric hindrance so towards the S_N2 reaction 1-bromopentane will be most reactive. **(1 Mark)**

(b) 2-Bromopentane (figure B) contain chiral carbon in it. So, this compound is optically active. **(1 Mark)**

(c) 2-Bromo-2-methylbutane will be most reactive towards the β-elimination since it will form most stable alkene (on account of highest no of α-hydrogens) **(1 Mark)**

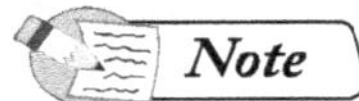

> **Note**
>
> *The identity of the nucleophile or base also determines which mechanism is favoured. E_2 reactions require strong bases whereas S_N2 reactions require good nucleophiles. Therefore, a good nucleophile (i.e., weak base) will favour S_N2 while a weak nucleophile (i.e, strong base) will favour E_2.*

22. For a first order reaction

$$t = 20 \text{ min. (given)}$$

$$t = \frac{2.303}{k} \log \frac{[R]_0}{[R]} \qquad \text{(½ Mark)}$$

$$\Rightarrow \quad k = \frac{2.303}{20} \log \frac{100}{100-25} = \frac{2.303}{20}(\log 4 - \log 3)$$

$$= \frac{2.303}{20}(0.6021 - 0.4771)$$

$$= 1.44 \times 10^{-2} \text{ min}^{-1} \qquad \text{(1 Mark)}$$

The time when 75% of the reaction completed can be calculated as

$$t = \frac{2.303}{k} \log \frac{100}{100-75} \qquad \text{(½ Mark)}$$

$$= \frac{2.303}{1.44 \times 10^{-2}} \log 4 = \frac{2.303}{1.44 \times 10^{-2}}(0.6021)$$

$$= 96.3 \text{ min (approximately)} \qquad \text{(1 Mark)}$$

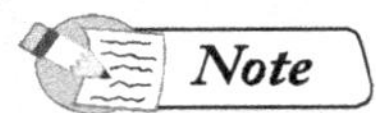

> **Note**
>
> *Some useful relationships between times for different fraction of reaction of Ist order are*
>
> $$t_{3/4} \text{ or } 75\% = 2\, t_{1/2}$$
> $$t_{87.5\%} = 3\, t_{1/2}$$
> $$t_{99.9\%} = 10\, t_{1/2}$$
>
> *These relations can be used to determined $t_{1/2}$ for different time intervals directly.*

23. (a) The values displayed by Rupali are self awareness, confidence, decision-making and concern towards adverse effect of harmful ingredients used in school canteen. **(1 Mark)**

(b) Polysaccharide component commonly present in bread is starch. **(1 Mark)**

(c) α-helix and β-pleated sheet are the two types of secondary structure of proteins. **(1 Mark)**

(d) Water soluble vitamins are B and C. **(1 Mark)**

24. (a) (i)

(1 Mark)

(ii)

(1 Mark)

(iii) $$CH_3 - CH = CH - CN \xrightarrow[\text{(b) } H_2O/HCl]{\text{(a) DIBAL-H}}$$

$$CH_3 - CH = CH - CHO$$

(1 Mark)

> **Note**
>
> *Equation (i) is an example of nucleophilic substitution reaction. Equation (ii) is an example of decarboxylation reaction. In this reaction the COOH or COONa group is removed and replaced with a hydrogen atom. In equation (iii) DIBAL being a reducing agents, reduces partially nitriles to imines then imines are hydrolysed to aldehyde.*

(b) (i) **Tollen's test :** Butanal gives positive test with Tollen's reagent whereas butan-2-one gives negative test.

$$CH_3CH_2CH_2CHO + 2\,[Ag(NH_3)_2]^+ + 3OH^-$$

$$\downarrow$$

$$CH_3CH_2CH_2CO\bar{O} + 2Ag + 2H_2O + 4NH_3$$

(1 Mark)

(ii) **$FeCl_3$ test :** Benzoic Acid gives a buff coloured ppt with neutral $FeCl_3$ solution whereas phenol gives a violet colour with neutral $FeCl_3$ solution.

(1 Mark)

OR

(a) (i) **Etard reaction.**

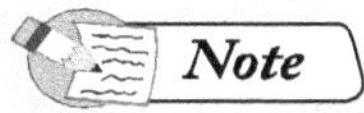

$$+ CrO_2Cl_2 \xrightarrow{CS_2} \text{CH(OCrOHCl}_2)_2$$

$$\xrightarrow{H_3O^+} \text{CHO}$$

(1 Mark)

> **Note**
>
> ***Etard Reaction:*** *Chromyl chloride (CrO_2Cl_2) oxidises methyl group of toluene to a chromium complex, which on hydrolysis gives corresponding benzaldehyde.*

(ii) **Stephen reaction.**

$$RCN + SnCl_2 + HCl \longrightarrow RCH=NH \xrightarrow{H_3O^+} RCHO$$

(1 Mark)

> **Note**
>
> ***Stephen Reaction:*** *Nitriles are reduced to corresponding imine with stannous chloride in the presence of hydrochloric acid, which on hydrolysis give corresponding aldehyde.*

(b) (*i*) Benzoic acid to benzaldehyde :

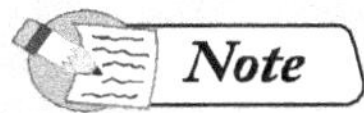

$$\xrightarrow[-SO_2,\,-HCl]{SOCl_2} \xrightarrow[\text{S or quinoline}]{H_2/Pd + BaSO_4}$$

(1 Mark)

(ii) Acetophenone to benzoic acid :

$$\xrightarrow[\Delta]{KMnO_4/KOH} \xrightarrow{H_3O^+}$$

Acetophenone   Benzoic acid

(1 Mark)

(iii) Ethanoic acid to 2-hydroxyethanoic acid :

$$CH_3 - COOH \xrightarrow[\text{(ii) H}_2\text{O}]{\text{(i) Cl}_2/\text{Red P}} CH_2(Cl) - COOH$$

Ethanoic acid

$$\xrightarrow{\text{aq·KOH}} CH_2(OH) - COOH$$

2−Hydroxyethanoic acid

(1 Mark)

25. (a) (i) Transition metals exhibit a variety of oxidation states. The variable oxidation states of transition metals are due to involvement of ns and $(n-1)$ d-electrons in bonding. The lower oxidation state is generally exhibited when only ns-electrons are involved in bonding and higher oxidation states when ns as well as $(n-1)\,d$ electrons are involved.

(1 Mark)

(ii) Zn, Cd and Hg are soft metals due to presence of completely filled orbitals. Therefore absence of any unpaired electrons results into weak metal-metal bonding. **(1 Mark)**

(iii) Mn^{2+} exists in half-filled d^5 state which is very stable while Mn^{3+} has d^4 configuration which is not so stable. Conversion from Mn^{3+} to Mn^{2+} will be quick and have negative ΔG value. Hence because of the stability factor the $E°$ value is high for this process. **(1 Mark)**

(b) **Similarity :** They both show contraction of radii, and progressive decrease in the radii of atoms of the lanthanoid and actionoid elements as the atomic number increases. **(1 Mark)**

Difference : Actionids show a large number of oxidation states whereas lanthanoids primarily show only three oxidation states $+2, +3, +4$. **(1 Mark)**

OR

(a)

Transition Metal ion	Number of unpaired electrons
$Ti^{4+}[Ar]3d^0$	0
$V^{2+}[Ar]3d^3$	3
$Mn^{3+}[Ar]3d^4$	4
$Cr^{2+}[Ar]3d^3$	3

(i) V^{2+} and Cr^{3+} are the most stable ions in aqueous solutions owing to stable t_{2g}^3 configuration.

(1 Mark)

(ii) Mn^{3+} ion are the strongest oxidising agents in aqueous solutions and itself reduced to Mn^{2+} state which has stable d^5 configuration. **(1 Mark)**

(iii) Those ions which have unpaired electrons in d-orbital and in which d-d transition is possible will be coloured while the ions in which d-orbitals are empty or completely filled will be colourless as no d-d transition is possible in those configuration.

Only Ti^{4+} has an empty d-orbital so it is colourless ion among these metal ions. **(1 Mark)**

(b) (i) $2MnO_4^- + 16H^+ + 5S^{2-} \longrightarrow 2Mn^{2+} + 8H_2O + 5S$

(1 Mark)

(ii) $2KMnO_4 \xrightarrow{heat} K_2MnO_4 + MnO_2 + O_2$

(1 Mark)

26. (a) Here $\Delta T_f = (273.15 - 269.15)\,K = 4\,K$

Molar mass of sugar $(C_{12}H_{22}O_{11})$
$= 12 \times 12 + 22 \times 1 + 11 \times 16 = 342\,g\,mol^{-1}$

10% solution (by mass) of sucrose (cane sugar) in water means 10 g of cane sugar is present in $(100 - 10)g = 90\,g$ of water.

Now, number of moles of cane sugar

$$= \frac{10}{342} = 0.0292\,mol$$

(1 Mark)

Therefore, molality (m) of the solution,

$$= \frac{0.0292 \times 1000}{90} = 0.3244\,mol\,kg^{-1}$$

Applying the relation, $\Delta T_f = K_f \times m$

$$\Rightarrow K_f = \frac{\Delta T_f}{m} = \frac{4}{0.3244}$$

$$= 12.33\,K\,kg\,mol^{-1}$$

(1 Mark)

Molar mass of glucose $(C_6H_{12}O_6)$
$= 6 \times 12 + 12 \times 1 + 6 \times 16$
$= 180\,g\,mol^{-1}$

10% glucose in water means 10 g of glucose is present in $(100 - 10)\,g = 90\,g$ of water.

$\therefore$ Number of mole of glucose

$$= \frac{10}{180}\,mol = 0.0555\,mol$$

Therefore, molality (m) of the solution

$$= \frac{0.0555 \times 1000}{90} = 0.6166\,mol\,kg^{-1}$$

Applying the relation, $\Delta T_f = K_f \times m$
$= 12.33\,K\,kg\,mol^{-1} \times 0.6166\,mol\,kg^{-1}$
$= 7.60\,K$ (approximately)

Hence, the freezing point of 10% glucose solution is $(273.15 - 7.60)\,K = 265.55\,K$ **(1 Mark)**

(b) **(i) Molality :** It is defined as the number of moles of a solute present in 1000 g (1kg) of a solvent.

$$\text{Molality}\,(m) = \frac{\text{Number of moles of solute}}{\text{Weight of solvent in kg}}$$

(1 Mark)

The relation between molarity and molality is

$$\text{Molality (m)} = \frac{\text{Molarity}(M)}{(\text{Density of the solution}(\rho) - \text{molarity})}$$
$$\times \text{molecular wt. of solute}$$

It can be used to determine the molarity if molality is given or vice versa.

(ii) Abnormal molar mass : Due to association or dissociation of molecules, the expected molar mass

is either lower or higher than calculated molar mass. Such molar mass is called abnormal molar mass.

(1 Mark)

Abnormal molar mass is the experimentally determined molar mass and is used to find the value of van't Hoff factor (i). To account for the extent of dissociation or association following relation can be used.

$$i = \frac{Normal\ molar\ mass}{Abnormal\ molar\ mass}$$

OR

(a) It is given that vapour pressure of water,
$P_1^\circ = 23.8\,mm\ of\ Hg$
Weight of water taken, $w_1 = 846\,g$
Weight of urea taken, $w_2 = 30g$
Molecular weight of water, $M_1 = 18\,g\,mol^{-1}$
Molecular weight of urea, $M_2 = 60\,g\,mol^{-1}$
Now, we have to calculate vapour pressure of water in the solution we take vapour pressure as P_1.

Relative lowering of vapour pressure equation can be written as :

$$\frac{P_1^0 - P_1}{P_1^0} = \frac{n_2}{n_1 + n_2}$$

For dilute solution $(n_2 << n_1)$

$$\frac{P_1^0 - P_1}{P_1^0} = \frac{n_2}{n_1}$$

(1 Mark)

$$\Rightarrow \frac{23.8 - P_1}{23.8} = \frac{(30/60)}{(846/18)}$$

(1 Mark)

$$\Rightarrow \frac{23.8 - P_1}{23.8} = \frac{1}{94}$$

$\Rightarrow P_1 = 23.5501\,mm\ of\ Hg$

Hence, the vapour pressure of water in the given solution is 23.5501 mm of Hg and its relative lowering is 0.0105. **(1 Mark)**

(b) Ideal solutions and non-ideal solutions

	Ideal Solutions	**Non-Ideal Solutions**
1.	Solutions which obey Raoult's law over the entire range of concentration are known as ideal solutions.	Solutions which do not obey Raoult's law over the entire range of concentration are know as non-ideal solutions.
2.	Intermolecular force of attraction between the molecules of solute (A – A) and those between the molecules of solvent (B – B) are nearly equal to those between solute and solvent molecules (A – B).	Intermolecular forces of attraction between molecules of solute (A – A) and those between the molecules of solvent (B – B) are not equal to those between solute and solvent molecules (A – B).

(1 + 1 = 2 Marks)

Delhi *2017*

CBSE Board Solved Paper

Time Allowed : 3 Hours   *Maximum Marks : 70*

General Instructions:
(i)   All questions are compulsory.
(ii) Section A : Question number **1** to **5** are very short answer questions and carry **1** mark each.
(iii) Section B : Question number **6** to **10** are short answer questions and carry **2** marks each.
(iv) Section C : Question number **11** to **22** are also short answer questions and carry **3** marks each.
(v)   Section D : Question number **23** is a value based question and carry **4** marks.
(vi) Section D : Question number **24** to **26** are long answer questions and carry **5** marks each.
(vii) Use log tables if necessary. Use of calculators is not allowed.

SECTION - A

1. Write the formula of an oxo-anion of Manganese (Mn) in which it shows the oxidation state equal to its group number.

2. Write IUPAC name of the following compound:

$(CH_3CH_2)_2NCH_3$

3. For a reaction $R \rightarrow P$, half-life $(t_{1/2})$ is observed to be independent of the initial concentration of reactants. What is the order of reaction ?

4. Write the structure of
1-Bromo-4-chlorobut-2-ene.

5. Write one similarity between Physisorption and Chemisorption.

SECTION - B

6. Complete the following reactions :

(i) $NH_3 + 3Cl_2(\text{excess}) \longrightarrow$

(ii) $XeF_6 + 2H_2O \longrightarrow$

OR

What happens when

(i) $(NH_4)_2Cr_2O_7$ is heated ?

(ii) H_3PO_3 is heated ?

Write the equations.

7. Define the following terms :

(i) Colligative properties

(ii) Molality (m)

8. Draw the structures of the following :

(i) $H_2S_2O_7$

(ii) XeF_6

9. Calculate the degree of dissociation (α) of acetic acid if its molar conductivity ($\wedge_m$) is 39.05 S cm^{2}mol^{-1}.

Given $\lambda^0(H^+) = 349.6$ S cm^2 mol^{-1} and $\lambda^0(CH_3COO^-) = 40.9$ S cm^2 mol^{-1}

10. Write the equations involved in the following reactions :

(i) Wolff-Kishner reduction

(ii) Etard reaction

SECTION - C

11. A 10% solution (by mass) of sucrose in water has freezing point of 269.15 K. Calculate the freezing point of 10% glucose in water, if freezing point of pure water is 273.15 K.

Given : (Molar mass of sucrose = 342 g mol^{-1}) (Molar mass of glucose = 180 g mol^{-1})

12. (a) Calculate the mass of Ag deposited at cathode when a current of 2 amperes was passed through a solution of $AgNO_3$ for 15 minutes.

(Given : Molar mass of Ag = 108 g mol^{-1} 1F = 96500 C mol^{-1})

(b) Define fuel cell.

13. (i) What type of isomerism is shown by the complex $[Co(NH_3)_6] [Cr(CN)_6]$?

(ii) Why a solution of $[Ni(H_2O)_6]^{2+}$ is green while a solution of $[Ni(CN)_4]^{2-}$ is colourless? (At. no. of Ni = 28)

(iii) Write the IUPAC name of the following complex : $[Co(NH_3)_5(CO_3)]Cl$.

14. Write one difference in each of the following :

    (i) Lyophobic sol and Lyophilic sol

    (ii) Solution and Colloid

    (iii) Homogeneous catalysis and Heterogeneous catalysis

15. Following data are obtained for the reaction :

    $N_2O_5 \rightarrow 2NO_2 + \frac{1}{2}O_2$

t/s	0	300	600
$[N_2O_5]/\,mol\,L^{-1}$	1.6×10^{-2}	0.8×10^{-2}	0.4×10^{-2}

    (a) Show that it follows first order reaction.

    (b) Calculate the half-life.

    (Given log 2 = 0.3010 log 4 = 0.6021)

16. Following compounds are given to you :

    2-Bromopentane, 2-Bromo-2-methylbutane, 1-Bromopentane

    (i) Write the compound which is most reactive towards S_N2 reaction.

    (ii) Write the compound which is optically active.

    (iii) Write the compound which is most reactive towards β-elimination reaction.

17. (a) Write the principle of method used for the refining of germanium.

    (b) Out of PbS and $PbCO_3$ (ores of lead), which one is concentrated by froth floatation process preferably ?

    (c) What is the significance of leaching in the extraction of aluminium ?

18. Write structures of compounds A, B and C in each of the following reactions :

    (i) $C_6H_5Br \xrightarrow{\text{Mg/dry ether}} A \xrightarrow[\text{(b) } H_3O^+]{\text{(a) } CO_2} B \xrightarrow{PCl_5} C$

    (ii) $CH_3CN \xrightarrow[\text{(b) } H_3O^+]{\text{(a) } SnCl_2/HCl} A \xrightarrow{\text{dil. NaOH}} B \xrightarrow{\Delta} C$

    OR

    Do the following conversions in not more than two steps :

    (i) Benzoic acid to Benzaldehyde

    (ii) Ethyl benzene to Benzoic acid

    (iii) Prapanone to Propene

19. Write the structures of the monomers used for getting the following polymers :

    (i) Dacron

    (ii) Melamine – formaldehyde polymer

    (iii) Buna-N

20. Define the following :

    (i) Anionic detergents

    (ii) Broad spectrum antibiotics

    (iii) Antiseptic

21. Give reasons:

    (i) Thermal stability decreases from H_2O to H_2Te.

    (ii) Fluoride ion has higher hydration enthalpy than chloride ion.

    (iii) Nitrogen does not form pentahalide.

22. Give reasons :

    (i) Acetylation of aniline reduces its activation effect.

    (ii) CH_3NH_2 is more basic than $C_6H_5NH_2$.

    (iii) Although $-NH_2$ is o/p directing group, yet aniline on nitration gives a significant amount of m-nitroaniline.

23. After watching a programme on TV about the presence of carcinogens(cancer causing agents) Potassium bromate and Potassium iodate in bread and other bakery products, Ritu a class XII student decided to aware others about the adverse effects of these carcinogens in foods. She consulted the school principal and requested him to instruct canteen contractor to stop selling sandwiches, pizza, burgers and other bakery products to the students. Principal took an immediate action and instructed the canteen contractor to replace the bakery products with some proteins and vitamins rich food like fruits, salads, sprouts etc. The decision was welcomed by the parents and students.

    After reading the above passage, answer the following questions :

    (i) What are the values (at least two) displayed by Ritu ?

    (ii) Which polysaccharide component of carbohydrates is commonly present in bread ?

    (iii) Write the two types of secondary structure of proteins.

    (iv) Give two examples of water soluble vitamins.

24. (a) Account for the following :

    (i) Transition metals form large number of complex compounds.

    (ii) The lowest oxide of transition metal is basic whereas the highest oxide is amphoteric or acidic.

    (iii) $E°$ value for the Mn^{3+}/Mn^{2+} couple is highly positive (+1.57 V) as compare to Cr^{3+}/Cr^{2+}.

    (b) Write one similarity and one difference between the chemistry of lanthanoid and actinoid elements.

OR

(a) (i)   How is the variability in oxidation states of transition metals different from that of the p-block elements ?

(ii) Out of Cu^+ and Cu^{2+}, which ion is unstable in aqueous solution and why?

(iii) Orange colour of $Cr_2O_7^{2-}$ ion changes to yellow when treated with an alkali. Why ?

(b) Chemistry of actinoids is complicated as compared to lanthanoids. Give two reasons.

25. (a) An element has atomic mass 93 g mol^{-1} and density 11.5 g cm^{-3}. If the edge length of its unit cell is 300 pm, identify the type of unit cell.

(b) Write any two differences between amorphous solids and crystalline solids.

OR

(a) Calculate the number of unit cells in 8.1 g of aluminium if it crystallizes in a f.c.c. structure.

(Atomic mass of Al = 27 g mol^{-1})

(b) Give reasons :

(i)   In stoichiometric defects, NaCl exhibits Schottky defect and not Frenkel defect.

(ii) Silicon on doping with Phosphorus forms n-type semiconductor.

(iii) Ferrimagnetic substances show better magnetism than antiferromagnetic substances.

26. (a) Write the product(s) in the following reactions :

(i) 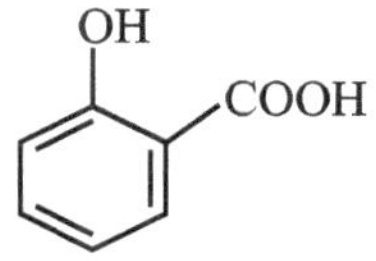   salicylic acid structure $\xrightarrow[H^+]{(CH_3CO)_2O}$?

(ii) $CH_3 - \underset{\underset{CH_3}{|}}{CH} - O - CH_2 - CH_3 \xrightarrow{HI} ? + ?$

(iii) $CH_3 - CH = CH - CH_2 - OH \xrightarrow{PCC} ?$

(b) Give simple chemical tests to distinguish between the following pairs of compounds:

(i)   Ethanol and Phenol

(ii) Propanol and 2-methylpropan-2-ol

OR

(a) Write the formula of reagents used in the following reactions :

(i)   Bromination of phenol to 2,4,6-tribromophenol

(ii) Hydroboration of propene and then oxidation to propanol.

(b) Arrange the following compound groups in the increasing order of their property indicated :

(i)   p-nitrophenol, ethanol, phenol (acidic character)

(ii) Propanol, Propane, Propanal (boiling point)

(c) Write the mechanism (using curved arrow notation) of the following reaction :

$$CH_3 - CH_2 - \overset{+}{O}H_2 \xrightarrow{CH_3CH_2OH} CH_3 - CH_2 - \underset{\underset{H}{|}}{\overset{+}{O}} - CH_2 - CH_3 + H_2O$$

Solutions

1. The formula of an oxo-anion of Manganese in which it shows the oxidation state equal to it's group number is permanganate MnO_4^- or $KMnO_4$. **(1 Mark)**

2. N-Ethyl-N-methylethenamine. **(1 Mark)**

3. First Order Reaction. **(1 Mark)**

> **Note**
>
> *Half life period of first order reaction is independent of the initial concentration of the reactant.*

4.

$$CH_2\!\!-\!\!CH\!\!=\!\!CH\!\!-\!\!CH_2$$
$$\underset{Cl}{|} \qquad\qquad \underset{Br}{|}$$

(1 Mark)

5. Physisorption and chemisorption both are a surface phenomenon *i.e.* both increase with increase in surface area. **(1 Mark)**

6. (i) $NH_3 + 3Cl_2 \xrightarrow{} NCl_3 + 3HCl$ **(1 Mark)**
      (excess)

(ii) $XeF_6 + 2H_2O \xrightarrow{} XeO_2F_2 + 4HF$ **(1 Mark)**

OR

(i) $(NH_4)_2 Cr_2 O_7$ (ammonium dichromate), decomposes on heating to produce N_2, H_2O and Cr_2O_3

$$(NH_4)_2 Cr_2O_7 \xrightarrow{heat} N_2 + 4H_2O + Cr_2O_3$$

(1 Mark)

(ii) When phosphorous acid (H_3PO_3) is heated, it gives phosphine (PH_3) and phosphoric acid (H_3PO_4).

$$4H_3PO_3 + heat \xrightarrow{} 3H_3PO_4 + PH_3$$ **(1 Mark)**

7. (i) Properties which depend on the number of solute particles irrespective of their nature relative to the total number of particles present in the solution are called colligative properties. **(1 Mark)**

(ii) Molality (m): The number of gram molecule or moles of solute dissolved in 1 kg of solvent represents the molality of solution.

$$Molality = \frac{Number\ of\ gram\ molecule\ of\ solute\,(mol)}{Mass\ of\ solvent\,(in\ kg)}$$

(1 Mark)

8. *Structure:*

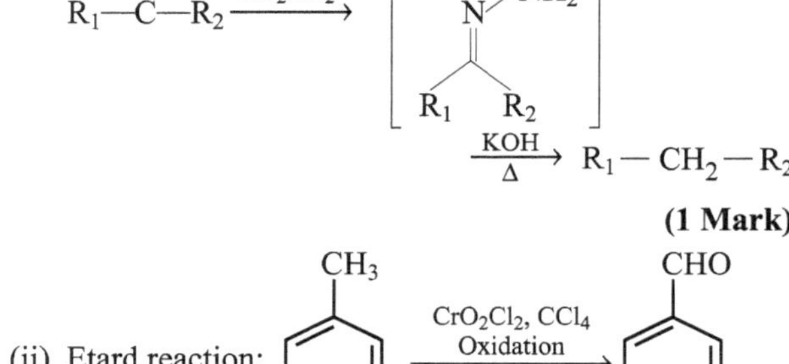

(i) $H-O-\overset{\displaystyle O}{\underset{\displaystyle O}{\overset{\|}{\underset{\|}{S}}}}-O-\overset{\displaystyle O}{\underset{\displaystyle O}{\overset{\|}{\underset{\|}{S}}}}-OH$ (ii)

(1 + 1 = 2 Marks)

9. $CH_3COOH \rightleftharpoons CH_3COO^- + H^+$

$$\Lambda^\circ_{(CH_3COOH)} = \lambda^\circ_{(CH_3COO^+)} + \lambda^\circ_{(H^+)}$$

$$= 40.9 + 349.6$$

$$= 390.5$$ **(1 Mark)**

Now degree of dissociation (α)

$$\alpha = \frac{\Lambda_m}{\Lambda^\circ} = \frac{39.05}{390.5} = 0.1$$ **(1 Mark)**

The degree of dissociation of acitic acid is 0.1.

10. (i) Wolff-kishner reduction

$$R_1-\overset{\displaystyle O}{\overset{\|}{C}}-R_2 \xrightarrow{NH_2NH_2} \left[\begin{array}{c} N^{\diagup NH_2} \\ \| \\ \underset{R_1 \quad R_2}{C} \end{array} \right]$$

$$\xrightarrow[\Delta]{KOH} R_1-CH_2-R_2$$

(1 Mark)

(ii) Etard reaction:

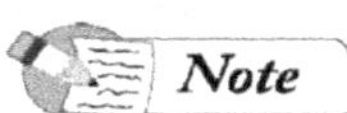

(1 Mark)

> **Note**
>
> *Chromyl chloride is a weak oxidising agent, it carry out partial oxidation of aromatic or heterocyclic bound methyl group to an aldehyde.*

11. Freezing point of surcose $(T_f) = 269.15$ K

Freezing point of water $(T^\circ_f) = 273.15$ K

Molar mass of surcose $= 342$ g mol^{-1}

$\Delta T_f = 273.15 - 269.15 = 4$ K

Molar mass of glucose $= 180$ g mol^{-1}

Freezing point of glucose = ?

For sucrose $m = \dfrac{\text{moles of solute}}{W(in\ \text{kg})}$ **(1 Mark)**

$$= \dfrac{w \times 1000}{M_{sucose} \times W} = \dfrac{10 \times 1000}{90 \times 342}$$

$$\Delta T_f = K_f \times m$$

$$4 = K_f \times \dfrac{10 \times 1000}{90 \times 342}$$

$$K_f = 12.30\ \text{K kg mol}^{-1}$$

For glucose $\Delta T_f = K_f \times m$ **(1 Mark)**

$$\Delta T_f = 12.30 \times \dfrac{10 \times 1000}{90 \times 180}$$

$$\Delta T_f = 7.7\ \text{K}$$

Freezing point of glucose = T_f = 273.15 − 7.7 = 265.45 K

(1 Mark)

12. (a) Reaction of cathode

$$Ag + e^- \longrightarrow Ag(s)$$

$$W = z \times I \times t \quad \text{where}\ z = \dfrac{E}{F} \quad \textbf{(½ Mark)}$$

$$W = \dfrac{E}{F} \times It$$

where E of Ag = 108

$$W = \dfrac{108 \times 2 \times 15 \times 60}{96500} \qquad \textbf{(½ Mark)}$$

$$= 2.015\ \text{g} \qquad \textbf{(1 Mark)}$$

(b) Fuel cells are the cells that are designed to convert the energy of combustion of fuel directly into electrical energy. The most common fuel cell is the hydrogen oxygen fuel cell.   **(1 Mark)**

13. (i) Coordination isomerism   **(1 Mark)**

This type of isomerism arises from the inter change of ligands between cationic and anionic entities of different metal ions present in a complex.

(ii) In case of $[Ni(H_2O)_6]^{2+}$, H_2O is weak field ligand so it does not cause the pairing of unpaired electron of Ni^{2+} ion. Thus there is possibility of intra d-d-transition. Thus light is absorbed from the visible region and colour is observed.

But in case of $[Ni(CN)_4]^{2-}$, CN^- is a strong field ligand. Therefore it will cause pairing of the unpaired electron of Ni^{2+} ion. There are no unpaired electron are present, so there are no d–d–transition and hence it is colourless.   **(1 Mark)**

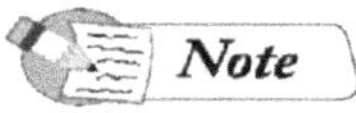

Some transition metal complexes are intensely coloured in solution but do not posses d-electrons. The intense colour is due to charge transfer from ligand to empty or partially filled metal d-orbitals.

(iii) Pentamminecarbonatocobalt(III)chloride   **(1 Mark)**

14. (i) Lyophilic sol: When dispersed phase has a greater affinity for the dispersion medium and shows the ease of solvation, the colloids are termed as lyophilic. These colloids are reversible in nature.

Lyophobic sol: When dispersed phase has less affinity for the dispersion medium, the colloids are termed as lyophobic. These colloids are irreversible in nature.

(1 Mark)

(ii) Solution: The size of solute particles in solution is smaller than 1 nanometer (10^{-7} cm) and the size of solute particles and solvent particles are almost same. Solutions are homogeneous and consists of only one phase.

Colloids: The solution in which size of solute particles lies between (1–200 nm) is known as colloidal solution. Colloids are hetrogeneous and consist of two phases.

(1 Mark)

(iii) Homogeneous Catalysis: When the phase of catalyst and reactant are same, then it is called homogeneous catalysis.

Example: $2SO_2(g) \xrightarrow{\ NO(g)\ } 2SO_3(g)$

Hetrogeneous catalysis: Catalyst and reactants both have different phase then it is called hetrogeneous catalysis.

Example: $2SO_2(g) \xrightarrow{\ Pt(s)\ } 2SO_3(g)$ **(1 Mark)**

15. (a) At 300 s

For the first order reaction

$$k = \dfrac{2.303}{t} \log \dfrac{[A]_\circ}{[A]}, \qquad \textbf{(½ Mark)}$$

where $[A]_0$ is initial concentration & $[A]$ is final concentration

$$= \dfrac{2.303}{300} \log \dfrac{1.6 \times 10^{-2}}{0.8 \times 10^{-2}}$$

$$= \dfrac{2.303}{300} \log 2$$

$$= 2.31 \times 10^{-3}\ \text{sec}^{-1} \qquad \textbf{(½ Mark)}$$

At 600 s

$$k = \dfrac{2.303}{t} \log \dfrac{[A]_\circ}{[A]}$$

$$= \frac{2.303}{600} \log \frac{1.6 \times 10^{-2}}{0.4 \times 10^{-2}}$$

$$= \frac{2.303}{600} \log 4$$

$$= \frac{2.303}{600} \times 0.6021$$

$$= 2.31 \times 10^{-3} \text{ sec}^{-1} \qquad \textbf{(1 Mark)}$$

In equal time interval, k is constant when using first order reaction, therefore it follows first order kinetics.

(b) $\qquad t_{1/2} = \dfrac{0.693}{k}, \ k = 2.31 \times 10^{-3}$

$$= \frac{0.693}{2.31 \times 10^{-3}} = 300 \text{ sec} \qquad \textbf{(1 Mark)}$$

half life is 300 sec.

16. (i) 1-Bromopentane is most reactive towards S_N2 reaction. It is a primary halide. **(1 Mark)**

Note

Primary halides are more reactive towards S_N2 reaction and tertiary halides are more reactive towards S_N1 reaction.

(ii) 2-Bromopentane $\overset{\text{Br}}{\underset{\ast}{\text{CH}_3 - \text{CH} - \text{CH}_2\text{CH}_2\text{CH}_3}}$ **(1 Mark)**

(iii) 2-Bromo-2-methylbutane is most reactive towards β-elimination reaction. **(1 Mark)**

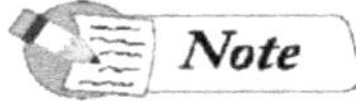

Note

$$\underset{\overset{|}{\text{Br}}}{\overset{\overset{\text{CH}_3}{|}}{\text{CH}_3 - \text{C} - \text{CH}_2 - \text{CH}_3}} \xrightarrow[\text{alc.}]{\text{KOH}} \text{CH}_3 - \text{C} = \text{CH}_2\text{CH}_3$$

(Highly substituted alkene)

17. (a) Zone refining method is used for the refining of germanium. The principle states that impurities are more soluble in the melt than in the solid state of the metal. **(1 Mark)**

(b) Froth floatation process is generally used for removing gangue from sulphide ores. So PbS is concentrated by froth floation methods. **(1 Mark)**

(c) In the extraction of aluminium, the significance of leaching is to concentrate pure alumina (Al_2O_3) from bauxite ore. **(1 Mark)**

Note

Bauxite usually contains silica, iron oxide, and titanium oxide as impurities. In the process of leaching, alumina is concentrated by heating the powdered ore with a concentrated solution of NaOH at 473-523 K and 35-36 bar.

18. (i) $C_6H_5Br \xrightarrow{\text{Mg/dry ether}} \underset{(A)}{C_6H_5 MgBr} \xrightarrow[(b)H_3O^+]{(a)CO_2}$

$\underset{(B)}{C_6H_5 COOH} \xrightarrow{\text{PCl}_5} \underset{(C)}{C_6H_5COCl}$

$(\frac{1}{2} + \frac{1}{2} + \frac{1}{2} = \textbf{1½ Marks})$

(ii) $CH_3CN \xrightarrow[(b)H_3O^+]{(a)SnCl_2/HCl} \underset{(A)}{CH_3CHO} \xrightarrow{\text{dil.NaOH}}$

$\underset{\overset{|}{\underset{(B)}{\text{OH}}}}{CH_3CH - CH_2CHO} \xrightarrow{\Delta} \underset{(C)}{CH_3CH = CHCHO}$

$(\frac{1}{2} + \frac{1}{2} + \frac{1}{2} = \textbf{1½ Marks})$

OR

(i) Benzoic acid to Benzaldehyde

$C_6H_5COOH \xrightarrow{\text{SOCl}_2} C_6H_5COCl$

$\xrightarrow{\text{H}_2, \text{Pd}-\text{BaSO}_4} C_6H_5CHO$

(1 Mark)

(ii) Ethyl Benzene to Benzoic acid

$\xrightarrow{\text{K}_2\text{Cr}_2\text{O}_7/\text{H}^+} C_6H_5COOH$ **(1 Mark)**

(iii) Propanone to propene

$CH_3COCH_3 \xrightarrow{\text{NaBH}_4} \underset{\overset{|}{\text{OH}}}{CH_3CHCH_3} \xrightarrow{\text{Conc.H}_2\text{SO}_4}$

$CH_3CH = CH_2$ **(1 Mark)**

19. (i) **Dacron:** It is a polymer of ethylene glycol and terphthalic acid.

Monomers:

$[\text{HO}-\text{CH}_2-\text{CH}_2-\text{OH}]$, ethylene glycol

terphthalic acid

(1 Mark)

(ii) **Melamine - formaldehyde polymer:** It is obtained by melamine and formaldehyde.

Monomers:

(1 Mark)

HCHO
Formaldehyde

Melamine

(iii) **Buna-N:** It is obtained from 1, 3-Butadiene and Acrylonitrile.

Monomers:

$$H_2C\!=\!HC\!-\!HC\!=\!CH_2$$

1, 3-Butadiene

$$CH_2\!=\!CH$$
$$|$$
$$CN$$

Acrylonitrile

(1 Mark)

20. (i) Anionic detergents are sodium salt of sulphonated long chain alcohol or hydrocarbons. For example; sodium lauryl sulphate.

(1 Mark)

(ii) **Broad spectrum antibiotics:**

Broad spectrum antibiotics are the drug which kill or inhibit a wide range of gram-positive and gram-negative bacteria.

Example: tetracycline, ofloxacin, ampicillin

(1 Mark)

(iii) **Antiseptic:** A drug which destroy or prevent the growth of micro-organism are called antiseptic. They are used in cleaning of wounds or in treatment of skin cut etc.

Example: Soframycine, terpineol, chloroxylenol.

(1 Mark)

21. (i) Thermal stability of hydrides decreases from H_2O to H_2Te, because size of central atom in hydrides increases from oxygen to tellurium. So the bond become weaker and thus breaks on heating easily.

(1 Mark)

(ii) Fluoride has higher hydration enthalpy than chloride ion due to the smaller size of fluoride ion. F^- ion has smaller size than chloride ion, so more water molecule can surround the fluoride ion.

(1 Mark)

(iii) Nitrogen does not form pentahalide (NCl_5), because nitrogen does not have d-orbital to form 5-bonds.

(1 Mark)

22. (i) Acetyl group is an electron withdrawing group which attracts the lone pair of electrons on the N-atom towards itself as a result, the activation effect of amino group is reduced.

Due to the resonance, the electron pair of nitrogen atom gets delocalised towards carbonyl group so activation effect is reduced.

 **(1 Mark)**

(ii) Due to resonance the lone pair of electron on the nitrogen in aniline get delocalised over benzene ring and electron density over nitrogen decreases thus making it less easily available for protonation. Hence aniline is weaker base than methyl amine. **(1 Mark)**

> **Note**
>
> *The order of basic strength of amines in aqueous solution is as follows:*
>
> $(CH_3)_2NH > CH_3NH_2 > (CH_3)_3N > NH_3 > C_6H_5NH_2$

(iii) Nitration is carried out with a mixture of conc. HNO_3 and conc H_2SO_4, (acidic medium). So in the presence of these acids aniline protonated to form anilinium ion. Anilinium ion is m-directing and deactivating. Therefore the nitration of anilinium ion gives m-nitroaniline as major product. **(1 Mark)**

> **Note**
>
> *Due to inductive effect anilinium nitrogen strongly withdraw electron density from the ortho position consequently deactivate the ortho position followed by meta and para position.*

SECTION D

23. (i) Caring, concerned, socially alert and leadership values displaced by Ritu. **(1 Mark)**

(ii) Starch is commonly present in bread. **(1 Mark)**

(iii) (a) α-Helix structure

(b) β-Pleated sheet structure **(1 Mark)**

(iv) water soluble vitamins: vitamin B, vitamin C

(1 Mark)

SECTION E

24. (a) (i) Due to small atomic radii and presence of high positive nuclear charge, transition metal have strong tendency to form complexes. Secondly these metal have vacant d-orbital in which the electron pair donated by ligands donor atom can be accommoded. Transition metals, therefore show strong tendency to form complexes and complex ions. **(1 Mark)**

(ii) In case of a lower oxides of a transition metal, the metal atom has a low oxidation state. This means that some of the valance electrons of the metal atom are not involved in bonding. As a result it can donate electron and behave as a basic metal oxides whereas highest oxide is acidic or amphoteric due to highest oxidation state.

(1 Mark)

(iii) Mn^{2+} exists in $3d^5$ configuration which is a half-filled configuration which provides extra stability to the metal ion while Mn^{3+} will exist in $3d^4$ configuration which is less stable than $3d^5$. Hence the conversion from 3+ to 2+ is very feasible. Hence E° value is more, while in Cr^{3+}, it exist in $3d^3$ half-filled d orbital ($3e^-$, electron in t_{2g}) extra stability is attain by Cr^{3+} than Cr^{2+}. Hence Cr^{3+} to Cr^{2+} is less feasible and hence it has less reduction potential as compare to Mn^{3+}/Mn^{2+}. **(1 Mark)**

(b) *Similarity:*

- Both show common oxidation state of +3.

- Both are electropositive elements

- Lanthenides and actinides show magnetic properties.

Difference: Lanthanoide have less tendency to form complex whereas actinoid have more tendency (great tendency) to form complex. Lanthanoids are colourless where as, actinoids are colourful. **(2 Marks)**

OR

(a) (i) The variability in oxidation state of transition metal is due to partially filled d-orbitals. Their oxidation state differ from each other by +1 *i.e.* Fe^{+2} and Fe^{3+}. In case of p block elements the oxidation state differ from each other by +2 for example: +3 and +5. **(1 Mark)**

(ii) Cuprous (Cu^+) ions are not stable in aqueous solution and get converted into Cu and Cu^{2+} due to self reduction and disproportion.

$$2Cu^+(aq) \longrightarrow Cu^{2+}(aq) + Cu$$

2nd ionisation enthalpy of copper is large but hydration enthalpy for Cu^{2+} is much more negative than that for Cu^+. So Cu^{2+} is stable than Cu^+. **(1 Mark)**

(iii) Orange colour of $Cr_2O_7^{2-}$ ion changes to yellow when treated with an alkali due to the formation of CrO_4^{2-}ion, which is yellow in colour.

$$\underset{\substack{\text{Dichromate ion} \\ \text{(orange)}}}{Cr_2O_7^{2-}} + 2OH^- \longrightarrow \underset{\substack{\text{Chromate ion} \\ \text{(yellow)}}}{2CrO_4^{2-}} + H_2O$$

(1 Mark)

(b) Chemistry of actinoids is complicated as compared to lanthanoids. The two reasons are as follows.

(i) Actinoids are radioactive and the radioactive decay gives out extremely energetic particles which may break bonds and distrupt crystal structure.

(ii) The breaking up of bonds by emitted particles due to higher energy associated with them also develops the process of self oxidation and it is therefore difficult to decides the more stable oxidation state. **(2 Marks)**

25. (a) $d = 11.5$ g cm^{-3}

edge length (a) = 300 pm = 300×10^{-10} cm

atomic mass (M) = 93 g mol^{-1}

$$d = \frac{Z\,M}{a^3 \times N_A} \qquad \textbf{(1 Mark)}$$

$$11.5 = \frac{Z \times 93}{(300 \times 10^{-10})^3 \times 6.023 \times 10^{23}}$$

$$Z = 2.009 \approx 2 \qquad \textbf{(1 Mark)}$$

So it is a body centric cubic unit cell. **(1 Mark)**

(b)

Amorphous Solid	Crystalline Solid
(i) In these solids particles are not arranged in a regular pattern.	In crystalline solid particles are arranged in regular pattern.
(ii) They melt over a range of temperature.	They have sharp and characteristic melting point.

(2 Marks)

OR

(a) number of atoms = no. of moles $\times N_A$

$$= n \times N_A = \frac{w}{M} \times N_A$$

$$= \frac{8.1}{27} \times 6.022 \times 10^{23} \qquad \textbf{(½ Mark)}$$

Number of atom in one unit cell in fcc = 4 **(½ Mark)**

So number of unit cells $= \dfrac{\text{Total number of atom}}{4}$

$$= \frac{8.1}{27} \times \frac{6.02 \times 10^{23}}{4}$$

$$= 4.5 \times 10^{23} \qquad \textbf{(1 Mark)}$$

(b) (i) NaCl exhibits schottky defects because of similar size of anion (Cl^-) and cation (Na^+). Whereas frenkel defect is generally found in those crystals which have large difference in their size of cation and anion. **(1 Mark)**

(ii) Silicon belongs to group-14 and phosphorus belongs to group-15. On doping, there will be a free electron. Hence it is n-type semiconductor.

(1 Mark)

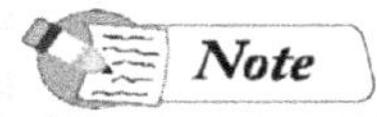

Note

Silicon an doping with group 13 elements form p-type semiconductors while with group 15 elements form n-type semiconductor.

(iii) In the presence of magnetic field, ferrimagnetic substances get oriented in the direction of the magnetic field. While in antiferromagnetic substance, domains are oppositevely oriented and cancel out each other. Hence ferrimagnetic substances show better magnetism than antiferromagnetic substances.

(1 Mark)

26. (a) (i)

$$\text{(salicylic acid)} \xrightarrow[H^+]{(CH_3CO)_2O}$$

Aspirin   + CH_3COOH Acetic acid

(1 Mark)

(ii) $CH_3\!-\!\overset{\overset{\displaystyle CH_3}{|}}{CH}\!-\!O\!-\!CH_2\!-\!CH_3 \xrightarrow{HI}$

$$CH_3\!-\!\overset{\overset{\displaystyle CH_3}{|}}{\underset{\underset{\displaystyle H}{|}}{C}}\!-\!I + CH_3CH_2OH$$

2-Iodopropane   ethanol

(1 Mark)

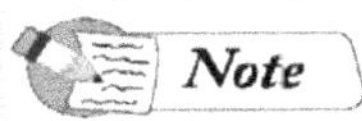

Note

In acidic cleavage of ethers alkyl halide is formed from the most stable carbocation.

(iii) $CH_3\!-\!CH\!=\!CH\!-\!CH_2\!-\!OH \xrightarrow{PCC}$

But-2-en-1-ol

$$CH_3\!-\!CH\!=\!CH\!-\!CHO$$

But-2-en-1-al

(1 Mark)

Note

PCC → Pyridinium chlorochromate it is a reagent which is used for oxidation of alcohol to form carbonyl.

(b) (i) Ethanol and Phenol

Iodoform test is used to distinguish between ethanol and phenol.

On heating with NaOH solution containing iodine, ethanol gives a yellow ppt of iodoform while phenol does not react.

$$C_2H_5OH + 4I_2 + 6NaOH \xrightarrow{\Delta}$$

$$CHI_3 + 5NaI + HCOONa + 5H_2O$$

Iodoform

(1 Mark)

(ii) Propanol and 2-methylpropan-2-ol

Propanol is primary alcohol while 2-methylpropan-2-ol is tertiary alcohol. Lucas test is used to distinguish bsoth of them.

Primary alcohol, i.e. propanol does not react with lucas reagent (conc.HCl + anhy. $ZnCl_2$) and no cloudiness is appeared.

Tertiary alcohol, i.e. 2-methylpropan-2-ol reacts with lucas reagent and give turbidity immediately.

(1 Mark)

OR

(a) (i) Bromination of Phenol to 2, 4, 6 tribromophenol

$$\xrightarrow{Aq.\ 3Br_2}$$

+ 3HBr, Reagent → Br_2

(1 Mark)

(ii) Hydroboration of propene and then oxidation to propanol.

$$6(CH_3\!-\!CH\!=\!CH_2) \xrightarrow{B_2H_6}$$

$$2(CH_3CH_2CH_2)_3B \xrightarrow[H_2O/OH^-]{H_2O_2} 2H_3BO_3$$

$$+ 6CH_3CH_2CH_2OH, \text{ reagent } B_2H_6,\ H_2O_2$$

(1 Mark)

(b) (i)   ethanol < phenol < p-nitrophenol

(1 Mark)

(ii) propane < propanal < propanol   **(1 Mark)**

Note

Nitrogroup is electron withdrawing group and it decreases the electron density in O – H bond therefore it easily loses a proton. Phenols and alcohols are weak acids but alcohols are less acidic than phenols.

(c) $CH_3CH_2\overset{+}{O}\!\!<^{H}_{H}$ $+$ $H-\overset{\cdot\cdot}{\underset{\cdot\cdot}{O}}-CH_2CH_3$

$$\longrightarrow CH_3CH_2-\overset{+}{\underset{H}{O}}-CH_2-CH_3 + H_2O$$

(1 Mark)

All India *2016*
CBSE Board Solved Paper

Time Allowed : 3 Hours   *Maximum Marks : 70*

General Instructions:

(i)   All question are compulsory.

(ii) Section A : Question number **1 to 5** are very short answer questions and carry **1** mark each.

(iii) Section B : Question number **6 to 10** are short answer questions and carry **2** marks each.

(iv) Section C : Question number **11 to 22** are also short answer questions and carry **3** marks each.

(v) Section D : Question number **23** is a value based question and carry **4** marks.

(vi) Section E : Question number **24 to 26** are long answer questions and carry **5** marks each.

(vii) Use log tables, if necessary. Use of calculator is not allowed.

SECTION - A

1. Write the IUPAC name of the given compound :

$$\text{C}_6\text{H}_5\text{—CH}_2\text{—CH}_2\text{—OH}$$

2. Write the structure of an isomer of compound C_4H_9Br which is most reactive towards S_N1 reaction.

3. What is the reason for the stability of colloidal sols ?

4. Give an example each of a molecular solid and an ionic solid.

5. $Pb(NO_3)_2$ on heating gives a brown gas which undergoes dimerization on cooling ? Identify the gas.

SECTION - B

6. For a reaction : $H_2 + Cl_2 \xrightarrow{hv} 2HCl$

Rate $= k$

(i)   Write the order and molecularity of this reaction.

(ii) Write the unit of k.

7. Write the chemical equations involved in the following reactions :

(i)   Hoffmann-bromamide degradation reaction

(ii) Carbylamine reaction

8. (i)   Gas (A) is more soluble in water than gas (B) at the same temperature. Which one of the two gases will have the higher value of K_H (Henry's constant) and why ?

(ii) In non-ideal solution, what type of deviation shows the formation of maximum boiling azeotropes ?

9. When a coordination compound $CoCl_3.6NH_3$ is mixed with $AgNO_3$, 3 moles of AgCl are precipitated per mole of the compound. Write

(i)   Structural formula of the complex

(ii) IUPAC name of the complex

10. Write the structures of the following :

(i) BrF_3

(ii) XeF_4

OR

What happens when :

(i) SO_2 gas is passed through an aqueous solution of Fe^{3+} salt ?

(ii) XeF_4 reacts with SbF_5 ?

SECTION - C

11. Write the final product(s) in each of the following reactions :

(a)
$$\underset{\overset{|}{\underset{CH_3}{}}}{\overset{\overset{CH_3}{|}}{CH_3 - C}} - O - CH_3 + HI \longrightarrow$$

(b)
$$CH_3 - CH_2 - \underset{\overset{|}{OH}}{CH} - CH_3 \xrightarrow{Cu/573K}$$

(c)
$$C_6H_5 - OH \xrightarrow[\text{(ii) } H^+]{\text{(i) } CHCl_3 + \text{aq.NaOH}}$$

12. How do you convert :

(i) Chlorobenzene to biphenyl

(ii) Propene to 1-iodopropane

(iii) 2-Bromobutane to but-2-ene

OR

Write the major product(s) in the following :

(i) O_2N—C$_6$H$_4$—CH_2—CH_3 $\xrightarrow{Br_2,\ UV\ light}$

(ii) $2CH_3$—$\underset{\underset{Cl}{|}}{CH}$—$CH_3$ $\xrightarrow[\text{dry ether}]{Na}$

(iii) CH_3—CH_2—Br $\xrightarrow{AgCN}$

13. (i) Write the structural difference between starch and cellulose.

(ii) What type of linkage is present in nucleic acids ?

(iii) Give one example each for fibrous protein and globular protein.

14. (i) Name the method of refining of nickel.

(ii) What is the role of cryolite in the extraction of aluminium ?

(iii) What is the role of limestone in the extraction of iron from its oxides ?

15. Give reasons :

(i) SO_2 is reducing while TeO_2 is an oxidizing agent.

(ii) Nitrogen does not form pentahalide.

(iii) ICl is more reactive than I_2.

16. (a) For the complex $[Fe(H_2O)_6]^{3+}$, write the hybridisation, magnetic character and spin of the complex.

(At. number : Fe = 26)

(b) Draw one of the geometrical isomers of the complex $[Pt(en)_2Cl_2]^{2+}$ which is optically inactive.

17. An element crystallizes in a *bcc* lattice with cell edge of 500 pm. The density of the element is 7.5 g cm^{-3}. How many atoms are present in 300 g of the element ?

18. (i) What is the role of sulphur in the vulcanization of rubber ?

(ii) Identify the monomers in the following polymer :

$$\left[\!-O-CH_2-CH_2-O-\overset{\overset{O}{\|}}{C}-C_6H_4-\overset{\overset{O}{\|}}{C}-\!\right]_n$$

(iii) Arrange the following polymers in the increasing order of their intermolecular forces : Terylene, Polythene, Neoprene.

19. For the first order thermal decomposition reaction, the following data were obtained :

$$C_2H_5Cl(g) \longrightarrow C_2H_4(g) + HCl(g)$$

Time/sec	Total pressure/atm
0	0.30
300	0.50

Calculate the rate constant.

(Given : log 2 = 0.301, log 3 = 0.4771, log 4 = 0.6021)

20. Give reasons for the following :

(i) Aniline does not undergo Friedel-Craft's reaction.

(ii) $(CH_3)_2NH$ is more basic than $(CH_3)_3N$ in an aqueous solution.

(iii) Primary amines have higher boiling point than tertiary amines.

21. Define the following terms :

(i) Lyophilic colloids

(ii) Zeta potential

(iii) Associated colloids

22. Calculate the boiling point of solution when 4g of MgSO$_4$ (M = 120 g mol^{-1}) was dissolved in 100 g of water, assuming MgSO$_4$ undergoes complete ionization.

(K_b for water = 0.52 K kg mol^{-1})

SECTION - D

23. Due to hectic and busy schedule, Mr. Singh started taking junk food in the lunch break and slowly became habitual of eating food irregularly to excel in his field. Once during meeting he felt severe chest pain and fell down. Mr. Khanna a close friend of Mr. Singh took him to doctor immediately. The doctor diagnosed that Mr. Singh was suffering from acidity and prescribed some medicines. Mr. Khanna advised him to eat home made food and change his lifestyle by doing yoga, meditation and some physical exercise. Mr. Singh followed his friend's advice and after few days he started feeling better.

After reading the above passage, answer the following :

(i) What are the values (at least two) displayed by Mr. Khanna ?

(ii) What are antacids ? Give one example.

(iii) Would it be advisable to take antacids for a long period of time ? Give reason.

SECTION - E

24. (a) Write the structures of A and B in the following reactions:

(i) $CH_3COCl \xrightarrow{H_2,Pd—BaSO_4} A \xrightarrow{H_2N–OH} B$

(ii) $CH_3MgBr \xrightarrow[2.\,H_3O^+]{1.\,CO_2} A \xrightarrow{PCl_5} B$

(b) Distinguish between :

(i) $C_6H_5–COCH_3$ and $C_6H_5–CHO$

(ii) CH_3COOH and $HCOOH$

(c) Arrange the following in the increasing order of their boiling points :

$CH_3CHO, CH_3COOH, CH_3CH_2OH$

OR

(a) Write the chemical reaction involved in Wolff-Kishner reduction.

(b) Arrange the following in the increasing order of their reactivity towards nucleophilic addition reaction.

$C_6H_5COCH_3, CH_3–CHO, CH_3COCH_3$

(c) Why a carboxylic acid does not give reactions of carbonyl group ?

(d) Write the product in the following reaction

$$CH_3CH_2CH = CH – CH_2CN \xrightarrow[2.\,H_2O]{1.\,(i–Bu)_2AlH}$$

(e) A and B are two functional isomers of the compound C_3H_6O. On heating with NaOH and I_2, isomer B forms yellow precipitate of iodoform, whereas isomer A does not form any precipitate. Write the formulae of A and B.

25. (a) Calculate E°_{cell} for the following reaction at 298 K:

$$2Al(s) + 3Cu^{2+}(0.01M) \longrightarrow 2Al^{3+}(0.01\,M) + 3Cu(s)$$

Given : $E_{cell} = 1.98$ V

(b) Using the E° values of A and B, predict which is better for coating the surface of iron $[E^\circ_{(Fe^{2+}/Fe)} = -0.44V]$ to prevent corrosion and why ?

Given : $E^\circ_{(A^{2+}/A)} = -2.37V$

$E^\circ_{(B^{2+}/B)} = -0.14$ V

OR

(a) The conductivity of 0.001 mol L^{-1} solution of CH_3COOH is 3.905×10^{-5} S cm^{-1}. Calculate its molar conductivity and degree of dissociation (α).

Given $\lambda^\circ(H^+) = 349.6$ S cm^2 mol^{-1} and $\lambda^0(CH_3COO^-) = 40.9$ S cm^2 mol^{-1}

(b) Define electrochemical cell. What happens if external potential applied becomes greater than E°_{cell} of electrochemical cell ?

26. (a) Account for the following :

(i) Mn shows the highest oxidation state of +7 with oxygen but with fluorine, it shows the highest oxidation state of +4.

(ii) Cr^{2+} is a strong reducing agent.

(iii) Cu^{2+} salts are coloured, while Zn^{2+} salts are white.

(b) Complete the following equations :

(i) $2MnO_2 + 4KOH + O_2 \xrightarrow{\Delta}$

(ii) $Cr_2O_7^{2-} + 14H^+ + 6I^- \longrightarrow$

OR

The elements of $3d$ transition series are given as :

Sc Ti V Cr Mn Fe Co Ni Cu Zn

Answer the following :

(i) Write the element which shows maximum number of oxidation states. Give reason.

(ii) Which element has the highest m.p ?

(iii) Which element shows only + 3 oxidation state ?

(iv) Which element is a strong oxidizing agent in +3 oxidation state and why ?

Solutions

SECTION - A

1. 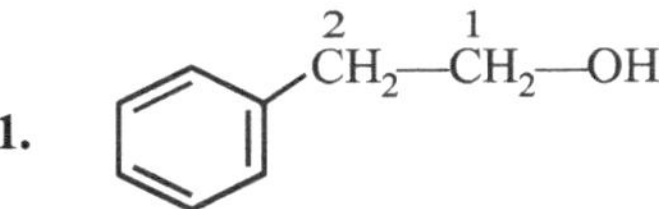

The IUPAC name of the given compound is 2-phenylethanol. **(1 Mark)**

2. The isomer of C_4H_9Br, which is most reactive towards S_N1 reaction, is the one that forms a tertiary carbocation upon the elimination of the leaving group. Its structure is shown below: **(1 Mark)**

3. Electrostatic stabilisation and solvation are two main reasons for the stability of colloidal sols. **(1 Mark)**

4. The example of molecular solids is ice (H_2O) and the examples of ionic solids is sodium chloride (NaCl). **(1 Mark)**

5. On heating $Pb(NO_3)_2$ undergoes decomposition reaction and gives nitrogen dioxide NO_2 which dimerises to give N_2O_4 gas.

$$2\,Pb(NO_3)_2 \longrightarrow 2PbO + 4\,NO_2\uparrow + O_2$$
$$\text{(brown)}$$
$$2\,NO_2 \xrightarrow{\text{dimerization}} N_2O_4 \qquad \textbf{(1 Mark)}$$

SECTION - B

6. (i) As the rate of the reaction does not depends on concentration of the reaction, its order will be zero whereas molecularity will be two. **(1 Mark)**

(ii) Since it is a zero-order reaction, the unit of rate constant is mole L^{-1} sec^{-1}. **(1 Mark)**

7. (i) Hoffmann bromamide degradation reaction

$$R - NH_2 + Na_2CO_3 + 2NaBr + 2H_2O$$
(1 Mark)

> **Note**
>
> *The reaction is an example of molecular rearrangement and involves migration of an alkyl or aryl group from the carbon group to the adjacent nitrogen atom.*

(ii) Carbylamine reaction

$$R - NH_2 + CHCl_3 + 3KOH(alc.) \xrightarrow{\Delta}$$
$$R - NC + 3KCl + 3H_2O \qquad \textbf{(1 Mark)}$$

> **Note**
>
> *The carbylamine reaction, also known as Hoffmann's cyanide test, is a chemical test for the detection of primary amine.*

8. (i) According to Henry's law, the solubility of a gas is inversely related to the Henry's constant (K_H) for that gas. Hence, gas (B), being less soluble, would have a higher K_H value than gas(A). **(1 Mark)**

> **Note**
>
> *Henry's law only works if the molecules are at equilibrium. It does not work for gases at high pressure and if there is a chemical reaction between the solute and solvent.*

(ii) The non-ideal solution which shows large negative deviation from Raoult's law form maximum boiling azeotrop at a specific composition. Example, nitric acid and water. **(1 Mark)**

9. (i) Since 3 moles of AgCl get precipitated, therefore 3 Cl^- ions in the coordination compound are present outside the coordination sphere. Thus structural formula of the complex is $[Co(NH_3)_6]Cl_3$. **(1 Mark)**

(ii) The IUPAC name of the complex is hexaamminecobalt (III) chloride. **(1 Mark)**

10. (i) **Structure of BrF_3 :** Bent T-shaped

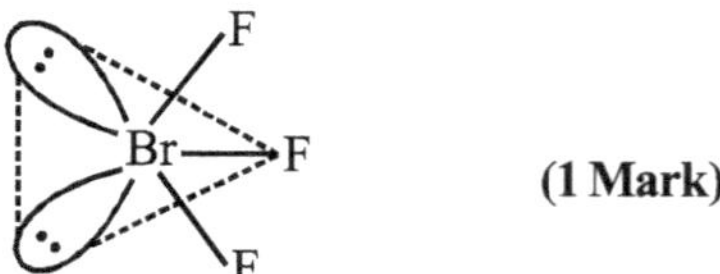

(1 Mark)

(ii) **Structure of XeF_4 :** Square planar

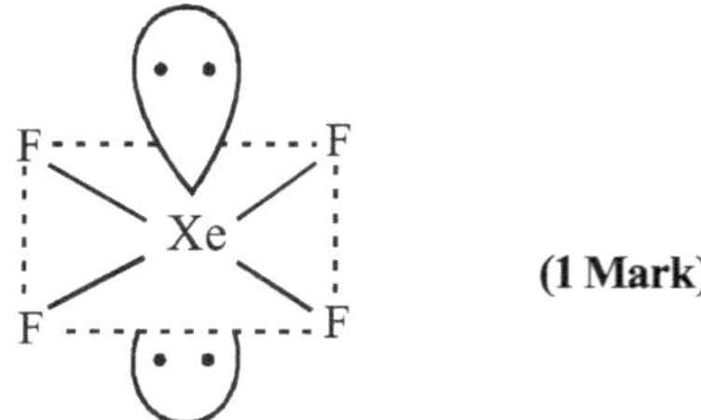

(1 Mark)

OR

(i) When SO_2 gas is passed through an aqueous solution of Fe^{3+} salt, SO_2 acts as a reducing agent, forming Fe^{2+} thereby turning the brown coloured solution green.

(1 Mark)

(ii) When XeF_4 reacts with SbF_5, the following reaction takes place :

$$XeF_4 + SbF_5 \rightarrow [XeF_3]^+ [SbF_6]^-$$ **(1 Mark)**

SECTION - C

11. The final products of the given reactions are :

(a)

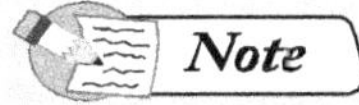

$$CH_3 - \underset{\underset{CH_3}{|}}{\overset{\overset{CH_3}{|}}{C}} - I + CH_3 - OH$$

(1 Mark)

> **Note**
>
> *Instead of CH_3I, the halide formed is a tertiary halide. Because in second step of the reaction a tertiary carbocation is formed by the departure of the leaving group, and the reaction follows $S_N 1$ mechanism.*

(b) $CH_3 - CH_2 - \underset{\underset{OH}{|}}{CH} - CH_3 \xrightarrow{Cu, 573K}$

Butan-2-ol

$$CH_3 - CH_2 - \underset{\underset{O}{\|}}{C} - CH_3 + H_2$$

Butan-2-one

(1 Mark)

> **Note**
>
> *When the vapours of a primary or a secondary alcohol are passed over heated copper at 573K, dehydrogenation takes place and an aldehyde or a ketone is formed while tertiary alcohols undergo dehydration.*

(c)

Phenol $+ CHCl_3 + 3NaOH \longrightarrow$

$\xrightarrow{\overset{+}{H}}$

Salicylaldehyde

(1 Mark)

12. (i)

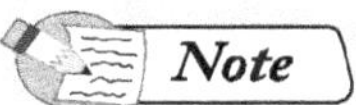

Chlorobenzene $2 \quad + 2Na \xrightarrow[\text{(Fittig reaction)}]{\text{Dry ether}}$

Biphenyl $+ 2NaCl$

(1 Mark)

> **Note**
>
> *Wurtz reaction is just for alkyl halides, wurtz fitting for alkyl and aryl halides together whereas fitting reaction is for only aryl halides. All these reactions result in formation of a new C–C bond.*

(ii) $\underset{\text{Propene}}{H_2C = CH - CH_3} + HBr \xrightarrow[\text{(anti-Markovnikov's)}]{\text{Peroxide}}$

$$CH_3CH_2CH_2Br \xrightarrow[\text{KI/acetone}]{\text{(Finkelstein reaction)}} \underset{\text{1-Iodopropane}}{CH_3CH_2CH_2I}$$

(1 Mark)

> **Note**
>
> *Propene can not be converted directly into 1-iodopropane. The addition of HBr to a unsymmetrical alkene (e.g. propene) in the presence of peroxide is free radical. In the case of HI, the H-I bond is weaker than H-Br bond and undergoes homolysis readily to from iodine free radical. But iodine free radicals have greater trendency to combine themselves to from iodine molecules rather than add to the ethylenic bond. Hence HI does not respond to the peroxide effect.*

(iii) $CH_3 - \underset{\underset{Br}{|}}{CH} - CH_2 - CH_3 \xrightarrow{\text{alc KOH}}$

2-Bromobutane

$$\underset{\text{But-2-ene}}{CH_3 - CH = CH - CH_3}$$

(1 Mark)

OR

(i)

$O_2N \quad \overset{CH_2 - CH_3}{} \xrightarrow[\text{UV light}]{Br_2}$

$O_2N \quad \overset{\overset{Br}{|}}{CH - CH_3}$

(1 Mark)

(ii) $2CH_3CH(Cl)CH_3 \xrightarrow[\substack{\text{dry ether} \\ \text{(Wurtz reaction)}}]{2Na}$

$$\begin{array}{l} CH_3 - CH - CH_3 \\ \quad\quad\;\; | \\ CH_3 - CH - CH_3 \end{array}$$

(1 Mark)

(iii) $CH_3 — CH_2 — Br \xrightarrow{AgCN} CH_3 - CH_2 - NC$

(1 Mark)

> **Note**
>
> *Haloalkanes react with KCN to form RCN as major product while AgCN forms iso-cyanide (RNC) as the major product. Because, KCN is ionic in nature, so provides CN^- ions in solution while AgCN is mainly covalent in nature and nitrogen is free to donate electron pair forming RNC as the major product.*

13.   (i)   Cellulose is a linear polymer made up of β-glucose having the C1-C4 glycosidic linkage, whereas starch is a polymer of α-glucose having two components: amylose and amylopectin. Amylose is a long, unbranched chain with 200-1,000 α-D-(+) glucose units held by the C1-C4 glycosidic linkage. Amylopectin is a branched-chain polymer of α-D-glucose unit in which the chain is formed by the C1-C4 glycosidic linkage and branching occurs at the C1-C6 glycosidic linkage.

(1 Mark)

(ii)   Three types of linkage are found in nucleic acids.
(1)   Hydrogen bonds
(2)   Glycosidic linkage
(3)   Phosphodiester linkage   **(1 Mark)**

(iii)   Fibrous protein: Keratin
Globular protein: Egg albumin   **(1 Mark)**

14.   (i)   The Mond's process is used for refining of nickel.

(1 Mark)

(ii)   Cryolite is used in the electrolytic reduction of alumina for lowering its melting point and making it as a good conductor of electricity.   **(1 Mark)**

(iii)   In the blast furnace, limestone decomposes to form CaO, which reacts with the silicate impurity to form slag.

$$CaCO_3 \longrightarrow CaO + CO_2$$

$$\underset{\text{Slag}}{CaO + SiO_2 \longrightarrow CaSiO_3}$$ **(1 Mark)**

15.   (i) SO_2 is a reducing agent because sulphur has empty d-orbitals and it can easily expand its oxidation state +4 to +6. However, Te is a heavy element; therefore, due to inert pair effect, its lower oxidation state is more stable, and TeO_2 acts as oxidising agent.   **(1 Mark)**

(ii)   Due to unavailability of empty d-orbitals in nitrogen, it cannot expand its valency. Hence, nitrogen does not form pentahalide.   **(1 Mark)**

(iii)   In general, interhalogen compounds are more reactive because of lower bond dissociation energy than halogen molecules (except F_2)   **(1 Mark)**

16.   (a)   Fe in ground state

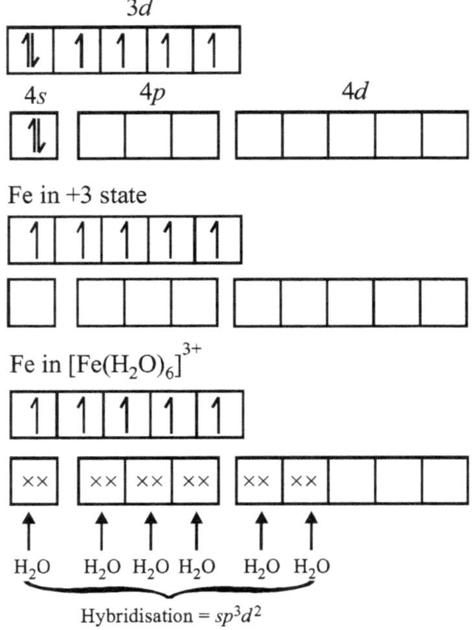

Hybridisation: sp^3d^2
Magnetic character: Paramagnetic
Spin: High spin   **(1 + 1 = 2 Marks)**

(b)   *trans*-isomer of $[Pt(en)_2Cl_2]^{2+}$ is optically inactive.

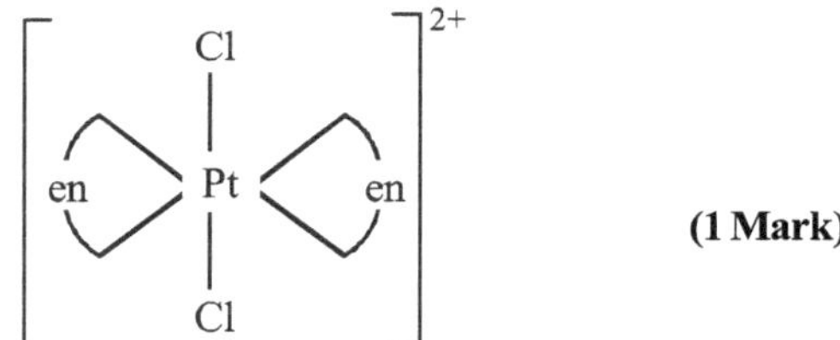

(1 Mark)

> **Note**
>
> *The complexes which are non-superimposable on their mirror images are optically active and optically active complexes are asymmetric in nature. Because trans isomer contains plane of symmetry, so it is optically inactive.*

17.   Volume of the unit cell $= (500\text{ pm})^3$

$$= (500 \times 10^{-10}\text{cm})^3$$

$$= 1.25 \times 10^{-22}\text{cm}^3$$

$$\text{Volume of 300 g of the element} = \frac{\text{Mass}}{\text{Density}}$$

$$= \frac{300\text{ g}}{7.5\text{ gcm}^{-3}}$$

$$= 40\text{ cm}^3 \qquad \textbf{(1 Mark)}$$

$$\text{Number of unit cell in } 40\ cm^3 = \frac{40}{1.25 \times 10^{-22}}$$
$$= 3.2 \times 10^{23} \qquad \textbf{(½ Mark)}$$

No. of atoms in a *bcc* unit cell = 2　　　　**(½ Mark)**

Total no. of atoms = no. of unit cells ×
　　　　　　　　　　no of atoms in a unit cell

$\therefore$ Number of atoms $= 3.2 \times 10^{23} \times 2$
$$= 6.4 \times 10^{23}$$

Therefore, the number of atoms present in 300 g of compound is 6.4×10^{23}.　　**(1 Mark)**

18. (i) Natural rubber becomes soft at high temperatures ($> 335K$) and brittle at low temperatures ($< 283K$).

Moreover, it is soluble in non-polar solvents and is non-resistant to the attacks by oxidising agents.

Therefore sulphur is added during its manufacturing to overcome these limitations. Sulphur forms cross linkages at reactive sites of double bonds and thus, the rubber gets stiffened.　　**(1 Mark)**

(ii) Name of the polymer : Glyptal

Monomers:

(a) Ethylene glycol

(b) Phthalic acid　　**(1 Mark)**

(iii) The increasing order of the intermolecular forces of the given polymers is as follows :

Neoprene < Polythene < Terylene　　**(1 Mark)**

 *Note*

Fibres have the strongest intermolecular forces, while elastomers have the least. Thermoplastics have the intermolecular forces intermediate between elastomers and fibres.

19. Given :

$P_i = 0.30\ atm$

$P_t = 0.50\ atm$

$$C_2H_5Cl(g) \longrightarrow C_2H_4(g) + HCl(g)$$

| | P_i | 0 | 0 | (At $t = 0$ s) |
| | $P_i - x$ | x | x | (At $t = 300$ s) |

$\therefore$　$P_i - x + x + x = P_t$
$$0.30 + x = 0.50$$
$$x = 0.20$$
$$P_i - x = 0.30 - 0.20$$
$$= 0.10\ atm \qquad \textbf{(1 Mark)}$$

For a first-order decomposition reaction, we know that

$$k = \frac{2.303}{t} \log\left(\frac{P_i}{P_i - x}\right) \qquad \textbf{(½ Mark)}$$

$$= \frac{2.303}{300} \log\left(\frac{0.30}{0.10}\right) \qquad \textbf{(½ Mark)}$$

$$= \frac{2.303 \times \log 3}{300}$$

$$= \frac{2.303 \times 0.4771}{300}$$

$$k = 0.0037\ s^{-1} \qquad \textbf{(1 Mark)}$$

20. (i) Aniline forms salt with aluminium chloride, the catalyst of the Friedel-Crafts reaction. As a result, the nitrogen atom in aniline acquires a positive charge, which deactivates the benzene ring towards the electrophillic reaction. Thus, aniline does not undergo the Friedel-Crafts reaction.　　**(1 Mark)**

(ii) There are two factors that affect the basicity of the amines in an aqueous solution : solvation of ammonium ions and inductive effect. Inductive effect of the alkyl group is greater in $(CH_3)_3N$ than in $(CH_3)_2NH$. However, due to greater stabilisation by increased hydrogen bonding in $(CH_3)_2NH$ on solvation with water molecules, $(CH_3)_2NH$ is more basic than $(CH_3)_3N$.　　**(1 Mark)**

(iii) Primary amines are engaged in intermolecular association because of hydrogen bonding between nitrogen of one molecule and hydrogen of another molecule, as shown below.

On the other hand, no such interaction is possible in tertiary amines because of absence of the hydrogen atom directly attached to nitrogen. Therefore, due to stronger intermolecular forces, the boiling point of primary amines is higher than that of secondary amines.

　　(1 Mark)

21. (i) **Lyophilic colloids :** Colloidal sols directly formed by mixing substances like gum, gelatine and starch with a suitable liquid are called lyophilic colloids.　**(1 Mark)**

Note

An important characteristic of these colloids is that if the dispersion medium is separated from the dispersed phase, the colloid can be reconstituted by simple remixing with the dispersion medium. Therefore, these colloids are also called reversible colloids.

(ii) Zeta potential: The charges of opposite signs on the fixed and diffused parts of the Helmholtz electrical double layer around the colloidal particles results in a difference in potential. This potential difference between the fixed layer and the diffused layer of opposite charges is called the electrokinetic potential or zeta potential. **(1 Mark)**

(iii) Associated colloids: There are some substances such as soaps and synthetic detergents that, at low concentrations, behave as normal strong electrolytes, but at higher concentrations, exhibit colloidal behaviour because of the formation of aggregates. The aggregated particles thus formed are called micelles. These are also known as associated colloids. **(1 Mark)**

22. $K_b = 0.52\ K\ kg\ mol^{-1}$

Mass of solute, $MgSO_4 = 4g$

Mass of solvent, water $= 100\ g$

So,

Molality of the solution, $m = \dfrac{4}{120} \times \dfrac{1000}{100}$

$$m = 0.33\ mol/kg \qquad \textbf{(1 Mark)}$$

Also, $MgSO_4$ undergoes complete ionisation, thereby yielding 2 moles of consituent ions for every mole of $MgSO_4$.

$\therefore \quad i = 2$ **(½ Mark)**

Now, elevation in boiling point is given as

$\Delta T_b = iK_b m$ **(½ Mark)**

$\quad = 2 \times 0.52 \times 0.33$

$\quad = 0.34\ K$

$\because \Delta T_b = T_b - T_b^\circ$

$0.34 = T_b - 373.15K$

$T_b \quad = 373.15 + 0.34$

$\quad = 373.49\ K$ **(1 Mark)**

Therefore, the new boiling point of the solution is 373.49 K.

SECTION - D

23. (i) The following values are displayed by Mr. Khanna :

(a) Care and concern : He cared for the well-being of his friend, Mr. Singh.

(b) Knowledge : He suggested effective measures to Mr. Singh to counter acidity and improve his health.

(c) Presence of mind : He acted immediately by taking his friend to doctor. **(2 Marks)**

(ii) Antacids is a class of drugs used to treat acidity. They contain either sodium hydrogen bicarbonate or aluminium/magnesium hydroxide.

For example, milk of magnesia **(1 Mark)**

(iii) Long time exposure to sodium bicarbonate can increase the pH of the stomach, making it alkaline. This will lead to more production of acid. Antacids only stop the symptoms of acidity. If the acidity advances, it leads to formation of ulcers whose only treatment is removal of the affected area of the stomach. Hence, it is not advisable to take antacids for a long period of time.

(1 Mark)

SECTION - E

24. (a) (i) $CH_3COCl \xrightarrow{H_2,\ Pd-BaSO_4} \underset{(A)}{CH_3CHO}$

$\xrightarrow{H_2N-OH} \underset{(B)}{CH_3CH = N - OH}$

(½ + ½ = 1 Mark)

(ii) $CH_3MgBr \xrightarrow[2.\ H_3O^+]{1.\ CO_2} \underset{(A)}{CH_3COOH}$

$\xrightarrow{PCl_5} \underset{(B)}{CH_3COCl}$

(½ + ½ = 1 Mark)

(b) (i) $C_6H_5 - COCH_3$ is a methyl ketone and therefore, gives a yellow precipitate of iodoform when reacted with NaOH and I_2 (haloform test).

$C_6H_5 - COCH_3 \xrightarrow[I_2]{NaOH} C_6H_5COONa + CHI_3$

$C_6H_5 - CHO$ does not give this reaction.

(1 Mark)

(ii) As shown below, methanoic acid gives silver mirror test, while ethanoic acid will not give this test.

$HCOOH + 2[Ag(NH_3)_2]NO_3$

$\longrightarrow 2Ag + CO_2 + 2NH_4NO_3 + 2NH_3$

(1 Mark)

(c) The increasing order of boiling points of the given compounds is as follows :

$CH_3CHO < CH_3CH_2OH < CH_3COOH$ **(1 Mark)**

Note

The boiling point of the given compounds can be compared on the basis of the extent of intermolecular hydrogen bond formation.

OR

(a)
$$CH_3 - \underset{\underset{H}{|}}{C} = O + NH_2NH_2 \xrightarrow{-H_2O}$$

Acetaldehyde

$$CH_3 - \underset{\underset{H}{|}}{C} = NNH_2 \xrightarrow[\text{Glycol}]{\text{KOH, 453–473 K}} CH_3 - CH_3 + N_2$$

Hydrazcne

(1 Mark)

(b) The increasing order of reactivity towards nucleophilic addition reaction for the given compounds is as follows:
$$CH_3COCH_3 < C_6H_5COCH_3 < CH_3 - CHO \qquad \textbf{(1 Mark)}$$

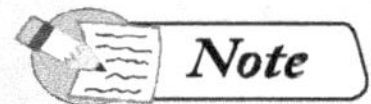

> ### Note
>
> *Aldehydes are more reactive than ketones towards the nucleophillic addition reaction. Among the ketones, aromatic ketones are more susceptible to nucleophilic attack than an aliphatic one.*

(c) The carbon of carboxylic acid is much less electrophilic as compared to aldehydes and ketones because the lone pair of oxygen attached to hydrogen is involved in resonance, as shown below:

$$R - \underset{}{C} - \overset{..}{\underset{..}{O}}H \longleftrightarrow R - C = \overset{+}{O}H$$

(1 Mark)

(d)
$$CH_3CH_2CH = CHCH_2CN \xrightarrow[\text{(ii) } H_2O]{\text{(i) } (i-Bu)_2\,AlH}$$
$$CH_3CH_2CH = CH - CH_2 - CHO$$

(1 Mark)

(e) The possible functional isomers of C_3H_6O are $CH_3 - CH_2 - CHO$ and CH_3COCH_3

Out of these, methyl ketone can give iodoform test as shown :
$$CH_3COCH_3 \xrightarrow[\Delta]{NaOH+I_2} CH_3COONa + CHI_3$$
$$\text{yellow ppt.}$$

Hence, isomer A is CH_3CH_2CHO and B is CH_3COCH_3

(1 Mark)

25. (a) Given: $2Al(s) + 3Cu^{2+}(0.01\ m) \longrightarrow$
$$2Al^{3+}(0.01\ m) + 3Cu(s)$$

$$E_{cell} = E^\circ_{cell} - \left[\frac{2.303\,RT}{nF} \log Q\right] \qquad \textbf{(1 Mark)}$$

$$E^\circ_{cell} = E_{cell} + \left[\frac{2.303\,RT}{nF} \log Q \frac{[Al^{3+}]^2}{[Cu^{2+}]^3}\right]$$

$$E^\circ_{cell} = 1.98 + \left[\frac{0.0591}{6} \log \frac{(0.01)^2}{(0.01)^3}\right]$$

$$E^\circ_{cell} = 1.98 + \left[\frac{0.0591}{6} \times \log 10^2\right] \qquad \textbf{(1 Mark)}$$

$$E^\circ_{cell} = 1.98 + \left[\frac{0.0591}{6} \times 2\right] = 1.99\ V \qquad \textbf{(1 Mark)}$$

(b) Corrosion is basically a process of oxidation, so oxidation potential is considered here.

Oxidation potential of Fe $= 0.44$ V

Oxidation potential of A $= 2.37$ V

Oxidation potential of B $= 0.14$ V

Since A has a higher oxidation potential than that of iron, so it will oxidise faster than Fe. Therefore A is better for coating. **(2 Marks)**

OR

(a)
$$\Lambda_m = \frac{\kappa}{C} \times 1000 = \frac{3.905 \times 10^{-5} \times 1000}{0.001}$$
$$= 39.05\ \text{S cm}^2\text{mol}^{-1} \qquad \textbf{(1 Mark)}$$

$$\Lambda^\circ_m = \lambda^\circ_{H^+} + \lambda^\circ_{CH_3COO^-}$$

$$\Lambda^\circ_m = 349.6 + 40.9$$

$$\Lambda^\circ_m = 390.5\ \text{S cm}^2\ \text{mol}^{-1} \qquad \textbf{(1 Mark)}$$

$$\alpha = \frac{\Lambda_m}{\Lambda^\circ_m} = 39.05/390.5 = 0.1 \qquad \textbf{(1 Mark)}$$

(b) An electrochemical cell is a device capable of generating electrical energy from chemical reaction. If external potential is higher than E°_{cell} potential value of the cell, the flow of current and cell reactions are reversed. The cell now functions as electrolytic cell, a device for using electrical energy to carry non-spontaneous chemical reactions. **(2 Marks)**

26. (a) (i) Mn shows the highest oxidation states of +7 with oxygen because it can form $p\pi - d\pi$ multiple bonds involving $2p$-orbitals of oxygen and $3d$ orbitals of Mn. On the other hand, Mn shows the highest oxidation state of +4 with F because it forms single bond with F due to unavailability of $2p$-orbitals in F for multiple bonding. **(1 Mark)**

(ii) Cr^{2+} has d^4 configuration while Cr^{3+} has d^3 configuration with half filled t_{2g} orbitals which makes Cr^{3+} more stable than Cr^{2+}. Cr^{2+} easily lose electron to attain stability and form Cr^{3+} and act as a reducing agent. **(1 Mark)**

(iii) Cu^{2+} has one unpaired e^- in d-orbitals, thereby allowing for the d-d transition and forming coloured salts, whereas Zn^{2+} has fully filled d-orbitals and does not form coloured salts.

(1 Mark)

(b) (i) $2MnO_2 + 4KOH + O_2 \longrightarrow 2K_2MnO_4 + 2H_2O$

(1 Mark)

(ii) $Cr_2O_7^{2-} + 14H^+ + 6I^- \longrightarrow 2Cr^{3+} + 3I_2 + 7H_2O$

(1 Mark)

OR

(i)   Mn shows maximum number of oxidation states. This is because the valence shell electronic configuration of Mn is $3d^5 4s^2$. In Mn, d-orbitals are half-filled so that it can lose all seven valence electrons.

(1½ Marks)

(ii)   Cr has the highest melting point due to availability of maximum number of unpaired electrons, which results an increase in strength of metallic bond.

(1 Mark)

(iii) Sc shows only the +3 oxidation state because it has one $3d$ and two $4s$ electrons. So, it can lose maximum of three electrons.

(1 Mark)

(iv)   Mn shows strong oxidising character in the +3 oxidation state because it acquires highly stable $3d^5$ configuration in the +2 oxidation state.

(1½ Marks)

CBSE Board Solved Paper

Time Allowed : 3 Hours   *Maximum Marks : 70*

General Instructions:
  (i)   All questions are compulsory.
 (ii)   Section A : Question number **1** to **5** are very short answer questions and carry **1** mark each.
(iii)   Section B : Question number **6** to **10** are short answer questions and carry **2** marks each.
 (iv)   Section C : Question number **11** to **22** are also short answer questions and carry **3** marks each.
  (v)   Section D : Question number **23** is a value based question and carry **4** marks.
 (vi)   Section D : Question number **24** to **26** are long answer questions and carry **5** marks each.
(vii)   Use log tables if necessary. Use of calculators is not allowed.

SECTION - A

1. Out of $CH_3 - \overset{\underset{\textstyle CH_3}{|}}{CH} - CH_2 - Cl$ and $CH_3 - CH_2 - \overset{\underset{\textstyle CH_3}{|}}{CH} - Cl$,

which is more reactive towards S_N1 reaction and why ?

2. On adding NaOH to ammonium sulphate, a colourless gas with pungent odour is evolved which forms a blue coloured complex with Cu^{2+} ion. Identify the gas.

3. What type of magnetism is shown by a substance if magnetic moments of domains are arranged in same direction ?

4. Write the IUPAC name of the given compound:

$$Br\text{-}\underset{\underset{\textstyle Br}{}}{\overset{\overset{\textstyle NH_2}{}}{\bigcirc}}\text{-}Br$$

5. Write the main reason for the stability of colloidal sols.

SECTION - B

6. From the given cells :

Lead storage cell, Mercury cell, Fuel cell and Dry cell

Answer the following :

  (i)   Which cell is used in hearing aids ?
 (ii)   Which cell was used in Apollo Space Programme ?
(iii)   Which cell is used in automobiles and inverters ?
 (iv)   Which cell does not have long life ?

7. When chromite ore $FeCr_2O_4$ is fused with NaOH in presence of air, a yellow coloured compound (A) is obtained which on acidification with dilute sulphuric acid gives a compound (B). Compound (B) on reaction with KCl forms a orange coloured crystalline compound (C).

  (i)   Write the formulae of the compounds (A), (B) and (C).
 (ii)   Write one use of compound (C).

OR

Complete the following chemical equations:

  (i) $8MnO_4^- + 3S_2O_3^{2-} + H_2O \rightarrow$
 (ii) $Cr_2O_7^{2-} + 3Sn^{2+} + 14H^+ \rightarrow$

8. When a co-ordination compound $CrCl_3.6H_2O$ is mixed with $AgNO_3$, 2 moles of AgCl are precipitated per mole of the compound. Write

  (i)   Structural formula of the complex.
 (ii)   IUPAC name of the complex.

9. For a reaction : $2NH_3(g) \xrightarrow{Pt} N_2(g) + 3H_2(g)$

$$Rate = k$$

  (i)   Write the order and molecularity of this reaction.
 (ii)   Write the unit of k.

10. Write the mechanism of the following reaction:

$$2CH_3CH_2OH \xrightarrow[413K]{Conc.\,H_2SO_4} CH_3CH_2 - O - CH_2 - CH_3$$

SECTION - C

11. Give reasons :

  (i)   C–Cl bond length in chlorobenzene is shorter than C–Cl bond length in CH_3–Cl.

 (ii)   The dipole moment of chlorobenzene is lower than that of cyclohexyl chloride.

(iii) S_N1 reactions are accompanied by racemization in optically active alkyl halides.

12. An element crystallizes in a f.c.c. lattice with cell edge of 250 pm. Calculate the density if 300 g of this element contain 2×10^{24} atoms.

13. The rate constant for the first order decomposition of H_2O_2 is given by the following equation :

$$\log k = 14.2 - \frac{1.0 \times 10^4}{T} K$$

Calculate E_a for this reaction and rate constant k if its half-life period be 200 minutes.

(Given: $R = 8.314\ J\ K^{-1}\ mol^{-1}$)

14. (i) Differentiate between adsorbtion and absorption.

(ii) Out of $MgCl_2$ and $AlCl_3$, which one is more effective in causing coagulation of negatively charged sol and why ?

(iii) Out of sulphur sol and proteins, which one forms multimolecular colloids ?

15. (i) Name the method of refining of metals such as Germanium.

(ii) In the extraction of Al, impure Al_2O_3 is dissolved in conc. NaOH to form sodium aluminate and leaving impurities behind. What is the name of this process ?

(iii) What is the role of coke in the extraction of iron from its oxides ?

16. Calculate e.m.f of the following cell at 298 K :

$2Cr(s) + 3Fe^{2+}(0.1M) \rightarrow 2Cr^{3+}(0.01M) + 3\ Fe(s)$

Given : $E°(Cr^{3+}\ |Cr) = -0.74V$, $E°(Fe^{2+}\ |\ Fe) = -0.44\ V$

17. Give reasons :

(i) Mn shows the highest oxidation state of +7 with oxygen but with fluorine it shows the highest oxidation state of +4.

(ii) Transition metals show variable oxidation states.

(iii) Actinoids show irregularities in their electronic configurations.

18. Write the main product(s) in each of the following reactions :

(i)
$$CH_3 - \overset{\overset{\displaystyle CH_3}{|}}{\underset{\underset{\displaystyle CH_3}{|}}{C}} - O - CH_3 + HI \longrightarrow$$

(ii) $CH_3 - CH = CH_2 \xrightarrow[\text{(ii) } 3H_2O_2/OH]{\text{(i) } B_2H_6}$

(iii) $C_6H_5 - OH \xrightarrow[\text{(ii) } CO_2, H^+]{\text{(i) } aq.NaOH}$

19. Write the structures of A, B and C in the following :

(i) $C_6H_5 - CONH_2 \xrightarrow{Br_2/aq.KOH} A \xrightarrow[0\text{-}5\ °C]{NaNO_2 + HCl}$

$B \xrightarrow{KI} C$

(ii) $CH_3 - Cl \xrightarrow{KCN} A \xrightarrow{LiAlH_4} B$
$$\xrightarrow[\Delta]{CHCl_3 + alc.KOH} C$$

20. (i) What is the role of t-butyl peroxide in the polymerization of ethene ?

(ii) Identify the monomers in the following polymer :
$$-[NH - (CH_2)_6 - NH - CO - (CH_2)_4 - CO -]_n$$

(iii) Arrange the following polymers in the increasing order of their intermolecular forces : Polystyrene, Terylene, Buna-S

OR

Write the mechanism of free radical polymerization of ethene.

21. (i) Write the name of two monosaccharides obtained on hydrolysis of lactose sugar.

(ii) Why Vitamin C cannot be stored in our body ?

(iii) What is the difference between a nucleoside and nucleotide ?

22. (a) For the complex $[Fe(CN)_6]^{3-}$, write the hybridization type, magnetic character and spin nature of the complex. (At. number : Fe = 26).

(b) Draw one of the geometrical isomers of the complex $[Pt(en)_2Cl_2]^{2+}$ which is optically active.

SECTION - D

23. Due to hectic and busy schedule, Mr. Angad made his life full of tensions and anxiety. He started taking sleeping pills to overcome the depression without consulting the doctor. Mr. Deepak, a close friend of Mr. Angad, advised him to stop taking sleeping pills and suggested to change his lifestyle by doing Yoga, meditation and some physical exercise. Mr. Angad followed his friend's advice and after few days he started feeling better.

After reading the above passage, answer the following :

(i) What are the values (at least two) displayed by Mr. Deepak ?

(ii) Why is it not advisable to take sleeping pills without consulting doctor ?

(iii) What are tanquilizers ? Give two examples.

SECTION - E

24. (a) Account for the following :

(i) Ozone is thermodynamically unstable.

(ii) Solid PCl_5 is ionic in nature.

(iii) Fluorine forms only one oxoacid HOF.

(b) Draw the structure of

(i) BrF_5 (ii) XeF_4

OR

(i) Compare the oxidizing action of F_2 and Cl_2 by considering parameters such as bond dissociation enthalpy, electron gain enthalpy and hydration enthalpy.

(ii) Write the conditions to maximize the yield of H_2SO_4 by contact process.

(iii) Arrange the following in the increasing order of property mentioned :

(a) H_3PO_3, H_3PO_4, H_3PO_2 (Reducing character)

(b) NH_3, PH_3, AsH_3, SbH_3, BiH_3 (Base strength)

25. (a) Write the structures of A, B, C, D and E in the following reactions :

$$C_6H_6 \xrightarrow[\text{Anhyd. AlCl}]{CH_3COCl} A \xrightarrow[\text{(ii) } H_3O^+]{\substack{\text{Zn–Hg/} \\ \text{conc.HCl}}} \xrightarrow[\text{(ii) } H_3O^+]{\substack{\text{(i) KMnO}_4 - \\ \text{KOH, } \Delta}} C$$

$$A \xrightarrow{\text{NaOI}} D + E$$

OR

(a) Write the chemical equation for the reaction involved in Cannizzaro reaction.

(b) Draw the structure of the semi-carbazone of ethanal.

(c) Why pK_a of $F - CH_2 - COOH$ is lower than that of $Cl - CH_2 - COOH$?

(d) Write the product in the following reaction:

$$CH_3 - CH = CH - CH_2CN \xrightarrow[\text{(ii) } H_2O]{\text{(i) DIBAL-H}}$$

(e) How can you distinguish between propanal and propanone ?

26. (a) Calculate the freezing point of solution when 1.9 g of $MgCl_2$ (M = 95 g mol^{-1}) was dissolved in 50 g of water, assuming $MgCl_2$ undergoes complete ionization. (K_f for water = 1.86 K kg mol^{-1})

(b) (i) Out of 1 M glucose and 2 M glucose, which one has a higher boiling point and why ?

(ii) What happens when the external pressure applied becomes more than the osmotic pressure of solution ?

OR

(a) When 2.56 g of sulphur was dissolved in 100 g of CS_2, the freezing point lowered by 0.383 K. Calculate the formula of sulphur (S_x).

(K_f for CS_2 = 3.83 K kg mol^{-1}, Atomic mass of Sulphur = 32 g mol^{-1}]

(b) Blood cells are isotonic with 0.9% sodium chloride solution. What happens if we place blood cells in a solution containing

(i) 1.2% sodium chloride solution ?

(ii) 0.4% sodium chloride solution ?

Solutions

SECTION - A

1. CH_3—CH_2—$\underset{\underset{CH_3}{|}}{CH}$—$Cl$ will form secondary carbocation

while

CH_3—$\underset{\underset{CH_3}{|}}{CH}$—$CH_2$—$Cl$ will form primary carbocation,

which is less stable than secondary carbocation.

So CH_3—CH_2—$\underset{\underset{CH_3}{|}}{CH}$—$Cl$ is more reactive towards S_N1

reaction. **(1 Mark)**

2. On adding NaOH to ammonium sulphate, ammonia gas is evolved.

$$(NH_4)_2\,SO_4(aq) + 2NaOH \longrightarrow$$
$$Na_2SO_4(aq) + 2H_2O(l) + 2NH_3(g)$$

it has a pungent odour and when ammonia reacts with solution of Cu^{2+} ion, form a deep blue coloured complex, $[Cu(NH_3)_4]^{2+}$. **(1 Mark)**

3. Ferromagnetism is shown by the substances for which the magnetic moments of domains are arranged in same direction. **(1 Mark)**

Iron, cobalt nickel are ferromagentic substance. When these substances are placed in magnetic field all the domains get oriented in the direction of magnetic field that produces a magnetic field which persists even after the removal of magnetic field and they get permanently magnetised.

4. 2, 4, 6-Tribromoaniline **(1 Mark)**

5. Colloid particles are extensively solvated due to strong particle solvent interaction because of which they acquire stability. **(1 Mark)**

SECTION - B

6. (i) Mercury cell is used in hearing aids. **(½ Mark)**

   (ii) Fuel cell was used in Apollo space Programme. **(½ Mark)**

   (iii) Lead storage cell is used in automobiles and inverters. **(½ Mark)**

   (iv) Dry cell does not have long life. **(½ Mark)**

7. (i) On fusing chromite ore $FeCr_2O_4$ with NaOH in presence of air it give yellow coloured compound(A)

$$4FeCr_2O_4 + 16NaOH + 7O_2 \longrightarrow$$
$$\underset{(A)}{8Na_2CrO_4} + 2Fe_2O_3 + 5H_2O$$

On acidification with dil. H_2SO_4 it forms sodium dichromate (B)

$$2Na_2CrO_4 + 2H^+ \longrightarrow \underset{(B)}{Na_2Cr_2O_7} + 2Na^+ + H_2O$$

$$\underset{(B)}{Na_2Cr_2O_7} + 2KCl \longrightarrow \underset{(C)}{K_2Cr_2O_7} + 2NaCl$$

So, the formula of compounds are

(A) Sodium chromate – Na_2CrO_4

(B) Sodium dichromate – $Na_2Cr_2O_7$

(C) Potassium dichromate – $K_2Cr_2O_7$

(1 Mark)

(ii) potassium dichromate $K_2Cr_2O_7$ is used as an oxidizing agent **(1 Mark)**

OR

(i) $8MnO_4^- + 3S_2O_3^{2-} + H_2O \longrightarrow 8MnO_2 + 6SO_4^{2-} + 2OH^-$

(1 Mark)

(ii) $Cr_2O_7^{2-} + 3Sn^{2+} + 14H^+ \longrightarrow 3Sn^{4+} + 2Cr^{3+} + 7H_2O$

(1 Mark)

8. (i) $[CrCl(H_2O)_5]\,Cl_2 . H_2O$ **(1 Mark)**

As 2 moles of AgCl are precipitated per mole of the compound so the structural formula would contain two Cl^- ion satisfying the primary valencies, while $5H_2O$ molecules and one Cl^- ion are present inside the co-ordination sphere, making the co-ordination no. 6. One H_2O molecule will be present as the molecule of hydration.

(ii) IUPAC name - pentaaquachloridochromium(III) Chloride **(1 Mark)**

9. (i) Rate = k, i.e Rate = $k[A]^0$

so order of reaction is zero order. **(½ Mark)**

Molecularity = 2 **(½ Mark)**

(ii) Unit of k = mol $L^{-1}s^{-1}$ **(1 Mark)**

10. Mechanism $H_2SO_4 \rightleftharpoons H^+ + HSO_4^-$

Step I:

$$CH_3-CH_2-\overset{\cdot\cdot}{\underset{\cdot\cdot}{O}}-H + H^+ \longrightarrow CH_3-CH_2-\overset{\cdot\cdot}{\underset{|}{\overset{+}{O}}}-H$$

(Proton from H_2SO_4)

Protonised alcohol

Step II: $CH_3-CH_2-\overset{\cdot\cdot}{\underset{\underset{H}{|}}{\overset{+}{O}}}-H \longrightarrow CH_3-\overset{+}{C}H_2 + H_2O$

Carbocation

Step III:

(i) $CH_3-\overset{+}{C}H_2 + :\overset{\underset{H}{|}}{O}-CH_2-CH_3 \longrightarrow$

$$CH_3-CH_2-\overset{\underset{H}{|}}{\overset{+}{O}}-CH_2-CH_3$$

(ii) $CH_3-CH_2-\overset{\underset{H}{|}}{\overset{+}{O}}-CH_2-CH_3 \xrightarrow{-H^\oplus}$

$$CH_3-CH_2-O-CH_2-CH_3$$

(2 Marks)

SECTION - C

11. (i) C – Cl bond in chlorobenzene has partial double bond character due to which it has shorter bond length than C – Cl bond in CH_3Cl. **(1 Mark)**

(ii) In cyclo-hexyl chloride, the carbon in C – Cl bond is sp^3 hybridized whereas in chlorobenzene C – Cl bond carbon is sp^2 hybridized. sp^2 carbon is more electronegative than sp^3 carbon. So C – Cl bond of chlorobenzene is less polar. **(1 Mark)**

(iii) In S_N1 reaction, formation of carbocation as an intermediate takes place. This carbocation has sp^2 hybridization and planar structure. This planar carbocation is attacked by nucleophile from both sides equally to form d and l isomers in equal proportion (50 : 50) such products are called racemic mixture. Hence S_N1 reaction are accompanied by racemisation in optically active alkyl halides. **(1 Mark)**

Note

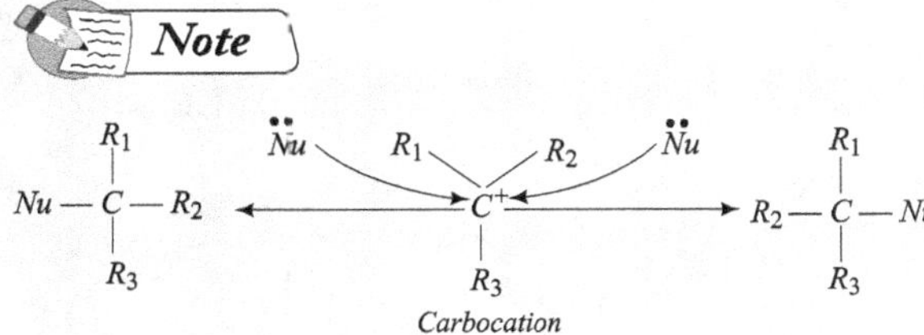

12. *Given:* $a = 250$ pm $= 250 \times 10^{-10}$ cm

For f.c.c $\quad Z = 4$

$$m = 300g$$

$$\therefore \quad M = \frac{6.02 \times 10^{23} \times 300}{2 \times 10^{24}}$$

$$M = 90.3 \qquad \textbf{(1 Mark)}$$

So

Now density $\quad d = \dfrac{Z\,M}{a^3\,N_A}$

$$= \frac{4 \times 90.3}{(250 \times 10^{-10})^3 \times 6.02 \times 10^{23}} \qquad \textbf{(1 Mark)}$$

$$= 38.4 \text{g/cm}^3 \qquad \textbf{(1 Mark)}$$

13. According to Arrhenius Equation

$$\log k = \log A - \frac{E_a}{2.303\ RT} \qquad ...(i)$$

Given Equation is $\ \log k = 14.2 - \dfrac{1.0 \times 10^4}{T}$ K $\qquad ...(ii)$

On Comparing Equation (i) or (ii) we get

$$\frac{E_a}{2.303\ RT} = \frac{1.0 \times 10^4}{T} \text{ K} \qquad \textbf{(1 Mark)}$$

$$E_a = \frac{1.0 \times 10^4 \times 2.303 \times R \times T}{T} K$$

$$= \frac{1.0 \times 10^4 \times 2.303 \times 8.314 \times T}{T} K$$

$$E_a = 19.14 \times 10^4 \text{ J/mol} \qquad \textbf{(1 Mark)}$$

For first order reaction, half life period will be

$$t_{1/2} = \frac{0.693}{k}$$

$$k = \frac{0.693}{t_{1/2}} = \frac{0.693}{200}$$

$$= 3.465 \times 10^{-3} \text{ min}^{-1}$$

$$= 5.7 \times 10^{-5} \text{ sec} \qquad \textbf{(1 Mark)}$$

14. (i)

	Adsorption	Absorption
1.	It is a surface phenomenon	It is a bulk phenomenon.
2.	It occurs at high rate initially but afterwards the rate decreases till the equilibrium is reached.	It occur at uniform rate and is slower than rate of adsorption.
3.	It is exothermic process Example: Adsorption of water molecule on the surface of silica gel.	No significant change occurs. Example: white colour of chalk become blue when dipped in blue ink (due to capillary action)

(1 Mark)

(ii) According to Hardy - Schulze law, ions carrying the opposite charge to that on sol are responsible for coagulation of the sol. Hence as sol is negative Mg^{2+} and Al^{3+} ions will cause coagulation.

As coagulation power of electrolyte is proportional to the valency of oppositevely charged ion, so $AlCl_3$ will be more effective than $MgCl_2$. **(1 Mark)**

(iii) Sulphur sol will form multimolecular colloids, because sulphur sol consists of particles containing a thousand or more S_8 molecules. On the other hand, proteins are macromolecular colloids. **(1 Mark)**

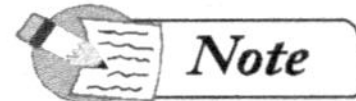
Note

Multimolecular colloids are formed when large number of atoms or small molecules having size less than 1 nm of a substance combine in a dispersion medium to form aggregates.

15. (i) Zone refining method is used for refining of metals such as germanium (semiconductor). **(1 Mark)**

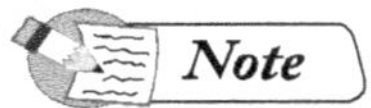
Note

Zone refining is based on the principle that the impurities are more soluble in the molten state than in the solid state of metal.

(ii) Leaching is the process which is used for the extraction of Al, impure Al_2O_3 is dissolved in conc. NaOH to form sodium aluminate and leaving impurities behind in this process. **(1 Mark)**

$$NaOH\ (aq) + 3H_2O(l) \longrightarrow 2Na[Al(OH)_4](aq)$$

(iii) Coke act as a reducing agent and it reduces the iron ore hematite. **(1 Mark)**

$$FeO + C \longrightarrow Fe + CO$$

16. The half cell reaction for the cell

$$[Cr \longrightarrow Cr^{3+} + 3e^-] \times 2,$$

$$[2e^- + Fe^{2+} \longrightarrow Fe] \times 3$$

$$E^{\circ}_{cell} = E^{\circ}_R - E^{\circ}_L = -0.44 - (-0.74)$$

$$E^{\circ}_{cell} = +0.30\ V \qquad \textbf{(1 Mark)}$$

Hence = n = 6, T = 298 K, R = 8.314 J K^{-1} mol^{-1}

Nearest equation for the cell

$$E_{cell} = E^{\circ}_{cell} - \frac{2.303RT}{nF}\log\frac{[Cr^{3+}]^2}{[Fe^{2+}]^3}$$

(1 Mark)

$$= 0.30 - \frac{2.303 \times 8.314 \times 298}{6 \times 96500}\log\frac{[0.01]^2}{[0.1]^3}$$

$$= 0.30 - \frac{0.059}{6}\log 10^{-1}$$

$$= 0.30 + \frac{0.059}{6}$$

$$E_{cell} = 0.3098\ V \qquad \textbf{(1 Mark)}$$

e.m.f. of the cell is 0.3098

17. (i) Mn shows the highest oxidation state of +7 with oxygen because it can form $p\pi - d\pi$ multiple bonds using $2p$ orbitals of oxygen and $3d$ orbitals of Mn. On the other hand with fluorine, Mn shows the highest oxidation state of +4 because it can form only single bond. **(1 Mark)**

(ii) The variable oxidation state of transition metal are due to the participation of ns and $(n-1)d$ electrons in bonding. **(1 Mark)**

(iii) Actinoids show irregularities in their electronic configuration because there are very less energy difference in $6d$, $7s$, and $5f$ subshell, hence an electron can be occupied in any of the subshells. **(1 Mark)**

Note

Due to contraction in size in Actinoid Series, energies of 6d, 7s and 5f orbitals become comparable. Therefore actinoid shows number of oxidation state and irregularity in their electronic configuration.

18. (i)

$$CH_3\!-\!\underset{\underset{CH_3}{|}}{\overset{\overset{CH_3}{|}}{C}}\!-\!O\!-\!CH_3 + HI \longrightarrow CH_3\!-\!\underset{\underset{CH_3}{|}}{\overset{\overset{CH_3}{|}}{C}}\!-\!I + CH_3OH$$

(1 Mark)

(ii) $3CH_3\!-\!CH\!=\!CH_2 \xrightarrow[\ (ii)\ 3H_2O_2/OH^-\ ]{(i)\ B_2H_6}$

$$3CH_3\!-\!CH_2\!-\!CH_2OH + B(OH)_3$$

(1 Mark)

(iii) $C_6H_5OH \xrightarrow[(ii)\ CO_2,\ H^+]{(i)\ aq.\ NaOH}$

Salicylic acid

(1 Mark)

19. (i) $C_6H_5CO\ NH_2 \xrightarrow{Br_2/aq.\ KOH} C_6H_5NH_2$

(A)
Aniline

$\xrightarrow{NaNO_2 + HCl} C_6H_5N_2^+Cl^- \xrightarrow{KI} C_6H_5I$

(B)
Benzene
diazonium
chloride

(C)
Iodobenzene

(½ + ½ + ½ = 1½ Mark)

(ii) $CH_3Cl \xrightarrow{KCN} CH_3CN \xrightarrow{LiAlH_2} CH_3CH_2NH_2$
                    (A)   (B)
              Ethanenitrile   Ethanamine

$\xrightarrow{CHCl_3 + \text{alc. KOH}} CH_3CH_2NC$
                                          (C)
                                         Ethyl
                                       isocynide

(½ + ½ + ½ = 1½ Mark)

20. (i) Decomposition of t-butyl peroxide produces free radical which initiate the chain reaction in the polymerisation of ethene. **(1 Mark)**

(ii) This is Nylon 6, 6 and it's monomers are hexamethylene diamine $H_2N—(CH_2)_6—NH_2$ and adipic acid $HOOC—(CH_2)_4—COOH$ **(1 Mark)**

(iii) Buna-S < Polystyrene < Terylene **(1 Mark)**

 **Note**

- *Buna-S is elastomer so it has weakest intermolecular force.*
- *Polystyrene is a thermoplast which has medium intermolecular forces.*
- *Terylene is a fibre so it has strongest intermolecular forces.*

OR

Mechanism:

Mechanism of polymerisation of ethene in the presence of benzoyl peroxide to form polythene is given below

(i) *Chain initiation step:* In this step benzoyl peroxide undergo homolysis to form phenyl free radical, which act as initiators.

$2C_6H_5—\overset{O}{\overset{||}{C}}—\overset{\bullet}{O} \xrightarrow{-2CO_2} 2\overset{\bullet}{C}_6H_5$
        Benzoyl free   Phenyl free
          radical   radical

(1 Mark)

$\overset{\bullet}{C}_6H_5 + CH_2 = CH_2 \longrightarrow C_6H_5 – CH_2 – \overset{\bullet}{C}H_2$
                    ethene

(ii) *Chain propagation step:* New free radical attacks on ethene to form now large free radical. This free radical further attacks on new monomer. Thus the chain initiated in first step is propagated continuously.

(1 Mark)

$C_6H_5 – CH_2\overset{\bullet}{C}H_2 + CH_2 = CH_2 \longrightarrow$

$C_6H_5 – CH_2 – CH_2 – CH_2 – \overset{\bullet}{C}H_2$

$C_6H_5 – CH_2 – CH_2 – CH_2 – \overset{\bullet}{C}H_2 + CH_2 = CH_2$

$\longrightarrow C_6H_5 – CH_2 – CH_2 – CH_2 – CH_2 – CH_2 – \overset{\bullet}{C}H_2$
                        or
$C_6H_5 \overset{}{(} CH_2 – CH_2 \overset{}{)}_n CH_2 – \overset{\bullet}{C}H_2$

(iii) *Chain termination step:* In this step, two free radicals unite and chain is terminated.

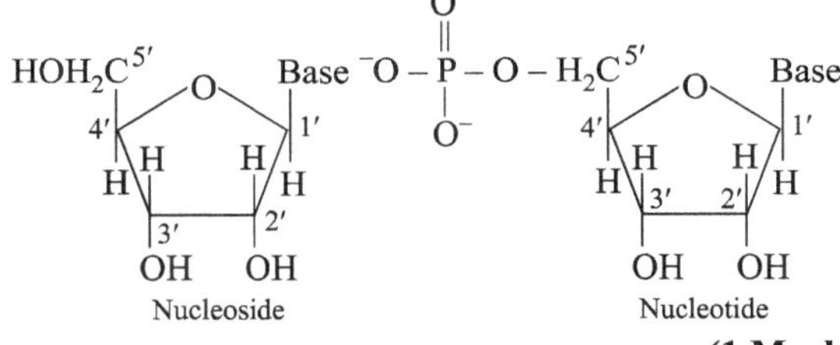

Polythene (Polymer)

(1 Mark)

21. (i) Two monosaccharides obtained on hydrolysis of lactose sugar are β-D-glucose and β-D-galactose.

(1 Mark)

(ii) Vitamin C cannot be stored in our body because it is water soluble in nature so it repeatedly gets eliminated through urine. **(1 Mark)**

(iii) When a base (purine or pyrimidine) get attached to 1′ position of a pentose sugar a nucleoside is formed.

When a nucleoside is further linked to phosphoric acid at 5′ position of the sugar moiety, we get a nucleotide.

Nucleoside   Nucleotide

(1 Mark)

22. (a) (i) Hybridisation type and shape - d^2sp^3, octahedral

(ii) Spin nature - low spin

(iii) Magnetic character - weakly paramagnetic (1 unpaired electron) **(2 Marks)**

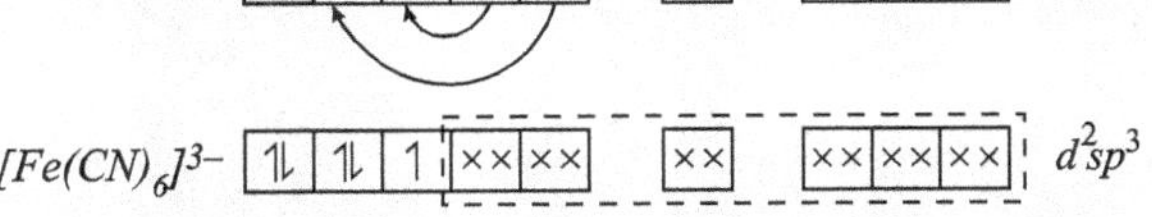 **Note**

$[Fe(CN)_6]^{3-}$

$Fe(26) = [Ar]4s^2\ 3d^6$

$Fe^{3+}\ ion = [Ar]\ 3d^5$

$[Fe(CN)_6]^{3-}$ ... d^2sp^3

as CN^- is a strong field ligand hence pairing will take place in d-orbital.

(b) 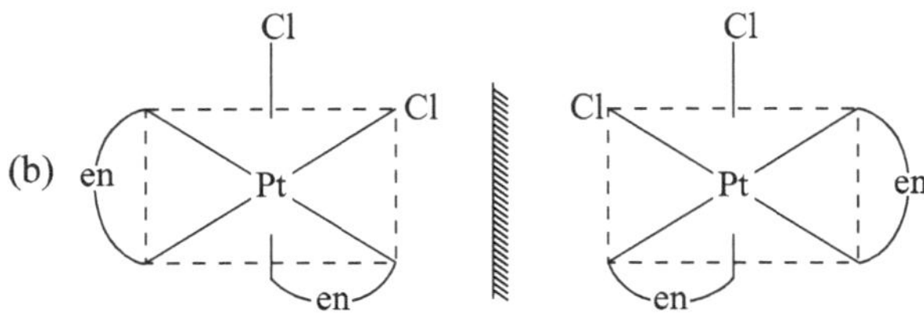

cis isomer of $[Pt(en)_2Cl_2]^{2+}$ is optically active.

(1 Mark)

SECTION - D

23. (i) Mr. Deepak shows care and concern for his friend. He also shows sense of awareness about the side effects of taking medicine without instructions. **(1 Mark)**

(ii) It is not advisable to take sleeping pills without consulting the doctor because sleeping pills are tranquillzers and they have several side effect like slowing down the working of brain and nervous system. **(1 Mark)**

(iii) Those medicines which are used to reduce mental excitement and stress are called tranquilizers. They are used in psychological disorders. Examples are chlordiazepoxide and meprobamate. **(2 Marks)**

SECTION - E

24. (a) (i) Ozone easily decomposes to give nascent oxygen.

$$O_3 \longrightarrow O_2 + [O]$$

because the reaction is exothermic, ($\Delta H = -$ ve) and results into increase in entropy ($\Delta S =$ positive) therefore overall gibb's energy change is quite high and negative. So O_3 becomes thermodynamically unstable. **(1 Mark)**

(ii) PCl_5 is ionic in solid state because it exists as $[PCl_4]^+ [PCl_6]^-$ in which the cation has tetrahedral geometry and the anion has octahedral geometry. **(1 Mark)**

(iii) Due to high electronegativity and small size of fluorine, forms only one oxoacid, HOF. **(1 Mark)**

(b) (i) BrF_5 **(ii)** XeF_4

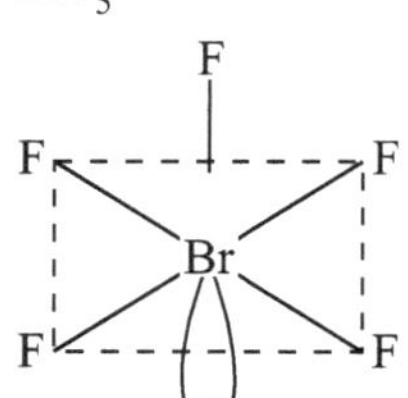

(2 Marks)

OR

(i) Fluorine is a much stronger oxidizing agent than chlorine. The oxidizing power depends on three factors.

    (a) Bond dissociation energy

    (b) Electron gain enthalpy

    (c) Hydration enthalpy

The electron gain enthalpy of chlorine is more negative than that of fluorine. However, the bond dissociation energy of fluorine is much lesser than that of chlorine. Also, because of it's small size, the hydration energy of fluorine is much higher than that of chlorine. Therefore, the latter two factors compensate more than for the less negative electron gain enthalpy of fluorine. Thus fluorine is a much stronger oxidizing agent than chlorine.

(2 Marks)

(ii) Contact process which is used to prepare sulphuric acid is exothermic, reversible and the forward reaction which leads to a decrease in volume. Hence, low temperature and high pressure are the optimum conditions for maximum yield. But if the temperature will be very low then the rate of reaction will become slow. Also, the presence of catalyst V_2O_5 fastens the reaction. **(1 Mark)**

(iii) (a) $H_3PO_4 < H_3PO_3 < H_3PO_2$ (Reducing character)

(1 Mark)

 *Note*

Higher the number of P–H bond, higher is the reducing power of the oxyacid of phosphorus. There are one P–H bond in H_3PO_3, two P–H bond in H_3PO_2 and no P–H bond in H_3PO_4. Therefore H_3PO_2 has highest reducing power followed by H_3PO_3 and least is H_3PO_4.

(b) $BiH_3 < SbH_3 < AsH_3 < PH_3 < NH_3$ (Base strength)

(1 mark)

 *Note*

NH_3 is the strongest base among the group 15 hydrides. On moving down the group atomic size increases therefore availability of lone pair of electron is maximum for NH_3 and minimum for BiH_3.

25.

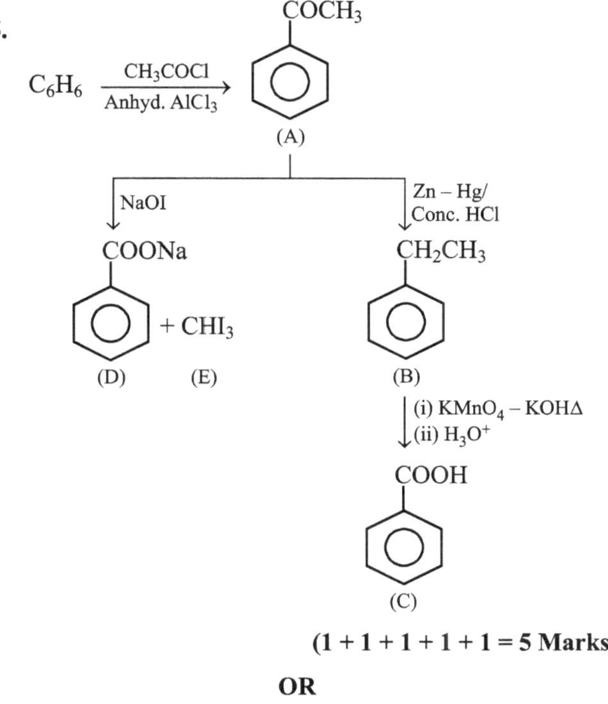

$$(1 + 1 + 1 + 1 + 1 = 5 \text{ Marks})$$

OR

(a) $\underset{\text{formaldehyde}}{HCHO + HCHO} \xrightarrow[\Delta]{\text{Conc. NaOH}} \underset{\substack{\text{methyl} \\ \text{alcohol}}}{CH_3\,OH} + \underset{\text{sodium formate}}{HCOONa}$

(1 Mark)

For aldehydes which do not have α-hydrogen atom undergoes self oxidation and reduction in the presence of concentrated alkali. This produces one mole of alcohol and one mole of salt of carboxylic acid. This is called cannizzaro's reaction.

(b) $\underset{\text{ethanal}}{\overset{H_3C}{\underset{H}{>}}C{=}O} + \underset{\text{semicarbazide}}{H_2N{-}NH{-}\overset{\overset{O}{\|}}{C}{-}NH_2} \longrightarrow$

$$\underset{\substack{\text{semicarbazone} \\ \text{of} \\ \text{ethanal}}}{CH_3{-}\overset{\overset{H}{|}}{C}{=}N{-}NH{-}\overset{\overset{O}{\|}}{C}{-}NH_2}$$

(1 Mark)

(c) Fluorine is more electronegative than chlorine. The presence of fluorine in a molecule will make it more acidic. Thus, the pKa of $F{-}CH_2COOH$ is lower than that of $Cl{-}CH_2COOH$. **(1 Mark)**

(d) $CH_3{-}CH{=}CH{-}CH_2CN \xrightarrow[\text{(ii) } H_2O]{\text{(i) DIBAL–H}}$

$$CH_3CH{=}CHCH_2CHO$$

(1 Mark)

(e) Tollen's reagent will give a positive test of silver mirror formation with propanal, while propanone does not give this test.

$$R{-}CHO + 2[Ag(NH_3)_2]^+ + 3OH^- \longrightarrow$$
$$2Ag{\downarrow} + R{-}COO^- + H_2O + NH_3$$

Tollen's Reagent

(1 Mark)

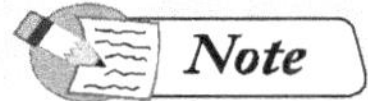

Ammonical silver nitrate solution act as mild oxidising agent and oxidises aldehyde to acetate ion and itself reduced to metallic silver.

26. (a) Given

$$K_f = 1.86 \text{ K kg mol}^{-1}$$
mass of solute $= 1.9$ g
mass of solvent $= 50$ g

Therefore

Molality of the solution, $m = \dfrac{\text{no. of mole of solute}}{\text{wt. of solvent in kg}}$

$$= \dfrac{1.9 \times 1000}{95 \times 50} = 0.4 \text{ m}$$ **(1 Mark)**

$$MgCl_2 \longrightarrow Mg^+ + 2Cl^-$$

No. of ion $= 3$

$$i = 3$$
$$\Delta T_f = i\,K_f\,m$$
$$= 3 \times 1.86 \times 0.4$$
$$= 2.232 \text{ K}$$ **(1 Mark)**
$$T_f(MgCl_2) = T_f(\text{water}) - \Delta T_f$$
$$= 273 - 2.232$$
$$= 270.77 \text{ K}$$ **(1 Mark)**

(b) (i) The elevation in the boiling point of a solution is a colligative property, therefore it is affected by the number of particles of the solute. Since the amount of solute is higher in 2M glucose solution as compared to 1M glucose solution, the elevation in the boiling point is higher. Hence, 2M glucose solution has a higher boiling point than 1 M glucose solution. **(1 Mark)**

(ii) When the external pressure applied become more than the osmotic pressure, pure solvent starts flowing out of the solution through the semipermeable membrane. This process is known as reverse osmosis. **(1 Mark)**

OR

(a) Weight of sulphur $(w_2) = 2.56$ g, $M_2 = 32$ g/mol

Weight of solvent $= 100$ g

$K_f = 3.83$ K kg/mol

$$\Delta T_f = K_f \times \frac{W_2}{M \times w_1} \times 1000 \qquad \textbf{(1 Mark)}$$

$$0.383 = \frac{3.83 \times 2.56 \times 1000}{M \times 100}$$

$M = 256$ g/mol **(1 Mark)**

Formula of sulphur

One atom of S $= 32$ g/mol^{-1}

so atoms of S in molecule $= \dfrac{256}{32} = 8$

Formula $= S_8$ **(1 Mark)**

(b) (i) 1.2% Sodium chloride is hypertonic with respect to 0.9% sodium chloride, hence cells will shrink and water flows out of the cells. Plasmolysis will take place. **(1 Mark)**

(ii) 0.41% Sodium chloride solution is hypotonic with respsect to 0.9% sodium chloride. Hence water flows into the cell and cells will swell. Endo osmosis will take place. **(1 Mark)**

Note

Isotonic solution : Concentration of solute inside the cell is same as in the solution outside.

Hypotonic solution : Outside solution has lower concentration of solute than inside the cell.

Hypertonic solution : Outside solution has greater solute concentration than inside the cell.

All India *2015*
CBSE Board Solved Paper

Time Allowed : 3 Hours   *Maximum Marks : 70*

General Instructions:
(i)   All question are compulsory.
(ii)   Section A : Question number **1 to 5** are very short answer questions and carry **1** mark each.
(iii) Section B : Question number **6 to 10** are short answer questions and carry **2** marks each.
(iv)   Section C : Question number **11 to 22** are also short answer questions and carry **3** marks each.
(v)   Section D : Question number **23** is a value based question and carry **4** marks.
(vi)   Section E : Question number **24 to 26** are long answer questions and carry **5** marks each.
(vii) Use log tables, if necessary. Use of calculator is not allowed.

SECTION - A

1. Zn^{2+} salts are white while Cu^{2+} salts are coloured. Why?

2. Which would undergo S_N1 reaction faster in the following pair?

$$CH_3 - CH_2 - Br \quad \text{and} \quad CH_3 - \underset{\underset{Br}{|}}{\overset{\overset{CH_3}{|}}{C}} - CH_3$$

3. How much charge is required for the reduction of 1 mol of Zn^{2+} to Zn ?

4. Write the dispersed phase and dispersion medium of butter.

5. Write the IUPAC name of the given compound.

$$CH_2 = \underset{\underset{CH_3}{|}}{C} - CH_2 - OH$$

SECTION - B

6. Write the structure of the following molecules.

(i) H_2SO_3 (ii) $XeOF_4$

7. Write down the IUPAC name of the complex $[Pt(en)_2Cl_2]^{2+}$. What type of isomerism is shown by this complex?

OR

Using IUPAC norms write the formulae for the following coordination compounds.

(i)   Hexaamminecobalt (III) chloride

(ii) Potassium tetrachloridonickelate (II)

8. Define rate of reaction ? Write two factors that affect the rate of reaction.

9. Arrange the following in increasing order of their basic strength.

(i) $C_6H_5 - NH_2, C_6H_5 - CH_2 - NH_2, C_6H_5 - NH - CH_3$

(ii)   (aniline, 4-nitroaniline, 4-methylaniline structures)

10. Why does a solution containing non-volatile solute have higher boiling point than the pure solvent?

Why is elevation of boiling point a colligative property?

SECTION - C

11. (i)   What is the principle behind the zone refining of metals?

(ii) What is the role of silica in the extraction of copper?

(iii) How is 'cast iron' different from 'pig iron'?

12. Give reasons for the following.

(i) N_2 is less reactive at room temperature.

(ii) H_2Te is the strongest reducing agent amongst all the hydrides of Group 16 elements.

(iii) Helium is used in diving apparatus as a diluent for oxygen.

13. (a) Write the hybridisation and shape of the following complexes.

(i) $[CoF_6]^{3-}$

(ii) $[Ni(CN)_4]^{2-}$

(Atomic number : Co = 27, Ni = 28)

(b) Out of NH_3 and CO, which ligand forms a more stable complex with a transition metal and why?

14. How do you convert the following.

  (i) $C_6H_5CONH_2$ to $C_6H_5NH_2$

  (ii)   Aniline to phenol

  (iii) Ethanenitrile to ethanamine

OR

Write the chemical equations involved when aniline is treated with the following reagents.

  (i) Br_2 water

  (ii) $CHCl_3 + KOH$

  (iii) HCl

15. Write the names and structures of the monomers of the following polymers.

  (i)   Buna-S

  (ii)   Glyptal

  (iii) Polyvinyl chloride

16. (i)   Write the product obtained when D-glucose reacts with H_2N–OH.

  (ii)   Amino acids show amphoteric behaviour. Why?

  (iii) Why cannot vitamin C be stored in our body?

17. Calculate the freezing point of the solution when 31 g of ethylene glycol ($C_2H_6O_2$) is dissolved in 500 g of water (K_f for water $= 1.86\,K\,kg\,mol^{-1}$)

18. Define the following terms.

  (i)   Primitive unit cells

  (ii)   Schottky defect

  (iii) Ferromagnetism

19. Write the structure of the major product in each of the following reactions.

  (i) $CH_3 - CH = C - CH_3 + HBr \longrightarrow$
                   $|$
                  CH_3

  (ii) $CH_3CH_2CH_2CH - CH_3 \xrightarrow[\Delta]{KOH\ (alc.)}$
                      $|$
                    Br

  (iii) (bromobenzene) $+ CH_3Cl \xrightarrow{anhyd.AlCl_3}$

20. Give reasons for the following.

  (i)   Phenol is more acidic than ethanol.

  (ii)   Boiling point of ethanol is higher in comparison to methoxymethane

  (iii) $(CH_3)_3C - O - CH_3$ on reaction with HI gives CH_3OH and $(CH_3)_3C - I$ as the main products and not $(CH_3)_3C - OH$ and CH_3I.

21. The rate constant of a first order reaction increases from 2×10^{-2} to 4×10^{-2} when the temperature changes from 300 K to 310 K. Calculate the energy of activation (E_a).

(log 2 = 0.301, log 3 = 0.4771, log 4 = 0.6021)

22. Define the following terms.

  (i)   Brownian movement

  (ii)   Peptization

  (iii) Multimolecular colloids

SECTION - D

23. Seeing the growing cases of diabetes and depression among young children, Mr. Lugani, the principal of a reputed school organized a seminar in which he invited parents and principals. They all resolved this issue by strictly banning junk food in schools and introducing healthy snacks and drinks like soup, lassi, milk, etc. in school canteens. They also decided to make compulsory half and hour of daily physical activities for the students in the morning assembly. After six months, Mr. Lugani conducted the health survey in most of the schools and discovered a tremendous improvement in the health of the students.

After reading the above passage, answer the following questions.

  (i)   What are the values (at least two) displayed by Mr. Lugani?

  (ii)   As a student, how can you spread awareness about this issue?

  (iii) What are antidepressant drugs? Give an example.

  (iv) Name the sweetening agent used in the preparation of sweets for a diabetic patient.

SECTION - E

24. Calculate e.m.f and ΔG for the following cell :

$Mg(s) \,|\, Mg^{2+}\,(0.001\ M) \,\|\, Cu^{2+}\,(0.0001\ M) \,|\, Cu\,(s)$

Given : $E^\circ_{(Mg^{2+}/Mg)} = -2.37V,$

          $E^\circ_{(Cu^{2+}/Cu)} = +0.34V.$

OR

  (a) The conductivity of 0.20 mol L^{-1} solution of KCl is $2.48 \times 10^{-2}S\ cm^{-1}$. Calculate its molar conductivity and degree of dissociation (α). Given $\lambda^\circ\,(K^+) = 73.5\ S\ cm^2\ mol^{-1}$ and $\lambda^\circ\,(Cl^-) = 76.5\ S\ cm^2\ mol^{-1}$.

  (b) What type of battery is mercury cell? Why is it more advantageous than dry cell?

25. (a) Account for the following.

(i) Zr and Hf have almost similar atomic radii.

(ii) Transition metals show variable oxidation states.

(iii) Cu^+ ion is unstable in aqueous solution.

(b) Complete the following equations.

(i) $2\,MnO_2 + 4\,KOH + O_2 \rightarrow$

(ii) $2\,Na_2CrO_4 + 2\,H^+ \rightarrow$

OR

(a)

$E^\circ_{M^{2+}/M}$	Cr	Mn	Fe	Co	Ni	Cu
	-0.91	-1.81	-0.44	-0.28	-0.25	$+0.34$

From the given data of E° values, answer the following questions.

(i) Why is $E^\circ_{(Cu^{2+}/Cu)}$ value exception-ally positive?

(ii) Why is $E^\circ_{(Mn^{2+}/Mn)}$ value highly negative as compared to other elements?

(iii) Which is a stronger reducing agent Cr^{2+} or Fe^{2+}? Give reason.

(b) Why do actinoids show a wide range of oxidation states? Write on similarity between the chemistry of lanthanoids and actinoids.

26. (a) A compound 'A' of molecular formula C_2H_3OCl undergoes a series of reactions as shown below. Write the structures of A, B, C and D in the following

reactions. $(C_2H_3OCl)A \xrightarrow{H_2/Pd-BaSO_4}$

$B \xrightarrow{\text{dil. NaOH}} C \xrightarrow{\text{Heat}} D$

(b) Distinguish between the following.

(i) $C_6H_5 - COCH_3$ and $C_6H_5 - CHO$

(ii) Benzoic acid and methyl benzoate

(c) Write the structure of 2-methylbutanal.

OR

(a) Write the structures of the main products when acetone $(CH_3 - CO - CH_3)$ reacts with the following reagents.

(i) $Zn - Hg/conc.\ HCl$

(ii) $H_2NNHCONH_2/H^+$

(iii) CH_3MgBr and then H_3O^+

(b) Arrange the following in the increasing order of their boiling points.

$C_2H_5OH,\ CH_3 - CHO,\ CH_3 - COOH$

(c) Give a simple chemical test to distinguish between the following pair of compounds:

CH_3CH_2CHO and $CH_3CH_2COCH_3$

Solutions

SECTION - A

1. Zn^{2+} salts are white due to the presence of completely filled d-orbitals, while Cu^{2+} has incompletely filled d-orbitals. **(1 Mark)**

2. $(CH_3)_3C-Br$ undergoes S_N1 reaction faster in comparison to C_2H_5Br. **(1 Mark)**

3. The electrode reaction is $Zn^2 + 2e^- \rightarrow Zn$

   Number of electrons involved = 2

   $\therefore$ Quantity of charge required for reduction of 1 mol of Zn^{2+} $= 2 \times F = 2 \times 96500\,C$

   $= 193000\,C$ **(1 Mark)**

4. Dispersed phase and dispersion medium in butter are liquid (H_2O) and liquid (oil) respectively. **(1 Mark)**

5. 2-Methylprop–2–ene–1– ol. **(1 Mark)**

SECTION - B

6. (i) Sulphurous acid (H_2SO_3) **(1 Mark)**

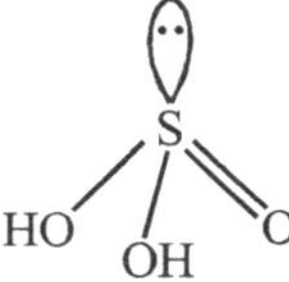

   (ii) Xenon oxytetrafluoride $(XeOF_4)$. **(1 Mark)**

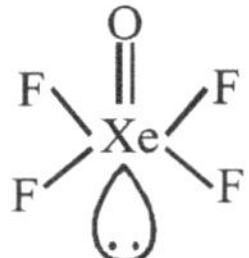

7. IUPAC name:

   Dichloridobis (ethylenediamine) platinum (IV)

   Geometrical isomerism is shown by this complex.

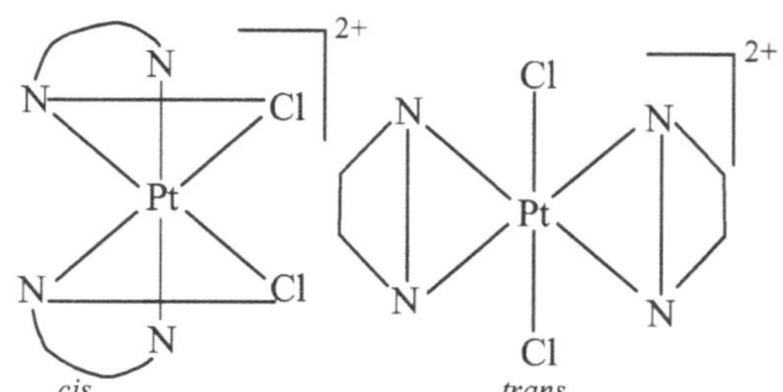

   (1 + 1 = 2 Marks)

   OR

   (i) $[Co(NH_3)_6]Cl_3$ **(1 Mark)**

   (ii) $K_2[NiCl_4]$ **(1 Mark)**

8. Rate of reaction is defined as the change in concentration of reactant or product per unit time.

   $$\text{Rate of reaction} = \frac{\text{Total change in concentration of reactant or product}}{\text{change in time}}$$

   Factors affecting rate of reaction are

   (a) Concentration of reactants

   (b) Temperature **(1 + 1 = 2 Marks)**

9. (i) The order of increasing basic strength is

   $$\underset{\text{least basic}}{C_6H_5NH_2} < C_6H_5NHCH_3 < \underset{\text{most basic}}{C_6H_5CH_2NH_2}$$ **(1 Mark)**

   Note

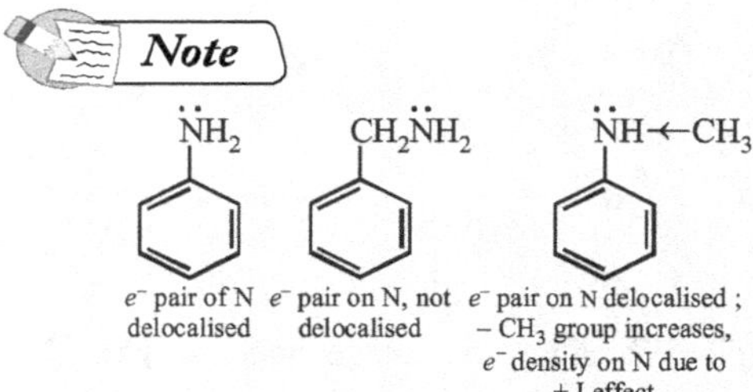

   A pair of electron of nitrogen in $C_6H_5CH_2.NH_2$ is available for donation.

   (ii)

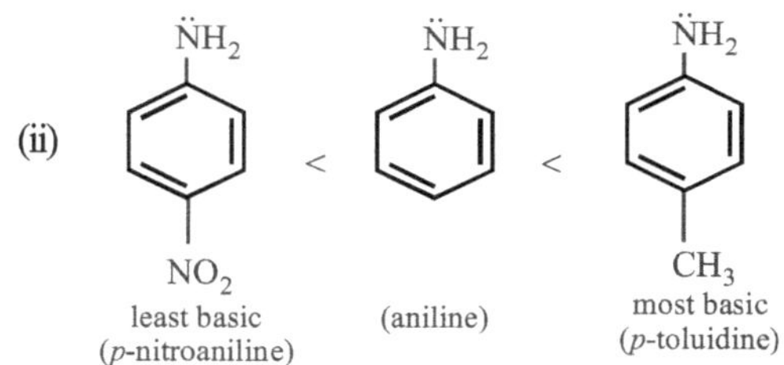

   (1 Mark)

   Note

   Nitro group is electron withdrawing hence reduces basic character, while methyl group is electron repelling hence increases basic character of aniline.

10. Boiling point is the temperature at which vapour pressure of the substance becomes equal to atmospheric pressure. As the vapour pressure of the solution containing non-volatile solute is lower than that of the pure solvent and vapour pressure increases with increase in temperature. Hence, the solution has to be heated more to make its vapour pressure equal to the atmospheric pressure so that it starts boiling.

    Elevation of boiling point is a colligative property because, it depends upon the number of particles of solute dissolved in solution. **(1 + 1 = 2 Marks)**

SECTION - C

11. (i) Zone refining is based on the fact that the impurities are more soluble in the liquid sthan in the solid state of the metal. In the process, one end of the impure metal rod is heated by means of a movable heater. The molten zone carrying impurities moves forward. In this way impurities are concentrated at the other end of the rod which is cut off. **(1 Mark)**

(ii) SiO_2 acts as an acidic flux. Copper ore is heated with silica in a reverberatory furnance when FeO is removed as $FeSiO_3$ (slag) and copper is produced in the form of copper matte. **(1 Mark)**

> **Note**
>
> *Acidic flux is the substance added to molten metals to bond with basic impurities that can be readily removed, while basic flux is the substance added to molten metals to bond with acidic impurities that can be readily removed.*

(iii) The iron obtained from blast furnace is called **pig iron**. It contains about 4% carbon and many other impurities in smaller amount (*e.g.*, S, P, Si and Mn).

Cast iron is made by melting pig iron with scrap iron and coke using hot air blast. It has slightly lower carbon content (about 3%) and is extremely hard and brittle. **(1 Mark)**

12. (i) Due to presence of triple bond between two N-atoms ($N \equiv N$), the bond dissociation energy of N_2 is very high. As a result, N_2 becomes less reactive at room temperature. **(1 Mark)**

> **Note**
>
> *Nitrogen is a colourless, odourless gas, which condenses at-195.8 °C to a colourless, mobile liquid. Because of high bond energy (approx. 226 k.cal) the activation energy for reaction of molecular nitrogen is usually very high, causing nitrogen to be relatively inert to most reagents under ordinary conditions.*

(ii) H_2Te is the strongest reducing agent among group 16 hydride because higher oxidation state is more stable in Te which is attained after oxidation. **(1 Mark)**

(iii) Because of low solubility of helium (as compared to N_2) in blood, a mixture of oxygen and helium is used in diving apparatus. **(1 Mark)**

13. (a) (i) $[CoF_6]^{3-}$ is sp^3d^2 hybridised, octahedral in shape and paramagnetic in nature.

Co (Z = 27) ground state :

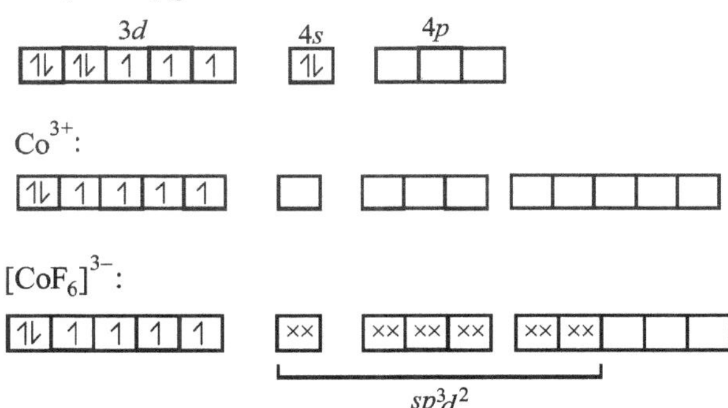

As F^- ions are weak ligands, pairing of electrons does not take place. **(1 Mark)**

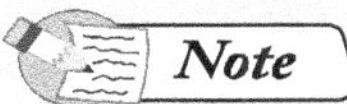

> **Note**
>
> *The nature of ligands either weak field or strong field can be predicted by the help of spectrochemical series. Weak field ligands cause less crystal fields splitting, so they form high spin complexes. The strong field ligands cause greater crystal field splitting, so they form low spin complexes. In general, ligands can be arranged in a series which is termed as spectrochemical series in the order of increasing field strength as given below.*
> $I^- < Br^- < SCN^- < Cl^- < S^{2-} < F^- < OH^- < H_2O < Py < NH_3 < en < Phen < NO_2^- < H^- < CN^- = CO$
> Ligands on the left are commonly referred to as weak-field ligands, and ligands on the right side are called strong filled ligands.

(ii) $[Ni(CN)_4]^{2-}$ is dsp^2 hybridised, square planar in shape and diamagnetic in nature.

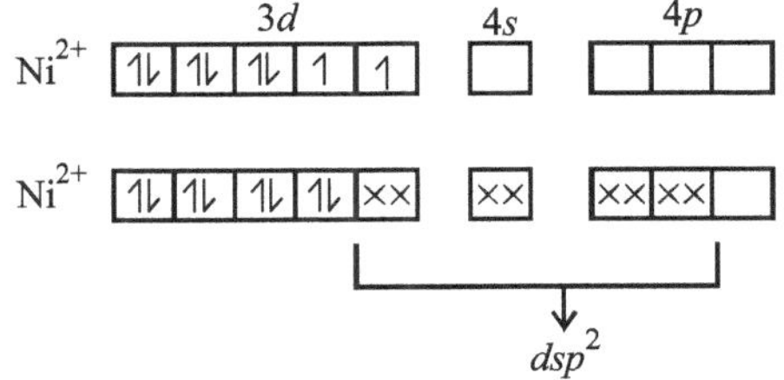

As CN^- ions are strong ligands, pairing of electrons will take place. **(1 Mark)**

(b) Since CO can form σ as well as π bond, whereas NH_3 has lone pair of electrons and can form σ bond only. Therefore, CO is better complexing reagent and forms a more stable complex than NH_3. **(1 Mark)**

> **Note**
>
> ***σ-donor ligands :*** *All ligands are σ-donors. The ligands lone pair that forms a bond with the metal will maximize its overlap with the metal's orbital by pointing directly at it . The more readily a ligand can share its lone pair, the higher its position on the spectrochemical series. For example hydride.*

π-donor ligand : *Some ligands have extra lone pairs on their bonding atom beyond the one that forms the σ-donor interaction.*

These additional lone pair electrons can also interact with the metal's d-orbital in side on fasion, creating an additional bond. For examples, halides can form strong bond with metal.

π-acceptor ligand : *Sometimes a ligands can donate electrons with its lone pair to form one bond, but also accept electrons from the metal with one of its empty orbitals. This phenomenon is sometime called back donation or back-bonding. The interaction is very strong, and results in very large Δ values.*

14. (i) Benzamide $\xrightarrow[\text{reaction)}]{\text{Br}_2/\text{NaOH}}$ (Hoffmann's bromamide reaction) Aniline **(1 Mark)**

(ii) Aniline $\xrightarrow{\text{NaNO}_2/\text{HCl}}$ Benzenediazonium chloride $\xrightarrow{\text{H}_2\text{O}}$ Phenol **(1 Mark)**

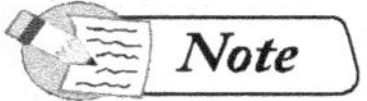

Note

Diazonium salts can directly form various compounds with different reagents.

$$\text{(Ar)}\overset{+}{N}_2X^-$$

$\xrightarrow{\text{CuCl}}$ Cl

$\xrightarrow{\text{CuBr}}$ Br

$\xrightarrow{\text{CuCN}}$ CN

$\xrightarrow{\text{KI}}$ I

$\xrightarrow[\Delta]{\text{H}_2\text{SO}_4, \text{H}_2\text{O}}$ OH

$\xrightarrow[\text{(ii) }\Delta]{\text{(i) HBF}_4}$ F

$\xrightarrow{\text{H}_3\text{PO}_2}$

(iii) $CH_3CH_2CN \xrightarrow{H_2O/H^+} CH_3CH_2COOH \xrightarrow[\Delta]{NH_3}$

Ethanenitrile   Propanoic acid

$CH_3CH_2CONH_2 \xrightarrow{Br_2/KOH} CH_3CH_2NH_2$ **(1 Mark)**

Propanamide   Ethylamine

OR

(i) Aniline $\xrightarrow{\text{Br}_2/\text{H}_2\text{O}}$ 2,4,6-Tribromoaniline **(1 Mark)**

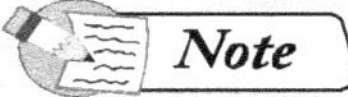

Note

The main problem enountered during electrophilic substitution reactions of aniline is that of their very high reactivity. Substitution tends to occur at ortho and para positions. If we have to prepare monosubstituted aniline derivative, first acetylation of aniline is carried out with acetic anhydride followed by the desired substitution of the substituted amide which is then hydrolysed to obtain the monosubstituted amine.

(ii) Aniline $\xrightarrow{\text{CHCl}_3/\text{KOH}}$ Benzene isocyanide **(1 Mark)**

(iii) Aniline $\xrightarrow{\text{HCl}}$ Anilinium chloride **(1 Mark)**

15. (i) Monomers of buna-S are

$$CH_2 {=\!\!=} CH \!-\! C_6H_5 \text{ and } CH_2 {=\!\!=} CH \!-\! CH {=\!\!=} CH_2$$
Styrene   Buta-1, 3-diene

(1 Mark)

(ii) Monomers of glyptal are phthalic acid and ethylene glycol. **(1 Mark)**

$HO \!-\! CH_2 \!-\! CH_2 \!-\! OH$ and (Phthalic acid, COOH, COOH)
Ethylene glycol

Phthalic acid

(iii) Monomer of polyvinyl chloride is vinyl chloride
$$CH_2 {=} CHCl$$
(1 Mark)
Vinyl chloride

16. (i) $HOH_2C - (CHOH)_4 - CHO + NH_2OH \xrightarrow{-H_2O}$
D-Glucose

$$HOH_2C - (CHOH)_4 - CH = NOH$$
Glucose oxime

(1 Mark)

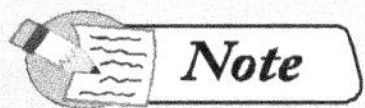

Note

The structure of glucose can be confirmed by various evidances which are as follows.

	Reagent	*Product*	*Conformation*
(i)	HI/Δ	*n-hexane*	*Confirms the presence of six carbon atoms which are linked in a straight chain.*
(ii)	NH_2OH/HCN	*Oxime/cyano hydrin*	*Confirms the presence of carbonyl group.*
(iii)	Br_2 *water*	*Gluconic acid*	*Confirms the presence of aldehyde group.*
(iv)	*Acetic anhydride*	*Glucose pentaacetate*	*Confirms the presence of 5 –OH group.*
(v)	HNO_3	*Saccharic acid*	*Confirms the presence of primary alcoholic group.*

(ii) Amino acids are amphoteric in nature because they exist as zwitterion and react with both acids as well as bases.

- **Reaction with acids**

$$R-\underset{\overset{|}{^+NH_3}}{CH}-COO^- \xrightarrow{H^+} R-\underset{\overset{|}{^+NH_3}}{CH}-COOH$$

- **Reaction with bases**

$$R-\underset{\overset{|}{^+NH_3}}{CH}-COO^- \xrightarrow{OH^-} R-\underset{\overset{|}{^+NH_2}}{CH}-COO^-$$

(1 Mark)

(iii) Vitamin C cannot be stored in the body because it is water soluble, so easily excreted through urine.

(1 Mark)

17. $W_2 = 31g$, $W_1 = 500$ g, $K_f = 1.86$ K kg mol^{-1}

M_2 $(C_2H_6O_2) = 24 + 6 + 32 = 62$ g mol^{-1}

$$\Delta T_f = \frac{1000 K_f \times W_2}{W_1 \times M_2} \qquad \textbf{(1 Mark)}$$

$$= \frac{1000 \times 1.86 \times 31}{500 \times 62} = 1.86\,K \qquad \textbf{(1 Mark)}$$

Freezing point of pure water $= 273.15$ K

$\therefore$ Freezing point of solution $= T_f^\circ - \Delta T_f$

$$= 273.15 - 1.86\,K$$
$$= 271.29\,K \qquad \textbf{(1 Mark)}$$

18. (i) Primitive unit cells are defined as the unit cells in which the constituent particles are present only at the corner positions. **(1 Mark)**

(ii) **Schottky defect:** It occurs when equal number of cations and anions are missing from the lattice sites. It decreases the density of the solid.

For example: NaCl, KCl. **(1 Mark)**

(iii) Ferromagnetism is the phenomenon shown by substances which are strongly attracted by magnetic field. These substances show magnetism even in the absence of a magnetic field. Examples are Fe, Co, Ni and CrO$_2$. **(1 Mark)**

19. (i)

$$CH_3-CH=\underset{\underset{CH_3}{|}}{C}-CH_3 + HBr \longrightarrow$$

2-Methylbut-2-ene

$$CH_3-CH_2-\underset{\underset{Br}{\overset{\overset{CH_3}{|}}{|}}}{C}-CH_3$$

2-Bromo-2-methylbutane

(1 Mark)

(ii)

$$CH_3-CH_2-CH_2-\underset{\underset{Br}{|}}{CH}-CH_3 \xrightarrow[\Delta]{KOH(alc.)}$$

2-Bromopentane

$$CH_3-CH_2-CH=CH-CH_3$$

Pent-2-ene
(Major)

(1 Mark)

Note

Alcoholic KOH, specially in ethanol, produces $C_2H_5O^-$ ions. Which is a stronger base than the OH^-. Thus, the former abstract the β-hydrogen of an alkyl halide to produce alkenes while aqueous KOH is alkaline in nature i.e., it dissociates to produce a hydroxide ion, which acts as a strong nucleophile and replaces the halogen atom in an alkyl halide.

(iii)

Bromobenzene $+ CH_3Cl \xrightarrow{anhyd.AlCl_3}$

p-Methylbromobenzene (Major) $+$ o-Methylbromobenzene

(1 Mark)

20. (i) Since the phenoxide ion formed after the removal of a proton is stabilized by resonance whereas alkoxide ion formed after the removal of a proton from alcohol is not resonance stabilized. Thus phenol is more acidic than alcohol. **(1 Mark)**

(ii) The boiling points of ethers are lower than their isomeric alcohols, due to the absence of hydrogen bonds between ether molecules. Low polarity in ethers does not allow hydrogen bonding and hence, their boiling points are low.

On the other hand, alcohol molecules are polar and get associated through intermolecular hydrogen bonds and hence their boiling points are high. **(1 Mark)**

(iii) Given reaction occurs by S_N1 mechanism and the formation of products is controlled by the stability of the carbocation resulting from the cleavage of C–O bond in protonated ether. Since tert-butyl carbocation is more stable than methyl carbocation, therefore $(CH_3)_3C - O–CH_3$ on reaction with HI gives methyl alcohol and the more stable tert-butyl iodide.

$$(CH_3)_3C - O - CH_3 \xrightarrow{H^+} (CH_3)_3 \overset{+}{C} + HOCH_3$$
$$\text{(more stable)}$$

(1 Mark)

21. Given, $k_1 = 2 \times 10^{-2}$, $k_2 = 4 \times 10^{-2}$
$T_1 = 300K$, $T_2 = 310\,K$

$$\log\left(\frac{k_2}{k_1}\right) = \frac{E_a}{2.303R}\left(\frac{T_2 - T_1}{T_1 T_2}\right)$$ **(1 Mark)**

$$\log 2 = \frac{E_a}{2.303 \times 8.314}\left(\frac{310 - 300}{300 \times 310}\right)$$

$$\Rightarrow E_a = \frac{0.301 \times 2.303 \times 8.314 \times 300 \times 310}{10}$$ **(1 Mark)**

$$= 53.598\,kJ\,mol^{-1}$$ **(1 Mark)**

22. (i) **Brownian movement :** The continuous zig-zag movement of the colloidal particles in a colloidal solution is called Brownian movement. The molecules of dispersion medium due to their kinetic motion strike against the colloidal particles from the sides with different forces. **(1 Mark)**

(ii) **Peptization :** The dispersion of freshly precipitated substance into colloidal solution by the addition of some electrolytes having one common ion is known as peptization. **(1 Mark)**

 *Note*

The electrolyte used is called peptizing agent e.g., a freshly precipitated $Fe(OH)_3$ is converted into colloidal solution by adding small quantity of $FeCl_3$ to the solution of $Fe(OH)_3$.

(iii) **Multimolecular colloids :** They are formed by the aggregation of a large number of atoms or molecules which generally have diameters less than 1 nm. Their molecular masses are not very high. Their atoms or molecules are held together by weak van der Waal's forces. *e.g.,* : sols of gold, sulphur, etc. **(1 Mark)**

SECTION - D

23. (i) Some of the values displayed by Mr. Lugani are awareness, intelligence, decision making and concern for health of students. **(1 Mark)**

(ii) A student can spread awareness about the concerned issue in following manners :

(a) One should take part and encourage others to be a part of nutritional awareness compaigns.

(b) One should educate friends and neighbourhood about the issue.

(c) One can convince and motivate other students to form a health commitee with catchy names i.e., "eat healthy stay healthy." **(1 Mark)**

(iii) **Antidepressants :** These drugs are given to patients with shattered confidence. These produce a feeling of well being and confidence in the person of depressed mood. Therefore, these are also called mood booster drugs. The common examples are vitalin, cocaine, methedrine etc. **(1 Mark)**

(iv) Saccharine, aspartame or alitame may be used in the preparation of sweets for a diabetic patient.

(1 Mark)

SECTION - E

24. $$Mg + Cu^{2+} \longrightarrow Mg^{2+} + Cu$$

$$E_{cell} = E^{\circ}_{cell} - \left[\frac{0.0591}{2} \log \frac{[Mg^{2+}]}{[Cu^{2+}]}\right]$$ **(1 Mark)**

$$= \left[0.34 - (-2.37)\right] - \left[\frac{0.0591}{2} \log \frac{10^{-3}}{10^{-4}}\right]$$ **(1 Mark)**

$$= 2.71 - 0.02955(\log 10)$$
$$= 2.68\,V$$ **(1 Mark)**

$$\Delta G = -nFE_{cell}$$ **(1 Mark)**
$$= -2 \times 96500 \times 2.68\,J$$
$$= -517240\,J\,mol^{-1} = -517.24\,kJ\,mol^{-1}$$ **(1 Mark)**

OR

(a) $$\lambda_m = \frac{\kappa \times 1000}{\text{Molarity}}$$ **(½ Mark)**

Molarity $= 0.20\,mol\,L^{-1}$,
$\kappa = 2.48 \times 10^{-2}\,S\,cm^{-1}$

$$\lambda_m = \frac{2.48 \times 10^{-2} \times 1000}{0.20}\,S\,cm^2\,mol^{-1}$$

$$= 124\,S\,cm^2\,mol^{-1}$$ **(1 Mark)**

Degree of dissociation,

$$\alpha = \frac{\lambda_m^c}{\lambda_m^\infty}$$

$$\lambda_m^\infty = \lambda^{\circ}_{(K^+)} + \lambda^{\circ}_{(Cl^-)}$$
$$= (73.5 + 76.5)\,S\,cm^2\,mol^{-1}$$
$$= 150.0\,S\,cm^2\,mol^{-1}$$ **(½ Mark)**

$$\alpha = \frac{124}{150} = 0.826$$

or 82.6% **(1 Mark)**

(b) Mercury cell is a type of primary battery. In primary batteries, the charging reaction occurs only once and after it has been used over a period of time, the battery becomes dead and cannot be reused.

Mercury cell is more advantageous than dry cell because dry cell has a very short life span due to the conversion of zinc to zinc chloride that makes the zinc casing porous. Due to this porous casing, the substance inside the cell leaks out and corrodes the metal, reducing the lifespan of the cell. While, in the case of mercury cell, the overall reaction does not involve formation of any ion in the solution whose concentration can change during its life time.

(1 + 1 = 2 Marks)

25. (a) (i) Zr and Hf have similar atomic radii due to lanthanide contraction. In lanthanoid series, with increasing atomic number, there is a progressive decrease in atomic as well as ionic radii of trivalent ions from La^{3+} to Lu^{3+}. This regular decrease in the atomic and the ionic radii of lanthanoids with increasing atomic number is known as lanthanoid contraction. Lanthanoid contraction, causes the radii of the members of the 3rd transition series to be very similar to those of the corresponding members of the 2nd series. **(1 Mark)**

(ii) The transition elements show variable oxidation states because the energies of $(n-1)d$ orbitals and ns orbitals are very close. Hence, electrons from both of these orbitals can participate in bonding. **(1 Mark)**

(iii) Copper (I) compound are unstable in aqueous solution and undergo disproportionation to give more stable Cu^{2+} and Cu.

$$2Cu^+ \longrightarrow Cu^{2+} + Cu$$

The high stability of Cu^{2+} (aq) rather than Cu^+ (aq) is due to the much more negative $\Delta_{hyd} H$ of Cu^{2+} (aq) than Cu^+ (aq), which is more than that compensates for the second ionisation enthalpy of Cu. **(1 Mark)**

(b) (i) $2MnO_2 + 4KOH + O_2 \longrightarrow$ **(1 Mark)**
$$2K_2MnO_4 + 2H_2O$$

(ii) $2Na_2CrO_4 + 2H^+ \longrightarrow Na_2Cr_2O_7$ **(1 Mark)**
$$+ 2Na^+ + H_2O$$

OR

(a) (i) $E^{\circ}_{M^{2+}/M}$ for any metal is related to the sum of enthalpy changes taking place in following steps :

$$M(s) + \Delta_a H \rightarrow M(g)$$

$$M(g) + \Delta_i H \rightarrow M^{2+}(g)$$
$$M^{2+}(g) \rightarrow M^{2+}(aq) + \Delta_{hyd}H$$

Cu has a high enthalpy of atomisation ($\Delta_a H$) and a low enthalpy of hydration ($\Delta_{hyd}H$). The high energy required to transform Cu(s) to Cu^{2+}(aq) is not balanced by its hydration enthalpy. Hence, $E^{\circ}(Cu^{2+}/Cu)$ is positive. **(1 Mark)**

(ii) $E^{\circ}_{Mn^{2+}/Mn}$ is highly negative because it is difficult to reduce Mn^{2+} to Mn as it has already half-filled d-orbital which leads to extra stability. However, Mn can be easily oxidized to Mn^{2+}. **(1 Mark)**

(iii) Cr^{2+} is a stronger reducing agent than Fe^{2+}. This is because $E^{\circ}(Cr^{3+}/Cr^{2+})$ is negative ($-0.41V$) whereas $E^{\circ}(Fe^{3+}/Fe^{2+})$ is positive ($+0.77V$). Thus, Cr^{2+} is easily oxidised to Cr^{3+} but Fe^{2+} cannot be easily oxidised to Fe^{3+}. **(1 Mark)**

(b) Actinoid elements show wide range of oxidation states due to comparable energies of $5f$, $6d$ and $7s$ levels.

(i) Electronic configuration: In both lathanoids and actionoids, f-orbitals are progressively filled. In lanthanoids $4f$- orbitals are progressively filled, whereas in actinoids $5f$-orbitals are progressively filled.

(ii) Oxidation states : Common oxidation state of lanthanoids and actinoids is +3. Some lanthanoids show +2 and +4 oxidation state also. Actinoids shows +3, +4, +5 +6, +7 oxidation states. Although +3 and +4 are most common.

(iii) Lanthanoids and actinoids both shows atomic/ionic size contraction.

(iv) Chemical reactivity: Both are highly reactive and exhibit similar chemical properties.

(1 + 1 = 2 Marks)

26. (a) $C_2H_3OCl \xrightarrow{H_2/Pd-BaSO_4} CH_3CHO$
(A)   Acetaldehyde (B)

$\downarrow$ dil NaOH Aldol reaction

$$CH_3 - \underset{\underset{\text{OH}}{|}}{CH} - CH_2 - CHO$$

β-hydroxy butyraldehyde (C)

$\downarrow$ Heat

$$CH_3CH = CHCHO$$
Crotonaldehyde (D)

(½ + ½ + ½ + ½ = 2 Marks)

$\therefore$ A = CH_3COCl

B = CH_3CHO

C = CH_3CH-CH_2CHO
                |
               OH

D = $CH_3CH=CH-CHO$

(b) (i) Benzaldehyde and acetophenone can be distinguished by iodoform test.

$C_6H_5COCH_3 + 3NaOI \longrightarrow$

$C_6H_5COONa + CHI_3 \downarrow + 2NaOH$
                         (Yellow ppt.)

$C_6H_5CHO + NaOI \longrightarrow$ No yellow ppt.

(1 Mark)

(ii) Benzoic acid and methyl benzoate can be distinguished by $NaHCO_3$ test.

$C_6H_5COOH + NaHCO_3 \longrightarrow$
Benzoic acid

$\qquad\qquad C_6H_5COO^-Na^+ H_2O + CO_2 \uparrow$
$\qquad\qquad$ Sodiumbenzoate

$C_6H_5COOCH_3 + NaHCO_3 \longrightarrow$ No CO_2
is formed   **(1 Mark)**

$$\overset{4}{C}H_3 - \overset{3}{C}H_2 - \overset{2}{\underset{\overset{|}{CH_3}}{C}}H - \overset{1}{C}HO$$

(c)   **(1 Mark)**
2-Methylbutanal

OR

(a) (i) $CH_3COCH_3 \xrightarrow{Zn-Hg/conc.HCl}$
Propanone

$\qquad\qquad\qquad CH_3CH_2CH_3$
$\qquad\qquad\qquad$ Propane

(1 Mark)

(ii) $CH_3COCH_3 \xrightarrow[H^+]{H_2N-NHCONH_2}$
Propanone

$CH_3-\underset{\overset{|}{CH_3}}{C}=NNHCONH_2 + H_2O$
Propanone semicarbazone

(1 Mark)

Note

H_2N, NH, $CONH_2$ contains three nucleophilc centre i.e., $-NH_2$, $-NH-$, $-CONH_2$, $-NH_2$ is more pronounce to attack on a electrophilic centre because its lone pair is more located at nitrogen atom compared to other which has its lone pair in conjugation with $-CO$ group.

(iii) $CH_3COCH_3 \xrightarrow[(ii)H_3O^+]{(i)CH_3MgBr} CH_3-\underset{\overset{|}{CH_3}}{\overset{\overset{OH}{|}}{C}}-CH_3$
Propanone
tert-butyl alcohol
(1 Mark)

(b) The increasing order of boiling points is :
$CH_3CHO < C_2H_5OH < CH_3COOH$ **(1 Mark)**

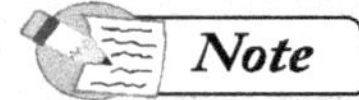

Note

The lowest boiling point of acetaldehyde is due to absence of H–bonding whereas both ethanol and acetic acid have H–bonding present in them. Now, the boiling point of acetic acid is higher due to stronger intermolecular H – bonding in it, which is due to the fact that the O – H bond in carboxylic acid is more polarized due to the presence of electron withdrawing carbonyl $\diagup C = O$ group. Moreover, the negatively polarized oxygen atom of one molecule of acetic acid can form H – bond with H-atom of the other molecule. Due to this acetic acid has higher boiling point than ethanol.

(c) $CH_3CH_2COCH_3$ gives iodoform test while CH_3CH_2CHO does not give this test.

$CH_3CH_2COCH_3 + 3NaOI \longrightarrow$

$\qquad CHI_3\downarrow + CH_3CH_2COONa + 2NaOH$
$\qquad$ Iodoform   **(1 Mark)**

CBSE Board Solved Paper

Time Allowed : 3 Hours   *Maximum Marks : 70*

General Instructions:
(i) All questions are compulsory.
(ii) Section A : Question number **1** to **5** are very short answer questions and carry **1** mark each.
(iii) Section B : Question number **6** to **10** are short answer questions and carry **2** marks each.
(iv) Section C : Question number **11** to **22** are also short answer questions and carry **3** marks each.
(v) Section D : Question number **23** is a value based question and carry **4** marks.
(vi) Section D : Question number **24** to **26** are long answer questions and carry **5** marks each.
(vii) Use log tables if necessary. Use of calculators is not allowed.

SECTION - A

1. What is the basicity of H_3PO_4 ?

2. Write the IUPAC name of the given compound:

NO_2–[ring]–OH / NO_2

3. Which would undergo S_N2 reaction faster in the following pair and why ?

$$CH_3 - CH_2 - Br \text{ and } CH_3 - \overset{\overset{\displaystyle CH_3}{|}}{\underset{\underset{\displaystyle Br}{|}}{C}} - CH_3$$

4. Out of $BaCl_2$ and KCl, which one is more effective in causing coagulation of a negatively charged colloidal sol ? Give reason.

5. what is the formula of a compound in which the element Y forms *ccp* lattice and atoms of X occupy $1/3^{rd}$ of tetrahedral voids ?

SECTION - B

6. What are the transition elements ? Write two characteristics of the transition elements.

7. (i) Write down the IUPAC name of the following complex:

$[Cr(NH_3)_2Cl_2(en)]Cl$ (en = ethylenediamine)

  (ii) Write the formula for the following complex :

Pentaamminenitrito-o-Cobalt (III).

8. Name the reagents used in the following reactions :

(i) $CH_3 - CO - CH_3 \xrightarrow{\ ?\ } CH_3 - \underset{\underset{\displaystyle OH}{|}}{CH} - CH_3$

(ii) $C_6H_5 - CH_2 - CH_3 \xrightarrow{\ ?\ } C_6H_5 - COO^-K^+$

9. What is meant by positive deviations from Raoult's law ? Give an example. What is the sign of $\Delta_{mix}H$ for positive deviation ?

OR

Define azeotropes. What type of azeotrope is formed by positive deviation from Raoult's law ? Give an example.

10. (a) Following reactions occur at cathode during the electrolysis of aqueous silver chloride solution :

$$Ag^+(aq) + e^- \longrightarrow Ag(s) \quad E° = +0.80 \text{ V}$$
$$H^+(aq) + e^- \longrightarrow \frac{1}{2}H_2(g) \quad E° = 0.00 \text{ V}$$

On the basis of their standard reduction electrode potential ($E°$) values, which reaction is feasible at the cathode and why ?

(b) Define limiting molar conductivity. Why conductivity of an electrolyte solution decreases with the decrease in concentration ?

SECTION - C

11. 3.9 g of benzoic acid dissolved in 49 g of benzene shows a depression in freezing point of 1.62 K. Calculate the van't Hoff factor and predict the nature of solute (associated or dissociated).

(Given : Molar mass of benzoic acid = 122 g mol^{-1}, K_f for benzene = 4.9 K kg mol^{-1})

12. (i) Indicate the principle behind the method used for the refining of zinc.

(ii) What is the role of silica in the extraction of copper ?

(iii) Which form of the iron is the purest form of commercial iron ?

13. An element with molar mass 27 g mol^{-1} forms a cubic unit cell with edge length 4.05×10^{-8} cm. If its density is 2.7 g cm^{-3}, what is the nature of the cubic unit cell ?

14. (a) How would you account for the following

    (i) Actinoid contraction is greater than lanthanoid contraction.

    (ii) Transition metals form coloured compounds.

  (b) Complete the following equation :

$$2MnO_4^- + 6H^+ + 5NO_2^- \longrightarrow$$

15. (i) Draw the geometrical isomers of complex $[Pt(NH_3)_2Cl_2]$.

  (ii) On the basis of crystal field theory, write the electronic configuration for d^4 ion if $\Delta_0 < P$.

  (iii) Write the hybridisation and magnetic behaviour of the complex $[Ni(CO)_4]$.

    (At.no. of Ni = 28)

16. Calculate emf of the following cell at 25 °C :

Fe | Fe^{2+} (0.001 M) || H$^+$(0.01 M) | H$_2$(g) (1 bar) | Pt(s)

$E°(Fe^{2+} | Fe) = -0.44$ V, $E°(H^+ | H_2) = 0.00$ V

17. Give reasons for the following observations :

  (i) Leather gets hardened after tanning.

  (ii) Lyophilic sol is more stable than lyophobic sol.

  (iii) It is necessary to remove CO when ammonia is prepared by Haber's process.

18. Write the names and structures of the monomers of the following polymers :

  (i) Nylon-6, 6

  (ii) PHBV

  (iii) Neoprene

19. Predict the products of the following reactions :

  (i) $CH_3 - C = O \xrightarrow[\text{(ii) KOH/Glycol, } \Delta]{\text{(i) } H_2N-NH_2} ?$ (with CH_3 below the carbonyl carbon)

  (ii) $C_6H_5 - CO - CH_3 \xrightarrow{NaOH/I_2} ? + ?$

  (iii) $CH_3 COONa \xrightarrow[\Delta]{NaOH/CaO} ?$

20. How do you convert the following :

  (i) Phenol to anisole

  (ii) Propan-2-ol to 2-methylpropan-2-ol

  (iii) Aniline to phenol

OR

  (a) Write the mechanism of the following reaction :

$$2CH_3CH_2OH \xrightarrow{H^+} CH_3CH_2 - O - CH_2CH_3$$

  (b) Write the equation involved in the acetylation of salicylic acid.

21. (i) Which one of the following is a disaccharide : Starch, Maltose, Fructose, Glucose ?

  (ii) What is the difference between fibrous protein and globular protein ?

  (iii) Write the name of vitamin whose deficiency causes bone deformities in children.

22. Give reasons :

  (a) *n*-Butyl bromide has higher boiling point than *t*-butyl bromide.

  (b) Racemic mixture is optically inactive.

  (c) The presence of nitro group ($-NO_2$) at o/p positions increases the reactivity of haloarenes towards nucleophilic substitution reactions.

SECTION - D

23. Mr. Roy, the principal of one reputed school organized a seminar in which he invited parents and principals to discuss the serious issue of diabetes and depression in students. They all resolved this issue by strictly banning the junk food in schools and to introduce healthy snacks and drinks like soup, lassi, milk etc. in school canteens. They also decided to make compulsory half an hour physical activities for the students in the morning assembly daily. After six months, Mr. Roy conducted the health survey in most of the schools and discovered a tremendous improvement in the health of students.

After reading the above passage, answer the following :

  (i) What are the values (at least two) displayed by Mr. Roy ?

  (ii) As a student, how can you spread awareness about this issue ?

  (iii) What are tranquilizers ? Give an example.

  (iv) Why is use of aspartame limited to cold foods and drinks ?

SECTION - E

24. (a) Account for the following :

    (i) Acidic character increases from HF to HI.

    (ii) There is large difference between the melting and boiling points of oxygen and sulphur.

    (iii) Nitrogen does not form pentahalide.

  (b) Draw the structures of the following :

    (i) ClF_3 (ii) XeF_4

OR

(i) Which allotrope of phosphorus is more reactive and why ?

(ii) How the supersonic jet aeroplanes are responsible for the depletion of ozone layers ?

(iii) F_2 has lower bond dissociation enthalpy than Cl_2. Why ?

(iv) Which noble gas is used in filling balloons for meteorological observations ?

(v)   Complete the equation :

$$XeF_2 + PF_5 \longrightarrow$$

25.   An aromatic compound 'A' of molecular formula C_7H_7ON undergoes a series of reactions as shown below. Write the structures of A, B, C, D and E in the following reactions :

$$(C_7H_7ON) \xrightarrow{Br_2 + KOH} C_6H_5NH_2 \xrightarrow[273\ K]{NaNO_2 + HCl} B \xrightarrow{CH_3CH_2OH} C$$

A

$C_6H_5NH_2 \xrightarrow{CHCl_3 + NaOH} D$

$B \xrightarrow{KI} E$

OR

(a)   Write the structures of main products when aniline reacts with the following reagents :

(i) Br_2 water

(ii)   HCl

(iii) $(CH_3CO)_2O$ / pyridine

(b)   Arrange the following in the increasing order of their boiling point :

$C_2H_5NH_2, C_2H_5OH, (CH_3)_3N$

(c)   Give a simple chemical test to distinguish between the following pair of compounds :

$(CH_3)_2NH$ and $(CH_3)_3N$

26.   For the hydrolysis of methyl acetate in aqueous solution, the following results were obtained :

t/s	0	30	60
$[CH_3COOCH_3]/mol\ L^{-1}$	0.60	0.30	0.15

(i)   Show that it follows pseudo first order reaction, as the concentration of water remains constant.

(ii)   Calculate the average rate of reaction between the time interval 30 to 60 seconds.

(Given $\log 2 = 0.3010$, $\log 4 = 0.6021$)

OR

(a)   For a reaction $A + B \longrightarrow P$, the rate is given by

$$Rate = k[A]\,[B]^2$$

(i)   How is the rate of reaction affected if the concentration of B is doubled ?

(ii)   What is the overall order of reaction if A is present in large excess ?

(b)   A first order reaction takes 30 minutes for 50% completion. Calculate the time required for 90% completion of this reaction.

$(\log 2 = 0.3010)$

Solutions

SECTION - A

1. Basicity of H_3PO_4 is 3. **(1 Mark)**

Note

H_3PO_4 *has three acidic hydrogen.*

2.

$$NO_2 \overset{5}{\underset{4}{\bigcirc}}\overset{6}{\underset{3}{}}\,OH,\ NO_2$$

2, 5-dinitrophenol or 2, 5-dinitrohydroxy benzene

(1 Mark)

3. $CH_3\ CH_2$—Br undergo S_N2 reaction faster than

$$H_3C-\underset{\underset{Br}{\overset{\overset{CH_3}{|}}{|}}}{C}-CH_3$$ because tertiary alkyl halides have more

stearic hinderence as compared to primary alkyl halides.

(1 Mark)

4. $BaCl_2$ is more effective in causing coagulation of a negatively charged colloidal sol. Because in KCl, K^+ and in $BaCl_2\ Ba^{2+}$ ions are present. According to Hardy-Schulze rule, greater the valency of a flocculating ion, greater will be its power to cause precipitation. **(1 Mark)**

5. Number of octahedral voids = Y

Number of tetrahedral voids = 2Y

'X' atoms occupics $=\dfrac{1}{3}\times$ no. of tetrahedral voids

$$=\dfrac{1}{3}\times 2Y\ =\dfrac{2}{3}Y$$

$\therefore$ Ratio $X:Y=\dfrac{2}{3}:1$

Hence formula of the compound is X_2Y_3. **(1 Mark)**

SECTION - B

6. The elements having incomplete $(n-1)d$-sub-shell are called d-block element or transition element.

The name transition given to the elements of d-block because they are placed between s-block and p-block elements. **(1 Mark)**

Characteristic of transition metal (element) are as follows.

1. Transition elements show variable oxidation state.

2. Transition elements have tendency to form complex.

(1 Mark)

7. (i) $[Cr(NH_3)_2\ Cl_2(en)]Cl$

diammindichloridoethylenediamine chromium (III) Chloride. **(1 Mark)**

(ii) Pentaaminenitrito o-cobalt(III)

$[(Co(NH_3)_5\ (ONO)]^{2+}$ **(1 Mark)**

8. (i) $CH_3-CO-CH_3 \xrightarrow{NaBH_4} CH_3-\underset{\underset{OH}{|}}{CH}-CH_3$

(1 Mark)

(ii) $C_6H_5-CH_2-CH_3 \xrightarrow[\text{Heat}]{KMnO_4-KOH} C_6H_5-COO^-\ K^+$

(1 Mark)

9. **Positive Deviation:** When the experimently determined vapour pressures of a binary liquid-liquid solution having different compositions are greater than calculated values of vapour pressure using Raoult's law, this is known as positive deviation.

In positive deviation the interaction between A-B is weaker than A-A and B-B. Where A and B are the two constituents liquid of binary solution. **(2 Marks)**

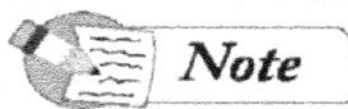

Note

In positive deviation the interaction between $A-B$ is weaker than $A-A$ and $B-B$ while in negative deviation the interaction between $A-A$ and $B-B$ is weaker than $A-B$. Where A and B are the two constituents liquids of binary solution.

OR

Azeotropes are the binary mixtures of solution that have the same composition in liquid and vapour phases and that have constant boiling points.

A minimum boiling azeotrope is formed by solutions showing a large positive deviation from Raoult's law at a specific composition.

Example: An ethanol – water mixture containing approximately 95% ethanol by volume. **(2 Marks)**

10. (a) We have given

$$Ag^+(aq) + e^- \longrightarrow Ag(s) \qquad E^\circ = +0.80\ V$$

$$H^+(aq) + e^- \longrightarrow \dfrac{1}{2}H_2(g) \qquad E^\circ = 0.00\ V$$

The relationship between the standard free energy change and emf of a cell reaction is given by

$$\Delta G^\circ = -nFE^\circ_{(cell)}$$

Thus, the more positive the standard reduction potential of a reaction, the more negative is the standard free energy change associated with the process, and consequently, the higher is the feasibility of the reaction.

Since $E^\circ_{Ag^+/Ag}$ has a greater positive value than $E^\circ_{H^+/H}$, the reaction which is feasible at the cathode is given by

$$Ag^+(aq) + e^- \longrightarrow Ag(s) \qquad \textbf{(1 Mark)}$$

(b) **Limiting Molar Conductivity:** At infinite dilution or at approximately zero concentration

$(V \to \infty, C \to 0)$ the molar conductivity attain limiting value and become constant. At infinite dilution, this limiting value of electrolyte is expressed by limiting molar conductivity (Λ°_m).

Conductivity of an electrolyte solution decreases with the decrease in concentration because with decrease in concentration number of ions per unit volume decreases. **(1 Mark)**

SECTION - C

11. $\Delta T_f = K_f \times \text{molality}$

$$\text{Molality} = \frac{3.9 \times 1000}{122 \times 49} = 0.612 \text{ m} \qquad \textbf{(½ Mark)}$$

Now, $\Delta T_f = 4.9 \times 0.612 = 2.99$ K **(1 Mark)**

$$i = \frac{\text{observed } \Delta T_f}{\text{calculated } \Delta T_f} \qquad \textbf{(½ Mark)}$$

ΔT_f observed $= 1.62$ K (given)

$$\therefore \quad i = \frac{1.62}{2.99} = 0.54$$

As $i < 1$, benzoic acid is an associated solute. **(1 Mark)**

12. (i) Zinc is refined using electrolytic refining process. In this method pure metal strip is used as cathode and impure metal as anode. Both cathode and anode are taken in electrolyte which is a soluble salt of the same metal. The more basic metal remains in the electrolytic solution and the less basic metals, present as impurities, precipitate as anode mud.

at anode: $Zn \rightarrow Zn^{2+} + 2e^-$
                          (from anode)

at cathode: $Zn^{2+} + 2e^- \rightarrow Zn$ **(1 Mark)**
                          (from electrolyte)

(ii) Ores of copper contain iron oxide as impurity. Silica reacts with iron oxide and forms iron silicate which is removed as slag.

$$FeO \; + \; SiO_2 \longrightarrow FeSiO_3$$

Iron oxide	Silica	Iron silicate
(impurity)	(flux)	(slag)

(1 Mark)

(iii) Wrought iron is the purest form of commercial iron. It contains 98.8–99.9% iron and rest is C, Si, P, Mn etc impurity. **(1 Mark)**

Puddling process is the method by which pig iron is converted to wrought iron by subjecting it to heat and frequent stirring in a furnace in the presence oxidizing substances.

13. Molar mass of the given element, $M = 27$ g mol^{-1}

Edge length, $a = 4.05 \times 10^{-8}$ cm

Density, $d = 2.7$ g cm^{-3}

We know that

$$d = \frac{Z \times M}{a^3 \times N_A} \qquad \textbf{(1 Mark)}$$

where, Z is the number of atom in the unit cell and N_A is the Avogadro number.

Thus,

$$Z = \frac{d \times a^3 \times N_A}{M}$$

$$= \frac{2.7 \times (4.05 \times 10^{-8})^3 \times 6.022 \times 10^{23}}{27} = 4 \quad \textbf{(1 Mark)}$$

So the number of atoms in the unit cell is 4. Therefore the given cubic unit cell has a face-centre cubic (*fcc*) or cubic closed structure. **(1 Mark)**

14. (a) (i) In actinoids, *5f*-orbitals are filled. So these element show actinoid contraction due to poor shielding effect of *5f*-subshells. So the effective nuclear charge experienced by electrons in valence shells in case of actinoids is much more than that experienced by electrons in valence shells in case of lanthanoids. Hence, the size contraction in actinoids is greater than that in lanthanoids. **(1 Mark)**

(ii) Transition metals form coloured compounds because under the influence of magnetic effect of ligands, *d*-subshell of metal is split into two groups name t_{2g} and e_g or t_{2g} this is called *d-d*-spliting, these two subsets have different energies and the difference between energies is equivalent to energy of visible light. Thus in a *d-d*-transition some wavelength of visible region are absorbed by the ion and complementary colour of reflected wavelength is seen. Hence they are coloured compound. **(1 Mark)**

(b) $2MnO_4^- + 6H^+ + 5NO_2^- \longrightarrow 2\,Mn^{2+} + 5\,NO_3^- + 3H_2O$
(1 Mark)

15. (i)

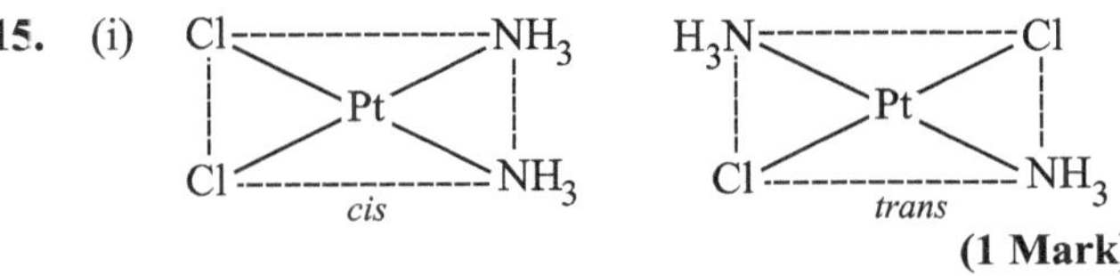

(1 Mark)

(ii) On the basis of crystal field theory, if $\Delta_o < P$, then high spin complex is formed. Therefore d^4 ion exhibit the electronic configuration as $t_{2g}^3 e_g^1$.

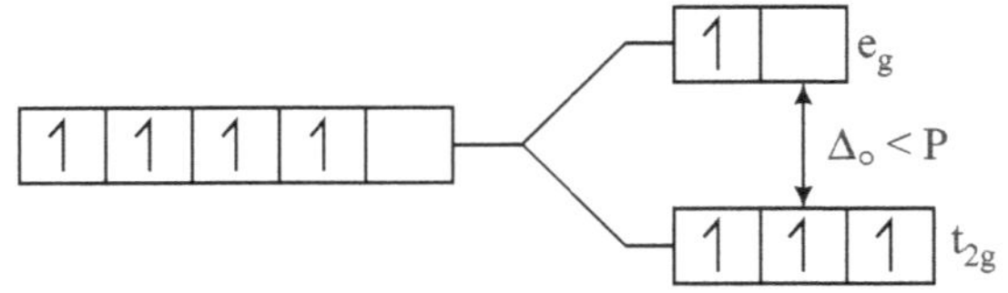

(1 Mark)

(iii) In $[Ni(CO)_4]$, Ni has zero oxidation state. **(1 Mark)** The hybridisation is sp^3 and complex is diamagnetic.

Note

Ni (28) $\Rightarrow 3d^8, 4s^2$

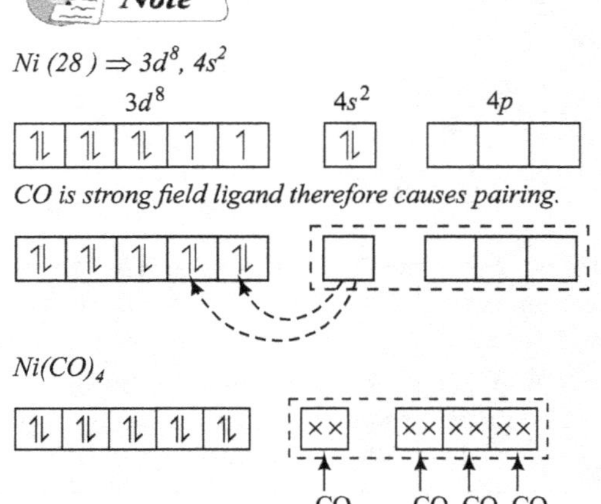

CO is strong field ligand therefore causes pairing.

$Ni(CO)_4$

16. For the given cell representation, the cell reaction will be
$$Fe(s) + 2H^+(aq) \longrightarrow Fe^{2+}(aq) + H_2(g)$$

The standard emf of the cell will be
$$E^\circ_{cell} = E^\circ_{(H^+/H_2)} - E^\circ_{(Fe^{2+}/Fe)}$$

$\Rightarrow E^\circ_{cell} = 0 - (-0.44) = 0.44\ V$ **(½ Mark)**

The Nernst equation for the cell
$$E_{cell} = E^\circ_{cell} - \left[\frac{0.0591}{2} \log \frac{[Fe^{2+}]}{[H^+]^2}\right]$$ **(1 Mark)**

$$= 0.44 - \left[\frac{0.0591}{2} \log \frac{0.001}{(0.01)^2}\right]$$

$$= 0.44 - [0.02955\ (\log 10)]$$ **(½ Mark)**

$$= 0.44 - 0.02955$$

$E_{cell} = 0.41\ V$ **(1 Mark)**

17. (i) The process of hardening of leather is known as tanning. Tanin contain negatively charged colloidal particles. Animal skin is also colloidal in nature and has positively charged particles. When they are soaked in tanin, mutual coagulation takes place and thus, leather becomes hard after tanning. **(1 Mark)**

(ii) Lyophilic sol is more stable than lyophobic sol due to two factors. One is charge and other is hydration of sol particles. In lyophilic colloids, a layer of dispersion medium is formed around the colloidal particles. Therefore colloidal particle do not come close to each other and the colloid gain stability.

(1 Mark)

(iii) CO is present as an impurity. The removal of impurities is necessary because they affect the catalytic activity of catalyst (iron catalyst). CO act as poison for iron catalyst in the Habber process.

(1 Mark)

18. (i) Nylon–6, 6 :

Monomer units:

$$H_2N—(CH_2)_6—NH_2 \text{ and } HO—\overset{O}{\overset{\|}{C}}—(CH_2)_4—\overset{O}{\overset{\|}{C}}—OH$$

Hexamethylene diamine Adipic acid

(1 Mark)

(ii) PHBV: Poly-β-hydroxybutyrate-co-β-hydroxy valerate

Monomer units :

$$CH_3—\overset{OH}{\overset{|}{CH}}—CH_2—\overset{O}{\overset{\|}{C}}—OH \text{ and}$$

3-Hydroxy butanoic acid

$$CH_3CH_2\overset{OH}{\overset{|}{CH}}—CH_2—\overset{O}{\overset{\|}{C}}—OH$$

3-Hydroxy pentanoic acid

(1 Mark)

(iii) Neoprene :

Monomer unit: $CH_2{=}CH—\overset{}{\underset{Cl}{\overset{|}{C}}}{=}CH_2$ **(1 Mark)**

Chloroprene

19. (i)
$$CH_3—\underset{CH_3}{\overset{|}{C}}{=}O \xrightarrow{H_2N—NH_2} \underset{H_3C}{\overset{H_3C}{>}}C{=}N—NH_2$$

Acetone phenyl hydrazine

$$\xrightarrow{KOH} \underset{H_3C}{\overset{H_3C}{>}}CH_2 + N_2$$

Propane

(1 Mark)

(ii) $C_6H_5—CO—CH_3 \xrightarrow{NaOH/I_2} CHI_3{\downarrow} + C_6H_5COONa$

Iodoform (yellow)

(1 Mark)

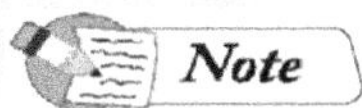

Note

The haloform reaction is the reaction of a methyl ketone with chlorine, bromine or iodine in the presence of hydroxide ions to give a carboxylate ion and a haloform. Only acetaldehyde is one among aldehydes which give haloform reaction. When the halogen used is iodine, the haloform reaction can be used to identify methyl ketones because iodoform is a yellow solid with a characteristic smell.

(iii) $CH_3COONa \xrightarrow{\text{NaOH/CaO}} CH_4 + Na_2CO_3$ **(1 Mark)**

Methane

20. (i) Phenol $+ NaOH \longrightarrow$ sodium phenoxide $\xrightarrow{CH_3Br}$ Anisole **(1 Mark)**

(ii) $CH_3-\underset{\underset{OH}{|}}{\overset{\overset{H}{|}}{C}}-CH_3 \xrightarrow[\text{(oxidation)}]{Cr_2O_7^{2-}/H^+} CH_3-\underset{\underset{O}{\|}}{C}-CH_3$

Propanone

$\xrightarrow{CH_3MgBr} CH_3-\underset{\underset{CH_3}{|}}{\overset{\overset{CH_3}{|}}{C}}-\bar{O}\overset{+}{M}g\,Br \xrightarrow{H_2O}$

Adduct

$Mg(OH)Br + CH_3-\underset{\underset{CH_3}{|}}{\overset{\overset{OH}{|}}{C}}-CH_3$

2-Methylpropan-2-ol **(1 Mark)**

(iii) aniline $\xrightarrow{NaNO_2 + HCl}$ Benzene diazonium chloride

$\xrightarrow[\text{warm}]{H_2O}$ phenol $+ N_2 + HCl$ **(1 Mark)**

OR

(a) The given reaction follows S_N2 mechanism as shown below.

Step 1:

$CH_3CH_2-\overset{..}{\underset{..}{O}}-H + H^+ \longrightarrow CH_3-CH_2-\underset{+}{\overset{\overset{H}{|}}{O}}-H$

(½ Mark)

Step 2:

$CH_3CH_2-\overset{..}{\underset{..}{O}}: + CH_3-CH_2-\overset{+}{O}\underset{\diagdown H}{\diagup H} \longrightarrow$

$CH_3CH_2-\underset{\underset{H}{|}}{\overset{+}{O}}-CH_2CH_3 + H_2O$ **(1 Mark)**

Step 3:

$CH_3CH_2-\underset{\underset{H}{|}}{\overset{+}{O}}-CH_2CH_3 \longrightarrow$

$CH_3CH_2-O-CH_2CH_3 + H^+$ **(½ Mark)**

(b) 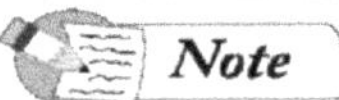 salicylic acid $+ (CH_3CO)_2O \xrightarrow{H^+}$

Acetic anhydride

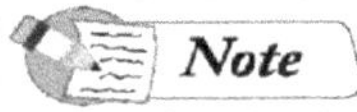 Aspirin $+ CH_3COOH$ **(1 Mark)**

Note

Synthesis of aspirin from salicylic acid occurs by acetylation in acidic medium. Salicylic acid react with acetic anhydride in presence of few drops of concentrated sulphuric acid. Acid initiate the process of detaching the acetate ion from aceticanhydride which later get associated with H+ ion from phenolic hydroxy group in salicylic acid to be eliminated as acetic acid.

21. (i) Maltose is a disaccharide, as it consist of two α-D glucose units. **(1 Mark)**

Note

Starch is a polysaccharide, whereas fructose and glucose are monosaccharides.

(ii)

Fibrous Protein	Globular Protein
(a) They are made up of parallel polypeptide chains which are held together with H-bond and disulphide bond.	The polypeptide chains in these protein are folded around themselves, giving these proteins a spherical structure.
(b) They are insoluble in water but soluble in strong acid and base	They are soluble in water, alkalies, salt solution and acid solution.

(1 Mark)

(iii) Deficiency of vitamin D causes bone deformities in children. **(1 Mark)**

22. (a) *n*-butyl bromide has higher boiling point than *t*-butyl bromide because in case of isomeric alkyl halide boiling point decrease as the branching in carbon increases. Straight chain molecule have larger surface area and therefore has stronger intermolecular forces. **(1 Mark)**

(b) Racemic mixture contains two enantiomers (*d*- and *l*-forms) in equal proportions and thus, the rotation due to one isomer is cancelled by the rotation due to another. Therefore, it has zero optical rotation and hence, it is optically inactive. **(1 Mark)**

(c) The presence of nitro groups ($-NO_2$) at-*o*/-*p* positions increases the reactivity of haloarenes towards nucleophilic substitution reaction because nitro groups ($-NO_2$) at-*o*/-*p* position withdraw the electron density from the benzene ring facilitating the attack of the nucleophile. The negative charge in the carbanion formed, at ortho and para position with respect to halogen atom, is stabilised through resonance and by the presence of nitro group ($-NO_2$). **(1 Mark)**

SECTION - D

23. (i) The values displayed by Mr. Roy are care and concern for the health of the students. He shows selfless service as he conducted seminars and health surveys in most of the schools. **(1 Mark)**

(ii) As a student, we can spread awareness about this issue by conducting seminars, health camps, debates, distribution of pamphlets, organising workshop by doctors, etc. **(1 Mark)**

(iii) Medicines which are used to reduce mental excitement and stress are called tranquillizers. They are used in psychological disorders. Example: chlorodiazepoxide **(1 Mark)**

(iv) Use of aspartame is limited to cold foods and drinks because it is unstable at temperatures achieved during cooking of food. **(1 Mark)**

SECTION - E

24. (a) (i) Acidic character increase from HF to HI due to increase in the size of the anion down the group $F^- < Cl^- < Br^- < I^-$, the size of iodine is largest, thus it has weakest bond with hydrogen and give largest acidity as removal of H^+ ion become easy. **(1 Mark)**

(ii) The oxygen exists as a diatomic molecule O_2 while sulphur exists as a polyatomic molecule S_8. Hence intermolecular forces of attraction are greater among sulphur molecule therefore sulphur is solids while oxygen is a gas. So there is a large difference between the melting and boiling point of oxygen and sulphur. **(1 Mark)**

(iii) Due to unavailability of vacant *d*-orbitals in outer shell of nitrogen, it can not expand it's octet. Hence, nitrogen does not form pentahalide. **(1 Mark)**

(b) (i) ClF_3 (ii) XeF_4

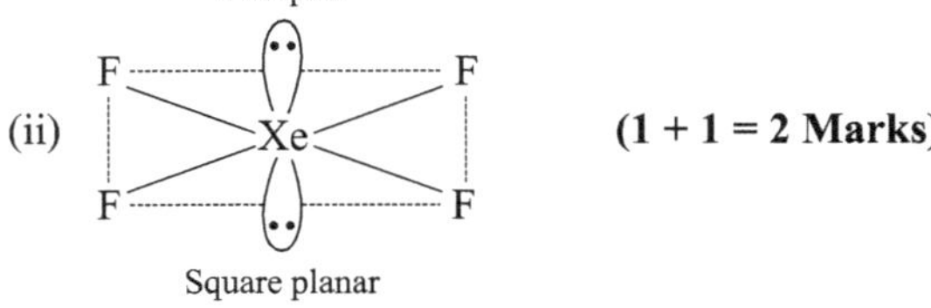

(i)

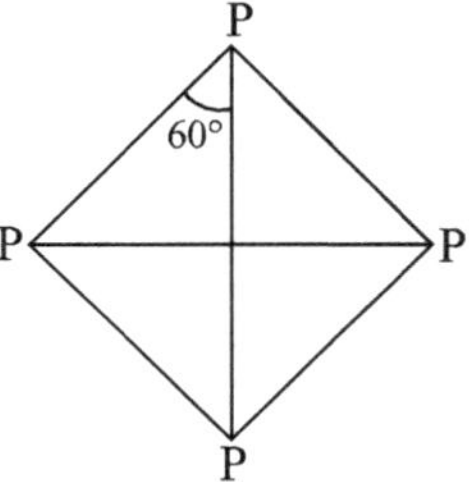

(ii)   **(1 + 1 = 2 Marks)**

OR

(i) White phosphorous is most reactive of all the allotropes of phosphorus because it is unstable due to the angular strain on P_4 molecule with the bond angle of 60°.

(1 Mark)

> *Note*
>
> *Diphosphorus (P_2) is the gaseous form of phosphorus that is thermodynamically stable above 1200°C and up to 2000°C. It can be generated by heating white phosphorus to 1100 K and is very reactive with bond dissociation energy 490 kJ/mol.*

(ii) Nitrogen oxide emitted from the exhausts of super sonic jet aeroplanes readily combine with ozone to form nitrogen dioxide and diatomic oxygen.

$$NO(g) + O_3(g) \longrightarrow NO_2(g) + O_2(g)$$

Since supersonic jets fly in the stratosphere near the ozone layer, they are responsible for the depletion of ozone layer. **(1 Mark)**

(iii) The size of a fluorine atom is very small as compared to a chlorine atom. Therefore the repulsion between electrons in the outer most shell of the two atoms in a fluorine molecule is much greater than that in chlorine molecule. Hence it required less energy to break up the fluorine molecule, making it's bond dissociation energy lesser than that of chlorine molecule. **(1 Mark)**

(iv) Helium gas is used in filling balloons for meteorological observation because it is light and non-inflammable and unreactive. **(1 Mark)**

(v) $XeF_2 + PF_5 \longrightarrow [XeF]^+ [PF_6]^-$ **(1 Mark)**

25. (a)

$$CONH_2 \xrightarrow{Br_2/KOH} (A) \longrightarrow NH_2 \xrightarrow[273\ K]{NaNO_2/HCl} (B) \longrightarrow N_2^+Cl^-$$

$$\xrightarrow{CHCl_3 + NaOH} NC \ (D)$$

$$N_2^+Cl^- \ (B) \xrightarrow{CH_3CH_2OH} (C)$$

$$\xrightarrow{KI} I \ (E)$$

(1 + 1 + 1 + 1 + 1 = 5 Marks)

OR

(a) (i)

$$NH_2 \ (Aniline) \xrightarrow{Br_2\ water} Br\text{-substituted } NH_2 \ (2,4,6\text{-tribromoaniline})$$ **(1 Mark)**

(ii)

$$NH_2 \ (Aniline) \xrightarrow{HCl} \overset{+}{N}H_3Cl^-$$ **(1 Mark)**

(iii)

$$NH_2 \ (Aniline) \xrightarrow{(CH_3CO)_2O/Pyridine} NHCOCH_3$$ **(1 Mark)**

(b) Increasing order of boiling point

$(CH_3)_2N < C_2H_5NH_2 < C_2H_5OH$ **(1 Mark)**

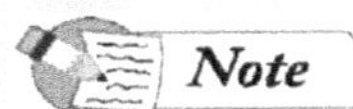

Note

Alcohols have higher boiling point as compared to that of amines because of strong intermolecular hydrogen bond. Oxygen is more electronegative than nitrogen, so, it forms strong hydrogen bond as compared to nitrogen. In tertiary amine, there is no hydrogen atom to form hydrogen bond and hence, it has the lowest boiling point.

(c) $(CH_3)_2$ NH reacts with benzenesulphonyl chloride to give sulfonamides.

$$\text{benzenesulphonyl chloride} + CH_3-\overset{H}{\underset{}{N}}-CH_3 \longrightarrow$$

$$O=\overset{O}{\underset{}{S}}-\overset{CH_3}{\underset{}{N}}-CH_3 + HCl$$

N, N-Dimethyl benzen sulphonamide

$(CH_3)_3$ N does not reacts with benzenesulphonyl chloride. **(1 Mark)**

26. (i) For the hydrolysis of methyl acetate to be a pseudo first-order reaction, the reaction should be first order with respect to ester when $[H_2O]$ is constant.

For first order reaction (rate constant is)

$$k = \frac{2.303}{t} \log \frac{a}{a-x}$$ **(½ Mark)**

Let $t_1 = 30$ sec, $t_2 = 60$ sec

$$k_1 = \frac{2.303}{30} \log \frac{0.60}{0.30}$$ **(½ Mark)**

$$= \frac{2.303}{30} \log 2$$

$$= \frac{2.303}{30} \times 0.3010 = 0.0231\ sec^{-1}$$ **(1 Mark)**

Now, $t_2 = 60$, $k_2 = ?$

$$k_2 = \frac{2.303}{t_2} \log \frac{0.60}{0.15}$$

$$= \frac{2.303}{60} \log 4 = \frac{2.303}{60} \times 0.6021 = 0.0231\ sec^{-1}$$

So $k_1 = k_2$ **(1 Mark)**

Hence the reaction is pseudo first order reaction.

(ii) Rate $= \dfrac{\Delta x}{\Delta t}$ **(½ Mark)**

$$= \frac{0.30 - 0.15}{60 - 30} = \frac{0.15}{30}$$ **(1 Mark)**

$$= 0.005\ mol\ L^{-1}\ sec^{-1}$$ **(½ Mark)**

OR

(i) It is given that the reaction is first order w.r.t reactant A and second order w.r.t reactant B.

$\therefore \quad r = k[A]\,[B]^2$ ...(i)

Where r is the rate of reaction and k is the rate constant of the reaction.

When concentration of B is doubled, then, let the new rate be r_1

$$r_1 = k[A][2B]^2 \qquad \qquad ...(ii)$$

Divide eqns (ii) by (i)

$$\frac{r_1}{r} = \frac{k[A][2B]^2}{k[A][B]^2}$$

$$\frac{r_1}{r} = 4$$

$\Rightarrow \quad r_1 = 4r$

thus if the concentration of B is doubled, rate of reaction increased by 4 times.   **(1 Mark)**

(ii) If A is present in large excess, then the reaction will be independent of the concentration of A and will be dependent only on the concentration of B. As $[B]^2$ will be the only determining factor in the rate equation the overall order of the reaction will be two.

(1 Mark)

(b) $t_1 = 30$ min, $a = 50\%$

Rate for 50%

$$k = \frac{2.303}{t_1} . \log \frac{100}{100 - 50}$$

$$k = \frac{2.303}{30} \log 2 \qquad \qquad ...(i) \quad \textbf{(1 Mark)}$$

For 90% completion, time required $t_2 = ?$, $a = 100$

$a - x = 100 - 90 = 10$

$$k = \frac{2.303}{t_2} \log \frac{a}{a - x} \qquad \qquad ...(ii)$$

$$k = \frac{2.303}{t_2} \log \frac{100}{100 - 90} = \frac{2.303}{t_2} \log 10$$

$$= \frac{2.303}{t_2} \qquad \qquad \textbf{(1 Mark)}$$

Put the value of k from eqn (i)

$$t_2 = \frac{2.303}{2.303} \times \frac{30}{\log 2} = \frac{30}{0.3010}$$

$$t_2 = 99.6 \text{ min} = 5.98 \times 10^3 \text{ sec.} \qquad \textbf{(1 Mark)}$$

All India *2014*
CBSE Board Solved Paper

Time Allowed: 3 Hours   *Maximum Marks: 70*

General Instructions:
(i) All question are compulsory.
(ii) Section A : Question number **1 to 8** are very short answer questions and carry **1** mark each.
(iii) Section B : Question number **9 to 18** are short answer questions and carry **2** marks each.
(iv) Section C : Question number **19 to 27** are also short answer questions and carry **3** marks each.
(v) Section D : Question number **28 to 30** are long answer questions and carry **5** marks each.
(vi) Use log tables, if necessary. Use of calculator is not allowed.

SECTION - A

1. What is the effect of temperature on chemisorption?

2. What is the role of zinc metal in the extraction of silver?

3. What is the basicity of H_3PO_3?

4. Identify the chiral molecule in the following pair:

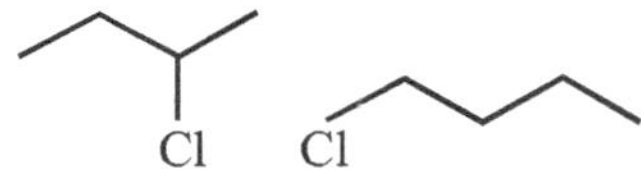

5. Which of the following is a natural polymer?
Buna-S, protein, PVC

6. The conversion of primary aromatic amines into diazonium salts is known as __________.

7. What are the products of hydrolysis of sucrose?

8. Write the structure of p-methylbenzaldehyde.

SECTION - B

9. An element with density 2.8 g cm^{-3} forms a *f.c.c.* unit cell with edge length 4×10^{-8} cm. Calculate the molar mass of the element.
(Given: $N_A = 6.022 \times 10^{23}$ mol^{-1})

10. (i) What type of non-stoichiometric point defect is responsible for the pink colour of LiCl?
(ii) What type of stoichiometric defect is shown by NaCl?

OR

How will you distinguish between the following pairs of terms:
(i) Tetrahedral and octahedral voids
(ii) Crystal lattice and unit cell

11. State Kohlrausch's law of independent migration of ions. Why does the conductivity of a solution decrease with dilution?

12. For a chemical reaction R $\longrightarrow$ P, the variation in the concentration (R) vs. time (t) plot is given as

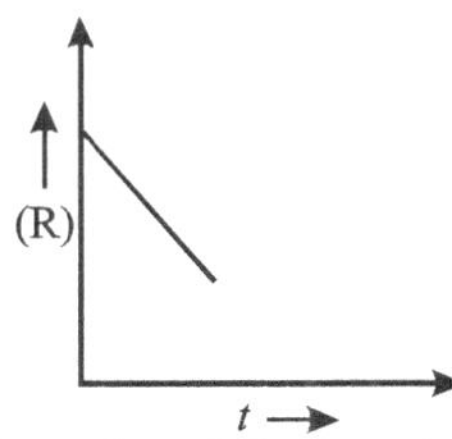

(i) Predict the order of the reaction.
(ii) What is the slope of the curve?

13. Explain the principle of the method of electrolytic refining of metals. Give one example.

14. Complete the following equations:
(i) $P_4 + H_2O \longrightarrow$ (ii) $XeF_4 + O_2F_2 \longrightarrow$

15. Draw the structures of the following:
(i) XeF_2 (ii) BrF_3

16. Write the equations involved in the following reactions:
(i) Reimer – Tiemann reaction
(ii) Williamson synthesis

17. Write the mechanism of the following reaction:
$$CH_3CH_2OH \xrightarrow{\text{HBr}} CH_3CH_2Br + H_2O$$

18. Write the names of monomers used for getting the following polymers:
(i) Bakelite
(ii) Neoprene

SECTION - C

19. (a) Calculate $\Delta_r G°$ for the reaction
$$Mg\ (s) + Cu^{2+}\ (aq) \rightarrow Mg^{2+}\ (aq) + Cu\ (s)$$
Given : $E°_{cell} = + 2.71$ V, 1 F = 96500 C mol^{-1}

(b) Name the type of cell which was used in Apollo space programme for providing electrical power.

20. The following data were obtained during the first thermal decomposition of SO_2Cl_2 at a constant volume.
$$SO_2Cl_2\ (g) \longrightarrow SO_2(g) + Cl_2(g)$$

Experiment	Time/s	Total pressure/atm
1	0	0.4
2	100	0.7

Calculate the rate constant.

(Given : log 4 = 0.6021; log 2 = 0.3010)

21. What are emulsions? What are their different types? Give one example of each type.

22. Give reasons for the following:
    (i) $(CH_3)_3P = O$ exists but $(CH_3)_3N = O$ does not.
    (ii) Oxygen has less electron gain enthalpy with negative sign than sulphur.
    (iii) H_3PO_2 is a stronger reducing agent than H_3PO_3.

23. (i)   Write the IUPAC name of the complex $[Cr(NH_3)_4Cl_2]Cl$.
    (ii) What type of isomerism is exhibited by the complex $[Co(en)_3]^{3+}$?
          (en = ethane-1,2-diamine)
    (iii) Why is $[NiCl_4]^{2-}$ paramagnetic but $[Ni(CO)_4]$ is diamagnetic?
          (At. nos. : Cr = 24, Co = 27, Ni = 28)

24. (a) Draw the structures of major monohalo products in each of the following reactions :
    (i)   ⬡—$CH_2OH \xrightarrow{PCl_5}$
    (ii) ⬡—$CH_2 – CH = CH_2 + HBr \longrightarrow$
    (b) Which halogen compound in each of the following pairs will react faster in S_N2 reaction:
    (i) CH_3Br or CH_3I
    (ii) $(CH_3)_3C – Cl$ or $CH_3– Cl$

25. Account for the following:
    (i)   Primary amines ($R\text{-}NH_2$) have higher boiling point than tertiary amines (R_3N).
    (ii) Aniline does not undergo Friedel - Crafts reactions:
    (iii) $(CH_3)_2NH$ is more basic than $(CH_3)_3N$ in an aqueous solution.

OR

Give the structures of A, B and C in the following reactions:

(i) $C_6H_5NO_2 \xrightarrow{Sn+HCl} A \xrightarrow[273K]{NaNO_2+HCl} B \xrightarrow{H_2O} C$

(ii) $CH_3CN \xrightarrow[A]{H_2O/H^+} A \xrightarrow[\Delta]{NH_3} B \xrightarrow{Br_2+KOH} C$

26. Define the following terms as related to proteins:
    (i)   Peptide linkage   (ii) Primary structure
    (iii) Denaturation

27. On the occasion of World Health Day, Dr. Satpal organized a 'health camp' for the poor farmers living in a nearby village. After check-up, he was shocked to see that most of the farmers suffered from cancer due to regular exposure to pesticides and many were diabetic. They distributed free medicines to them. Dr. Satpal immediately reported the matter to the National Human Rights Commission (NHRC). On the suggestions of NHRC, the government decided to provide medical care, financial assistance, setting up of super-speciality hospitals for treatment and prevention of the deadly disease in the affected villages all over India.

(i)   Write the values shown by
      (a) Dr. Satpal   (b) NHRC
(ii) What type of analgesics are chiefly used for the relief of pains of terminal cancer?
(iii) Give an example of artificial sweetener that could have been recommended to diabetic patients.

SECTION - D

28. (a) Define the following terms :
        (i)   Molarity
        (ii) Molal elevation constant (K_b)
    (b) A solution containing 15 g urea (molar mass = 60 g mol^{-1}) per litre of solution in water has the same osmotic pressure (isotonic) as a solution of glucose (molar mass = 180 g mol^{-1}) in water. Calculate the mass of glucose present in one litre of its solution.

OR

(a) What type of deviation is shown by a mixture of ethanol and acetone? Give reason.
(b) A solution of glucose (molar mass = 180 g mol^{-1}) in water is labelled as 10% (by mass). What would be the molality and molarity of the solution?
     (Density of solution = 1.2 g mL^{-1})

29. (a) Complete the following equations :
        (i) $Cr_2O_7^{2-} + 2OH^- \longrightarrow$
        (ii) $MnO_4^- + 4H^+ + 3e^- \longrightarrow$
    (b) Account for the following :
        (i)   Zn is not considered as a transition element.
        (ii) Transition metals form a large number of complexes.
        (iii) The E° value for the Mn^{3+}/Mn^{2+} couple is much more positive than that for Cr^{3+}/Cr^{2+} couple.

OR

(i)   With reference to structural variability and chemical reactivity, write the differences between lanthanoids and actinoids.
(ii) Name a member of the lanthanoid series which is well known to exhibit +4 oxidation state.
(iii) Complete the following equation :
      $MnO_4^- + 8H^+ + 5e^- \longrightarrow$
(iv) Out of Mn^{3+} and Cr^{3+}, which is more paramagnetic and why?
      (Atomic nos. : Mn = 25, Cr = 24)

30. (a) Write the products formed when CH_3CHO reacts with the following reagents:
        (i)   HCN   (ii) $H_2N–OH$
        (iii) CH_3CHO in the presence of dilute NaOH
    (b) Give simple chemical tests to distinguish between the following pairs of compounds:
        (i)   Benzoic acid and Phenol
        (ii) Propanal and Propanone

OR

(a) Account for the following:
    (i) $Cl–CH_2COOH$ is a stronger acid than CH_3COOH.
    (ii) Carboxylic acids do not give reactions of carbonyl group.
(b) Write the chemical equations to illustrate the following name reactions:
    (i)   Rosenmund reduction (ii) Cannizzaro's reaction
(c) Out of $CH_3CH_2–CO–CH_2–CH_3$ and $CH_3CH_2–CH_2–CO–CH_3$, which gives iodoform test?

Solutions

SECTION - A

1. Chemical adsorption increases with increase of temperature upto certain limit and than after it starts decreasing. **(1 Mark)**

2. During leaching, Ag forms a soluble complex with CN^- i.e. $[Ag(CN)_2]^-$. The metal is recovered from this complex by displacement reaction using a more electropositive zinc metal.

$$2[Ag(CN)_2]^-\,(aq) + Zn(s) \longrightarrow 2Ag(s) + [Zn(CN)_4]^{2-}\,(aq)$$

(1 Mark)

3. The structure of H_3PO_3 is:

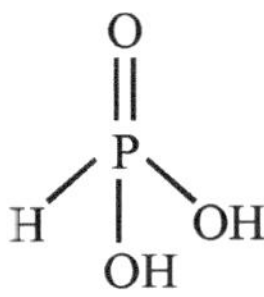

Thus basicity of H_3PO_3 is two. **(1 Mark)**

> **Note**
>
> *Generally, Basicity depends on the number of H-atoms attached to O.*

4.     **(1 Mark)**

> **Note**
>
> *A chiral molecule has atleast one C-atom in which all the four groups are different (chiral carbon).*

5. Protein is a natural polymer. **(1 Mark)**

> **Note**
>
> *Polymers which are found in nature are called natural polymers.*

6. The conversion of primary aromatic amines into diazonium salts is known as **diazotization.** **(1 Mark)**

7. The products of hydrolysis of sucrose are: D-glucose and D-fructose **(½ + ½ = 1 Mark)**

8. The structure of *p*-methylbenzaldehyde is:

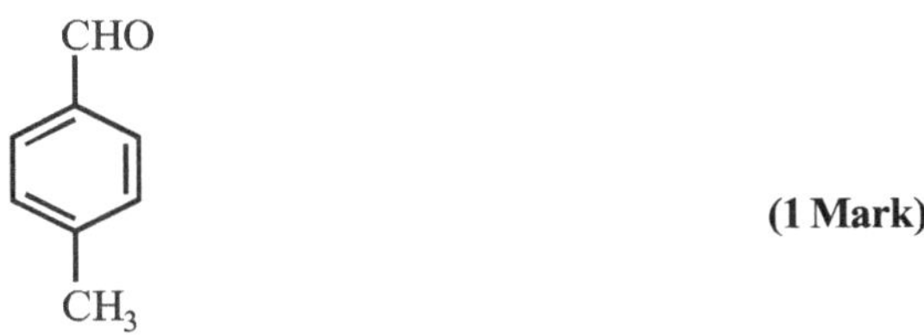

(1 Mark)

SECTION - B

9. **Given:** Density, $d = 2.8$ g cm^{-3}
edge length, $a = 4 \times 10^{-8}$ cm
fcc unit cell, $\therefore$ Z = 4
To find: molar mass, M = ?

$$d = \frac{Z.M}{N_A.a^3}$$ **(½ Mark)**

$$2.8 \text{ g cm}^{-3} = \frac{4 \times M}{6.022 \times 10^{23}\,mol^{-1} \times (4 \times 10^{-8}\,cm)^3}$$

$$M = \frac{2.8 \text{ g cm}^{-3} \times 6.022 \times 10^{23}\,mol^{-1} \times 64 \times 10^{-24}\,cm^3}{4}$$

(½ Mark)

$M = 269.785 \times 10^{-1} = 26.97$ g mol^{-1}
$\therefore$ Molar mass $= 26.97$ g mol^{-1} **(1 Mark)**

10. (i) Metal excess defect caused by *anionic* vacancies is responsible for pink colour of LiCl. **(1 Mark)**

(ii) Schottky defect is the stoichiometric defect shown by NaCl. **(1 Mark)**

OR

(i)

	Tetrahedral Voids	Octahedral Voids
1.	It is a simple triangular void surrounded by four spheres.	It is a double triangular void surrounded by six spheres.
2.		

(½ + ½ = 1 Mark)

(ii)

Crystal lattice	Unit cell
It is a regular arrangement of constituent particles in a 3D space.	It is the smallest 3D portion of a complete space lattice which when repeated over and over again in different directions produces the space lattice.

(1 Mark)

11. According to Kohlrausch law of independent migration of ions, the limiting molar conductivity of an electrolyte is the sum of the limiting ionic conductivities of the cation and the anion each multiplied with the number of ions present in one formula unit of the electrolyte.

i.e., Λ_m° for $A_x B_y = x\lambda_+^\circ + y\lambda_-^\circ$ **(1 Mark)**

The conductivity of a solution decreases with dilution because the number of current carrying particles, i.e., ions per cm^3 of the solution become less and further decreases on dilution. **(1 Mark)**

12. 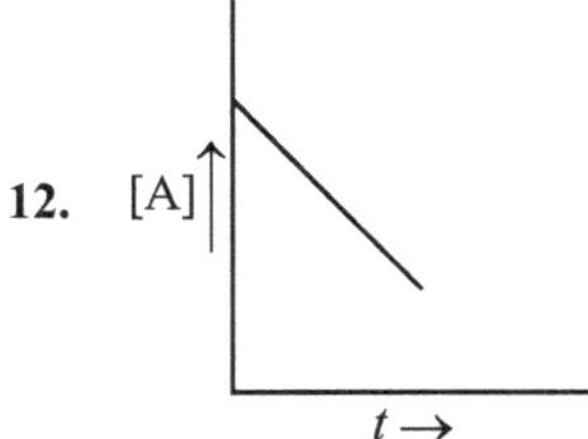

For zero order,

$$k = \frac{1}{t}\{[A]_0 - [A]\} \text{ or } [A] = -kt + [A]_0$$

$\therefore$ (i)   Order of reaction = zero

      (ii)   Slope of the curve = $-k$ **(1 + 1 = 2 Marks)**

13. Electrolytic refining is the process of refining in puremetal by using electricity. This process impure metal is made as the anode while a thin strip of pure metal is made the cathode. The electrodes are suspended in solution of soluble salt of same metal (i.e., electrolyte). On passing electric current, metal dissolves from anode and pass into electrolyte solution as metal ions. An equivalent amount of metal ions from electrolyte are deposited at cathode in form of pure metal. The impurities in the impure mental gets collected below the anode which is called as anode mud. **(1 Mark)**

For example: In electrolytic refining of Cu,

Anode: Crude copper metal

Cathode: pure Cu

Electrolyte: $CuSO_4$ solution.

Net result: Transfer of Cu from anode to cathode in pure form.

Anode: $Cu \longrightarrow Cu^{2+} + 2e^-$

Cathode: $Cu^{2+} + 2e^- \longrightarrow Cu$

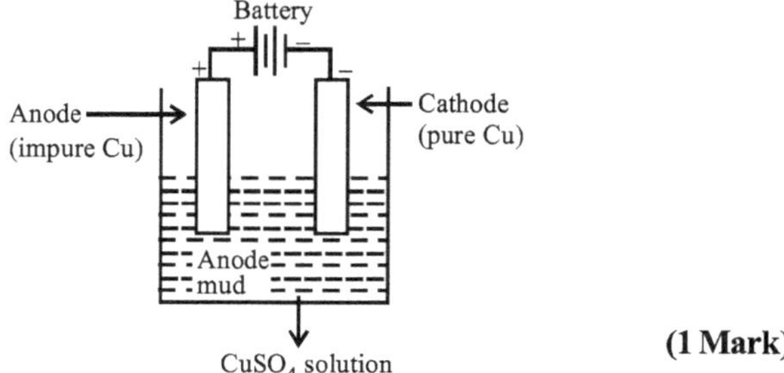

(1 Mark)

14.   (i) $P_4 + 6H_2O \longrightarrow 2PH_3 + 2H_3PO_3$

     (ii) $XeF_4 + O_2F_2 \longrightarrow XeF_6 + O_2$ **(1 + 1 = 2 Marks)**

 *Note*

Hydrolysis of XeF_6 :

XeF_6 gives different products on hydrolysis. XeO_3 is formed on complete hydrolysis whereas oxyfluorides is formed on partial hydrolysis.

Complete hydrolysis:

$$XeF_6 + 3H_2O \longrightarrow XeO_3 + 6HF$$

Partial hydrolysis :

$$XeF_6 + H_2O \longrightarrow XeOF_4 + 2HF$$
$$XeF_6 + 2H_2O \longrightarrow XeO_2F_2 + 4HF$$

15.   The structure of

(i) XeF_2: 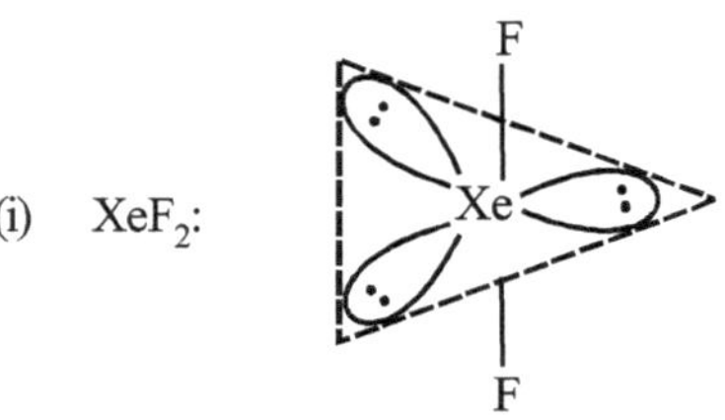

(ii) BrF_3: 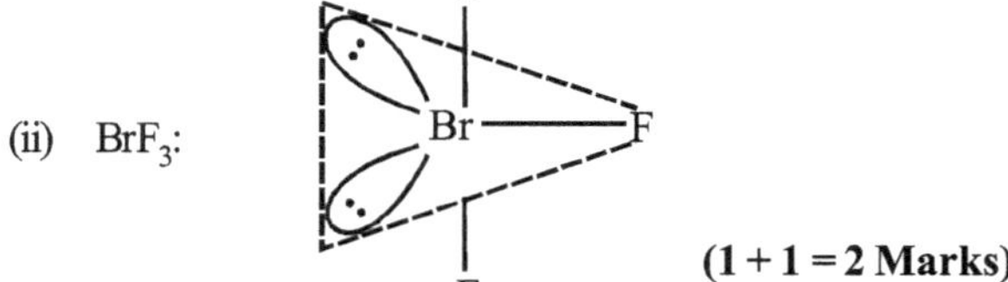

(1 + 1 = 2 Marks)

 *Note*

XeF_2 and BrF_3 both have sp^3d hydridisation but the shapes are different. The shape of XeF_2 is linear while shape of BrF_3 is bent T-shape. The difference in shape in these two compound is due to the presence of lone pairs. XeF_2 has 3 lone pairs and BrF_3 has 2 lone pairs.

16.   (i)   **Reimer-Tiemann reaction:**

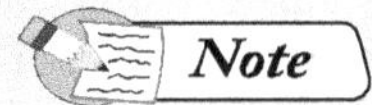

Heterocyclic organic compounds that are quite rich in electrons, such as pyrroles and indoles can also undergo the Reimer Tiemann reaction.

(ii) Williamson synthesis :

$$RO^-Na^+ + R'-X \xrightarrow{S_N2} R'-O-R + NaX$$

(1 + 1 = 2 Marks)

17. $H^{\delta+}Br^{\delta-} \longrightarrow H^+Br^-$

$$CH_3CH_2OH \xrightarrow{H^+} CH_3CH_2\overset{+}{O}H_2$$

(2 Marks)

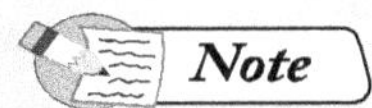

An acid protonates the most basic atom in a molecule. Primary alcohols cannot undergo S_N1 reactions because primary carbocations are too unstable to be formed even when the reaction is heated. Therefore, when a primary alcohol reacts with a hydrogen halide, it must do so in S_N2 reaction pathway.

18. (i) Bakelite: The monomers of bakelite are phenol and formaldehyde. **(½ + ½ = 1 Mark)**

(ii) Neoprene: It is a polymer of chloroprene (2-Chloro - 1, 3-butadiene) **(1 Mark)**

SECTION - C

19. (a) $Mg(s) + Cu^{2+}(aq) \longrightarrow Mg^+(aq) + Cu(s)$

Given: $E°_{cell} = 2.71V$

$1\,F = 96500\,C\,mol^{-1}$

To find: $\Delta G° = ?$

$\Delta G° = -nFE°_{cell}$ **(½ Mark)**

For this reaction, $n = 2$

$\therefore \Delta G° = -2 \times 96500 \times 2.71$ **(½ Mark)**

$= -523030\,J$

$\therefore \Delta G° = -523030\,J = -523.03\,kJ.$ **(1 Mark)**

(b) The hydrogen-oxygen fuel cell was used in Apollo space programme for providing electrical power.

(1 Mark)

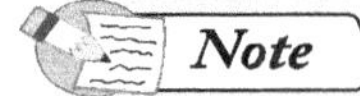

The usage of hydrogen itself is purely CO_2 emission free system since hydrogen is used as a fuel and results only in H_2O without CO_2, unlike in fossil fuel engines.

20.

$$SO_2Cl_2(g) \longrightarrow SO_2(g) + Cl_2(g)$$

At t = 0	P_o atm	0	0
At t = 100 sec	$(P_o - x)$ atm	x atm	x atm

$P_x = (P_o - x) + (x) + (x) = P_o + x$

$x = P_t - P_o$

$P_A = P_o - x = P_o - (P_t - P_o)$

$= 2P_o - P_t$ **(½ Mark)**

Given: $P_o = 0.4$ atm

$P_t = 0.7$ atm

$$k = \frac{2.303}{t} \log \frac{P_o}{P_A}$$ **(½ Mark)**

When $t = 100$ sec, $k = \dfrac{2.303}{100} \log \dfrac{0.4}{(2 \times 0.4) - 0.7}$

$= \dfrac{2.303}{100} \log \dfrac{0.4}{0.8 - 0.7}$ **(1 Mark)**

$= \dfrac{2.303}{100} \log \dfrac{0.4}{0.1} = \dfrac{2.303}{100} \log 4 = \dfrac{2.303}{100} \times 0.6021$

rate constant (k) $= 1.38 \times 10^{-2}\,s^{-1}$ **(½ + ½ = 1 Mark)**

21. An emulsion is a colloidal suspension in which both, dispersed phase and dispersion medium are liquid. **(1 Mark)**

Emulsions are of two types:

(i) Oil in water: Dispersed phase is oil and dispersion medium is water. For example: milk. **(½ + ½ = 1 Mark)**

(ii) Water in oil: Dispersed phase is water and dispersion medium is oil. For example: butter. **(½ + ½ = 1 Mark)**

22. (i) N does not have vacant d-orbitals and thus cannot expand its covalency beyond four to form $(CH_3)_3N = O$. On the other hand, P can expand its covalency beyond four and hence can form $(CH_3)_3P = O$. **(1 Mark)**

(ii) Due to very small size of O, interelectronic repulsions are high and hence, it does not accept e^-s with ease. On the other hand, S is much larger in size than O, so no interelectronic repulsions and hence, it can accept e^- with much ease than O. Thus, O has less negative e^- gain enthalpy than sulphur. **(1 Mark)**

(iii)

H_3PO_2 has two P–H bonds while H_3PO_3 has only one. As a result, H_3PO_2 acts as a stronger reducing agent than H_3PO_3. **(1 Mark)**

23. (i) IUPAC name of $[Cr(NH_3)_4Cl_2]Cl$ is

tetraamminedichloridochromium (III) chloride **(1 Mark)**

(ii) $[Co(en)_3]^{3+}$ exhibits optical isomerism as follows:

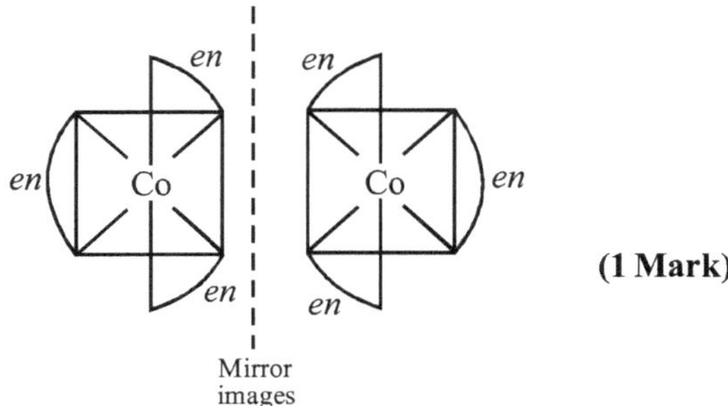

(1 Mark)

(iii) In $[NiCl_4]^{2-}$, Ni is in +2 oxidation state.

$Ni\,(28) : 3d^8 4s^2 \quad Ni^{2+} : 3d^8\,4s^0$

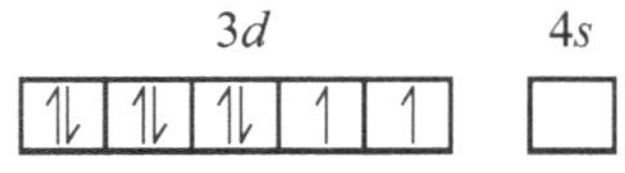

Cl^- is weak field ligand. It does not pair up electrons. Hence, it is paramagnetic.

In $[Ni\,(CO)_4]$, Ni is in 0 O.S. $\quad Ni\,(28) : 3d^8\,4s^2$

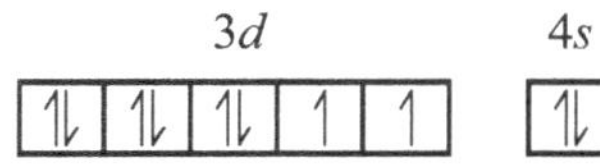

CO is strong field ligand, as it pairs up the $4s$ electrons with $3d$ electrons to give $3d^{10}\,4s^0$. So, there is no unpaired electron and hence, the complex is diamagnetic. **(1 Mark)**

24. (a) (i)

$$\langle\!\!\rangle\!-\!CH_2OH \xrightarrow{PCl_5} \langle\!\!\rangle\!-\!CH_2Cl$$

(1 Mark)

(ii)

$$\langle\!\!\rangle\!-\!CH_2CH = CH_2 + HBr \longrightarrow$$

$$\langle\!\!\rangle\!-\!\underset{\underset{Br}{|}}{CH_2CHCH_3}$$

(1 Mark)

(b) (i) CH_3I reacts faster by S_N2 reaction because I^- is a better leaving group than Br^- **(½ Mark)**

(ii) CH_3Cl being 1° alkyl halide reacts faster by S_N2 reaction. **(½ Mark)**

 *Note*

Primary alkyl halides react faster in S_N2 reactions. Nucleophile attack from the back side in S_N2 reaction therefore less stearic hindrance at the substrate in the transition state favoured the reaction.

25. (i) RNH_2 have higher boiling point than 3° amines (R_3N). This is because of intermolecular H-bonding in RNH_2 which is absent in 3° amines. **(1 Mark)**

(ii) Aniline being a Lewis base reacts with Lewis acid $(AlCl_3)$ to form a salt.

$C_6H_5NH_2 + AlCl_3 \longrightarrow C_6H_5NH_2^+AlCl_3^-$

As a result, N of aniline acquires positive charge and hence it acts as a strong deactivating group for electrophilic substitution reactions. Consequently, aniline does not undergo Fridel Crafts reaction.

(1 Mark)

(iii) $(CH_3)_2NH$ is a stronger base than $(CH_3)_3N$ in aqueous solution because in aqueous solution, basicity is controlled by three factors: +I-effect of alkyl group, H-bonding and steric factors. All these factors are favourable for 2° amines and hence 2°amines are strongest bases in solution. **(1 Mark)**

OR

(i) $C_6H_5NO_2 \xrightarrow[HCl]{Sn} \underset{(A)}{C_6H_5NH_2} \xrightarrow[273\ K]{NaNO_2 + HCl}$

$\underset{(B)}{C_6H_5N_2^+Cl^-} \xrightarrow{H_2O} \underset{(C)}{C_6H_5OH} + N_2 + HCl$

(1½ Marks)

(ii) $CH_3CN \xrightarrow{H_2O/H^+} \underset{(A)}{CH_3COOH} \xrightarrow[\Delta]{NH_3}$

$\underset{(B)}{CH_3CONH_2} \xrightarrow{Br_2 + KOH} \underset{(C)}{CH_3NH_2}$

(½ + ½ + ½ = 1½ Marks)

26. (a) **Peptide linkage:** A peptide bond is an amide linkage formed between – COOH group of one α-amino acid and NH_2 group of other α-amino acid by loss of a water molecule. For example:

$$\underset{}{H_2N - CH_2 - \overset{\overset{\textstyle O}{\|}}{C} - OH + H - \underset{\underset{H}{|}}{N} - \underset{\underset{CH_3}{|}}{CH} - COOH}$$

$$\longrightarrow H_2N\!-\!CH_2\!\overset{\overset{\textstyle O}{\|}}{C}\!-\!NH\!-\!CH\!-\!COOH$$
$$\text{Peptide bond}$$

(1 Mark)

(b) **Primary structure:** Each polypeptide chain of proteins has a large number of α-amino acids which are linked to one another in a specific manner. The specific sequence in which various α-amino acids present in a protein are linked to one another is called its primary structure. Any change in sequence of α-amino acids creates a different protein. **(1 Mark)**

(c) **Denaturation:** When a protein in its native form is subjected to physical changes such as change in temperature, pH, etc., H-bonds are broken. Due to cleavage of H-bonds, unfolding of protein molecule occurs and the protein loses its biological activity. This loss of biological activity is called denaturation.

(1 Mark)

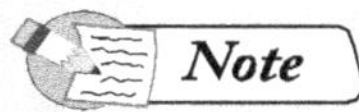 **Note**

Denaturation of proteins involves the disruption of both secondary and tertiary structures. Denaturation reactions are not enough strong to break the peptide bonds therefore primary structure of proteins remain intact. Denaturation process disrupt the normal alpha-helix and beta sheets in protein and uncoils them into random shape.

27. (i) (a) Dr. Satpal performed his duty very well and showed awareness about World Health Day and tried to benefit poor people. **(½ Mark)**

(b) NHRC responded quickly and so showed concern for the villagers. **(½ Mark)**

(ii) Non-narcotic analgesics are used for relieving pains of terminal cancer. **(1 Mark)**

(iii) The artificial sweetening agent that can be given to diabetic patients are aspartame, saccharin, etc. **(1 Mark)**

SECTION - D

28. (a) (i) **Molarity:** It is defined as number of moles of solute per litre of the solution. Its units are mol L^{-1}.

$$\text{Molarity (M)} = \frac{\text{No. of moles of solute}}{\text{Volume of solution}}$$

(1 Mark)

(ii) **Molal elevation constant (K_b):** It is defined as the elevation in boiling point when the molality of the solution is unity, i.e., 1 mole of the solute is dissolved in 1 kg of the solvent. **(1 Mark)**

(b) **Given:**

Urea	Glucose
$w_1 = 15$ g	$M_2 = 180$ g
$M_1 = 60$ g	

To find: $w_2 = ?$

As the solutions are isotonic, we have

$$\pi_1 = \pi_2 \qquad \text{(½ Mark)}$$
$$C_1RT = C_2RT$$
$$C_1 = C_2 \qquad \text{(½ Mark)}$$
$$\frac{n_1}{V_1} = \frac{n_2}{V_2}$$
$$\Rightarrow \quad n_2 = \frac{n_1}{V_1} \times V_2$$

$V_1 = V_2$ as vol. is 1 litre

$\therefore$
$$n_2 = n_1$$
$$\frac{w_2}{M_2} = \frac{w_1}{M_1} \qquad \text{(1 Mark)}$$
$$w_2 = \frac{w_1}{M_1} \times M_2$$
$$= \frac{15}{60} \times 180 = 45$$

$\therefore$ mass of glucose = 45 g **(½ + ½ = 1 Mark)**

OR

(a) A mixture of ethanol and acetone shows positive deviation from Raoult's law. This is because acetone molecules enter between alcohol molecules thus breaking the H-bonds between ethanol molecules and hence showing +ve deviation. **(1 + 1 = 2 Marks)**

(b) **Given:** 10% solution of glucose $\Rightarrow$ 10 g of glucose in 100 g of solution

molar mass of glucose, $M_2 = 180$ g mol^{-1}

density of solution, $d = 1.2$ g mL^{-1}

To find: (i) molality, m

(ii) molarity, M

(i) Molality,

$$m = \frac{\text{Moles of solute}}{\text{Mass of solvent (in g)}} \times 1000 \quad \text{(½ Mark)}$$
$$m = \frac{(10/180)}{(100-10)} \times 1000$$
$$m = \frac{10}{180 \times 90} \times 1000$$
$$= \frac{100}{18 \times 9}$$
$$m = 0.617 \text{ mol kg}^{-1} \qquad \text{(1 Mark)}$$

(ii) Molarity,

$$m = \frac{\text{Moles of solute}}{\text{Volume of solution (in mL)}} \times 1000$$

(½ Mark)

$$M = \frac{(10/180)}{V_{sol}} \times 1000$$
$$V_{sol} = \frac{m_{sol}}{d} = \frac{100}{1.2}$$
$$\therefore \quad M = \frac{10/180}{100/1.2} \times 1000 = \frac{2}{3}$$
$$\therefore \quad M = 0.66 \text{ mol L}^{-1} \qquad \text{(1 Mark)}$$

29. (a) (i) $Cr_2O_7^{2-} + 2OH^- \longrightarrow 2CrO_4^{2-} + H_2O$

(1 Mark)

(ii) $MnO_4^- + 4H^+ + 3e^- \longrightarrow MnO_2 + 2H_2O$

(1 Mark)

(b) (i) Zinc is not considered as a transition element because it does not contain vacant d-orbitals in either the ground state or its common oxidation state (+2) **(1 Mark)**

(ii) Transition elements form a large number of complexes because of:
   (a) smaller size of their ions
   (b) high ionic charges
   (c) availability of vacant d-orbitals. **(1 Mark)**

(iii) $Mn(25) \xrightarrow{-e^-} Mn^+ \xrightarrow{-e^-} Mn^{2+} \xrightarrow{-e^-} Mn^{3+}$
   $\quad\quad 3d^5 4s^2 \quad\quad 3d^5 4s^1 \quad\quad 3d^5 4s^0 \quad\quad 3d^4 4s^0$

   $Cr(24) \xrightarrow{-e^-} Cr^+ \xrightarrow{-e^-} Cr^{2+} \xrightarrow{-e^-} Cr^{3+}$
   $\quad\quad 3d^5 4s^1 \quad\quad 3d^5 4s^0 \quad\quad 3d^4 4s^0 \quad\quad 3d^3 4s^0$

The reduction of $Mn^{3+} \longrightarrow Mn^{2+}$ gives stable half-filled configuration of $3d^5$, which is not the case when $Cr^{3+} \longrightarrow Cr^{2+}$. Thus, $E°$ value for Mn^{3+}/Mn^{2+} couple is more positive than Cr^{3+}/Cr^{2+} couple. **(1 Mark)**

OR

(i) **Lanthanoids :**
   1. They are non-radioactive.
   2. Their compounds are less basic.
   3. They show only one O.S, 3. This is due to large energy gap between $4f$ and $5d$ subshells.
   4. They are less reactive chemically.

   Actinoids :
   1. They are radioactive.
   2. Their compounds are more basic.
   3. They show many O.S. like, $+3, +4, +5, +6, +7$ due to small energy gap between $5d$, $6s$ and $7s$ subshells.
   4. They are highly reactive. **(2 marks)**

(ii) Cerium (Ce) shows $+4$ O.S. due to stable configuration $[Xe]4f^0$ **(1 Mark)**

(iii) $MnO_4^- + 8H^+ + 5e^- \longrightarrow Mn^{2+} + 4H_2O$
  (1 Mark)

(iv) $Mn(25) \xrightarrow{-3e^-} Mn^{3+}$
   $\quad 3d^5 4s^2 \quad\quad\quad 3d^4 4s^0$

$3d$

| ↑ | ↑ | ↑ | ↑ | | → 4 unpaired e^-

$Cr(24) \xrightarrow{-3e^-} Cr^{3+}$
   $\quad 3d^5 4s^1 \quad\quad\quad 3d^3 4s^0$

$3d$

| ↑ | ↑ | ↑ | | | → 3 unpaired e^-

Due to presence of 4 unpaired, e^- in Mn^{3+} as compared to 3 in Cr^{3+}, Mn^{3+} is more paramagnetic than Cr^{3+}. **(1 Mark)**

30. (a) (i) $CH_3CHO \longrightarrow CH_3CH(OH)CN$ **(1 Mark)**
   Cyanohydrin

(ii) $CH_3 - \overset{\overset{\displaystyle H}{|}}{C} = \boxed{O + H_2} - NOH \longrightarrow$

   $CH_3 - CH = \underset{\text{Oxime}}{NOH}$ **(1 Mark)**

(iii) $CH_3CHO + CH_3CHO \xrightarrow[\text{NaOH}]{\text{dil.}}$
   $CH_3 - CH(OH) - CH_2 - CHO$ **(1 Mark)**

(b) (i) **Ferric chloride test :** Phenol reacts with neutral $FeCl_3$ to form an iron phenol complex giving violet colouration.
   $6C_6H_5OH + FeCl_3 \longrightarrow$
   $\quad\quad\quad [Fe(OC_6H_5)_6]^{3-} + 3H^+ + 3Cl^-$
   Violet colour

   But benzoic acid reacts with neutral $FeCl_3$ to give a buff coloured ppt. of ferric benzoate.
   $3C_6H_5COOH + FeCl_3 \longrightarrow$
   $\quad\quad\quad (C_6H_5COO)_3 Fe + 3HCl$
   Buff colour **(1 Mark)**

(ii) Proponal is an aldehyde, thus, it reduces Tollen's reagent. But propanone being a ketone does not reduce Tollen's reagent. **(1 Mark)**

OR

(a) (i) $ClCH_2COOH$ is a stronger acid than CH_3COOH. This is because Cl atom exhibits $-$ I effect, withdraw electron denstity from O–H bond. As a result, polarity of O–H bond increases and hence release of H^+ becomes easier. **(1 Mark)**

(ii) Carboxylic acids do not give reactions of carbonyl group because carbonyl carbon in carboxyl group is less electropositive than carbonyl carbon in aldehydes and ketones due to resonance.
  (1 Mark)

(b) (i) **Rosenmund Reduction** is used to prepare aldehydes from acid chloride by passing H_2 gas through xylene in presence of Pd catalyst and partially poisoned by addition of S or quinoline.

   $CH_3 - \overset{\overset{\displaystyle O}{||}}{C} - Cl + H_2 \xrightarrow[\text{boiling xylene}]{Pd, BaSO_4, S}$
   $CH_3 - \overset{\overset{\displaystyle O}{||}}{C} - H + HCl$ **(1 Mark)**

(ii) **Cannizzaro reaction:** Aldehydes which do not contain α-hydrogen atom, when treated with conc. alkali solution undergo self oxidation and reduction to form alcohol and carboxylate ion.

   $\underset{\text{Formal dihyde}}{HCHO} + \underset{\text{(conc)}}{NaOH} \longrightarrow \underset{\text{Methanol}}{CH_3OH} + \underset{\text{Sodium formate}}{HCOO^-Na^+}$
  (1 Mark)

(c) $CH_3CH_2CH_2COCH_3$ will give iodoform test due to presence of $CH_3 - CO -$ group. **(1 Mark)**

CBSE Board Solved Paper

Time Allowed : 3 Hours   *Maximum Marks : 70*

General Instructions:
  (i)   All question are compulsory.
  (ii)   Section A : Question number **1 to 8** are very short answer questions and carry **1** mark each.
  (iii) Section B : Question number **9 to 18** are short answer questions and carry **2** marks each.
  (iv) Section C : Question number **19 to 27** are also short answer questions and carry **3** marks each.
  (v)   Section D : Question number **28 to 30** are long answer questions and carry **5** marks each.
  (vi) Use log tables, if necessary. Use of calculator is not allowed.

SECTION - A

1. Give one example each of 'oil in water' and 'water in oil' emulsion.

2. Which reducing agent is employed to get copper from the leached low grade copper ore ?

3. Which of the following is more stable complex and why ?
   $[Co(NH_3)_6]^{3+}$ and $[Co(en)^3]^{3+}$

4. Write the IUPAC name of the compound.

   $$CH_3 - \underset{\underset{\displaystyle OH}{|}}{CH} - CH_2 - COOH$$

5. Which of the following isomers is more volatile :
   o-nitrophenol or *p*-nitrophenol

6. What are isotonic solutions ?

7. Arrange the following compounds in increasing order of solubility in water :
   $C_6H_5NH_2, (C_2H_5)_2NH, C_2H_5NH_2$

8. Which of the two components of starch is water soluble ?

SECTION - B

9. An element with density 11.2 g cm^{-3} forms a *f.c.c.* lattice with edge length of 4×10^{-8} cm. Calculate the atomic mass of the element.
   (Given : $N_A = 6.022 \times 10^{23} \, mol^{-1}$)

10. Examine the given defective crystal

A^+	B^-	A^+	B^-	A^+
B^-	0	B^-	A^+	B^-
A^+	B^-	A^+	0	A^+
B^-	A^+	B^-	A^+	B^-

Answer the following questions :
  (i)   What type of stoichiometric defect is shown by the crystal ?
  (ii)   How is the density of the crystal affected by the defect?
  (iii) What type of ionic substances show such defect ?

11. Calculate the mass of compound (molar mass $= 256$ g mol^{-1}) to be dissolved in 75 g of benzene to lower its freezing point by 0.48 K ($K_f = 5.12$ K kg mol^{-1}).

12. Define an ideal solution and write one of its characteristics.

13. Write two differences between 'order of reaction' and 'molecularity of reaction'.

14. Outline the principles behind the refining of metals by the following methods :
    (i)   Zone refining method
    (ii) Chromatographic method

15. Complete the following chemical equations :
    (i) $Ca_3P_2 + H_2O \longrightarrow$
    (ii) $Cu + H_2SO_4 \, (conc.) \longrightarrow$

    OR

    Arrange the following in the order of property indicated against each set :
    (i)   HF, HCl, HBr, Hl - increasing bond dissociation enthalpy.
    (ii) H_2O, H_2S, H_2Se, H_2Te - increasing acidic character.

16. Write the IUPAC name of the complex $[Cr(NH_3)_4Cl_2]^+$. What type of isomerism does it exhibit ?

17. (i) Which alkyl halide from the following pair is chiral and undergoes faster S_N2 reaction ?

(a) [structure: CH₃CH₂CH₂CH₂Br]   (b) [structure: sec-butyl bromide]

(ii) Out of S_N1 and S_N2, which reaction occurs with (a) Inversion of configuration (b) Racemisation ?

18. Draw the structure of major monohalo product in each of the following reactions :

(i) [cyclohexyl]—OH $\xrightarrow{SOCl_2}$

(ii) [benzyl]—$CH_2 - CH = CH_2 + HBr \xrightarrow{Peroxide}$

SECTION - C

19. (a) In reference to Freundlich adsorption isotherm write the expression for adsorption of gases on solids in the form of an equation.

(b) Write an important characteristic of lyophilic sols.

(c) Based on type of particles of dispersed phase, give one example each of associated colloid and multimolecular colloid.

20. Draw the structures of the following molecules.

(a) (i) $XeOF_4$ (ii) H_2SO_4

(b) Write the structural differences between white phosphorus and red phosphorus.

21. Account for the following :

(i) PCl_5 is more covalent than PCl_3.

(ii) Iron on reaction with HCl forms $FeCl_2$ and not $FeCl_3$

(iii) The two O-O bond lengths in the ozone molecule are equal.

22. The following data were obtained during the first order thermal decomposition of SO_2Cl_2 at a constant volume.

$$SO_2Cl_2(g) \longrightarrow SO_2(g) + Cl_2(g)$$

Experiment	Times/s	Total pressure/atm
1	0	0.4
2	100	0.7

Calculate the rate constant.

(Given : log 4 = 0.06021; log 2 = 0.3010)

23. (i) Give two examples of macromolecules that are chosen as drug targets.

(ii) What are antiseptics ? Give an example.

(iii) Why is use of aspartame limited to cold food and soft drinks ?

24. (i) Deficiency of which vitamin causes night blindless?

(ii) Name the base that is found in nucleotide of RNA only.

(iii) Glucose on reaction with HI gives n-hexane. What does it suggest about the structure of glucose ?

25. After the ban of plastic bags, students of one school decided to make the people aware of the harmful effects of plastic bags on environment and Yamuna River. To make the awareness more impactful, they organized rally by joining hands with other schools and distributed paper bags to vegetable vendors, shopkeepers and departmental stores.

All students pledged not to use polythene bags in future to save Yamuna River.

After reading the above passage, answer the following questions.

(i) What values are shown by the students?

(ii) What are biodegradable polymers? Give an example.

(iii) Is polythene a condensation or an addition polymer?

26. (a) Write the mechanism of the following reaction:

$$CH_3CH_2OH \xrightarrow{HBr} CH_3CH_2Br + H_2O$$

(b) Write the equation involved in Reimer-Tiemann reaction.

27. Give the structures of A, B and C in the following reactions :

(i) $CH_3Br \xrightarrow{KCN} A \xrightarrow{LiAlH_4} B \xrightarrow[273K]{HNO_2} C$

(ii) $CH_3COOH \xrightarrow[\Delta]{NH_3} A \xrightarrow{Br_2 + KOH}$

$B \xrightarrow{CHCl_3 + NaOH} C$

OR

How will you convert the following :

(i) Nitrobenzene into aniline

(ii) Ethanoic acid into methanamine

(iii) Aniline into N-phenylethanamide

(Write the chemical equations involved.)

SECTION - D

28. (a) Define the following terms :

(i) Limiting molar conductivity

(ii) Fuel cell

(b) Resistance of a conductivity cell filled with 0.1 mol L^{-1} KCl solution is 100Ω. If the resistance of the same cell when filled with 0.02 mol L^{-1} KCl solution is 520Ω, calculate the conductivity and molar conductivity of 0.02 mol L^{-1} KCl solution. The conductivity of 0.1 mol L^{-1} KCl solution is $1.29 \times 10^{-2} \ \Omega^{-1} \ cm^{-1}$.

OR

(a) State Faraday's first law of electrolysis. How much charge in terms of Faraday is required for the reduction of 1 mol of Cu^{2+} to Cu.

(b) Calculate *emf* of the following cell at 298 K :

Mg (s) | Mg^{2+} (0.1 M) || Cu^{2+} (0.01) | Cu(s)

[Given $E^{\circ}_{cell} = +2.71$ V, 1F = 96500 C mol^{-1})

29. (a) How do you prepare :

(i) K_2MnO_4 from MnO_2 ?

(ii) $Na_2Cr_2O_7$ from Na_2CrO_4 ?

(b) Account for the following :

(i) Mn^{2+} is more stable than Fe^{2+} towards oxidation to +3 state.

(ii) The enthalpy of atomization is lowest for Zn in 3*d* series of the transition elements.

(iii) Actinoid elements show wide range of oxidation states.

OR

(i) Name the element of 3*d* transition series which shows maximum number of oxidation states. Why does it show so ?

(ii) Which transition metal of 3*d* series has positive E° (M^{2+}/M) value and why ?

(iii) Out of Cr^{3+} and Mn^{3+}, which is a stronger oxidizing agent and why ?

(iv) Name a member of the lanthanoid series which is well known to exhibit +2 oxidation state.

(v) Complete the following equation :

$$MnO_4^- + 8H^+ + +5e^- \longrightarrow$$

30. (a) Write the products of the following reactions :

(i) 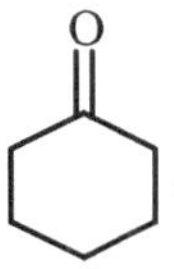 (cyclohexanone structure) $+ H_2N - OH \xrightarrow{H^+}$

(ii) $2C_6H_5CHO + $ conc. NaOH $\longrightarrow$

(iii) $CH_3COOH \xrightarrow{Cl_2/P}$

(b) Give simple chemical tests to distinguish between the following pairs of compounds:

(i) Benzaldehyde and Benzoic acid

(ii) Propanal and Propanone

OR

(a) ˙Account for the following :

(i) CH_3CHO is more reactive than CH_3COCH_3 towards reaction with HCN.

(ii) Carboxylic acid is a stronger acid then phenol.

(b) Write the chemical equations to illustrate the following name reactions :

(i) Wolff-Kishner reduction

(ii) Aldol condensation

(iii) Cannizzaro reaction

Solutions

SECTION - A

1. An example of :

   (i)   Oil in water emulsion : Milk   (½ Mark)

   (ii)   Water in oil emulsion : Butter   (½ Mark)

2. Iron in employed to get copper from leached low grade copper ore.   (1 Mark)

3. Out of $[Co(NH_3)_6]^{3+}$ and $[Co(en)_3]^{3+}$, $[Co(en)_3]^{3+}$ is more stable because of the formation of a chelate (i.e. ring) which makes it more stable.

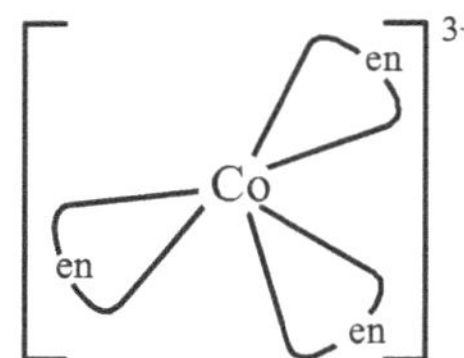

                       (1 Mark)

4. The IUPAC name of

$$CH_3 - \underset{\underset{OH}{|}}{CH} - CH_2 - COOH \text{ is 3- Hydroxybutanoic acid}$$

                       (1 Mark)

5. o-Nitrophenol is more volatile than p-nitrophenol.   (1 Mark)

> **Note**
>
> *Various types of interactions present in the molecule affect the properties of that molecule. o-Nitrophenol has intramolecular H-bonding where as p-Nitrophenol has intermolecular H-bonding. Intramolecular H-bonding in o-Nitrophenol make it more volatile than p-Nitrophenol.*

6. Two solutions having same osmotic pressure at a given temperature are called isotonic solutions.   (1 Mark)

7. The order of solubility in water is :

$$C_6H_5NH_2 < (C_2H_5)_2NH < C_2H_5NH_2$$

                       (1 Mark)

> **Note**
>
> *Solubility of amines in water depends upon the extent of H-bonding between amine and water molecules. Extent of intermolecular H-bonding is highest for primary amine followed by secondary amine. Aniline does not form intermolecular H-bond with water to very large extent due to bulky hydrophobic phenyl group.*

8. Amylose is water soluble component of starch which constitute about 15-20%.   (1 Mark)

SECTION - B

9. **Given:** Density (d) = 11.2 g cm^{-3}

   fcc lattice $\Rightarrow$ z = 4

   Edge length (a) = 4×10^{-8} cm

   To find : Atomic mass, M = ?

   We know, $d = \dfrac{zM}{a^3 N_A}$ (½ Mark)

$$\Rightarrow M = \dfrac{d.a^3.N_A}{z}$$

$$\Rightarrow M = \dfrac{11.2 \times (4 \times 10^{-8})^3 \times 6.022 \times 10^{23}}{4}$$ (½ Mark)

$$\Rightarrow M = 1079.14 \times 10^{-24} \times 10^{23} \text{ g}$$

   $M = 107.9 \text{ g} \approx 108 \text{ g}$ (1 Mark)

10. (i)   The given crystal shows schottky defect.   (½ Mark)

   (ii)   The density of the crystal decreases.   (½ Mark)

   (iii)   Schottky defect is shown by ionic substances in which the cation and anion are of almost similar size. Ex : NaCl, KCl, AgBr.   (1 Mark)

11. **Given :** $\Delta T_f = 0.48$ K

   $M_2 = 256$ g mol^{-1}

   $w_1 = 75$ g

   $K_f = 5.12$ K kg mol^{-1}

   To find : $w_2 = ?$

   Solution $\Delta T_f = K_f m$ (½ Mark)

$$\Delta T_f = K_f \times \dfrac{w_2}{M_2} \times \dfrac{1000}{w_1}$$

$$\Rightarrow \quad w_2 = \dfrac{\Delta T_f \times M_2 \times w_1}{K_f \times 1000}$$ (½ Mark)

$$= \dfrac{0.48 \times 256 \times 75}{5.12 \times 1000}$$

$$\Rightarrow \quad w_2 = 1.8 \text{ g}$$ (1 Mark)

12. The solutions which obey Raoult's law over the entire range of concentration are known as ideal solutions. For an ideal solution, the A-B interactions are nearly same as the A-A and B-B interactions. Where A and B are the two components of the solution. **(2 Marks)**

13.

	Order of reaction	Molecularity of reaction
(i)	The sum of powers of the concentration of the reactant in the rate law expression is the order of reactant.	The number of reacting species taking part in an elementary reaction is called molecularity of a reaction.
(ii)	It is an experimental entity. It can be zero and even a fraction.	It cannot be zero or a non-integer.

(2 Marks)

14. (i) **Zone-refining method :** It is based on the principle that the impurities are more soluble in the melt than in the solid state of the metal. **(1 Mark)**

(ii) **Chromatographic method :** It is based on the principle that different components of a mixture are absorbed to different extent on an absorbent.

(1 Mark)

15. (i) $Ca_3P_2 + 6H_2O \longrightarrow 3Ca(OH)_2 + 2PH_3$ **(1 Mark)**

(ii) $Cu + 2H_2SO_4(Conc.) \longrightarrow CuSO_4 + SO_2 + 2H_2O$

(1 Mark)

OR

(i) The order of increasing bond dissociation energy is:

$$HI < HBr < HCl < HF \qquad \textbf{(1 Mark)}$$

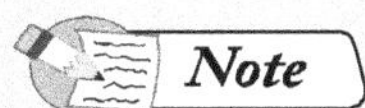

> *Note*
>
> *As we move from HF to HI in a group, size of the halogen atom increases. Therefore bond length increase and bond strength decreases consequently bond breaks easily.*

(ii) The order is :

$$H_2O < H_2S < H_2Se < H_2Te \qquad \textbf{(1 Mark)}$$

> *Note*
>
> *Acidic strength depends upon the ease of release of H. More easily the H can be replaced, more in the acidic strength. As we move from H_2O to H_2Te, size increases, bond length increases, bond strength decreases and hence, ease of release of H increases, so does the acidic strength.*

16. IUPAC name : Tetrammine dichloridochrominium (III) ion

It shows geometrical and optical isomerism as shown below :

(i) Geometrical isomers

(ii) The *cis* form is optically active.

(1 + 1 = 2 Marks)

17. (i) is chiral due to presence of asymmetric carbon atom and undergoes S_N2 reaction faster. **(1 Mark)**

(ii) S_N2 occurs with inversion of configuration and S_N1 occurs with racemisaiton. **(1 Mark)**

> *Note*
>
> *Primary alkyl halides undergo S_N2 mechanism because primary substrates have little steric hindrance to nucleophilic attack. As more alkyl groups added to α carbon atom, the substrate becomes less susceptible to S_N2 attack. In S_N2 reactions nucleophile will always attack from the backside and results into inversion of configuration.*

18. (i) OH $\xrightarrow{SOCl_2}$ Cl **(1 Mark)**

(ii) $-CH_2-CH=CH_2 + HBr \xrightarrow{Peroxide} -CH_2-CH_2-CH_2-Br$ **(1 Mark)**

SECTION - C

19. (a) According to Freundlich adsorption isotherm, the quantity of gas adsorbed by unit mass of solid adsorbent and pressure at a particular temperature is given by the following equation :

$$\frac{x}{m} = kp^{1/n} \quad (n > 1)$$

where x = mass of adsorbate

m = mass of adsorbent

p = pressure

k and n = constants at a particular temperature **(1 Mark)**

(b) Lycophilic sols are liquid-loving. An improtant characteristic of these sols is that if dispersion medium is separated from dispersed phase, the sol can be reconstituted by simply remixing the dispersion medium. **(1 Mark)**

(c) An example of :

(i) Multimolecular colloid : gold sol, sulphur sol **(½ Mark)**

(ii) Associated colloid : soaps, synthetic detergents **(½ Mark)**

20. (a) Structure of :

(i) $XeOF_4$: Square - pyramidal

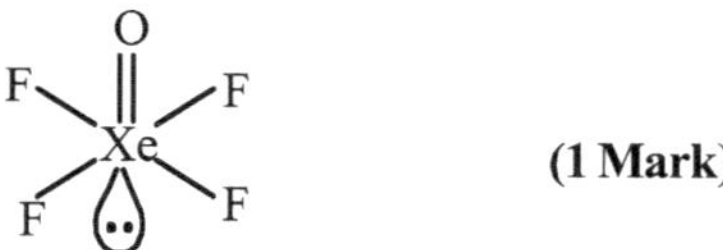

(1 Mark)

(ii) H_2SO_4: Tetrahedral

(1 Mark)

(b) **White Phosphorus:** It consists of discrete tetrahedral molecules held together by weak van der Waals forces.

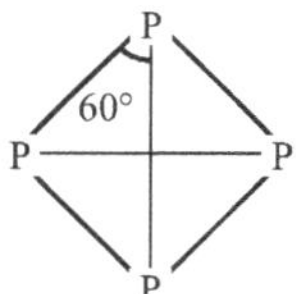

Red Phosphorus: In this P_4 molecules are linked by covalent bonds in the polymeric structure.

(1 Mark)

21. (a) PCl_5 is more covalent than PCl_3. This is because ionization energy required for the formation of P^{5+} is very high. Hence, rather than forming ionic bonds, P in +5 oxidation state forms covalent bonds. **(1 Mark)**

(b) Iron on reaction with HCl forms readily $FeCl_2$ and not $FeCl_3$ because second ionization energy is less as compared to third ionization energy. The additional energy required to remove third electron is fairly high, so even though Fe^{3+} is more stable, its formation is less. **(1 Mark)**

(c) The two O–O bond lengths is ozone are equal due to resonance. Ozone is a resonance hybrid of two forms shown below and the molecule is angular with a bond angle of about $117°$.

(1 Mark)

22.

$$SO_2Cl_2(g) \longrightarrow SO_2(g) + Cl_2(g)$$

Initial	P_0	0	0
after time t	$P_0 - P$	P	P

Total pressure after time t

$(P_t) = P_0 - P + P + P = P_0 + P$

or, $P = P_t - P_0$

$\therefore a = P_0$ and $(a - x) = P_0 - P = P_0 - (P_t - P_0)$

$= 2P_0 - P_t$ **(½ Mark)**

$$k = \frac{2.303}{t} \log \frac{a}{a - x}$$ **(½ Mark)**

$$= \frac{2.303}{t} \log \frac{P_0}{2P_0 - P_t} = \frac{2.303}{100} \log \frac{0.4}{(2 \times 0.4) - 0.7}$$

$$\Rightarrow k = \frac{2.303}{100} \log \frac{0.4}{0.8 - 0.7}$$ **(½ Mark)**

$$= \frac{2.303}{100} \log \frac{0.4}{0.1} = \frac{2.303}{100} \log (2^2)$$

$$\Rightarrow k = \frac{2.303}{100} \times 2 \log 2$$ **(½ Mark)**

$$= \frac{2.30 \times 2 \times 0.3010}{100}$$

$k = 1.38 \times 10^{-2} \text{ sec}^{-1}$ **(1 Mark)**

23. (i) Macromolecules chosen as drug targets are proteins, nucleic acids, etc. **(1 Mark)**

(ii) Antiseptics kill or stop the growth of microorganisms. They are applied to living issues such as wounds, cuts, ulcers and diseased skin surfaces.

For ex : soframicine. **(1 Mark)**

(iii) Use of asparatame is limited to cold foods and soft drinks because it is unstable at cooking temperature.

(1 Mark)

24. (i)   The deficiency of vitamin A causes night blindness.
(1 Mark)

(ii)   Uracil (U) is the base that is found in nucleotide of RNA only.   **(1 Mark)**

(iii)   On prolonged heating with HI, glucose forms n-hexane. This shows that all the six carbon atoms in glucose are linked in a straight chain.   **(1 Mark)**

25. (i)   The students showed awareness about the environmental hazards and were eco-friendly and trying to save and de-pollute the environment.
(1 Mark)

(ii)   Biodegradable polymers are those which degrade in the environment and thus do not cause environmental pollution.

For example : Poly urethanes.   **(1 Mark)**

(iii)   Polythene is an addtion polymer as it is formed by the repeated addition of various ethene molecules as shown below :

$$nCH_2 = CH_2 \longrightarrow (-CH_2 - CH_2)_n$$
Ethene   Polythene   **(1 Mark)**

26. (a) $CH_3CH_2OH \xrightarrow{HBr} CH_3CH_2Br + H_2O$

This is an example of nucleophilic substitution reaction :

As ethanol (CH_3CH_2OH) is a primary alcohol, it will undergo substitution by S_N2 mechanism. The mechanism is shown below :

$$HBr \rightleftharpoons H^+ + Br^-$$

(2 Marks)

(b)   **Reimer-Tiemann reaction**

Phenol $\xrightarrow[\text{aq. NaOH}]{CHCl_3}$ [Intermediate] $\xrightarrow{NaOH}$ $\xrightarrow{H^+}$ Salicylaldehyde

(1 Mark)

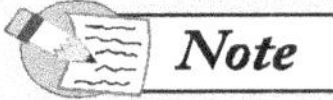

Dichlorocarbene is the reactive intermediate which form in the first step of reaction.

$$H-C\begin{array}{c}Cl\\Cl\\Cl\end{array} \xrightarrow{NaOH} {}^-C\begin{array}{c}Cl\\Cl\\Cl\end{array} \longrightarrow :C\begin{array}{c}Cl\\Cl\end{array}$$

Dichlorocarbene act as a electrophile in the reaction.

27. (i) $CH_3Br \xrightarrow{KCN} \underset{(A)}{CH_3CN} \xrightarrow{LiAlH_4}$

$$\underset{(B)}{CH_3CH_2NH_2} \xrightarrow[273K]{HNO_2} \underset{(C)}{CH_3CH_2OH} + N_2 + H^+$$

(½ + ½ + ½ = 1½ Marks)

(ii) $CH_3COOH \xrightarrow[\Delta]{NH_3} \underset{(A)}{CH_3CONH_2}$

$$\xrightarrow[KOH]{Br_2} \underset{(B)}{CH_3NH_2} \xrightarrow[NaOH]{CHCl_3} \underset{(C)}{CH_3NC}$$

(½ + ½ + ½ = 1½ Marks)

OR

(i)   Nitrobenzene into aniline

$$\text{NO}_2 \xrightarrow[HCl]{Fe} \text{NH}_2 + 2H_2O$$ **(1 Mark)**

(ii)   Ethanoic acid to methanamine

$$CH_3COOH \xrightarrow{SOCl_2} CH_3COCl$$
$$\xrightarrow{NH_3} CH_3CONH_2 \xrightarrow{Br_2/KOH} CH_3NH_2$$

(1 Mark)

(iii)   Aniline into N-phenylethanamide

$$\text{NH}_2 \xrightarrow[\text{Pyridine}]{(CH_3CO)_2O} \text{HNCOCH}_3$$ **(1 Mark)**

28. (a)   (i)   **Limiting molar conductivity :** It is that value of molar conductivity which is obtained at infinite dilution i.e. when the concentration of the solution approaches zero. It is denoted by Λ_m^0.

(1 Mark)

(ii) **Fuel cell :** Galvanic cells that are designed to convert the energy of combustion of fuels like hydrogen, methane, methanol etc. directly into other form of energy are called fuel cells.

(1 Mark)

(b) **Given :**

$$R_1 = 100\Omega \qquad R_2 = 520\ \Omega$$
$$C_1 = 0.1\ mol\ L^{-1} \qquad C_2 = 0.02\ mol\ L^{-1}$$
$$\kappa_1 = 1.29 \times 10^{-2}\ \Omega^{-1}\ cm^{-1}$$

To find: κ and $\wedge_m$ of $0.02\ mol^{-1}$ KCl solution.

Sol : Cell constant $= R\kappa_1 = 100 \times 1.29 \times 10^{-2}$
$$= 1.29\ cm^{-1} \qquad \textbf{(½ Mark)}$$

As cell constant will be same,

$$\therefore \quad \kappa = \frac{Cell\ constant}{R} = \frac{1.29\,cm^{-1}}{520\Omega} \qquad \textbf{(½ Mark)}$$
$$= 2.48 \times 10^{-3}\ \Omega^{-1}\ cm^{-1}\ and, \qquad \textbf{(½ Mark)}$$
$$\wedge_m = \frac{\kappa \times 1000}{C_2} = \frac{1.29}{520}\Omega^{-1}cm^{-1} \times \frac{1000}{0.02\,mol^{-1}} \quad \textbf{(½ Mark)}$$
$$= 124.038\ \Omega^{-1}\ cm^{-1} \qquad \textbf{(1 Mark)}$$

OR

(a) According to Faraday's first law of electrolysis, the amount of chemical reaction which occurs at any electrode during electrolysis by a current is proportional to the quantity of electricity passed through the electrolyte.

Reduction of 1 mol of Cu^{2+} of Cu is given by :

$$Cu^{2+} + 2e^- \longrightarrow Cu$$

$\therefore$ The charge required for 1 mole of $Cu^{2+} = 2F$

(2 Marks)

(b) **Given:**

Mg (s)| Mg^{2+} (0.1M)) || Cu^{2+} (0.01M) | Cu(s)

$E°_{cell} = 2.71\ V,\ 1F = 96500\ C\ mol^{-1}$

To find : $E_{cell} = ?$

Solution : Using Nernst equation,

$$E_{cell} = E°_{cell} - \left[\frac{0.059}{n}\log\frac{[P]}{[R]}\right] \qquad \textbf{(½ Mark)}$$

The redox equation for the above cell is :

$$Mg(s) + Cu^{2+}(aq) \longrightarrow Mg^{2+}(aq) + Cu(s)$$

$$\therefore \quad E_{cell} = E°_{cell} - \left[\frac{0.059}{n}\log\frac{[Mg^{2+}]}{[Cu^{2+}]}\right]$$

$$= 2.71 - \left[\frac{0.059}{2}\log\frac{[0.1]}{[0.01]}\right] \qquad \textbf{(½ Mark)}$$

$$= 2.71 - \left[\frac{0.059}{2}\log 10\right] \qquad \textbf{(½ Mark)}$$

$$= 2.71 - \left[\frac{0.059}{2}\times 1\right] \quad (\because\ \log 10 = 1) \qquad \textbf{(½ Mark)}$$

$$= 2.68\ V \qquad \textbf{(1 Mark)}$$

29. (a) (i) $2MnO_2 + 4KOH + O_2 \longrightarrow$
$$2K_2MnO_4 + 2H_2O$$
(1 Mark)

(ii) $Na_2CrO_4 + 2H^+ \longrightarrow$
$$Na_2Cr_2O_7 + 2Na^+ + H_2O$$
(1 Mark)

(b) (i) Mn is stable in +2 state with $3d^5$ half-filled configuration. So, it does not tend to get oxidised to +3 state. On the other hand, Fe in +2 state has $3d^6$ configuration and in +3 state, it has $3d^5$ stable configuration hence Fe^{2+} readily gets oxidised to Fe^{3+}. **(1 Mark)**

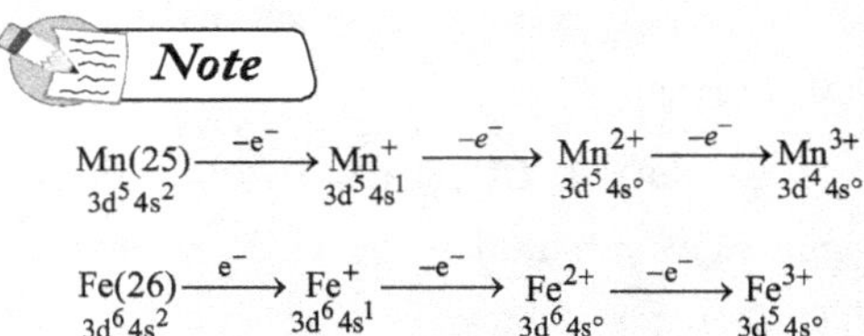

(ii) Enthalpy of atomization depends upon the number of unpaired electrons. More the number of unpaired electrons, more the number of bonds formed and hence more is the enthalpy of atomization. Zn has $3d^{10}\ 4s^2$ configuration. So it has no unpaired electrons and so it has lowest enthalpy of atomization. **(1 Mark)**

(iii) Actinoid elements shows wide range of oxidation states due to comparable energies of $5f$, $6d$ and $7s$ levels. **(1 Mark)**

OR

(i) Mn shows the maximum no. of oxidation states in $3d$-series. This is because variability of oxidation states depends upon the no. of unpaired electrons in d-orbitals. As Mn has maximum no. of unpaired electrons ($3d^5$), so it shows maximum number of oxidation states. **(1 Mark)**

(ii) Cu has positive $E°$ (M^{2+}/M) value. This is because standard reduction potential depends upon three factors :

1. Enthalpy of atomization.
2. Enthalpy of submination
3. Hydration enthalpy

The sum of the above three gives $E°$ value. For copper, enthalpy of atomization is very high while its hydration enthalpy is low. As a result, $E°$ comes to be +ve. **(1 Mark)**

(iii) $$\underset{3d^4 4s^0}{Cr^{2+}} \xrightarrow{-e^-} \underset{3d^3 4s^0}{Cr^{3+}} \quad \underset{3d^5 4s^0}{Mn^{2+}} \xrightarrow{-e^-} \underset{3d^4 4s^0}{Mn^{3+}}$$

Reduction of $Mn^{3+} \longrightarrow Mn^{2+}$ gives stable configuration of $3d^5$. Hence, Mn^{3+} is a stronger oxidising agent than Cr^{3+}. **(1 Mark)**

(iv) Europium (Eu) shows + 2 oxidation state because of formation of stable f^7 configuration after loss of two s-electrons. **(1 Mark)**

(v) $MnO_4^- + 8H^+ + 5e^- \longrightarrow Mn^{2+} + 4H_2O$

(1 Mark)

30. (a) (i) 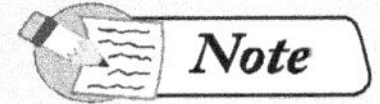

$$\bigcirc = O + H_2N - OH \xrightarrow{H^+}$$

$$\bigcirc = N - OH$$

(1 Mark)

(ii) $2C_6H_5CHO + conc.NaOH \longrightarrow$

$C_6H_5CH_2OH + C_6H_5COOH$ **(1 Mark)**

(iii) $CH_3COOH \xrightarrow{Cl_2+P\ (red)} \underset{\underset{Cl}{|}}{CH_2COOH}$ **(1 Mark)**

> **Note**
>
> *Cannizzaro Reactions are the base induced disproportionation of two molecules of a non-enolizable aldehyde to yield a carboxylic acid and a primary alcohol. The reaction is also said to be redox process because one aldehyde oxidised to give carboxylic acid while other aldehyde undergoes reduction to yield the alcohol.*

(b) (i) $NaHCO_3$ is used distinguish benzaldehyde and benzoic acid,

$$\underset{CHO}{\bigcirc} + NaHCO_3 \longrightarrow \text{No reaction}$$

$$\underset{COOH}{\bigcirc} + NaHCO_3 \longrightarrow$$

$C_6H_5COONa + CO_2\uparrow + H_2O$ **(1 Mark)**

(ii) Fehling's test is used to distinguish propanal and propanone

$$\underset{\text{propanal}}{CH_3CH_2CHO} + 2Cu^{2+} + 5OH^- \longrightarrow$$

$$Cu_2O + CH_3CH_2COO^- + 3H_2O$$
$$\text{(Red Colour)}$$

$$\underset{\text{propanal}}{CH_3COCH_3} + Cu^{2+} + OH^- \longrightarrow \text{No reaction}$$

(1 Mark)

OR

(a) (i) CH_3CHO is more reactive than CH_3COCH_3 towards reaction with HCN. This is because there is more steric hindrance in case of CH_3COCH_3, so the attack by the nucleophile (CN^-) becomes difficult. This is not the case in CH_3CHO.

(1 Mark)

(ii) Carboxylic acid is a stronger acid than phenol. This is because in the resonating structures of carboxy anion, the –ve charge is on the more electro –ve O-atom whereas in phenoxide ion, –ve charge is on less electronegative carbon atom. Moreover, the –ve charge is delocalised over two oxygen atoms in carboxylate anion whereas is phenoxide ion, it is delocalised over one oxygen atom and less electro negative carbon-atoms.

(1 Mark)

(b) (i) Wolff-Kishner reduction

$$\underset{\text{ald/ketone}}{\diagdown C = O} \xrightarrow[-H_2O]{NH_2NH_2} \diagdown C = NNH_2$$

$$\xrightarrow[\Delta]{KOH/glycol} \underset{\text{alkane}}{\diagdown CH_2} + N_2$$

(1 Mark)

(ii) Aldol condensation

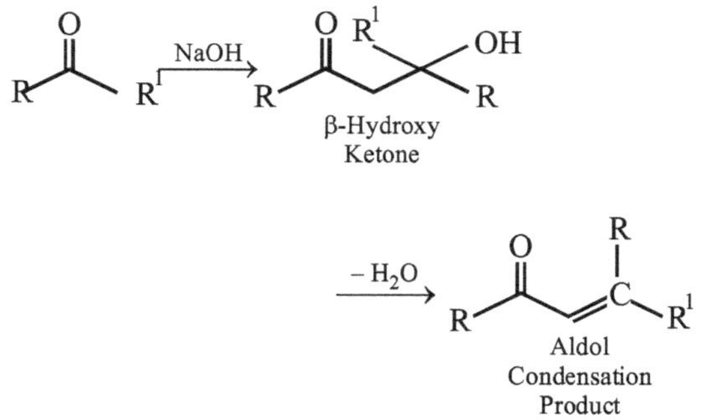

$$\underset{R'}{\overset{O}{\underset{\|}{R-C}}} \xrightarrow{NaOH} \underset{\substack{\beta\text{-Hydroxy} \\ \text{Ketone}}}{R-C-C-R}$$

$$\xrightarrow{-H_2O} \underset{\substack{\text{Aldol} \\ \text{Condensation} \\ \text{Product}}}{R-C-C=C-R^1}$$

(1 Mark)

(iii) Cannizaro Reaction

$$2HCHO \xrightarrow[\text{NaOH}]{\text{conc}} CH_3OH + HCOONa$$

(1 Mark)

All India *2013*
CBSE Board Solved Paper

Time Allowed : 3 Hours   *Maximum Marks : 70*

General Instructions:
- (i) All questions are compulsory.
- (ii) Section A : Questions number **1** to **8** are very short answer questions and carry **1** mark each.
- (iii) Section B : Questions number **9** to **18** are short answer questions and carry **2** marks each.
- (iv) Section C : Questions number **19** to **27** are also short answer questions and carry **3** marks each.
- (v) Section D : Questions number **28** to **30** are long answer questions and carry **5** marks each.
- (vi) Use of log tables, if necessary. Use of calculators is not allowed.

SECTION - A

1. Of physisorption or chemisorption, which has a higher enthalpy of adsorption?

2. Name the method used for refining of copper metal.

3. Name two poisonous gases which can be prepared from chlorine gas.

4. Write the IUPAC name of the following compound:

$$CH_3 - \underset{\underset{CH_3}{|}}{\overset{\overset{CH_3}{|}}{C}} - \underset{\underset{Cl}{|}}{CH} - CH_3$$

5. Rearrange the following compounds in the increasing order of their boiling points :

$$CH_3 - CHO, \; CH_3 - CH_2 - OH, \; CH_3 - CH_2 - CH_3$$

6. Write the structure of N-methylethanamine.

7. What are the products of hydrolysis of sucrose?

8. Is $\left(\!-CH_2-\underset{\underset{Cl}{|}}{CH}-\!\right)_n$ a homopolymer or a copolymer ?

SECTION - B

9. Account for the following :
- (i) Schottky defects lower the density of related solids.
- (ii) Conductivity of silicon increases on doping it with phosphorus.

10. Aluminium crystallizes in an *fcc* structure. Atomic radius of the metal is 125 pm. What is the length of the side of the unit cell of the metal?

11. The standard electrode potential ($E°$) for Daniel cell is $+ 1.1$ V. Calculate the $\Delta G°$ for the reaction $Zn(s) + Cu^{2+}(aq) \longrightarrow Zn^{2+}(aq) + Cu(s)$

$(1F = 96500 \, C\, mol^{-1})$.

12. (a) For a reaction $A + B \rightarrow P$, the rate law is given by,

$r = k\,[A]^{1/2}\,[B]^2$.

What is the order of this reaction?

   (b) A first order reaction is found to have a rate constant $k = 5.5 \times 10^{-14}\,s^{-1}$. Find the half life of the reaction.

13. (a) Name the method used for removing gangue from sulphide ores.

   (b) How is wrought iron different from steel?

14. Draw the structures of the following molecules :

   (i) $XeOF_4$ (ii) H_3PO_3

15. How are interhalogen compounds formed? What general compositions can be assigned to them?

16. Explain the mechanism of the following reaction:

$$CH_3 - CH_2 - OH \xrightarrow[443\,K]{H^+} CH_2{=}CH_2 + H_2O$$

17. Write the equations involved in the following reactions :
- (i) Reimer – Tiemann reaction
- (ii) Williamson's ether synthesis

18. Define thermoplastic and thermosetting polymers. Give one example of each.

OR

What is a biodegradable polymer? Give an example of a biodegradable aliphatic polyester.

19. The rate of a reaction becomes four times when the temperature changes from 293 K to 313 K. Calculate the energy of activation (E_a) of the reaction assuming that it does not change with temperature.

$[R = 8.314 \, J \, K^{-1} \, mol^{-1}, \log 4 = 0.6021]$

20. What are the characteristics of the following colloids? Give one example of each.

(i)   Multimolecular colloids

(ii) Lyophobic sols

(iii) Emulsions

21. Give reasons for the following :

(i)   Where R is an alkyl group, $R_3P = O$ exists but $R_3N = O$ does not.

(ii) $PbCl_4$ is more covalent than $PbCl_2$.

(iii) At room temperature, N_2 is much less reactive.

22. For the complex $[NiCl_4]^{2-}$, write

(i)   the IUPAC name.

(ii) the hybridization type.

(iii) the shape of the complex.

(atomic no. of Ni = 28)

OR

What is meant by crystal field splitting energy? On the basis of crystal field theory, write the electronic configuration of d^4 in terms of t_{2g} and e_g in an octahedral field when

(i) $\Delta_o > P$

(ii) $\Delta_o < P$

23. Give reasons for the following :

(i)   Ethyl iodide undergoes S_N2 reaction faster than ethyl bromide

(ii) ($\pm$) 2-Butanol is optically inactive.

(iii) $C - X$ bond length in halobenzene is smaller than $C - X$ bond length in $CH_3 - X$.

24. Complete the following reactions :

(i) $CH_3CH_2NH_2 + CHCl_3 + KOH \, (alc.) \longrightarrow$

(ii) $C_6H_5N_2^+Cl^- \xrightarrow[\text{(Room temp.)}]{H_2O}$

(iii) (structure: aniline, $C_6H_5NH_2$) $+ HCl \, (aq.) \longrightarrow$

25. (i)   What class of drug is Ranitidine ?

(ii) If water contains dissolved Ca^{2+} ions, out of soaps and synthetic detergents, which will you use for cleaning clothes?

(iii) which of the following is an antiseptic ?

0.2% phenol, 1% phenol.

26. Calculate the emf of the following cell at 25°C :

$$Ag \, (s) \, | \, Ag^+ \, (10^{-3} \, M) \, || \, Cu^{2+} \, (10^{-1} \, M) \, | \, Cu \, (s)$$

Given $E^°_{cell} = + 0.46 \, V$ and $\log 10^n = n$.

27. Shanti, a domestic helper of Mrs. Anuradha, fainted while mopping the floor. Mrs. Anuradha immediately took her to the nearby hospital where she was diagnosed to be severely 'anaemic'. The doctor prescribed an iron rich diet and multivitamins supplement to her. Mrs. Anuradha supported her financially to get the medicines. After a month, Shanti was diagnosed to be normal.

After reading the above passage, answer the following questions :

(i)   What values are displayed by Mrs. Anuradha?

(ii) Name the vitamin whose deficiency causes 'pernicious anaemia'.

(iii) Give an example of a water soluble vitamin.

28. (a)   State Raoult's law for a solution containing volatile components. How does Raoult's law become a special case of Henry's law?

(b)   1.00 g of a non-electrolyte solute dissolved in 50 g of benzene lowered the freezing point of benzene by 0.40 K. Find the molar mass of the solute. (K_f for benzene = 5.12 K kg mol^{-1})

OR

(a) Define the following terms :

   (i) Ideal solution

   (ii) Azeotrope

   (iii) Osmotic pressure

(b) A solution of glucose ($C_6H_{12}O_6$) in water is labelled as 10% by weight. What would be the molality of the solution?

   (Molar mass of glucose = 180 g mol^{-1})

29. (a) Give reasons for the following :

   (i) Mn^{3+} is a good oxidising agent.

   (ii) $\overset{\circ}{E}_{M^{2+}/M}$ values are not regular for first row transition metals (3d series).

   (iii) Although 'F' is more electronegative than 'O', the highest Mn fluoride is MnF_4, whereas the highest oxide is Mn_2O_7.

(b) Complete the following equations :

   (i) $2CrO_4^{2-} + 2H^+ \longrightarrow$

   (ii) $KMnO_4 \xrightarrow{\text{heat}}$

OR

(a) Why do transition elements show variable oxidation states?

   (i) Name the element showing maximum number of oxidation states among the first series of transition metals from Sc (Z = 21) to Zn (Z = 30).

   (ii) Name the element which shows only +3 oxidation state.

(b) What is lanthanoid contraction ? Name an important alloy which contains some of the lanthanoid metals.

30. (a) How will you convert the following :

   (i) Propanone to propan-2-ol

   (ii) Ethanal to 2-hydroxy propanoic acid

   (iii) Toluene to benzoic acid

(b) Give simple chemical test to distinguish between :

   (i) Pentan-2-one and pentan-3-one

   (ii) Ethanal and propanal

OR

(a) Write the products of the following reactions :

   (i) $CH_3 - \underset{\underset{O}{\|}}{C} - CH_3 \xrightarrow[\text{conc.HCl}]{\text{Zn-Hg}} ?$

   (ii) $CH_3 - \underset{\underset{O}{\|}}{C} - Cl + H_2 \xrightarrow{\text{Pd-BaSO}_4} ?$

   (iii) 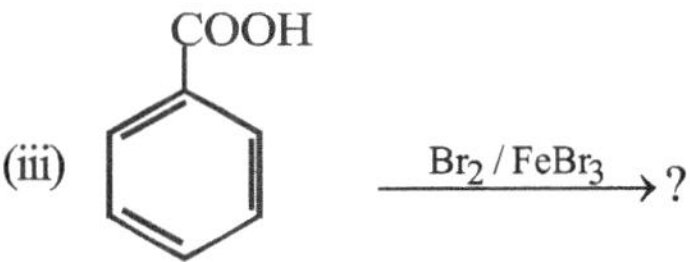 $\xrightarrow{Br_2/FeBr_3} ?$

(b) Which acid of each pair shown here would you expect to be stronger?

   (i) $F - CH_2 - COOH$ or $Cl - CH_2 - COOH$

   (ii) (benzoic acid structure, C_6H_5COOH) or CH_3COOH

Solutions

SECTION - A

1. Chemisorption has higher enthalpy of adsorption. **(1 Mark)**

2. Electrolytic refining is used for refining of copper metal. **(1 Mark)**

3. Phosgene ($COCl_2$), tear gas (CCl_3NO_2). **(1 Mark)**

 *Note*

$CO + Cl_2 \rightarrow COCl_2$
Industrially, phosgene is produced by passing purified carbon monoxide and chlorine gas through a bed of porous activated carbon, which serves as a catalyst.
Chloropicrin (CCl_3NO_2) is one of the tear gas and it has been used in chemical warfare.
$CH_3NO_2 + 3\,NaOCl \rightarrow Cl_3CNO_2 + 3NaOH$

4. 2-Chloro-3, 3-dimethylbutane. **(1 Mark)**

5. $CH_3-CH_2-CH_3 < CH_3-CHO < CH_3-CH_2-OH$ **(1 Mark)**

6. $CH_3-CH_2-NH-CH_3$. **(1 Mark)**

7. Glucose and fructose.

$$C_{12}H_{22}O_{11} + H_2O \xrightarrow{\ HCl\ } C_6H_{12}O_6 + C_6H_{12}O_6$$
$$\text{Glucose} \qquad \text{Fructose}$$

(1 Mark)

8. It is a homopolymer as it is derived from only one type of monomer (vinyl chloride) units. **(1 Mark)**

SECTION - B

9. **(i)** In Schottky defect, equal number of cations and anions are missing from their lattice sites. As a result number of ions decreases and thus mass decreases but volume remains same. Thus causes decrease in density $\left(\text{density} = \dfrac{\text{mass}}{\text{volume}}\right)$ of the solids having Schottky defect.

(1 Mark)

(ii) Phosphorus is a group 15 element and has five electrons in its valence shell. Upon doping silicon with phosphorus four out of 5 valence electrons forms four covalent bonds with neighbouring silicon atoms, the fifth extra electron is free and gets delocalised which increases the conductivity of the silicon. **(1 Mark)**

10. For *fcc* edge length, $a = 2\sqrt{2}r$ **(½ Mark)**

$= 2 \times 1.414 \times 125$ **(½ Mark)**

$= 353.5\,pm$ **(1 Mark)**

 *Note*

The relation between edge length (a) and radius of atom (r) for bcc lattice is
$\sqrt{3}\,a = 4r$
$a = \dfrac{4}{\sqrt{3}}r$

11. $\Delta G^\circ = -n\,FE^\circ_{cell}$ **(½ Mark)**

$= -2 \times 96500\ C\,mol^{-1} \times 1.1\ V$ **(½ Mark)**

$= -212300\ J\,mol^{-1}\ (J = C.V)$

$= -212.3\ kJ\,mol^{-1}$ **(1 Mark)**

12. **(a)** Order $= \dfrac{1}{2} + 2 = \dfrac{5}{2} = 2.5$ **(1 Mark)**

(b) For a first order reaction,

$t_{\frac{1}{2}} = \dfrac{0.693}{k} = \dfrac{0.693}{5.5 \times 10^{-14}s^{-1}} = 1.26 \times 10^{13}\ sec.$ **(1 Mark)**

13. **(a)** Froth floatation method. **(1 Mark)**

(b) Wrought iron is the purest form of commercial iron. It has low carbon content with 1-3% siliceous slag. Steel is an alloy of iron, carbon and other elements. **(1 Mark)**

14. (i) 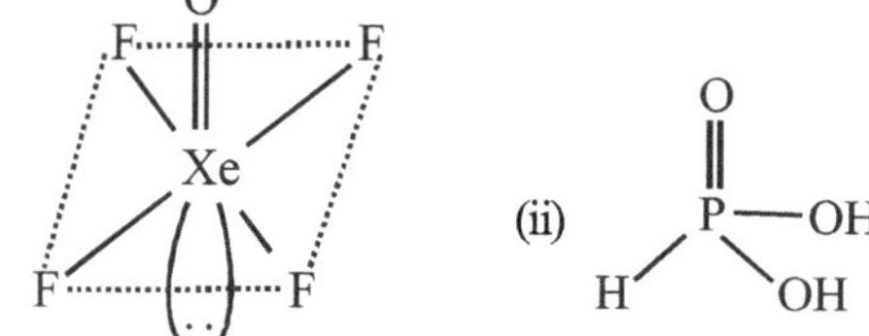   (ii) 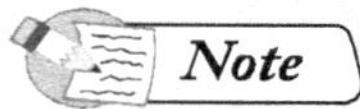

(1 + 1 = 2 Marks)

15. Halogens react with each other to form covalent interhalogen compounds. They are formed either by direct combination of the halogens or by the action of a halogen on a lower interhalogen.

e.g., $Cl_2(g) + F_2(g) \xrightarrow{\ 473K\ } 2ClF(g)$
Equal Volumes

$ClF(g) + F_2(g) \xrightarrow{\ 475-575K\ } ClF_3(g)$

General composition of interhalogen compounds can be given as XY_n, where X is a less electronegative halogen, while Y is a more electronegative halogen and n can have the values 1, 3, 5 and 7. **(2 Marks)**

Note

Interhalogen compounds are of four general types:
1. XY (e.g., ClF)   2. XY_3 (e.g., ClF_3)
3. XY_5 (e.g., BrF_5)   4. XY_7 (e.g., IF_7)
The interhalogen compounds of type XY and XY_3 are formed between the halogen having very low electronegative difference. The interhalogen compounds of type XY_5 and XY_7 are formed by larger atoms having low electronegativity with the smaller atoms having high electronegativity.

16. **Step 1.** Formation of protonated alcohol :

$$CH_3CH_2 - \ddot{O} - H + H^+ \rightleftharpoons CH_3 - CH_2 - \overset{\oplus}{\underset{..}{O}} \overset{H}{\underset{H}{<}}$$

(½ Mark)

Step 2. Formation of carbocation

$$CH_3 - CH_2 - \overset{\oplus}{\underset{..}{O}} \overset{H}{\underset{H}{<}} \xrightarrow{slow} CH_3 - \overset{\oplus}{C}H_2 + H_2O$$

(½ Mark)

It is the rate determining step.

Step 3. Elimination of a proton to form ethene

$$H - \overset{\oplus}{C}H_2 - CH_2 \xrightarrow{Fast} \underset{\text{Ethene}}{CH_2 = CH_2} + H^+$$

(½ Mark)

17. (i)

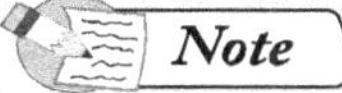

(1 Mark)

(ii) $R + X + Na\,OR' \longrightarrow R - O - R' + NaX$

$$CH_3 - CH_2 + I + Na + O - CH_2 - CH_3$$

Ethyl Iodide   Sodium ethoxide

$$\longrightarrow CH_3 - CH_2 - O - CH_2 - CH_3 + NaI$$

(1 Mark)

18. Thermoplastic Polymers : In these polymers, the intermolecular forces of attraction are in between those of elastomers and fibres. They are hard at room temperature, become soft and viscous on heating and again rigid on cooling.

e.g., Polythene, PVC etc. **(1 Mark)**

Thermosetting polymers : They are semifluid substances with low molecular masses which when heated become hard, infusible and insoluble because of sufficiently large number of cross links. They cannot be remelted and reworked. e.g., Bakelite. **(1 Mark)**

OR

Biodegradable polymer : These polymers disintegrate over a period of time due to environmental degradation by bacteria. An example of biodegradable aliphatic polyester is PHBV i.e., Poly hydroxybutyrate-co-β-hydroxy valerate.

(2 Marks)

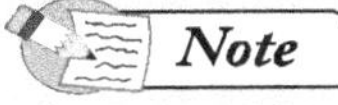

$$nCH_3 - \overset{OH}{\underset{|}{CH}} - CH_2 - COOH +$$
3-Hydroxybutanoic acid

$$nCH_3 - CH_2 - \overset{OH}{\underset{|}{CH}} - CH_2 - COOH \longrightarrow$$
3–Hydroxy pentanoic acid

$$+O - \overset{}{\underset{CH_3}{CH}} - CH_2 - \overset{}{\underset{O}{C}} - O - \overset{}{\underset{CH_2CH_3}{CH}} - CH_2 - \overset{}{\underset{O}{C}} +_n$$
PHBV

19. Let $k_1 = k$, $T_1 = 293$ K

$\therefore$ $k_2 = 4k_1$, $T_2 = 313$ K

$$\log \frac{k_2}{k_1} = \frac{E_a}{2.303R} \left[\frac{T_2 - T_1}{T_1 T_2} \right]$$ **(½ Mark)**

$$\log \frac{4k_1}{k_1} = \frac{E_a}{2.303 \times 8.314} \left[\frac{313 - 293}{293 \times 313} \right]$$ **(½ Mark)**

$$\log 4 = \frac{E_a}{2.303 \times 8.314} \left[\frac{20}{91709} \right]$$

$$0.6021 = \frac{E_a \times 20}{2.303 \times 8.314 \times 91709}$$ **(½ Mark)**

$\therefore$ $E_a = \dfrac{0.6021 \times 2.303 \times 8.314 \times 91709}{20}$ **(½ Mark)**

     $= 52863.33$ J mol^{-1}

     $= 52.863$ kJ mol^{-1} **(1 Mark)**

20. (i) Multimolecular colloids : They are formed by the aggregation of a large number of atoms or molecules which generally have diameters less than 1 nm. Their molecular masses are not very high. Their atoms or molecules are held together by weak van der Waal's forces. eg : sols of gold, sulphur, etc. **(1 Mark)**

(ii) Lyophobic sols : Lyophobic sols are the sols in which the dispersed phase has no attraction for the dispersion medium or the solvent. For example, dispersion of gold, iron and sulphur in water. **(1 Mark)**

Note

Lyophobic sols are not stable, they can be readily precipitated by adding small amount of electrolyte or heating. They are also called irreversible sols. They are not much hydrated. e.g., gold sol.

(iii) Emulsions : A colloidal dispersion in which both the dispersed phase and the dispersion medium are liquids is called an emulsion. Emulsions are stabilised by emulsifiers. Emulsions exhibit properties like Tyndall effect, electrophoresis etc. Their constituent liquids can be separated by boiling, freezing etc. e.g., vanishing cream, butter etc. **(1 Mark)**

21. (i) Due to presence of vacant d-orbitals phosphorus forms $p\pi$-$d\pi$ multiple bonds and hence can expand its covalency beyond four. Therefore, $R_3P = O$ exists. In $R_3N = O$, the covalency of N is also 5, but due to absence of d-orbitals N cannot form $p\pi - d\pi$ bonds and thus cannot expand its covalency beyond 4. Hence $R_3N = O$ does not exist. **(1 Mark)**

(ii) O.S. of Pb in $PbCl_4$ is $+4$ while in $PbCl_2$ it is $+2$. According to Fajan's rule for similar anion cation with small size and high charge causes greater polarisation of anion hence more will be covalent character. Ionic radii of Pb^{4+} is smaller than Pb^{2+} thus $PbCl_4$ is more covalent than $PbCl_2$. **(1 Mark)**

> **Note**
>
> *Fajan's Rule can be stated on the basis of three factors:*
> 1. *Size of the ion: Smaller the size of cation, the larger the size of the cation, greater is the covalent character of the bond.*
> 2. *The charge of cation: Greater the charge of cation, greater is the covalent character of the bond.*
> 3. *Electronic configuration: For cation with charge and size, the one with $(n-1)d^{\,n}\,ns^0$ have greater covalent character than the cation with $ns^2\,np^6$ electronic configuration.*

(iii) N_2 (which is a gas at room temperature), is triply bonded ($N \equiv N$). Due to its high bond dissociation energy ($941.410\ kJ\ mol^{-1}$), it is unreactive at room temperature. **(1 Mark)**

22. (i) Tetrachloridonickelate (II) ion
(ii) sp^3
(iii) Tetrahedral   **(1 + 1 + 1 = 3 Marks)**

OR

The d-orbitals present in metal have the same energy in the free state. This is called degenerate state of d-orbital. But, when a complex is formed the ligands destroy the degeneracy of these orbitals. The d-orbitals gets split into two sets one with lower and one with higher energy. The difference of energy between two sets is called crystal field splitting energy. **(1 Mark)**

(i) When $\Delta_o > P$, the d^4 has configuration i.e., $t_{2g}^4 e_g^0$

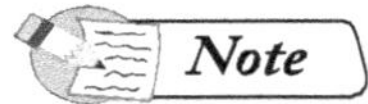

(1 Mark)

(ii) When $\Delta_o < P$, the d^4 has configuration i.e., $t_{2g}^3 e_g^1$

(1 Mark)

23. (i) Ethyl iodide undergoes S_N2 reaction faster than ethyl bromide because I^- is a better leaving group than Br^-. **(1 Mark)**

(ii) $(\pm)$ 2-Butanol represents a racemic mixture of two enantiomers. Two enantiomers always show opposite optical activities. i.e., they rotate the plane of polarized light by equal amounts in opposite directions. The optical rotation of an equimolar mixture of a pair of enantiomers is zero because the optical rotations of the enantiomers cancel out. **(1 Mark)**

(iii) $C - X$ bond in haloarene acquires partial double bond character due to rasonance and also carbon atom in $C - X$ bond in haloarene is sp^2 hybridised while in alkyl halide it is sp^3 hybridised. Therefore C–X bond length is shorter in haloarene. **(1 Mark)**

24. (i) $CH_3CH_2NH_2 + CHCl_3 + 3\ KOH\,(alc.) \xrightarrow{\ \Delta\ }$
$$CH_3CH_2N \cong C + 3KCl + 3H_2O$$
Ethylisocyanide

(1 Mark)

(ii) $C_6H_5N_2^+Cl^- \xrightarrow[\text{Room temp.}]{H_2O} C_6H_5OH + N_2 + HCl$
Phenol

(1 Mark)

(iii)

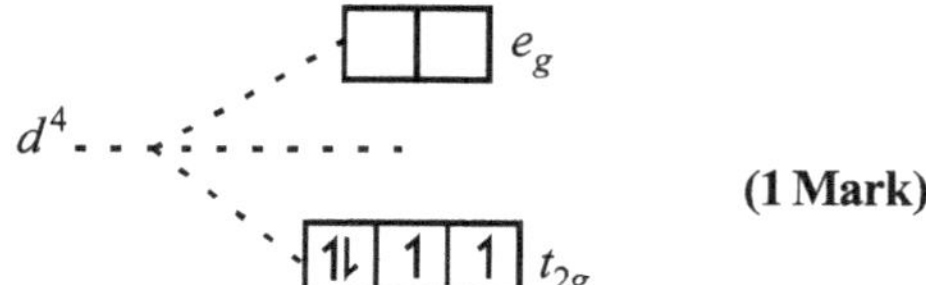

(1 Mark)

25. (i) Ranitidine belongs to antacids class of drugs. **(1 Mark)**
(ii) Water containing dissolved Ca^{2+} is hard. Synthetic detergents are preferred over soaps for cleaning clothes in hard water because calcium salts of detergents are soluble in water while calcium salts of soaps are insoluble and thus appears as a sticky scum. **(1 Mark)**
(iii) 0.2% solution of phenol is used as an antiseptic. **(1 Mark)**

26. For the given cell, the redox reaction is
$$2Ag(s) + Cu^{2+}(aq) \longrightarrow 2Ag^+(aq) + Cu(s)$$
$$\therefore \quad n = 2$$

$$E_{cell} = E_{cell}^{\circ} - \left[\frac{0.0591}{n}\log\frac{[Ag^+]^2}{[Cu^{2+}]}\right] \quad \textbf{(½ Mark)}$$

$$= 0.46 - \left[\frac{0.0591}{2}\log\frac{(10^{-3})^2}{10^{-1}}\right] \quad \textbf{(½ Mark)}$$

$$= 0.46 - [0.02955 \log 10^{-5}]$$
$$= 0.46 - [0.02955 \times (-5)] \quad \textbf{(1 Mark)}$$
$$= 0.46 + 0.14775$$
$$= 0.60775\ V. \quad \textbf{(1 Mark)}$$

27. (i) The incident displayed that Mrs. Anuradha is a nice human being associated with some values like presence of mind, kind hearted, helping nature, concern for others etc. **(1 Mark)**

(ii) Vitamin B_{12} deficiency causes pernicious anaemia. **(1 Mark)**

(iii) Vitamin C is a types of water soluble vitamin. **(1 Mark)**

SECTION - D

28. **(a)** **Raoult's law :** For a solution of volatile liquids, the partial vapour pressure of each component of the solution is directly proportional to its mole fraction present in solution.

For two components A and B

$$p_A = p_A^{\circ} x_A \qquad p_B = p_B^{\circ} x_B \qquad \textbf{(1 Mark)}$$

Raoult's law as a special case of Henry's law :

According to Raoult's law, for any volatile component of the solution.

$$p_A = p_A^{\circ} \times x_A$$

Now, for a solution in which a gas is the solute and liquid is the solvent, then according to Henry's law

$$p_A = k_H \times x_A$$

i.e., partial pressure of the volatile component (gas) is directly proportional to the mole fraction of that component (gas) in the solution.

Thus, Raoult's law and Henry's law become identical except that their proportionality constants are different. **(2 Marks)**

(b) $W_2 = 1.00\,g$

$W_1 = 50\,g$

$\Delta T_f = 0.40\,K$

$K_f = 5.12\,K\,kg\,mol^{-1}$

$$M_2 = \frac{1000 \times K_f \times W_2}{W_1 \times \Delta T_f} \qquad \textbf{(1 Mark)}$$

$$= \frac{1000 \times 5.12 \times 1.00}{50 \times 0.40}$$

$$= 256\,g\,mol^{-1} \qquad \textbf{(1 Mark)}$$

OR

(a) (i) **Ideal solution :** (I) The solution which obey Raoult's law at all temperatures and concentrations (II) $\Delta H_{mix} = 0$ i.e. no heat is evolved or absorbed when components are mixed to form the solution (III) $\Delta V_{mix} = 0$ i.e. no change in volume. **(1 Mark)**

(ii) **Azeotrope :** A liquid mixture, having a definite composition, and boiling point like a pure liquid, is called a constant boiling mixture or an azeotrope. **(1 Mark)**

(iii) **Osmotic pressure :** The minimum excess pressure that has to be applied to the solution to prevent the entry of the solvent into the solution through the semipermeable membrane due to osmosis is called the osmotic pressure. **(1 Mark)**

(b) 10% glucose solution by weight means

Mass of solute $(W_2) = 10\,g$

Mol. mass of solute $(M_2) = 180\,g\,mol^{-1}$

Mass of solvent $(W_1) = 100 - 10 = 90\,g$

$$\text{Molality (m)} = \frac{W_2}{M_2} \times \frac{1000}{W_1} \qquad \textbf{(1 Mark)}$$

$$= \frac{10}{180} \times \frac{1000}{90}$$

$$= 0.617\,m \qquad \textbf{(1 Mark)}$$

29. **(a)** (i) $_{25}Mn = [Ar]\,3d^5 4s^2$

$_{25}Mn^{+3} = [Ar]\,3d^4 4s^0$

Mn^{3+} is a good oxidizing agent. A good oxidising agent reduces itself i.e. gains electron(s) from others. Mn^{3+} tends to gain one electron to acquire stable $3d^5$ configuration hence Mn^{3+} is a good oxidizing agent. **(1 Mark)**

(ii) $E^{\circ}_{M^{2+}/M}$ values are the sum of sublimation enthalpy, ionisation enthalpy, hydration enthalpy etc. The irregularity in the E° values is, because of irregular variation of ionisation enthalpies $(IE_1 + IE_2)$ and also the sublimation enthalpies. **(1 Mark)**

(iii) Oxygen stabilises the highest oxidation state even more than fluorine, e.g., the highest fluoride of Mn is MnF_4 whereas highest oxide is Mn_2O_7. The reason for this is the ability of oxygen to form multiple bonds with metal atoms. **(1 Mark)**

(b) (i) $2CrO_4^{2-} + 2H^+ \longrightarrow Cr_2O_7^{2-} + H_2O$ **(1 Mark)**

(ii) $2KMnO_4 \xrightarrow{\ 513K\ } K_2MnO_4 + MnO_2 + O_2$ **(1 Mark)**

OR

(a) The transition elements show variable oxidation states because the energies of $(n-1)d$ orbitals and ns orbitals are very close. Hence, electrons from both of these orbitals can participate in bonding. **(1 Mark)**

(i) In the first series of transition elements, Mn shows maximum number of oxidation states. **(1 Mark)**

(ii) Scandium shows only +3 O.S. **(1 Mark)**

(b) In lanthanoid series, with increasing atomic number, there is a progressive decrease in atomic as well as ionic radii of trivalent ions from La^{3+} to Lu^{3+}. This regular decrease in the atomic and the ionic radii of lanthanoids with increasing atomic number is known as lanthanoid contraction.

'Mischmetal' is an alloy which contains some of the lanthanoid metals. **(2 Marks)**

 **Note**

Lanthanoid contraction is a unique feature in the chemistry of lanthanoids, lanthanoid contraction, results due to improper shielding of 4f electrons. Similar effect is also observe in actinoid series which is due to improper shielding of 5f electrons. However effect is more pronounced in actionoid series due to greater deshielding effect of 5f electrons in comparison to 4f electrons.

30. (a)

(i)

$$CH_3 - \overset{\displaystyle O}{\overset{\|}{C}} - CH_3 + H_2 \xrightarrow{\text{Ni, Pt or Pd}} CH_3 - \overset{\displaystyle OH}{\overset{|}{C}}H - CH_3$$

Propanone　　　　　　　　　　　　Propan-2-ol

(1 Mark)

(ii)

$$CH_3 - CHO \xrightarrow{HCN} CH_3 - \overset{\displaystyle H}{\underset{\displaystyle OH}{\overset{|}{\underset{|}{C}}}} - CN$$

Ethanal

$$\xrightarrow{H^+ / H_2O} CH_3 - \overset{\displaystyle OH}{\overset{|}{C}}H - COOH$$

2 – Hydroxy propanoic acid

(1 Mark)

(iii)

Toluene $\xrightarrow[\text{(ii) H}^+ / H_2O]{\text{(i) KMnO}_4 / OH^-, \Delta}$ Benzoic acid (COOH)

(1 Mark)

(b) Chemical tests to distinguish between :

(i) Pentan-2-one and pentan-3-one : On treating with NaOI (I_2/NaOH) pentan-2-one gives yellow ppt. of iodoform but pentan-3-one does not. (only methyl ketones give iodoform test)

$$CH_3 - CH_2 - CH_2 - \overset{\displaystyle O}{\overset{\|}{C}} - CH_3 + 3NaOI \rightarrow$$

Pentan-2-one

$$CH_3CH_2CH_2COONa + CHI_3 \downarrow + 2NaOH$$

Iodoform
(Yellow ppt.)

$$CH_3 - CH_2 - \overset{\displaystyle O}{\overset{\|}{C}} - CH_2 - CH_3 \xrightarrow{NaOI} \text{No yellow}$$

Pentan-3-one　　　　　　　　　　　ppt. of iodoform

(1 Mark)

(ii) Ethanal and propanal : Ethanal when treated with I_2/NaOH (or NaOI) gives yellow ppt. of iodoform but propanal does not.

$$CH_3CHO + 3NaOI \longrightarrow CHI_3 \downarrow + HCOONa + 2NaOH$$

Ethanal　　　　　　　Yellow
　　　　　　　　　　　ppt.

$$CH_3CH_2CHO$$

Propanal $\Big\downarrow I_2/NaOH$

No yellow ppt.
of iodoform

(1 Mark)

OR

(a) (i)

$$CH_3 - \overset{\displaystyle O}{\overset{\|}{C}} - CH_3 + 4[H] \xrightarrow[\text{conc.HCl}]{\text{Zn–Hg}} CH_3CH_2CH_3 + H_2O$$

Acetone　　　　　　　　　　　　　Propane

(1 Mark)

(ii)

$$CH_3 - \overset{\displaystyle O}{\overset{\|}{C}} - Cl + H_2 \xrightarrow{Pd - BaSO_4} CH_3CHO + HCl$$

Ethanoyl chloride　　　　　　　　Ethanal

(1 Mark)

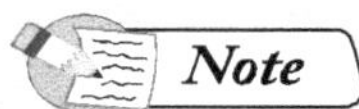

> **Note**
>
> *The rosenmund reaction is catalysed by palladium on barium sulphate. Barium sulphate reduces the activity of palladium due to its low surface area hence decreases the reducing power of palladium in order to prevent over-reduction of the acid.*

(iii)

Benzoic acid (COOH) $\xrightarrow{Br_2/FeBr_3}$ *m*-Bromo benzoic acid (COOH, Br) $+ HBr$ **(1 Mark)**

(b) (i) $F - CH_2COOH$ is stronger acid than $Cl - CH_2COOH$ because F is more electronegative than Cl. F withdraws electrons from $O - H$ bond more strongly than Cl and helps in easier release of H^+ ions by making $O - H$ bond weaker relative to Cl. The stronger - I effect of F also disperses the –ve charge on carboxylate anion and stabilises it to a greater extent than Cl. **(1 Mark)**

(ii) In benzoic acid, benzene ring is present which is an electron withdrawing group and hence it makes the $O - H$ bond more polar and easier to break. This means benzoic acid is more acidic, while, there is no electron withdrawing group in ethanoic acid. Therefore, benzoic acid is more acidic than ethanoic acid. **(1 Mark)**

Delhi *2013*
CBSE Board Solved Paper

Time Allowed : 3 Hours   *Maximum Marks : 70*

General Instructions:
- (i) All question are compulsory.
- (ii) Section A : Question number **1 to 8** are very short answer questions and carry **1** mark each.
- (iii) Section B : Question number **9 to 18** are short answer questions and carry **2** marks each.
- (iv) Section C : Question number **19 to 27** are also short answer questions and carry **3** marks each.
- (v) Section D : Question number **28 to 30** are long answer questions and carry **5** marks each.
- (vi) Use log tables, if necessary. Use of calculator is not allowed.

SECTION - A

1. How many atoms constitute one unit cell of a face-centered cubic crystal?

2. Name the method used for the refining of nickel metal.

3. What is the covalency of nitrogen in N_2O_5?

4. Write the IUPAC name of

$$CH_3\overset{\underset{\displaystyle |}{Cl}}{CH}-CH_2CH=CH_2.$$

5. What happens when CH_3-Br is treated with KCN?

6. Write the structure of 3-methyl butanal.

7. Arrange the following in increasing order of their basic strength in aqueous solution :

$CH_3NH_2, (CH_3)_3N, (CH_3)_2NH$

8. What are three types of RNA molecules which perform different functions?

SECTION - B

9. 18 g of glucose, $C_6H_{12}O_6$ (Molar Mass = 180 g mol^{-1}) is dissolved in 1 kg of water in a sauce pan. At what temperature will this solution boil?

(K_b for water = 0.52 K kg mol^{-1}, boiling point of pure water = 373.15 K)

10. The conductivity of 0.20 M solution of KCl at 298 K is 0.025 S cm^{-1}. Calculate its molar conductivity.

11. Write the dispersed phase and dispersion medium of the following colloidal systems :

- (i) Smoke   (ii) Milk

OR

What are lyophilic and lyophobic colloids? Which of these sols can be easily coagulated on the addition of small amounts of electrolytes?

12. Write the differences between physisorption and chemisorption with respect to the following :

- (i) Specificity   (ii) Temperature dependence
- (iii) Reversibility and   (iv) Enthalpy change

13. (a) Which solution is used for the leaching of silver metal in the presence of air in the metallurgy of silver?

    (b) Out of C and CO, which is a better reducing agent at the lower temperature range in the blast furnace to extract iron from the oxide ore?

14. What happens when :

- (i) PCl_5 is heated?   (ii) H_3PO_3 is heated?

Write the reactions involved.

15. (a) Which metal in the first transition series ($3d$ series) exhibits +1 oxidation state most frequently and why?

    (b) Which of the following cations are coloured in aqueous solutions and why?

    $Sc^{3+}, V^{3+}, Ti^{4+}, Mn^{2+}$

    (At. nos. Sc = 21, V = 23, Ti = 22, Mn = 25)

16. Chlorobenzene is extremely less reactive towards a nucleophilic substitution reaction. Give two reasons for the same.

17. Explain the mechanism of the following reaction:

$$2CH_3-CH_2-OH \xrightarrow[413K]{H^+} CH_3\,CH_2\,\ddot{O}-CH_2-CH_3+H_2O$$

18. How will you convert :
    (i) Propene to Propan-2-ol?
    (ii) Phenol to 2, 4,6-trinitrophenol?

SECTION - C

19. (a) What type of semiconductor is obtained when silicon is doped with boron?

    (b) What type of magnetism is shown in the following alignment of magnetic moments?

    (c) What type of point defect is produced when AgCl is doped with $CdCl_2$?

20. Determine the osmotic pressure of solution prepared by dissolving 2.5×10^{-2} g of K_2SO_4 in 2 L of water at 25°C, assuming that it is completely dissociated.

    ($R = 0.0821$ L atm K^{-1} mol^{-1}, Molar mass of $K_2SO_4 = 174$ g mol^{-1}).

21. Calculate the emf of the following cell at 298 K :

    $Fe(s)\,|\,Fe^{2+}\,(0.001\,M)\,\|\,H^+\,(1\,M)\,|\,H_2\,(g)\,(1\,bar),\,Pt\,(s)$

    (Given $E^{\circ}_{cell} = +0.44V$)

22. How would you account for the following ?
    (i) Transition metals exhibit variable oxidation states.
    (ii) Zr $(Z = 40)$ and Hf $(Z = 72)$ have almost identical radii.
    (iii) Transition metals and their compounds act as catalyst.

OR

Complete the following chemical equations :

    (i) $Cr_2O_7^{2-} + 6Fe^{2+} + 14H^+ \longrightarrow$

    (ii) $2CrO_4^{2-} + 2H^+ \longrightarrow$

    (iii) $2MnO_4^- + 5C_2O_4^{2-} + 16H^+ \longrightarrow$

23. Write the IUPAC names of the following coordination compounds :

    (i) $[Cr(NH_3)_3Cl_3]$

    (ii) $K_3[Fe(CN)_6]$

    (iii) $[CoBr_2(en)_2]^+$, (en = ethylenediamine)

24. Give the structures of A, B and C in the following reaction :

    (i) $C_6H_5N_2^+Cl^- \xrightarrow{CuCN} A \xrightarrow{H_2O/H^+} B \xrightarrow[\Delta]{NH_3} C$

    (ii) $C_6H_5NO_2 \xrightarrow{Sn+HCl} A$

    $\xrightarrow[273\,K]{NaNO_2+HCl} B \xrightarrow[\Delta]{H_2O/H^+} C$

25. Write the name and structures of the monomers of the following polymers :
    (i) Buna-S   (ii) Neoprene
    (iii) Nylon-6, 6

26. After watching a programme on TV about the adverse effects of junk food and soft drinks on the health of school children, Sonali, a student of Class XII, discussed the issue with the school principal. Principal immediately instructed the canteen contractor to replace the fast food with the fibre and vitamins rich food like sprouts, salad, fruits etc. This decision was welcomed by the parents and the students. After reading the above passage, answer the following questions :

    (a) What values are expressed by Sonali and the Principal of the school?

    (b) Give two examples of water-soluble vitamins.

27. (a) Which one of the following is a food preservative ?
        Equanil, Morphine, Sodium benzoate
    (b) Why is bithional added to soap?
    (c) Which class of drugs is used in sleeping pills ?

SECTION - D

28. (a) A reaction is second order in A and first order in B.
        (i) Write the differential rate equation.
        (ii) How is the rate affected on increasing the concentration of A three times?
        (iii) How is the rate affected when the concentrations of both A and B are doubled?

    (b) A first order reaction takes 40 minutes for 30% decomposition. Calculate $t_{1/2}$ for this reaction. (Given log $1.428 = 0.1548$)

OR

    (a) For a first order reaction, show that time required for 99% completion is twice the time required for the completion of 90% of reaction.

(b) Rate constant 'k' of a reaction varies with temperature 'T' according to the equation :

$$\log k = \log A - \frac{E_a}{2.303R}\left(\frac{1}{T}\right)$$

Where E_a is the activation energy. When a graph is plotted for $\log k$ Vs. $\frac{1}{T}$, a straight line with a slope of -4250 K is obtained. Calculate 'E_a' for the reaction. $(R = 8.314 \text{ JK}^{-1}\text{ mol}^{-1})$

29. (a) Give reasons for the following :

(i) Bond enthalpy of F_2 is lower than that of Cl_2.

(ii) PH_3 has lower boiling point than NH_3.

(b) Draw the structures of the following molecules :

(i) BrF_3

(ii) $(HPO_2)_3$

(iii) XeF_4

OR

(a) Account for the following :

(i) Helium is used in diving apparatus.

(ii) Fluorine does not exhibit positive oxidation state.

(iii) Oxygen show catenation behaviour less than sulphur.

(b) Draw the structures of the following molecules :

(i) XeF_2 (ii) $H_2S_2O_8$

30. (a) Although phenoxide ion has more number of resonating structures than carboxylate ion. Carboxylic acid is a stronger acid than phenol. Give two reasons.

(b) How will you bring about the following conversion?

(i) Propanone to propane

(ii) Benzoyl chloride to benzaldehyde

(iii) ethanal to but-2-enal.

OR

(a) Complete the following reactions :

(i) $2H-\underset{\underset{O}{\|}}{C}-H \xrightarrow{\text{Conc. KOH}}$

(ii) $CH_3COOH \xrightarrow{Br_2/P}$

(iii) C₆H₅CHO (benzaldehyde) $\xrightarrow[273-278\,K]{HNO_3/H_2SO_4}$

(b) Give simple chemical tests to distinguish between the following pairs of compounds:

(i) Ethanal and Propanal

(ii) Benzoic acid and Phenol.

Solutions

SECTION - A

1. In face-centered cubic crystal, there are 8 atoms at the corners and 6 at face-centres.

$$\therefore \text{ Total no. of atoms per unit cell} = \left(8 \times \frac{1}{8}\right) + \left(6 \times \frac{1}{2}\right) = 4$$

(1 Mark)

2. Mond process is used for the refining of nickel metal.

(1 Mark)

3. Covalency of nitrogen in N_2O_5 is 4. **(1 Mark)**

4. 4-Chloropent-1-ene **(1 Mark)**

5. $CH_3Br + KCN \longrightarrow \underset{\text{Acetonitrile}}{CH_3CN} + KBr$ **(1 Mark)**

6. $\underset{\text{3 -Methyl butanal}}{CH_3 - \overset{\overset{\displaystyle CH_3}{|}}{CH} - CH_2 - CHO}$ **(1 Mark)**

7. $(CH_3)_2NH > CH_3NH_2 > (CH_3)_3NH$ **(1 Mark)**

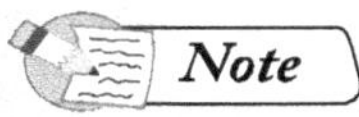

> **Note**
>
> *Basic strength of alkyl amines in the aqueous state is determined by inductive effect, solvation effect and stearic hinderance of the alkyl group. As $-CH_3$ group is smaller than $-C_2H_5$, it offers less stearic hinderance to hydrogen bonding. Therefore order of basic strength will be different for ethyl substituted amines.*
>
> $$(C_2H_5)_2NH > (C_2H_5)_3N > C_2H_5NH_3 > NH_3$$
> $$(CH_3)_2NH > CH_3NH_2 > (CH_3)_3N > NH_3$$

8. The three types of RNA which perform different functions are :
(i)   Transfer RNA or tRNA.
(ii) Ribosomal RNA or rRNA.
(iii) Messenger RNA or mRNA. **(1 Mark)**

SECTION - B

9. $W_2 = 18\,g$
$M_2 = 180\,g\,mol^{-1}$
$W_1 = 1\,kg = 1000\,g$
$K_b = 0.52\,K\,kg\,mol^{-1}$

$$\Delta T_b = K_b \times \frac{W_2}{M_2} \times \frac{1000}{W_1}$$

(½ Mark)

$$= 0.52 \times \frac{18}{180} \times \frac{1000}{1000} = \frac{0.52}{10}$$

(½ Mark)

$$= 0.052\,K$$

Now, $\Delta T_b = T_s - T°$ **(½ Mark)**
$0.052 = T_s - 373.15$
$\therefore \quad T_s = 373.15 + 0.052 = 373.202\,K$
$\therefore \quad$ Boiling point of solution $= 373.202\,K.$ **(½ Mark)**

10. Conductivity $(\kappa) = 0.025\,S\,cm^{-1}$
Molarity $= 0.20\,M$

$$\wedge_m = \frac{\kappa \times 1000}{\text{Molarity}} = \frac{0.025 \times 1000}{0.20}$$

(1 Mark)

$$= 125\,S\,cm^2\,mol^{-1}.$$

(1 Mark)

11. (i) Dispersed phase of smoke is solid and dispersion medium is gas. **(1 Mark)**
(ii) Dispersed phase of milk is liquid and dispersion medium is also liquid. **(1 Mark)**

OR

Lyophilic sols: Lyophilic sols are those sols in which the particles of dispersed phase have great affinity for the dispersion medium, e.g., sols of gum, gelatine, starch, etc. **(1 Mark)**

Lyophobic sols: In this type of sols the particles of dispersed phase have little or no affinity for the dispersion medium, e.g., gold sol, $Fe\,(OH)_3$ sol, As_2O_3 sol., etc.
Lyophobic sols easily coagulate on the addition of small amount of electrolyte because these are not stable. **(1 Mark)**

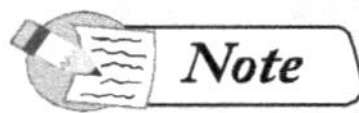

> **Note**
>
> *The stability of Lyophobic sols is only due to the presence of charge on the colloidal particles, on the other hand stability of lyophilic sol is due to charge as well as solvation of colloidal particles.*

12.

		Physisorption	Chemisorption
(i)	Specificity	It is not specific in nature.	It is highly specific in nature and occurs only when there is some possibility of compound formation between gas being adsorbed and the solid adsorbent.
(ii)	Temperature dependence	It occurs at low temperature and decreases with increase of temperature.	It occurs at high temperature and increases with increase of temperature.
(iii)	Reversibility	It is reversible.	It is irreversible.
(iv)	Enthalpy change	It has low enthalpy change, 20 – 40 kJ / mol.	It has high enthalpy change, 80 – 240 kJ / mol.

(2 Marks)

13. (a) In the metallurgy of silver, the metal is leached with dilute solution of NaCN or KCN in the presence of air. **(1 Mark)**

(b) CO is a better reducing agent at lower temperature range in blast furnace to extract iron from iron oxide. **(1 Mark)**

14. (i) When heated, PCl_5 sublimes and decomposes into PCl_3 and Cl_2

$$PCl_5 \xrightarrow{\Delta} PCl_3 + Cl_2$$

(1 Mark)

(ii) When H_3PO_3 is heated, it follows disproportionation reaction and forms PH_3 and H_3PO_4.

$$4\overset{+3}{H_3PO_3} \xrightarrow{\Delta} \overset{-3}{PH_3} + 3\overset{+5}{H_3PO_4} \qquad \textbf{(1 Mark)}$$

15. (a) Copper exhibits + 1 O.S. because after loss of one electron, it acquire $3d^{10}$ configuration and becomes fully filled and hence stable. **(1 Mark)**

(b) V^{3+} $(3d^2)$, Mn^{2+} $(3d^5)$ ions are coloured in aqueous solution because they have unpaired electrons in d-subshell. **(1 Mark)**

16. chloro benzene (like vinyl halides) are less reactive towards nucleophilic substitutions under ordinary conditions. This low reactivity is due to
  (i) resonance effect,
  (ii) sp^2 hybridisation of carbon atom holding the halogen atom and
  (iii) less polarity of the C–X bond. **(2 Marks)**

17. Step-I : $C_2H_5 - \overset{..}{\underset{..}{O}} - H + H^+ \longrightarrow C_2H_5 - \overset{H}{\underset{..}{\overset{|}{O}}}{}^+ - H$ **(½ Mark)**

Step-II :

$C_2H_5 - \overset{..}{\underset{..}{O}} - H + C_2H_5 - \overset{H}{\underset{..}{\overset{|}{O}}}{}^+ - H \longrightarrow C_2H_5 - \overset{H}{\underset{..}{\overset{|}{O}}}{}^+ - C_2H_5 + H_2O$

(1 Mark)

Step-III $C_2H_5 - \overset{H}{\underset{..}{\overset{|}{O}}}{}^+ - C_2H_5 \longrightarrow C_2H_5 - \overset{..}{\underset{..}{O}} - C_2H_5 + H^{\oplus}$
Diethyl ether

(½ Mark)

18. (i) $CH_3 - CH = CH_2 + H_2SO_4 \xrightarrow[\text{(Markovnikov Addition)}]{H_2O,\ Boil}$
  Propene

$$CH_3 - \underset{\underset{OH}{|}}{CH} - CH_3 \qquad \textbf{(1 Mark)}$$
  Propene-2-ol

(ii) 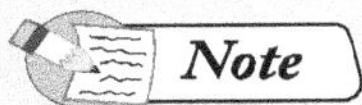
  Phenol $\xrightarrow[\text{conc. }H_2SO_4]{\text{conc. }HNO_3}$ 2, 4, 6-Trinitrophenol **(1 Mark)**

SECTION - C

19. (a) p-type (positive type) extrinsic semiconductor is formed when silicon is doped with boron. **(1 Mark)**

Note

Boron is a trivalent atom. It shares three electrons with three neighboring silicon atoms in the lattice, the fourth silicon atom demands an electron but born does not have extra electron to share. This creates a void or hole in lattice.

(b) Given alignment of magnetic moments is for ferromagnetic substance. **(1 Mark)**

(c) When AgCl is doped with $CdCl_2$ two Ag^+ ions are replaced by one Cd^{2+} ion to maintain electrical neutrality. Thus, a hole is created at the lattice site for every Cd^{2+} introduced. This gives rise to impurity defect. **(1 Mark)**

20. $\pi = iCRT = i\dfrac{W}{M} \times \dfrac{R \times T}{V}$ **(½ Mark)**

For $K_2SO_4 \rightleftharpoons 2K^+ + SO_4^{2-}$
$i = 3$ **(½ Mark)**

$$\dfrac{3 \times 2.5 \times 10^{-2}\,(\text{gram}) \times 0.0821\ \text{L atm K}^{-1}\text{mol}^{-1} \times 298\text{K}}{174(\text{g mol}^{-1}) \times 2\ \text{L}}$$

(1 Mark)

$= 5.27 \times 10^{-3}$ atm **(1 Mark)**

21. $Fe + 2H^+ \rightarrow Fe^{2+} + H_2, n = 2$ **(½ Mark)**

$E_{cell} = E_{cell}^{\circ} - \left[\dfrac{0.0591}{2}\log\dfrac{[Fe^{2+}]}{[H^+]^2}\right]$ **(½ Mark)**

$= (0.44) - \left[\dfrac{0.0591}{2}\log\dfrac{10^{-3}}{(1)^2}\right]$ **(1 Mark)**

$= 0.44 + 0.0886 = 0.5286\ V$ **(1 Mark)**

22. (i) The energy difference between $(n-1)\,d$ and ns orbitals of transition metal atoms is very small, so the electrons from both these orbitals can participate in bonding and hence they show variable oxidation states. **(1 Mark)**

(ii) Due to Lanthanoid contraction, Hf has size similar to that of Zr. **(1 Mark)**

Note

Lanthanoid contraction is due to the poor shielding of one 4f electron by another in the same sub-shell. Lanthanoid contraction causes the radii of the members of the third transition series to be very similar to those of the corresponding members of the second series.

(iii) The transition metals and their compounds behave as catalyst due to the presence of partly filled d-orbitals and exhibiting various oxidation states. They form unstable intermediate complex with reactants and thus lowering the energy of activation. They also provide a suitable surface for the reaction to occur. **(1 Mark)**

OR

(i) $Cr_2O_7^{2-} + 6Fe^{2+} + 14H^+ \longrightarrow$
$2Cr^{3+} + 6Fe^{3+} + 7H_2O$ **(1 Mark)**

(ii) $2CrO_4^{2-} + 2H^+ \longrightarrow Cr_2O_7^{2-} + H_2O$ **(1 Mark)**

(iii) $2MnO_4^- + 5C_2O_4^{2-} + 16H^+ \longrightarrow$
$2Mn^{2+} + 8H_2O + 10CO_2$ **(1 Mark)**

23. (i)   Triamminetrichloridochromium (III).   **(1 Mark)**

(ii) Potassiumhexacyanoferrate (III).   **(1 Mark)**

(iii) Dibromidobis(ethylenediamine) cobalt (III) ion.
                                                                  (1 Mark)

24. (i) $C_6H_5N_2^+Cl^- \xrightarrow{CuCN} C_6H_5CN \xrightarrow{H_2O/H^+}$
                                  (A)

$$C_6H_5COOH \xrightarrow[\Delta]{NH_3} C_6H_5CONH_2$$
$\quad\quad$ (B) $\quad\quad\quad\quad\quad\quad\quad$ (C)
                          (½ + ½ + ½ = 1½ Marks)

(ii) $C_6H_5NO_2 \xrightarrow{Sn+HCl} C_6H_5NH_2 \xrightarrow[273K]{NaNO_2+HCl}$
                                        (A)

$$C_6H_5N_2^+Cl^- \xrightarrow[\Delta]{H_2O/H^+} C_6H_5OH$$
$\quad\quad$ (B) $\quad\quad\quad\quad\quad\quad$ (C)
                          (½ + ½ + ½ = 1½ Marks)

25.

Polymer	Monomers	
	Name	**Structure**
Buna-S	1, 3 Butadiene Styrene	$CH_2 - CH - CH = CH_2$ $C_6H_5 - CH - CH_2$
Neoprene	Chloroprene	$CH_2 = CH - \underset{\underset{Cl}{\mid}}{C} = CH_2$
Nylon-6, 6	Adipic acid Hexamethy-lenediamine	$HOOC - (CH_2)_4 - COOH$ and $H_2N - (CH_2)_6 - NH_2$

                                        (1 + 1 + 1 = 3 Marks)

26. (a) The values expressed by Sonali are concern for health of her school mates, observation and analysis of a problem. Taking initiative for a good cause agreeing to valuable ideas of others, taking prompt action for the valuable ideas given by Sonali are some values expressed by Principal of the school.   **(2 Marks)**

(b) Two water soluble vitamins are Vitamin B_{12} and Vitamin C.   **(1 Mark)**

27. (a) Sodium benzoate   **(1 Mark)**

(b) Bithional is an antiseptic and reduces the foul odour produced by the bacterial decomposition of organic matter on the skin.   **(1 Mark)**

(c) Tranquilizers relieve stress and fatigue by inducing sense of well being thus they are used in making of sleeping pills.   **(1 Mark)**

SECTION - D

28. (a) (i)   Differential equation for the respective reaction will be, $\dfrac{dx}{dt} = k[A]^2[B]$ **(1 Mark)**

(ii) Now since,

Rate $= k[A]^2[B]$

$\therefore$ If conc. of A is increased three times.

The rate will increase nine times.   **(1 Mark)**

(iii) Rate $= k[A^2][B]$

New rate $= k'[2A]^2[2B]$

$\quad\quad\quad = k'8[A]^2[B]$

When conc. of both A and B are doubled, then the rate will become eight time.   **(1 Mark)**

(b) 30% decomposition means $x = 30\%$ of $a = 0.30\,a$.
Now, for a first order reaction

$$k = \frac{2.303}{t} \log \frac{a}{a-x} \quad\quad\quad \textbf{(½ Mark)}$$

$$= \frac{2.303}{40} \log \frac{a}{a - 0.30a} \quad\quad \textbf{(½ Mark)}$$

$$= \frac{2.303}{40} \log \frac{10}{7}\, min^{-1}$$

$$= \frac{2.303}{40} \log 1.428\, min^{-1}$$

$$= \frac{2.303}{40} \times 0.1548\, min^{-1}$$

$$= 8.91 \times 10^{-3}\, min^{-1} \quad\quad \textbf{(½ Mark)}$$

For a first order reaction

$$t_{1/2} = \frac{0.693}{k} = \frac{0.693}{8.91 \times 10^{-3}\, min^{-1}}$$

$$= 77.7\, min \quad\quad\quad\quad \textbf{(½ Mark)}$$

OR

(a) For a first order reaction

$$t = \frac{2.303}{k} \log \frac{a}{a-x} \quad\quad\quad \textbf{(½ Mark)}$$

99% completion means
$x = 99\%$ of $a = 0.99a$

$$t_{99\%} = \frac{2.303}{k} \log \frac{a}{a - 0.99a} \quad\quad \textbf{(½ Mark)}$$

$$= \frac{2.303}{k} \log 10^2 = 2 \times \frac{2.303}{k} \quad \textbf{(½ Mark)}$$

90% completion means that
$x = 90\%$ of $a = 0.90a$

$$\therefore \quad t_{90\%} = \frac{2.303}{k} \log \frac{a}{a - 0.90a} \quad \textbf{(½ Mark)}$$

$$= \frac{2.303}{k} \log 10 = \frac{2.303}{k}$$

$$\therefore \quad \frac{t_{99\%}}{t_{90\%}} = \left(\frac{2 \times 2.303}{k} \right) \Big/ \frac{2.303}{k} = 2 \quad \textbf{(½ Mark)}$$

$$\therefore \quad t_{99\%} = 2 \times t_{90\%} \quad\quad\quad \textbf{(½ Mark)}$$

(b) For the equation

$$\log k = \log A - \frac{E_a}{2.303R}\left(\frac{1}{T}\right)$$

Slope of line $= -\dfrac{E_a}{2.303R} = -4250K$ **(1 Mark)**

$E_a = 4250 \text{ K} \times 2.303 \times 8.314 \,(JK^{-1}\,mol^{-1})$

$\quad = 81,375.35 \text{ J mol}^{-1}$ **(1 Mark)**

29. (a) (i) Bond enthalpy of F_2 is lower than that of Cl_2 because $F - F$ bond is weak as F atom is very small. This strengthen the electron-electron repulsions between the lone pairs of electrons.   **(1 Mark)**

(ii) This is due to the fact that NH_3 molecules are associated with intermolecular hydrogen bonding which increases the bond strength. A larger amount of energy is then required to overcome attractive force among NH_3 molecules which is not so in case of PH_3.   **(1 Mark)**

(b) (i) BrF_3 : Trigonal bipyramidal

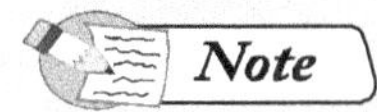

(1 Mark)

(ii) $(HPO_2)_3$

(1 Mark)

(iii) XeF_4 : Square bipyramidal

(1 Mark)

OR

(a) (i) Helium is very little soluble in blood and causes less discomfort to the diver in breathing therefore helium is used in diving apparatus.   **(1 Mark)**

At extreme depths the pressure is high enough that if you had nitrogen in the tank it would become saturated enough in your blood that you would develop nitrogen narcosis. Helium would not be absorbed across the alveoli and will not react with your body, so it is used for diving.

(ii) Being the most electronegative element. It exhibits a negative O.S. of -1. Further, since it has no vacant d-oribitals, it does not exhibit any higher O.S. of $+1, +3, +5, +7$.   **(1 Mark)**

(iii) S–S bond is much stronger than O–O bond and hence sulphur has a much greater tendency for catenation than oxygen.   **(1 Mark)**

The strength of $S = S$ bond is less than $S - S$ bond. While $O = O$ bond is stronger than $O - O$ bond. Consequently S_2 form does not exist as element. However it is possible in ion form S_2^{2-}.

(b) (i) XeF_2

(1 Mark)

(ii) $H_2S_2O_8$

(1 Mark)

30. (a) Reasons for carboxylic acid being stronger acid than phenols are as follows.

(i) Carboxylate ion, the conjugate base of carboxylic acid is stablised by two equivalent resonance structures in which the negative charge is effectively delocalised between two more electronegative oxygen atoms.

(ii) The conjugate base of phenol, a phenoxide ion has non equivalent resonance structures in which the negative charge is at the less electronegative carbon atom.   **(2 Marks)**

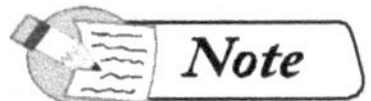

Note

Consider the resonating structures of carboxylate and phenoxide ion

$$RCOOH \rightleftharpoons RCOO^- + H^+$$

Carboxylate ion

≡ Resonance hybrid

In case of phenoxide ion, structures (II – IV) carry a negative charge on the less electronegative carbon atom. Therefore, their contribution towards the resonance stabilization of phenoxide ion is very small.

(b) (i) $CH_3COCH_3 + 4[H] \xrightarrow{Zn-Hg,HCl}$
Propanone
$$CH_3CH_2CH_3 + H_2O$$
Propane   **(1 Mark)**

Note

Clemmensen reduction is complementary to wolf-kishner reduction, which also convert aldehyde and ketones to hydrocarbons. Clemmensen reduction carried out in strongly acidic conditions and wolf kishner reduction carried out in strongly basic conditions.

(ii) COCl $\xrightarrow[H_2]{Pd-BaSO_4}$ CHO   **(1 Mark)**

Benzoyl chloride   Benzaldehyde

(iii) $2CH_3CHO \xrightarrow[Aldol\ condensation]{Dil.NaOH}$
Ethanal

$$CH_3 - \overset{OH}{\underset{|}{CH}} - CH_2 - CHO$$

$$\xrightarrow[\Delta,-H_2O]{H^+/H_2O} CH_3 - CH = CH - CHO$$ **(1 Mark)**
But-2-enal

OR

(a) (i) $2H - \overset{O}{\overset{||}{C}} - H \xrightarrow{Conc.\ KOH}$
Formaldehyde   cannizzaro reaction

$$CH_3OH \quad + \quad HCOOK$$ **(1 Mark)**
Methyl alcohol   Potassium formate

(ii) $CH_3COOH \xrightarrow{Br_2/P} Br - CH_2 - COOH$
Acetic acid   Bromoacetic acid

(1 Mark)

Note

Hell-volhard-zelinsky reaction:

Carboxylic acids having an α-hydrogen are halogenated at the α-position on treatment with chlorine or bromine in the presence of small amount of red phosphoms to give α-halocarboxylic acids. The reaction fails to accomplish the fluorination and iodination of carboxylic acids.

(iii) CHO $\xrightarrow[273-283\ K]{HNO_3/\ H_2SO_4}$ (m-Nitrobenzaldehyde) $+ H_2O$

Benzaldehyde   m-Nitrobenzaldehyde

(1 Mark)

(b) (i) **Ethanal and propanal :** On reacting with I_2/NaOH (or NaOI) ethanal gives yellow precipitate of iodoform but propanal does not.

$$CH_3CHO + 3I_2 + 4NaOH \xrightarrow{heat}$$

$$CHI_3 + HCOONa + 3NaI + 3H_2O$$
Iodoform
(Yellow ppt.

$$CH_3CH_2CHO + I_2 + NaOH \longrightarrow$$
No yellow ppt.   **(1 Mark)**

(ii) **Benzoic acid and phenol :** On reacting with $NaHCO_3$ solution, benzoic acid evolves CO_2 but phenol does not.

$$C_6H_5COOH + NaHCO_3 \longrightarrow$$
Benzoic acid

$$C_6H_5COONa + CO_2 \uparrow + H_2O$$
Sodium benzoate

$$C_6H_5OH \xrightarrow{NaHCO_3} No\ evolution\ of\ CO_2$$
Phenol

(1 Mark)